Selling Hollywood to the World

U.S. AND EUROPEAN STRUGGLES FOR MASTERY OF THE GLOBAL FILM INDUSTRY, 1920–1950

The global expansion of Hollywood and American popular culture in the first decades of the twentieth century met with strong opposition throughout the world. Determined to defeat such resistance, the Hollywood moguls created a powerful trade organization that worked closely with the State Department in an effort to expand the U.S. film industry's dominance worldwide. This book offers insight into and analysis of European efforts to overcome the U.S. film industry's preeminence. It focuses particularly on Britain, Hollywood's largest overseas market of the interwar years; France, a nation with an alternative vision of cinema; and Belgium, which was entrusted by the Vatican with coordination of the international movement against depravity in films. In contributing to the understanding of American popular culture at home and abroad, this study demonstrates Hollywood's role in orchestrating the American Century.

John Trumpbour is Research Director at the Harvard University Trade Union Program. Editor of *The Dividing Rhine: Politics and Society in Contemporary France and Germany,* he has also published articles in the *New York Times, Monthly Review, Queen's Quarterly,* and the *South Asia Bulletin.* His dissertation, which served as the basis for this work, received the Allan Nevins Prize for Literary Distinction in the Writing of History from the Society of American Historians.

CAMBRIDGE STUDIES IN THE HISTORY OF MASS COMMUNICATIONS

General Editors
Kenneth Short, *University of Houston*
Garth Jowett, *University of Houston*

Cambridge Studies in the History of Mass Communications includes books that examine the communications processes and communications systems within social, cultural, and political contexts. Inclusive of empirical, effects-based research, works in this series proceed from the basis that the histories of various media are an important means to understanding their role and function in society. The history of a medium – its pattern of introduction, diffusion, acceptance, and effects – varies in each society, interacting with and, in turn, shaping its culture. Moreover each society reacts differently to the introduction of a medium, and regulatory policies are shaped by both political and cultural forces. The detailed study of various communications forms and their complex message systems is now understood to be the key to unraveling the evolution of modern society and its culture.

Other Books in the Series:

Selling Hollywood to the World

U.S. AND EUROPEAN STRUGGLES FOR MASTERY OF THE GLOBAL FILM INDUSTRY, 1920–1950

JOHN TRUMPBOUR
Harvard University

CAMBRIDGE
UNIVERSITY PRESS

PUBLISHED BY THE PRESS SYNDICATE OF THE UNIVERSITY OF CAMBRIDGE
The Pitt Building, Trumpington Street, Cambridge, United Kingdom

CAMBRIDGE UNIVERSITY PRESS
The Edinburgh Building, Cambridge CB2 2RU, UK
40 West 20th Street, New York, NY 10011–4211, USA
477 Williamstown Road, Port Melbourne, VIC 3207, Australia
Ruiz de Alarcón 13, 28014 Madrid, Spain
Dock House, The Waterfront, Cape Town 8001, South Africa

http://www.cambridge.org

First published 2002

Printed in the United Kingdom at the University Press, Cambridge

Typefaces Sabon 10/13 pt. with Gill Sans   *System* Quark XPress™ [MG]

A catalog record for this book is available from the British Library

Library of Congress Cataloging-in-Publication Data
Trumpbour, John.
Selling Hollywood to the world : U.S. and European struggles for mastery of the global
film industry, 1920–1950 / John Trumpbour.
    p.   cm. – (Cambridge studies in the history of mass communications)
Includes bibliographical references and index.
ISBN 0 521 65156 5
    1. Motion pictures, American – Marketing.   2. Motion picture industry – United States –
History.   3. Motion picture industry – Europe – History.   I. Title.   II. Cambridge
studies in the history of mass communications
PN1995.9.M29 T78 2001
384´.8´0973 – DC21   2001037562

ISBN 0 521 65156 5 hardback

To my parents

Contents

Illustrations

Preface

A decade ago, I attended a series of lectures on films by Gore Vidal in which the writer immediately confessed that "the only thing I ever really liked to do was go to the movies. Naturally, Sex and Art always took precedence over the cinema. Unfortunately, neither ever proved to be as dependable. . . ." For Vidal, "Movies are the lingua franca of the twentieth century. The Tenth Muse, as they call the movies in Italy, has driven the other nine right off Olympus – or off the peak, anyway."

A few weeks after winning the 2001 Nobel Prize for Literature, V. S. Naipaul seconded Vidal's sentiments in admitting that "the movies in the twentieth century were much more important as a forum for shaping people's feelings and educating people than literature." Though ill at ease with the "technical exhibitionism" of contemporary movies, he glories in his "favorite film," *High Sierra* starring Ida Lupino and Humphrey Bogart. The gangster Bogart perishes in what Warner Brothers billed as "The blazing mountain manhunt for Killer Mad-Dog Earle!"

I fear that my own excursions into cinema policy and moral crusades against Hollywood may be weighed down by representatives of a very different sensibility; that is, those who harbor feelings of betrayal by the Tenth Muse. The talk-show host Jay Leno captured their view of the U.S. culture industry when he did a promotion for the pan-European NBC Super Channel: "We're going to ruin your culture just like we ruined our own!"

At the end of the twentieth century, clouds of gloominess thickened in Europe about the future of film policy, those measures seeking to strengthen avenues of expression outside corporate Hollywood. In 1998, thirty-nine of the top forty most successful films in global sales came from U.S. companies. Long in the vanguard of European cinema, France watched as national production dwindled from over 53 percent of domestic box-office receipts in 1982 to 27 percent in 1998. Nine out of the top ten films in France during 1999 came from the United States. While Great Britain via the multiplex revolution experienced a remarkable threefold leap in cinema attendance during the 1990s over the nadir of the 1980s, Hollywood soon grabbed levels of market dominance that decades ago would have provoked parliamentary outcries of national crisis. After reaching 27 percent of the national market in 1997, the share of box-office receipts for British films plunged by half the following year. Germany actually dropped below 10 percent of the domestic market in 1998.

In light of the latest achievements of Denmark, a miniature nation of five million that has exceeded a 20 percent market share for national producers in 1999 and 2000, the performance of Europe's large nations seems rather embarrassing. Some commentators are calling for European countries to find out what's behind the Danish film renaissance, so that they can emulate its model of film schools and national subsidies. (There may be some hope for other small nations such as Belgium, after all.) Other observers call on Europeans to broaden their horizons. Asian cinema, particularly in India, Korea, Hong Kong, Taiwan, China, and Iran, has shown a creativity in recent years that belies the narratives of international despair. After the dismantling of quotas in the late 1990s, Korea went from a 20 percent to a 40 percent national market share at the turn of the century, and it is becoming a favored model for free-market opponents of European state intervention.

State intervention is, however, far from dying. Recently said to be afflicted with stuporous decline, the Gallic Rooster is once again crowing, as French films have secured close to 50 percent of the nation's box-office receipts in the first half of 2001. Some of the French cinematic surge of the early twenty-first century is due to the arrival of the big-budget films of Gaulywood, a development that some fear could extinguish the nation's heritage of small-scale, artisanal movie production. For certain critics, the enemy of France is the large multinational media conglomerate, and they spurn fixation on Hollywood or the United States alone as the danger to French culture. Instead of a simple assault against the American colossus, the fin-de-siècle European uprisings against globalization have much more to do with opposing the depredations of transnational capital. (For that matter, the French New Wave of the earlier postwar era revered the best Hollywood directors, and their rebellion could not properly be construed as some narrow nativist backlash.)

My own historical work takes up some of the more feverish debates of an earlier epoch, 1920–50. If History (Clio) is one of the Nine Muses who have been knocked off Olympus by the Tenth Muse (Cinema), I am grateful to the few of you who continue to search the great peak's base for signs of life among those left waylaid. I hope that my work might in some small way help to deepen understanding of the struggles over popular culture of the previous century.

Acknowledgments

I want to thank the series editor, Professor K. R. M. Short, for many helpful suggestions and also thank Cambridge University Press arts editor Beatrice Rehl. Michael Gnat of Cambridge University Press has rescued me not only from perpetuating the blunders of other scholars, but also from several of my own creation. Gnat has constructed the filmographies and copyedited the masterworks of an entire lineup of cinema-studies scholars far more distinguished than myself. It has been a considerable privilege to have an editor of his talent on my work.

The Belgian American Educational Foundation and the Harvard Center for European Studies/Krupp Foundation long ago gave me grants that helped to launch this work. I am also grateful to the Society of American Historians for honoring the larger project with the Allan Nevins Prize.

In recent years, I have enjoyed teaching film studies to labor leaders at the Harvard Trade Union Program. My coworkers Elaine Bernard, Lorette Baptiste, Laurie Fafard, and Margy Rydzynski have made the HTUP a welcome place for a whole range of interdisciplinary teaching and scholarship on the worlds of work and culture. At the Department of History at Harvard, I benefited from the workshops of Akira Iriye, as well as the regular concern of Laura Johnson, David Nickles, Susan Hunt, John Womack, and Dennis Skiotis. Professor emeritus Daniel Aaron of the Department of English and American Literature and Language has reached out to me, as well as to so many other young scholars whose work may not have won over the guardians of academic orthodoxy at the Crimson university. There are many other friends and individuals thanked for specific contributions in the book's notes.

Finally, I have a special word of gratitude for Abi Husainy of the Public Record Office (U.K.). Her sound advice and South Indian charm have always helped me to keep things in perspective.

Selling Hollywood to the World

U.S. AND EUROPEAN STRUGGLES FOR MASTERY OF THE
GLOBAL FILM INDUSTRY, 1920–1950

Introduction

"Death to Hollywood" – J. M. Keynes

Before the twentieth century, few Europeans judged the cultural production of the United States to be of global significance. The British essayist Sydney Smith voiced this consensus when in 1820 he posed his famous question: "In the four quarters of the globe, who reads an American book? or goes to an American play? or looks at an American picture or statue?"[1] Even Alexis de Tocqueville, who admired Americans for their indomitable energy and spirit of voluntarism in civic life, concluded that the literary production of the entire United States could hardly measure up to that of European cities of medium size and stature.

With the rise of the culture industry in the twentieth century, such serene faith in the perpetual marginality of U.S. culture was severely shaken. The United States soon dominated the most influential cultural institutions of the epoch, first overcoming the French lead in cinema and then conquering the international trade in television. Such a momentous shift in cultural power filled European elites with fear and revulsion, a hostility directed at what were often described as barbarous upstarts who threatened the very space necessary for the survival of national traditions.

In describing the impact of the U.S. culture industry, the political and intellectual authorities employed language laden with the metaphors of disease and of military conquest, as "contagion" and "invasion" became the operative words in their ideological riposte. In testimony before Parliament in the 1950s, Lord Reith, the former director-general of the BBC, compared the prospect of American-style commercial television to the introduction of bubonic plague in the fourteenth century, and in 1931 the French writer Charles Pomaret had declared that: "The conquest of Europe has advanced and the little outposts of the American invasion have already been installed at the gates of France, Italy, Germany, and all the nations of the Old World."[2] Britain's *World Film News* (November 1937) judged that

The American drive to obliterate every vestige of a native British film industry is succeeding admirably. Cynics are comparing the situation with the Italian conquest of Abyssinia, and there are indeed certain resemblances. The Americans, with their impressive supply of Hollywood pictures, have the necessary tank power to put native exhibitors at their mercy. They are using it remorselessly.[3]

The loss of national control over popular culture seemed particularly subversive of the traditional authority of religious, educational, and political institutions in reproducing the customs and moral codes of European societies. To the consternation of many, the British film-industry paper *Bioscope* (1919) boldly proclaimed cinema the church's "legitimate competitor in moulding the character of the nation," and in a report of 28 July 1924, Julien Luchaire, director of the International Institute of Intellectual Cooperation of the League of Nations, testified to the "striking fact that only the Bible and the Koran have an indisputably larger circulation than that of the latest film from Los Angeles. . . . Today the lower classes derive from the cinema show . . . a large part of the emotions and thoughts which make up their mental life." Even so implacable a foe of U.S. imperialism as Joseph Stalin later admitted his handicap in not possessing this pervasive a force for shaping modern life. "If I could control the medium of the American motion picture," he once declared, "I would need nothing else to convert the entire world to Communism."[4]

Throughout the twentieth century, European governments, as well as cultural and religious institutions, have erected an array of organizations and policies designed to protect their national cultures from the vast tidal wave of Hollywood production in cinema and television. In the second half of the 1920s, most major European countries imposed a panoply of quotas and managed trade in film imports, and in the postwar period a virtual commercial-free zone of public television from the Atlantic to the Urals was set into place – a not-so-veiled repudiation of the U.S. model of broadcasting and the continental experiments in sponsored programming during the interwar years.

This book explores the clash between U.S. and European societies in the politics of culture by focusing on cinema as the dominant medium during the first half of the twentieth century. It builds upon a diverse body of scholarship on cinema and the state for this period, including the transnational approaches of Ian Jarvie, Kristin Thompson, Ruth Vasey, H. Mark Glancy, K. R. M. Short, Pierre Sorlin, René Bonnell, Thomas Guback, Heide Fehrenbach, Thomas Saunders, Sarah Street, Margaret Dickinson, Manjunath Pendakur, and Victoria DeGrazia.[5] Part I of the present work tries to establish the aims of the U.S. film industry in conquering overseas markets and spreading American values, with special focus on the relations between the main trade organization, the Motion Picture Producers and Distributors of America (MPPDA), and its critics at home and abroad. The role of U.S.-based crusaders against Hollywood is seen as critical in shaping the MPPDA's overseas campaigns, and fears of impending economic sanctions conditioned capitulation to their demands. For all its pious talk of elevating cinematic art and ensuring high moral standards, the MPPDA, through its Production Code Administration (PCA), saved the studios enormous costs by vetting scripts and preventing the shooting of scenes that would have run afoul of censorship boards around the globe. As a source for the dislocations of modernity, Hollywood would have inevitably generated opposition; but it was also the sole hegemonic institution in U.S. society to be under non-WASP (White Anglo-Saxon Protestant) control, which created a potential for dangerously volatile ideological interventions. The Jewish leaders of the industry found themselves caught between the scissors of domestic opponents, who castigated them for insufficient display of American patriotism, and foreign enemies who loathed them for trumpeting the superiority of American civilization.

Despite pockets of cultural resistance in the interwar State Department, Washington chose to run overseas interference for the film industry on the grounds that "trade follows the film." In an age of protectionism that included advancing quarantine against Hollywood in the heartlands of Nazism and Bolshevism, the U.S. government gave its film industry an ample boost of support. After World War II, the U.S. State Department pursued broader policy aims in Western Europe and soon found itself in increasing conflict with the demands of the later renamed MPEAA (Motion Picture Export Association of America), a story that illuminates the relationship of the state to powerful corporate interests. The MPPDA – which sometimes treated the interwar State and Commerce departments as messenger boys, in New Dealer Josephus Daniels's inimitable phrase – now faced a government apparatus seeking greater autonomy from corporate interest groups. Retaining the goal of expanding U.S. film industry dominance abroad, the State Department shifted its tactics. It would no longer directly represent the film industry in negotiations with foreign regimes.

The chapters focusing on Great Britain, Belgium, and France (Parts II–III) take up the attempt of European governments to establish the defense of national culture, a task rendered precarious by the enormous popular appeal of Hollywood entertainment. (In a forthcoming book, this problem will also be seen through the lens of empire, in the vision of many elites who saw Hollywood as colonizing Europe and decolonizing Europe's vast imperial order.)

The rise of alternative national film industries is explored, as well as their stormy relationship with pressure groups dedicated to thwarting hedonistic excess and depravity in film. Exhorted by an encyclical of Pope Pius XI to imitate the U.S. Catholic Legion of Decency in resisting Hollywood, European Catholicism tried to alter the U.S. film industry's impact on the continent's varied cultures, though it soon proved a greater irritant to representatives of alternative cinematic traditions.

The narrative seeks to shed light on four major questions that intersect with social, cultural, and cinema history: (1) the politics of state intervention and organization of the cinema industry; (2) industrial versus artisanal film production; (3) film and imperialism; and (4) the international role of religion in film regulation.

Politics of State Intervention and Organization of the Cinema Industry. In conquering the world cinema market, the U.S. industry created vertically integrated enterprises of production, distribution, and exhibition, as well as oligopoly conditions in its national market. In the 1920s, the major film moguls accepted the need to surrender some autonomy in favor of a corporatist leadership of the industry, capable of moderating intra-industry disputes, winning over sometimes suspicious publics, and conducting foreign policy in cooperation with the U.S. government. The U.S. State Department, as overseas negotiator for the film industry, and the U.S. Commerce Department, in carrying out annual market research and relaying business intelligence, gave the corporatist leadership important assistance in consolidating Hollywood's global supremacy [Fig. 1].

In Europe of the early interwar period, by contrast, most national film industries produced acute fissures among production, distribution, and exhibition, the last sector typically favoring heavy importation of cheap and profitable U.S. movies. Britain, France, Germany, and Italy all imposed production quotas in the 1920s, despite determined exhibitor opposition. Only Belgium, with a tiny production sector, generally retained a liberal market, a victory for its exhibitors, who also succeeded in keeping special cinema taxes at comparatively mild levels. Aside from support of documentary filmmakers, Belgium did not rally substantial state resources for feature production until as late as 1963. A liberal import policy also held sway throughout the postwar epoch.

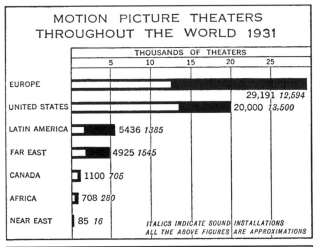

MOTION PICTURE THEATERS THROUGHOUT THE WORLD 1931

THOUSANDS OF THEATERS

	5	10	15	20	25
EUROPE					29,191 12,594
UNITED STATES					20,000 13,500
LATIN AMERICA	5436 1385				
FAR EAST	4925 1545				
CANADA	1100 705				
AFRICA	708 280				
NEAR EAST	85 16				

ITALICS INDICATE SOUND INSTALLATIONS
ALL THE ABOVE FIGURES ARE APPROXIMATIONS

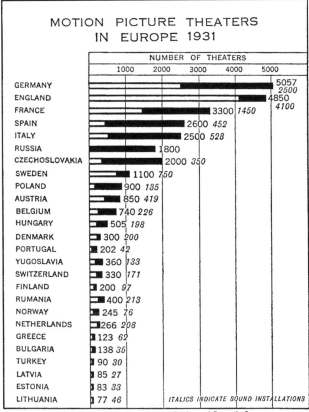

MOTION PICTURE THEATERS IN EUROPE 1931

NUMBER OF THEATERS

	1000	2000	3000	4000	5000
GERMANY					5057 2500
ENGLAND					4850 4100
FRANCE			3300 1450		
SPAIN		2600 452			
ITALY		2500 528			
RUSSIA	1800				
CZECHOSLOVAKIA		2000 350			
SWEDEN	1100 750				
POLAND	900 135				
AUSTRIA	850 419				
BELGIUM	740 226				
HUNGARY	505 198				
DENMARK	300 200				
PORTUGAL	202 42				
YUGOSLAVIA	360 133				
SWITZERLAND	330 171				
FINLAND	200 97				
RUMANIA	400 213				
NORWAY	245 76				
NETHERLANDS	266 208				
GREECE	123 62				
BULGARIA	138 35				
TURKEY	90 30				
LATVIA	85 27				
ESTONIA	83 33				
LITHUANIA	77 46				

ITALICS INDICATE SOUND INSTALLATIONS

*Table compiled by M. P. Dennis, Bureau of Foreign and Domestic Commerce

FIGURE I. Charts prepared by the U.S. Department of Commerce on the distribution of motion picture theaters throughout the world. As can be seen, many European nations were slow in converting to sound. The Department of Commerce regularly provided valuable market research for the U.S. film industry.

Theorists of state intervention on behalf of cinema have categorized government policies as restrictive, supportive, or comprehensive.[6] (*Restrictive* refers to the establishment of market barriers such as quotas; *supportive,* to direct state aid; and *comprehensive,* to a policy with both restrictive and supportive features.) For the interwar period, Britain and France practiced a mildly restrictive policy via quotas but eschewed supportive legislation, whether direct aid, subsidies, or credit schemes such as Germany's film bank. In France, with an industry comprising myriad small, often ephemeral firms, the government frequently watered down its restrictive policy. For instance in 1936, those conducting Franco–U.S. trade negotiations scuttled local production interests in favor of U.S. concessions toward the champagne industry. The absence of true corporatist integration left the film industry at the mercy of a capricious state. The French state in the interwar period, for example, lodged film policy in three different ministries, occasionally making of it a jumble. It took the Vichy regime to impose state integration of the film industry and France's first comprehensive policy, a combination of restrictive and supportive measures that were later repackaged in the postwar period under more salubrious democratic auspices.

In Britain of the late 1930s and 1940s, J. Arthur Rank moved to attain vertical integration and promotion of the national film interest; but after a brief run of glory, his operation sputtered, hurt in a crucial historical showdown by the failure to achieve state and capitalist cooperation. Though the British state imposed the rudiments of a comprehensive policy after the industry's near collapse in the late 1940s, Rank often chose to forsake aid, bitter at a meddling state that had imposed on his cinemas some of the highest special taxes in all Europe.

British film policy was conducted mainly by the Board of Trade and the Foreign Office. For a short phase of the 1920s, the Department of Overseas Trade (DOT) sought to harmonize policy between these two bodies, but it was an experiment quickly abandoned. After briefly exploring Britain's DOT as a means of improving State and Commerce department cooperation, U.S. Secretary of Commerce Herbert Hoover rejected such a model.

Finally, the U.S. example serves as a concrete historical case study that raises serious questions about the leading social-science theories on power and the nature of the capitalist state. In the 1970s, British Marxist Ralph Miliband and his Parisian rival Nicos Poulantzas argued, respectively, that capitalist interests had either an instrumentalist or a structuralist relationship to the state.[7] *Instrumentalists* asserted that the capitalist class exercised direct control over the state; *structuralists* countered that the state required relative autonomy, necessary for mediating conflicting interests and resolving crises that would otherwise threaten the long-term survival of capital-ism. Although these competing theories are vastly simplified here, the his-torical approach in this book suggests that theoreticians of power may need to break from such essentialist constructs. In the case of film politics, the interwar MPPDA and U.S. State Department interacted in a fashion much closer to the instrumentalist model; but in the postwar period, John Mc-Cloy, John Foster Dulles, and others made a strong case that the U.S. State Department could best achieve the long-term interests of the film industry and other capitalists by amplifying structural autonomy.[8] Instrumentalism or structuralism may work better depending on the specific historical con-juncture in state–capitalist relations. Each concept may also vary by nation-al context: France's state technocrats typically exercise bureaucratic ration-ality with a greater autonomy from capitalist interests than, for example, the Commerce Department of Calvin Coolidge–era America. There is a need, in short, to apply these concepts with greater historical specificity, rather than viewing either structuralism or instrumentalism as a quality in-trinsic to the entire history of the state under capitalism.

Industrial versus Artisanal Film Production. Interwar Germany's UFA, Britain's J. Arthur Rank, and, to a lesser extent, Alexander Korda sought large-scale organization as a means of competing with Hollywood. As the standard-bearer of the movement for Film Europa during the 1920s, UFA carried the hopes of those seeking a European Goliath to rival Film Amer-ica. UFA conquered much of the Germanic market, but the national market was often not big enough to amortize its line of high-budget productions (*Grossfilme*) and even medium-budget ones. It has been estimated that only one in six of its *Grossfilme* productions between 1924 and 1930 made inter-national profits and, meanwhile, 75 percent of German films by 1927 had to turn to U.S. sources for their financing.[9] UFA's own financial instability in the mid-1920s led it to borrow profusely from U.S. giants Paramount and MGM, firms that demanded in exchange half of UFA's theater slots in its German exhibition sector. While the U.S. films basked in glory in Ber-lin's first-run theaters, UFA productions were exiled to the cinemas of York-ville, a predominantly German sector of New York City.[10] In any case, the emergence of the talking picture rendered hopes for a Film Europa ever more precarious. The U.S. arts critic Gilbert Seldes expressed the yearning that Europe would continue to develop the art of the silent film while Holly-wood mastered the talking picture; but the possibilities of a dual cinema market disappeared. Even though Nazism later sought to purge the morbid and macabre themes of Weimar cinema, German film since the days of *Das*

Cabinet des Dr. Caligari (*The Cabinet of Dr. Caligari*, 1920) and *Nosferatu* (1922) had trouble shaking its sinister image, one in which a critic complained: "It has the odor of tainted food. It leaves a taste of cinders in the mouth."[11] There is now a vast body of scholarship on UFA, and my work takes up only the postwar breakup of this cartel, which remains a major issue of contention for critics of U.S. cultural imperialism.[12]

Rank's and Korda's own talk of a Hollywood-on-the-Thames sometimes elicited a negative response from partisans of John Grierson, who favored the small producer, the lone artisan bent on escaping the machinery of the industrial cultural Goliaths. While Grierson himself thought the documentary filmmaker could construct only a small alternative island in the vast Hollywood sea, France spawned a large cohort of artisanal feature film producers who sought a commanding share of the national market. They championed the cinematic atelier as more hospitable than industrialized studios to great art. Their celebration of the artisan and French national genius led to an ideological formation that in this book is called *artisanal populism*, a major rallying point for opponents of Hollywood universalism. The artisanal organizing principle in interwar France succeeded in creating several outstanding works of cinema, but it came at a cost: low capital investment, frequent boom-and-bust cycles, and a feeble international distribution network. The French state in the postwar period sought to remedy these defects and, though never able to dislodge Hollywood, generally secured the most consistent share of the national market of any European nation. Though Belgium produced several outstanding documentarists, as well as artists whose careers flourished in other European nations, its miniature national market and absence of restrictive policy consigned small producers to a single-digit share of screen time throughout the twentieth century.

The U.S. film industry is sometimes described as a triumph of the Fordist model of production over artisans and cottage industry. The automobile-industry metaphors have a compelling quality insofar as France had the world's leading film and auto industries prior to World War I and then rapidly surrendered global supremacy to the United States in these fields. Nevertheless, as the literary scholar Kristin Ross is at pains to point out, the concept of Fordism implies a rationalization of production, the triumph of Taylorism, and the notion that workers would have enough income to consume the costly product they were manufacturing. The film industry did not have the same direct consumerist agenda in paying most of its work force. Moreover, while millions of French people regularly watched U.S. films, few owned U.S. automobiles.[13] This could be another way of saying that Hollywood developed a full-fledged program of globalization well before many other industries [Fig. 2]. As Alan Wood explained it in 1952:

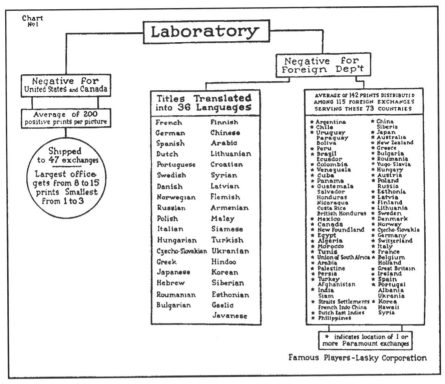

Chart Nº1

Laboratory

Negative for
Foreign Dep't

Negative for
United States and Canada

Average of 200
positive prints per picture

Shipped
to 47 exchanges
Largest office
gets from 8 to 15
prints Smallest
from 1 to 3

Titles Translated
into 36 Languages

French	Finnish
German	Chinese
Spanish	Arabic
Dutch	Lithuanian
Portuguese	Croatian
Swedish	Syrian
Danish	Latvian
Norwegian	Flemish
Russian	Armenian
Polish	Malay
Italian	Siamese
Hungarian	Turkish
Czecho-Slovakian	Ukranian
Greek	Hindoo
Japanese	Korean
Hebrew	Siberian
Roumanian	Esthonian
Bulgarian	Gaelic
	Javanese

AVERAGE OF 142 PRINTS DISTRIBUTED
AMONG 115 FOREIGN EXCHANGES
SERVING THESE 73 COUNTRIES

★ Argentina	★ China
★ Chile	Siberia
★ Uruguay	★ Japan
Paraguay	★ Australia
Bolivia	★ New Zealand
★ Peru	★ Greece
★ Brazil	★ Bulgaria
Ecuador	★ Roumania
★ Colombia	★ Yugo-Slavia
★ Venezuela	★ Hungary
★ Cuba	★ Austria
★ Panama	★ Poland
★ Guatemala	Russia
Salvador	★ Esthonia
Honduras	★ Latvia
Nicaragua	★ Finland
Costa Rica	★ Lithuania
British Honduras	★ Sweden
★ Mexico	★ Denmark
★ Canada	★ Norway
★ New Foundland	★ Czecho-Slovakia
★ Egypt	★ Germany
★ Algeria	★ Switzerland
★ Morocco	★ Italy
★ Tunis	★ France
★ Union of South Africa	★ Belgium
★ Arabia	Holland
★ Palestine	★ Great Britain
★ Persia	★ Ireland
★ Turkey	★ Spain
★ Afghanistan	★ Portugal
★ India	Albania
Siam	Ukrania
★ Straits Settlements	★ Korea
French Indo China	Hawaii
★ Dutch East Indies	★ Syria
★ Philippines	

★ indicates location of 1 or
more Paramount exchanges

Famous Players-Lasky Corporation

FIGURE 2. A chart from the early 1930s showing the global marketing strategies of Famous Players–Lasky Corporation, better known by the trade name of Paramount Pictures.

[A]ny attempt to break Hollywood's monopoly would be a grim fight indeed, owing to a peculiarity of film economics: *it is the only industry where increasing the geographical extent of the market does not increase the demand for the product.* The requirement of a small town like Reading [U.K.], for instance, can be met by 400 films a year. Open new cinemas in Iceland and the South Sea Islands, and you will still only need 400 films a year. And Hollywood was quite prepared to make every one of the 400 films itself.[14]

Hollywood's integration of production, distribution, and exhibition proved to be an asset to its global triumph, but it lost this advantage in the postwar period. Some European media conglomerates of the 1990s have actually achieved integration of these sectors, yet it has not been enough to turn the tide against the domination of U.S. film productions. Industrial organization remains an important component of Hollywood's preeminence, but message still matters, despite the cultural protestation that the product is vapid.

Film and Imperialism. The extraordinary scope of British imperialism in the eighteenth and nineteenth centuries paved the way for U.S. cultural domination in the twentieth: The global size of the English-language market has been a distinct advantage to Hollywood.[15] One of the major schools of thought on U.S. popular culture, influential in UNESCO and state ministries of culture, is that of cultural imperialism. Curiously most historical and social-science literature bathed in the concept give scant exploration of U.S. popular culture and the classical phase of modern imperialism, the European empires. Although, as mentioned earlier, this book will be followed by a companion volume that explores film and imperialism in much greater depth, a few brief preliminary observations are in order here.

While European intellectual and political elites feared film's effects on the metropolis, on the masses who had only recently gained the right to vote, they were especially alarmed about cinema's deleterious moral lessons for "the child-like natives," who seemed increasingly prone to disobedience toward the colonial authorities. Film became a major culprit in the rise of anticolonialism, according to the imperial imagination of interwar Europe.

There is a massive literature on the purported "effects" of film on the "mass mind," a social-science tradition that has its origins in studies of World War I propaganda and in the project of the Motion Picture Research Council, founded by the Protestant cleric William Harrison Short. Much of it holds that the "masses" can easily be manipulated by popular culture. In the case of imperialism, however, Hollywood's subsequent efforts to glorify the British Empire throughout the 1930s inadvertently ended up fanning the flames of Indian unrest, whereas Belgium's decision in 1945 to ban Hollywood productions for Congolese viewers failed to prevent the rise of violent anticolonial struggle. Although Hollywood film does have "effects" on audiences, it surely is never as simple as the cultural Cassandras would have it. Film becomes a scapegoat absolving nations from the righteous indignation that confronts regimes of social injustice.

Recognizing such imperialist discourse as self-serving, economic liberals are quick to advance demands for free trade in cultural commodities. Swept up in strong belief in the universal mission of American ideals, the United States has not been a society particularly receptive to foreigners crying out for the preservation of their national culture. In *Men of Destiny* (1927), Walter Lippmann explained that:

All the world thinks of the United States today as an empire, except the people of the United States. We shrink from the word "empire" and insist that it should not be used to describe the dominion we exercise from Alaska to the Philippines, from Cuba to Panama, and beyond. We feel there ought to be some other name for the civilizing work which we do so reluctantly in these backward countries.[16]

The cultural politics of film may be a fresh means of understanding interimperialist conflict and responses to the rise of the United States as a global power.

The International Role of Religion in Film Regulation. The Catholic Church's construction of an international film movement during the late 1920s and 1930s revealed new wells of religious vitality when confronting the challenge of modernity. European Catholics built a network of cinema publications and movie theaters, and then inspired leading cadres of the U.S. Legion of Decency, a body founded during a moral campaign of 1933 and 1934. The papacy soon advised European Catholicism to follow the example of their American brethren, a rare instance of U.S. Catholics receiving the Vatican's imprimatur in supplying moral leadership for the rest of Christendom.

Both the French and Belgian church built exhibition and media outlets, unlike the U.S. body, which focused on moral monitoring of Hollywood and communication to the Catholic masses through established diocesan press organs. Hollywood feared the Legion, in part because it also received support from leading U.S. Protestant and Jewish organizations. Belgium played a special role on the international plane, entrusted by the Vatican with the coordination of national Catholic film movements. It should be stressed that the Holy See called for a variety of national responses, as Pius XI downplayed universalism in favor of moral regulation responsive to historical differences in standards and customs in specific communities.

In Protestant Britain, Catholic activists failed to make the same impact as in Belgium, France, and the United States, though a Roman Catholic did ascend to the leadership of the British Board of Film Censors. Instead Protestantism took the major initiative in the movement for morality in films, a gauntlet picked up by the Methodist J. Arthur Rank. Though his relations with leading U.S. Catholic film regulators such as Joseph Breen were cordial, Rank found that commercialism and morals in movies sometimes collided, and he did not relish finding himself under attack for allegedly straying from Christian rectitude.

Many contemporary accounts have delivered a strong civil-libertarian condemnation of the Legion of Decency for preventing works of social import from reaching the screen.[17] While regarding myself as a civil libertarian and hence prone to spasms of moral outrage at episodes of "thought control," I do not believe that censorship regimes inevitably lead to a diminution in the quality of art. Moral regulation in the United States may have expanded the quantity of films best described as mediocre, but censorship regimes are often productive, creating struggles for new ways of expressing ideas. In some circumstances, this magnified the growth of outstanding works of cinematic art. Moreover, commercialism, not simply Catholicism, conditioned film majors to steer clear of the controversial, the burning social issues of the age. Voltairean denunciations of religious intolerance do little to explain how some directors persistently managed to produce outstanding films in a climate said to be one of enveloping sterility.

Social theorists have long tried to explain American exceptionalism, the uniqueness of the U.S. social formation in relation to its European counterparts. Religion continues to have a power and force in the civil society of the United States, whereas it has diminished substantially in other advanced industrial societies. The apparent paradox of the United States, with its separation of church and state, is the increased salience of religion in civil society.[18] Further comparative attention to religious movements in advanced industrial societies may help to unlock the causes and meanings of America's distinctive cultural formation, a task for a twenty-first-century Tocqueville. The Enlightenment confidently assumed that modernity over the long haul dissolves devotion to the sacred. Nevertheless, the power of televangelism in the hypermodern United States, the Islamic uprising in the midst of Iran's breakneck modernization, the cult of Mary pervading communist-ruled Poland, and the successful campaign to canonize Czar Nicholas in the Orthodox Church of postcommunist Russia suggest that history may have other destinations for its discontents: The wounds of modernity could be healed by new waves of religiosity and messianic devotion.

This introduction has sought to provide some comparative perspective to the national histories that follow. Britain receives special attention because this empire long swallowed the majority of Hollywood's international sales and because the increasingly ravenous cinemagoing habits of its citizenry rescued the U.S. studios from the Nazi obstruction of continental European markets; Belgium, because it sought to coordinate a global Catholic resistance to the film industry and illustrates the travail of small nations in securing cultural production; and finally France, a nation that once led the global film industry and crafted an artisanal vision opposed to Hollywood's industrial universalism. The focus on Britain, Belgium, and France makes special sense when it comes to my subsequent work on imperialism, as all three empires judged the new globalized popular culture as destructive of colonial order. Beyond this, both books will help supply some of the materials necessary for what Perry Anderson regards as the new frontier for historical inquiry, what he calls "the transitive impact of one society on another that poses the most demanding and, often least ventilated, questions of a true international history." He elaborates that by this he does not "mean comparative history, which has a wide welcome and is much on the increase today." Rather, there needs to be "a *relational* history, that studies the incidence – reciprocal or asymmetrical – of different national or territorial units and cultures on each other."[19]

Declaring this true international approach to be "still fairly rare," he finds that "the bulk of our history writing, be it radical, liberal or conservative, remains national in focus." While "national histories can be compared, or even set within some large global complex, as world-system theory does," he finds that "what is less often either attempted or achieved, however, is a reconstruction of their dynamic interrelationships over time."

The eruption of the U.S. culture industry on a world scale is one of the topics that will have to undergo this type of historical reconstruction. Although my project focuses most on the British Empire, where Hollywood conducted the vast majority of its overseas business (an annual $101.2 million out of $135 million just prior to World War II), it shows how the U.S. culture industry generated political responses and religious movements on every one of the globe's inhabited continents.[20] Through film, Will Hays believed, the planet could be remade in America's image. Customs and cultures have long appeared in retreat; yet their tenacity is testimony that we remain far from that fool's paradise, the end of history.

PART ONE

THE UNITED STATES

CHAPTER ONE

The Domestic Roots of Hollywood's Foreign Policy

CENSORSHIP AND CORPORATISM IN THE FORMATION OF THE MPPDA, 1921–1941

"SELL AMERICA TO THE WORLD"

On 5 October 1923, Will H. Hays, the head of the newly formed Motion Picture Producers and Distributors of America, delivered a speech in London outlining the international aims of the U.S. motion picture industry. In it, he proclaimed that the

Members of our Association have taken . . . definite steps to make certain that every film that goes from America abroad, wherever it shall be sent, shall correctly portray to the world the purposes, the ideals, the accomplishments, the opportunities, and the life of America.[1]

He then boldly declared: "We are going to sell America to the world with American motion pictures." In such an enterprise, he assured the British audience that he could count on the support of the U.S. State Department: "The possibilities are as great as all the tomorrow. Immediate understandings with many of the foreign countries have to be worked out . . . and in all these matters our own State Department is cooperating splendidly."[2]

Upon Hays's return to the United States, his office issued a press release declaring that "he came back filled with enthusiasm over one outstanding fact – that ninety percent of all motion pictures are American made pictures and that they please the great number of Britons who go to see them." Of this "outstanding fact," Hays himself stated in his inimitable portly prose: "The international understanding by the peoples of the world, each of the other, which will be brought about by the right kind of American motion pictures all over the world, will move us very far indeed in the direction of World peace."[3] Backed by the Daughters of the American Revolution, Hays convinced the most illustrious director of the epoch, D. W. Griffith, to produce the marathon film *America,* a star-spangled celebration of the War of Independence and U.S. visions of liberty.[4]

In spreading the Good News of the coming of the motion picture, Hays at first seemed blissfully unaware that his dream of selling America to the world inflamed elite opinion in Great Britain and Western Europe. Throughout these lands in the 1920s, U.S. films faced blame for (1) abetting U.S. economic supremacy over the rest of the world, (2) shredding the fabric of national cultures and customs, and (3) threatening European rule in colonial dominions by showing the white man, particularly figures of authority, in scenes thought likely to elicit responses of contempt and ridicule. Indeed the Griffith spectacle so highly touted by Hays depicted the English as villains in America's colonial history, and the epic, retitled *Love and Sacrifice,* was effectively banned by the British Board of Film Censors, whose members compelled substantial prunings before granting it a certificate in the autumn of 1924.[5] The booster Hays and his European critics shared one fundamental assumption: that film is an extremely powerful force, able to alter centuries-old habits and traditions.

For Hays, film under public-spirited supervision could be a source of boundless good able to remake the world in its own image; his overseas opponents, however, were apt to agree with the assessment of British critic Ernest Betts, who later in the decade wrote that

chiefly as a result of American films, a large part of the world, and especially the youthful world, now has a cabaret outlook, full of feeble passion, Woolworth glitter, and trumpery heroics. . . .
But . . . there is a difference between entertaining a man by making him drink and entertaining a man by making him drunk. The American film has doped the world with rotten juices. By a strength of purpose which is staggering and its one superb virtue, it has flung at us, year by year, in unending deluge, its parcel of borrowed stories and flashy little moralities.[6]

Hays had certain occasion for his brimming confidence. From a purely business yardstick, the U.S. industry had displaced France from its former domination of the film industry in the first decade of the twentieth century, first by gaining majority control over British Commonwealth and Latin American markets from 1911 to 1914 and then by overwhelming Europe during the First World War. The belief of some Europeans that they could expect to recover dominance in the film trade once the war ended proved increasingly illusory. As the interwar period progressed, the U.S. industry exploited several advantages over its rivals:

1. The world's largest domestic market by a substantial margin – fifteen to twenty thousand theaters in the U.S. compared to between three and five thousand in the major European nations – made it more likely that the costs of film could be amortized at home.

2. A nation of immigrants, a sort of world audience, forced producers to learn how to create spectacles appealing to peoples from many backgrounds. In Will Hays's explanation,

There is a special reason why America should have given birth and prosperous nurture to the motion picture and its world-wide entertainment. America in the very literal sense is truly the world state. All races, all creeds, all men are to be found here. . . .[7]

3. Industrial organization of production and distribution were reflected in studios rich in land, labor, and equipment, the star system, professional advertising, and later extensive investment networks – all a stark contrast to the largely artisanal production of film abroad.

4. An ideology of optimism and happy endings repudiated the tragic realism of much European film and theatrical performance that, as MGM's Louis B. Mayer repeatedly warned, represented box-office poison. Arguing that "the public should not patronize shows which offer only these depressing endings," the *Moving Picture World* back in 1909 exhorted exhibitors: "Give the public good cheer and watch the increased stream of dimes and nickels which will flow into your coffers."[8] In "Radicalism – An Industry Peril," a speech to southern theater owners in late 1937, the trade-journal editor Martin Quigley forewarned of a crucial reason to keep communists at bay:

They want the film to be realistic – to deal with the facts of life in the raw. They are unhappy because the people are made happy in the theatres. They want the screen to shock and embitter patrons so that the ranks of the discontented will be enlarged, giving to them recruits in greater numbers to flock to their magical cures for what's wrong with the world.[9]

Quigley insisted that the entertainment film generate "contentment and happiness." For others, the good cheer and Barnumizing ambience of commercial theater threatened art. "The fetish of a happy ending . . . does more to keep good stories from the screen in recognizable form than the Hays Code and the sinful and slothful nature of man combined," lamented Elliot Paul in 1942. "When Hemingway's *A Farewell to Arms* was in the works, Don Ernesto suggested two versions, one for the large cities in which the heroine dies in childbirth, modestly screened from public view, and another in which she gives birth to the American flag which fills the fade-out." But Paul was quick to admit: "Most attempts at grim endings have resulted in box-office flops."[10] German expressionism in the 1920s had represented one of the prized alternatives to the Hollywood aesthetic, but this cinematic tradition, it was frequently said, left the mouths of audiences with the taste of ashes.

5. Corporatist leadership of the industry under the aegis of the MPPDA and substantial vertical integration in production, exhibition, and distribution was in marked contrast to the sharp divisions between these three sectors in most European nations. The U.S. State Department and the Commerce Department could represent the overall interests of a film industry under oligopoly capitalism, whereas rival European governments constantly encountered fierce infighting among these three sectors with clashing interests: the desire for cheap, plentiful Hollywood imports among European exhibitors versus the anti-import bias of domestic producers. European distributors tended to divide between those renting U.S. wares and others primarily serving national producers.

"RESCUE THE MOTION PICTURE FROM THE HANDS OF THE DEVIL"

Far from the glamour of the West Coast studios, the New York–based MPPDA played the central role in the formation of state–film industry relations in the United States, particularly concerning censorship issues and foreign policy. Founded in the winter of 1921–2, the MPPDA became known in the popular mind as an organization dedicated to cleaning up the morals of motion pictures, a crisis seen as acute to the point of peril for the industry. Earlier in September 1921, police had arrested actor Roscoe "Fatty" Arbuckle on charges of raping and murdering actress Virginia Rappe in the aftermath of a wild drinking party in San Francisco. Rumors abounded that the popular 320-pound actor had repeatedly used a Coke bottle in the fatal rupturing of the actress's bladder. Rappe's apparent fiancé, the director Henry Lehrman, peered over a copy of H. G. Wells's *Outline of History* and then proclaimed Arbuckle a symptom of a decaying civilization:

That's what comes of taking vulgarians from the gutter and giving them enormous salaries and making idols of them. Some people don't know how to get a kick out of life, except in a beastly way. They are the ones who resort to cocaine and the opium needle and who participate in orgies that surpass the orgies of degenerate Rome.[11]

The industry's leadership feared the mobilization of a populist backlash against Hollywood as a bottomless pit of immorality, a specter heightened in February 1922 with the murder of producer William Desmond Taylor. This case brought in its wake further tales of sex and drug-soaked debauchery. Only after three trials, the first two featuring hung juries, did Arbuckle receive an acquittal; but the outcome hardly reversed the damage done to his career, nor to an industry already suspect in the predominantly Protestant republic for its Jewish ownership and the prominence of actors from foreign lands and of southern European émigré stock. Evangelist Billy Sunday in early 1921 preached that "No foreign bunch can come over here and tell us how we ought to observe the Lord's day," a reference to his opposition to the showing of movies on Sundays, while the Reverend Wilbur Fisk Crafts frequently mobilized his International Reform Bureau, a crusade formed in 1895 against opium, alcohol, sex, and subsequently celluloid.[12] Crafts, who had several times testified before Congress against "'smutty' and crime-breeding films," announced in a press release of December 1920 that his lobby "voted tonight to rescue the motion pictures from the hands of the Devil and 500 un-Christian Jews." He added that he "would crash into Congress backed by the Christian Churches and reform organizations, which was the only way to defeat the $40,000,000 slush fund the movie men had come to Washington with."[13] In the 1 January 1921 issue of Henry Ford's *Dearborn Independent,* the editors kicked off the New Year with a multipart series on the danger of Jewish preeminence in Hollywood and the world of theater. Movies, they wrote, are

Jew-controlled, not in spots only, not 50 per cent merely; but entirely; with the natural consequence that now the world is in arms against the trivializing and demoralizing influences of that form of entertainment as presently managed. . . . As soon as the Jews gained control of the "movies," we had a movie problem. . . . It is the genius of that race to create problems of a moral character in whatever business they achieve a majority.[14]

So certain that Jews "create problems of a moral character in whatever business they achieve a majority," the *Dearborn Independent* also traced the decline of wholesome Shakespearean plays to the rise of Jewish ownership of the stage since 1885. While a Jewish stage manager allegedly proclaimed, "Shakespeare spells ruin," the newspaper asserted that "the Jews may be credited also with having introduced Oriental sensuality to the American stage. . . . The scenes are most Oriental in their voluptuous abandonment." Though the article avoids mention of Jewish ownership in the garment industry as the cause of racy fashions, it decries a theatrical world of "Men in breech-clouts, leopard skins and buck skins, women in flimsy gowns of gossamer texture, slashed to the hips. . . . It is perfectly natural . . . that the complete Judaization of the theater should result in its being transformed into 'the show business,' a mere matter of trade and barter."[15] Elsewhere the series held that popular song had become "the most active agent of moral miasma in the country, or if not the most active, then neck and neck with the movies." Naturally "the time of entry of Jews into control of the popular song is the exact time when the morality of popular song began to decline."[16] Jewish-owned clubs had banished traditional song and classical music in favor of jazz and jungle rhythms. The movies represented just one part of a multipronged assault on Western civilization. "Many of these producers don't know how filthy their stuff is – it is so natural to them," concluded the journalists of the *Dearborn Independent.* Making the connection between the foulness of the films and the stage, Frederick Boyd Stevenson of the *Brooklyn Eagle* affirmed that "the reels are reeking with filth. They are slimy with sex plays."[17]

With scandal afoot and open rumblings of complaint about Jewish preeminence in the entertainment industry, the movie moguls had reached the first of several crossroads: They would have to reverse some of these grotesque perceptions. On 8 December 1921, Lewis J. Selznick, the president of Selznick Pictures, and Saul Rogers, an attorney for Fox Pictures, approached Will H. Hays, former chairman of the Republican National Committee and now postmaster general in the Harding Administration. They asked him if he would like to assume the leadership of a new organization of the nine major film corporations. In their round-robin letter to Hays dated 2 December 1921, the several movie chieftains declared their goal to be "attaining and maintaining the highest possible standard of motion picture film production," while "striving to have the industry accorded the consideration and dignity to which it is justly entitled, and proper representation before the people of this country so that its position, at all times, may be presented in an unbiased and unprejudiced manner."[18] Hays, a Presbyterian elder basking in a reputation as an ace reformer of a postal service previously thought to be in disarray, modestly referred to himself as a "tenderfoot" in the matter of films [Fig. 3]. His neophyte status did not stop the movie moguls from offering him a salary variously estimated at between $100,000 and $250,000 per annum – a substantial raise from his $12,000 remuneration as postmaster general and well in excess of that of the president of the United States and the CEOs of most major corporations. Under Hays, noted Terry Ramsaye in 1926, "The post-office which had been intensely unpopular became popular. Even the dextrine on the back of the stamps tasted better after Hays got ahold."[19]

Nevertheless, Reverend Crafts immediately condemned Hays for allowing himself to be "bought" by the film industry, while the *Dearborn Independent* jabbed at him as the new hired mouthpiece for alien interests. Indubitably, the moguls hoped that Hays could allay the fears of a provincial

FIGURE 3. Looking confident in pinstripes and flannel, Will H. Hays, former chairman of the Republican National Committee, poses with the actress Constance Talmadge and the director Sidney Franklin. A master of public relations and the first leader of the Motion Picture Producers and Distributors of America (MPPDA), Hays called himself a "tenderfoot" when it came to understanding the making of movies. *Source:* Hirz/Hulton|Archive.

Protestant middle class brazenly vocal about those thought noxious to the values of the heartland: Jews, immigrants, and other urbanized carriers of cosmopolitan culture.[20] In the era before the "breakdown of the Gentile theater," argued Henry Ford's journalists, entertainers had "worked first for the approval of the people of 'the provinces,' which is the contemptuous Jewish term for the rest of the United States."[21]

The forces triggering the turn to Hays, however, lie beyond the storms swirling from the Arbuckle case, the Ford-sponsored campaigns against the Jewish presence in popular entertainment, and the mobilization of Christian morality campaigns against the industry's leadership. Following the collapse of the Edison-led Motion Picture Patent Company (MPPC, often

Come Out of It, Mr. Exhibitor!

FIGURE 4 *(here and facing).* The Hollywood movie moguls regarded themselves as pro–free enterprise and champions of people from ordinary walks of life. In his battles to defeat the MPPC (aka Film Trust), Carl Laemmle published cartoons and text in the *Moving Picture Herald* during May and June 1909 expressing his world view: "I want you to remember one thing always, namely, that I built up the biggest and best film renting business in the world by catering to the so-called 'little fellows.' . . . I owe my success to them more than anyone else." The founder of Universal Studios in 1912 and an executive sometimes credited with inventing the concept of the "movie star," Laemmle would later resent attacks on the movie moguls as monopolists. He and his generation of moguls hired Republican Postmaster General Will Hays during the early 1920s in hopes of shielding the film majors from chal-lenge and attack.

called "the Film Trust"), which represented mainly WASP-owned film enter-prises [Fig. 4], the film industry had tried to organize itself twice, first in 1915 under the aegis of the Motion Picture Board of Trade led by J. W. Binder and then in 1916 under the National Association of the Motion Pic-ture Industry (NAMPI) headed by the San Francisco–based vaudevillian William Brady. Brady, an associate of movie mogul Adolph Zukor, defended the industry against raging critics in 1920 during the city of Chicago's hear-ings into film's contribution to crime and juvenile delinquency. Later that

"NEXT!"

"Have You A Little White Elephant In Your Home?"

year, he lashed out in the *New York Times* (12 December 1920) against the critics of the immigrant presence in the industry. "If these slanderers, Jew-baiters, and Catholic haters are not silenced," he declared, "we must fight to the finish with no quarter." Despite his fervor in defending the moguls, the industry's leadership increasingly lost faith in Brady. In Hays's version of events, NAMPI had been rife with division and lacked the clout at both the national and international level necessary for an industry now of global scope.

THE CORPORATIST MOMENT

Hays's rise to power is better understood in the context of corporatism, an ideology and form of industrial organization that gained increasing adherence among public-service-oriented representatives of the capitalist class. Herbert Hoover, who as secretary of Commerce in the Harding and Coolidge administrations paid careful attention to the needs of the film industry, stood in the vanguard of the corporatist movement, doctrines he preferred labeling "associationalism." His friend and cabinet colleague Hays proved to be a vocal defender of many cherished tenets of corporatism:

1. developing self-regulation among the industry in part to prevent the lurking dangers of state intervention,
2. in appropriate spheres, building state–corporate cooperation, and
3. providing a critique of the anarchic stage of capitalism to the degree that it allowed unscrupulous operators and exploitative elements too easy access to the marketplace.

In one of his first interviews as head of the MPPDA, Hays in a dazzling display of mixed metaphors agreed with the correspondent of the *Boston Globe* (9 April 1922) who wondered if his mission was more than just "solely concerned with improving the morality of pictures. . . ." Hays replied in the affirmative, stating that:

the industry has just settled down to a period of calmness . . . [I]n the beginning it was like a rush to a new gold field, like the races there used to be for free lands in newly opened Government areas. Everyone, seeing fortune in the pictures, raced into the business.
    There was no team play. Any man who could grab the ball grabbed it and tore down the field trying to make a touchdown for himself. The various branches of the business did not understand each other and took no particular interest in each other.
    Now they have come to a stage where the early confusion is all over, and men can look at each other and say: ". . . Let's get together and work for our mutual good and for the good of our patrons." . . .
    And right here I would like to point out to the public that the idea of getting together and working harmoniously and noncompetitively (just like a Board of Trade or a Chamber of Commerce) was the idea of the producers and exhibitors, not of Will Hays. I just chanced to be the man they selected to head the organization. . . .[22]

In his memoirs, Hays gave a more explicit rendition of corporatist ideology. Observing that "in a democratic commonwealth each business, each industry, and each art has as much right to, and as much duty toward self-regulation as has the general citizenry to self-government," he called this "the fundamental idea behind the medieval trade guilds – the ancestors of our professional associations as well as of our labor unions." In an analysis that suggests a departure from the earlier model in which the moguls had a fellow showman (Brady) lead the industry, Hays called the movie owners "shrewd enough to see that they needed an outsider, an 'impartial chairman,' to bind them into an effective group and to mediate between them and the public."[23]

Raymond Moley, regarded as the head of FDR's original brain trust and an unreconstructed booster for the Hays Office, declared that

The MPPDA turned out to be an association quite unlike any of the others, in fact an organization unique in American industrial life. . . . It was to be an expression and fulfillment of their cooperative impulses. It was to be the industry governing itself – in its own and in the public interest.

In producing the first major study of the Hays Office, Moley proved quick to dispel the traditional accent on the Arbuckle affair and the censorship campaigns in the formation of the MPPDA. Referring to Hays's reputation as "the Czar of all the Rushes," he noted that

Hays was not being chosen as "Czar" of the Industry. But neither was he being employed merely to ward off the impending danger of Federal and State censorship legislation. There was an abundance of problems the perturbed film men were finally willing to recognize as common – the protection of the interest of producers and distributors in foreign countries; the theft and piracy of films; the revenue, copyright and tariff laws affecting the industry.[24]

In responding to the shortcomings of Brady's NAMPI, the MPPDA elevated foreign policy to a central place in promoting the future frontiers of the film industry. In their vision of corporatism, the industry's leadership recognized the value of having a single body represent their interests in Washington and in foreign capitals. Hays later pronounced the foreign division of the MPPDA to be "almost an adjunct of our State Department," and he found himself plunged in foreign-policy issues almost immediately.[25] In contrast to Moley's neat separation, however, Hays found censorship issues clouding his efforts to tackle such mundane concerns as tariff policy and free access to foreign markets. Only through the proper management of censorship politics could the MPPDA be freed to pursue its broader corporatist mission.[26]

Indeed his first crisis upon accepting the leadership of the MPPDA came from foreign sources: Mexico issued a protest and a ban on Hollywood films for their repeated portrayal of her people as a nation of "bad men."

World War I had interrupted the "greaser" cycle of films: *Tony the Greaser* (1911), *Broncho Billy and the Greaser* (1914), and *The Greaser's Revenge* (1914). No longer the villain of choice, the Mexican greaser became replaced by the kaiser and the horrible Hun. Then, much to the consternation of the Mexican government, Hollywood resumed interwar production featuring the Mexican as villain, as well as a cycle of "films of squalor" in 1919. The latter exaggerated the prevalence of filth and decrepit living conditions in Mexico, a type of tourist gaze that by nauseating counterexample sought to validate the superiority of U.S. civilization. The Mexican government's formal letters of protest to the Hollywood producers in 1919 had limited impact, and in 1922 the state sought an embargo on all U.S. films.[27] At the opening business meeting of the MPPDA on 13 April 1922, Hays helped pass "a resolution prohibiting the production of any picture derogatory to Mexico." He later sent Bernon T. Woodle, an Ivy Leaguer versed in the arts of diplomacy, to Mexico to seek a resolution of the dispute. "[M]aintaining the attitude of an ambassador negotiating a bi-lateral 'treaty' to preserve the honor and interests of both sides," wrote Hays, Woodle found problems escalating beyond Mexico: In May 1922 Honduras suddenly imposed censorship regulations akin to draconian measures already in place in Costa Rica, and in June and November, respectively, Spain and Germany aired their own grievances about U.S. films. As Woodle successfully negotiated the lifting of the ban on U.S. films to Mexico by the close of 1922 – and Hays later exalted in the announcement of early 1926, "Motion Pictures Gain Favor over Mexican Bullfighting" – the MPPDA realized the urgency of creating a more developed foreign-policy apparatus.[28]

Elite opinion in the United States had already become agitated about the dangers of motion pictures in subverting long-term foreign-policy aims, an awareness heightened by the role of propaganda in World War I. In the July 1921 issue of *Atlantic Monthly*, Kathleen Gerould warned that, "according to unquestionable authority," films had been causing

such harm among the brown and yellow races . . . I have heard it said and corroborated, in unimpeachable quarters, that to the movies is due a large part of the unrest of India. For a decade, the East Indian has been gazing upon the white man's movie; and it is inevitable that he should ask why the people who behave that way at home should consider that they have a divine mission to civilize and govern other races.

Her "unimpeachable" authorities included J. O. P. Bland, a man "who has been observing alien races in their own habitat for many years, with patient precision, [and] avers that the American (and perhaps European) movie is doing incalculable harm to the mixed populaces of the South American republics." She then drew special attention to the reprobate behavior of Western females on celluloid:

[W]e can perfectly see that to the Hindu and the Mohammedan, the Japanese and the South American of Hispano–Moorish social tradition, the spectacle of the movie heroine who is not only unchaperoned but scantily dressed, who more or less innocently "vamps" every man within striking radius, who drives her own car through the slums at midnight, who places herself constantly in perilous or unworthy contact yet who is on the whole considered a praiseworthy and eminently marriageable young woman, is not calculated to enhance the reputation of Europe or the United States. She violates every law of decency, save one, that is known to the Hindu, the Japanese, or the mestizo of South America. It is scarcely conceivable to them that anyone but a prostitute should behave like that. Yet they have it on good authority – the film – that she is the daughter of the American millionaire, or the British peer, who considers himself immeasurably the poor Hindu's, the poor Jap's, the poor peon's superior.[29]

Eighteen months into Hays's reign at the MPPDA, former U.S. Secretary of State Charles Evans Hughes declared:

I wish indeed that the important educational instrument, the moving picture, was not so frequently used in foreign countries to give a false impression of American life. It is most discouraging to reflect upon the extent to which the best efforts of educators and the men of public affairs are thwarted by a pernicious distortion among other people with respect to the way in which our people live and the prevalence of vice and crime.[30]

Most critics left the impression that the interwar film industry operated in a sea of unrestraint and therefore became a vessel of licentiousness steered toward bacchanalia and orgy. Quite the contrary, film emerged as a controlled medium under growing levels of constraint:[31]

State and Municipal Censorship Boards. These gained additional clout from the Supreme Court's refusal to grant film First Amendment protections of freedom of speech. In 1907, Chicago became the first major city to establish a censorship board, and it soon found multifarious emulators. At the time Hays came to power, thirty-six states had bills pending that advocated censorship. The Christian moral crusaders Fred Eastman and Edward Ouellette, nevertheless, bemoaned the Film Czar's triumphs:

Mr. Hays succeeded in his job so well that every one of the thirty-six state censorship battles was called off. Now, only seven states – Pennsylvania, Kansas, Ohio, Maryland, New York, Massachusetts, and Virginia – have any kind of censorship provision – all these laws were passed before the advent of Mr. Hays.[32]

Domestic Pressure Groups, Particularly Women's Clubs and Religious Organizations. The Daughters of the American Revolution proved assertive in the early Hays years but, as will be seen, other groups agitating for film reform multiplied rapidly in the 1920s and 1930s.

Foreign Governments, Censorship Boards, and International Pressure Groups. Most European nations launched movements for a morally hygienic cinema prior to World War I and even before the advent of Hollywood. In Berlin during 1907, activists started the *Kinematographische Reformvereinigung*, often described in the Anglo–American world as the Kino Reform Movement. Seeking a wider array of educational and nature films as well as the protection of women and children, the German movement gained a second wave of momentum after 1918, when the lifting of censorship led to an outpouring of sexually explicit cinema fare. By 1921, the "smut-merchants" were throttled when parliamentary lobbying produced a resumption of censorship.[33]

Well before the German "smut" floodgates had been opened in 1918, the British Home Office and the British Board of Film Censors (BBFC) had objected to flagrant Teutonic output. The Incorporated Association of Kinematograph Manufacturers had told Home Secretary Herbert Samuel on 19 April 1916 that "The Board [BBFC] have done much to stop objectionable films; most of those relating to sexual matters are of German and Scandinavian origins. It is believed that the German manufacturers took up this line of film because the Police disallowed anything touching on breaches of law and order, thus limiting the choice of subject."[34] Back in 1909, Britain's Parliament had given local authorities wider powers to shut down cinemas, ostensibly for fire safety but in reality to check impresarios of sleaze. Founded in 1912, the British Board of Film Censors came under film-trade control as a means of granting exhibition certificates to individual movies, thus ensuring their morally upright quality. A variety of efforts to strengthen the BBFC by, for instance, putting the body under Home Office control floundered because the film-trade leadership had fears of creeping state control. With support from Boy Scout founder Robert Baden-Powell and the Lord Bishop of Birmingham, the National Council on Public Morals sought in vain a system of national state censorship that could supplant the BBFC.

The artiste held U.S. films of the 1930s up to ridicule for the convention of separate beds for husband and wife, but this was just one of many restrictions imposed by the British Board of Film Censors, representing a nation that received compliance because it remained Hollywood's largest overseas market.

Elsewhere the anthropologist Hortense Powdermaker told of a Hollywood studio that

feared that a picture that was supposed to open with several Mexicans embroiled in a street fight might be offensive to Mexicans. Since a fight was a necessary part of the plot they kept it, but changed the fighting characters from Mexicans to gypsies. The studio representative blandly remarked that the gypsies had no country or organization to register a protest.[35]

Indeed in 1937 Mexico banned importation of Columbia Pictures' *Lawless Riders* "Because a character depicted as a Mexican, wearing a big sombrero, is kicked around and laughed at."[36] When the U.S. State Department appeared puzzled in 1928 that the Mexican government had failed to protest the movie *The Dove*, apparently featuring a prominent Mexican villain, the MPPDA's Frederick L. Herron claimed that "the quiescent attitude of Mexico results from the fact that certain motion picture interests in the United States have bought or may buy scenarios from a third secretary of the Mexican Embassy, who appears to consider himself a budding writer of scenarios."[37] Upon closer examination, the film's villain Don José María y Sandoval (played by Noah Beery) described himself as "the bes' dam *caballero* in Costa Roja," which the title cards cautiously locate as somewhere in the Mediterranean. When RKO remade the film as a talkie in 1932 with the title *Girl of the Rio*, its producers inconveniently forgot such subtleties and located the story in the Mexican borderlands. Leo Carillo plays a corrupt, hard-drinking womanizer named Señor Tostada (Toast), who frames a wholesome American for murder while boasting he is "the best *caballero* in all Mexico." Setting off a chain of sanctions forbidding its display in Mexico, Panama, and Nicaragua, *Girl of the Rio* initiated unofficial discussions that culminated in debates at the Inter-American Conference at Buenos Aires (1936) and a series of bilateral treaties between Spain and Latin American nations throughout 1935 and 1936 in which the parties agreed to ban films offensive to each other. Spain signed treaties with Nicaragua, El Salvador, Peru, and Chile, while Peru reached similar accords with Chile and Argentina. In the text that served as the model for these agreements, the 1935 Film Treaty between Spain and El Salvador pledged these countries to

regard as disparaging to and to prohibit the trade and circulation and exhibition in both countries of cinematographic films or reels, sound or silent . . . which attack, slander, defame, or ridicule, insult, or misrepresent directly or indirectly, the uses, institutions, habits, characteristics, or peculiarities of or incidents occurring in Spain and Salvador.[38]

It should be conceded that Hollywood had early on found that frequent use of false locales did not prevent nationalist uprisings against its productions. Hoping to avoid trouble from either Spain or France, Universal in its film *The Boudoir Diplomat* (1930) instead sought to locate the action in "a mythical kingdom or Russia or some kingdom where it will do no harm." The company settled on "the Kingdom of Luvaria." Even so, Major Herron had to get them to drop the names "Belgra" and "Slavia" for the cities of "Luvaria," as he argued that the similarities to Belgrade and Yugoslavia could outrage citizens of that strife-torn Balkan nation. This same company would at least feel beyond reproach against nationalist agitation in the making of *Dracula* (1931) when James B. Fisher of the Studio Relations Committee (SRC) judged that "Dracula is not really a human being so he cannot conceivably cause any trouble." Meanwhile, Pathé decided to make a film called *Her Man* (1930) about a pimp-dominated prostitute, a story vaguely claimed to be on the "scarlet streets of the wickedest pleasure-mad city of the Universe." When Cubans noticed a picture of Morro Castle in the background of the publicity posters, the protests began, with the Cuban embassy leading the charge. The company pledged to eliminate this famous Cuban site from the film. The upshot and perhaps irony of these protests, as the distinguished film scholar Ruth Vasey has suggested, is that Hollywood's heightened attention to Latin sensitivities and nuances rendered the U.S. film industry better able to know what it would take to retain its dominance over South American markets. Alas, she laments, "The industry was only intent on appeasing its foreign territories in order to occupy them."[39]

The Emerging Bodies for Self-Regulation and Precensorship Organized by the Hays Organization. Hays met grass-roots initiatives with the gradual development of a Production Code responsive to pressure groups and censorship boards, both domestic and foreign. Meanwhile, he built up overseas staff and offices, while cultivating MPPDA links with the Departments of State and Commerce. Frederick L. Herron, whose sister later became Hays's second wife, had served in the U.S. diplomatic corps prior to World War I; he would lead the MPPDA's Foreign Department during 1922–41.

Concerning the Production Code, Hays oversaw three stages of evolution before its adoption in 1930. First, in 1924, the MPPDA agreed to "The Formula," a Hays directive to avoid filming salacious books and winning audiences through "dishonest advertising." Then, in 1926, he reassigned his Director of Public Relations, Jayson S. Joy, to run the Studio Relations

Committee, a body that sought greater compliance with the Formula. Finding the Formula too vague, Colonel Joy worked in 1927 with the West Coast Association in establishing standards. Stressing the autonomy of the West Coast group from the MPPDA because "the adoption of a practical production policy . . . might well have constituted a restraint of trade," Hays declared that "I am lawyer enough to know there is sometimes a distinction between what is morally right and what is legally defensible."[40] Spurred by talks with Hays, the West Coast Association appointed a committee including MGM production head Irving G. Thalberg, film editor E. H. Allen, and Fox Films producer Sol Wurtzel. They adopted what later came to be known as the MPPDA's "pre-Code" or its "Don'ts and Be Carefuls." The original draft provided eleven prohibitions ("Don'ts") designed to placate critics of the industry in the United States and abroad. These included the avoidance of:

Pointed profanity – by either title or lip: this includes the words God, Lord, Jesus Christ (unless they be used reverently in connection with proper religious ceremonies), hell, damn, gawd, and every other profane and vulgar expression however it may be spelled.
   Any licentious or suggestive nudity – in fact or in silhouette; and any lecherous or licentious notice thereof by other characters in the picture.
   The illegal traffic in drugs.
   Any inference of sex perversion.
   White slavery.
   Miscegenation (sex relationships between the white and black races).
   Sex hygiene and venereal diseases.
   Scenes of actual childbirth – in fact or in silhouette.
   Children's sex organs.
   Ridicule of the clergy.
   Willful offense to any nation, race, or creed.[41]

In retrospect, Hays recognized several problems with this effort: Most important were the absence of a philosophical rationale for its principles and its optional nature, subject to the choice of individual producers "submitting or declining to submit scenarios to Joy's committee in advance of shooting." From a purely business standpoint, Hays thought it prudent for the moguls to subject themselves regularly to the stick of precensorship. Of those who gave advance scripts to Joy, they found on average only 1.9 percent of their film footage trimmed by censorship boards; of those not submitted for consultation, nearly 6 percent had been chopped, representing hundreds of thousands of dollars in lost studio expenses.[42]

The industry soon found itself economically squeezed by Warner Brothers' introduction of the talking film, which raised substantially the cost of producing and exhibiting films. On top of this came the ravages of the Depression. A turn to sensational and lurid themes became one means of attracting audiences, claimed Hays, a strategy that brought occasional short-term financial triumph at the expense of the long-term industry health. The gangster cycle of films in the late 1920s and early 1930s emerged as among the most assailed of these developments.

THE CATHOLIC TWIST TO FILM REGULATION

In mid-1929, Hays turned to a pair of Catholics, the exhibitor and film critic Martin Quigley and the Jesuit Daniel Lord, to formulate the philosophical bases of a code for film precensorship. Weaving together a triad of natural law, Thomistic theology, and strictures culled from the Ten Commandments, Quigley and Lord came up with the doctrine of "compensating values," the view that criminality and immorality in some forms could be depicted so long as the perpetrator received just punishment in the end. Well after they finished this project, Jason Joy clung to the hope that producers could create a symbolic universe "from which conclusions might be drawn by the sophisticated mind, but which would mean nothing to the unsophisticated and inexperienced."[43] In the formation of the code, Lord and Quigley did not repudiate this view, although they appreciated the difficulty of producing art for a more democratic audience. According to the 1930 Production Code,

Most arts appeal to the mature. . . . Music has its grades for different classes; so has literature and drama. . . .
  [I]t is difficult to produce films intended for only certain classes of people. The exhibitor's theatres are built for the masses, for the cultivated and the rude, the mature and the immature, the self-respecting and the criminal. Films, unlike books and music, can only with difficulty be confined to certain selected groups.[44]

The Catholic layperson Joseph I. Breen, who would soon enforce Lord and Quigley's strictures for the MPPDA, pressed filmmakers to develop the distinction between "suggestion" and "depiction," the former producing the subtlety and nuance that would achieve Joy's goal; that is, appeal to the "sophisticated mind" without corrupting those thought rude and barbarous, or at best innocent.

In contrast to literature, film had a power and "vividness" capable of overwhelming the faculties of even the most elevated spectator. As the code expressed it:

The reaction of a reader to a book depends largely on the keenness of the reader; the reaction to a film depends on the vividness of presentation. Hence many things which might be described or suggested in a book could not possibly be presented in a film.[45]

In shaping the moral regulation of film, Hays's turn to the Catholics may seem incongruous with his devout Presbyterianism and the Jewish background of the moguls. However, the film industry developed a curious division of labor: Jews produced the films, Catholics took charge of their moral dimension, and Protestants represented the industry before the public and in foreign policy. It became known as a Jewish-owned industry selling Catholic theology to Protestant America.[46]

Operating in a WASP republic, Catholics and Jews did run into limits in their spheres of influence. Rather than impose their views on the industry, the Jewish moguls sparingly represented their own people on celluloid, while the Catholics serving in the Production Code office reluctantly found themselves approving the depiction of divorce and other affronts to their moral sensibility.

Hays's decision to lean more and more toward Catholics on matters of morality had several bases: (1) the importance of the Catholic working classes in filling theatres in key urban markets, (2) the need to retain markets in Catholic nations, and (3) his bubbling frustration with many Protestant sects whose leadership called for federal censorship laws and for added measure accused him, in the words of the liberal Episcopalian journal *The Churchman* (June 1929), of serving "shrewd Hebrews . . . as a smokescreen to mask their meretricious methods." Protestant enthusiasm for government censorship went against the predominant U.S. Catholic approach favoring organized boycotts of offending films and the expansion of mechanisms for industry self-regulation carried out in cooperation with Christian moralists. "We are not striving for censorship at all," declared the Jesuit Wilfrid Parsons in 1934. "Quite the contrary. The responsibility does not belong to the state, and we are throwing it back where it belongs, on the producers of pictures."[47]

Pope Pius XI initially hailed the Quigley–Lord document approved by the MPPDA membership on 31 March 1930;[48] but the gangster cycle of films continued to run its course, causing the industry many problems at home and abroad, particularly Italy. At home, Hays faced billingsgate from enemies of the industry. In a letter of 17 February 1931 to Hays, a person identifying him- or herself as "Disgusted" wrote: "You are responsible for the morality of our films. Such pictures as *Little Caesar* and other gang pictures are more destructive to the morality of the people and the civilization of our country than any other single force today. The public expects you to censor these pictures as well as the characters of stars." On 26 June 1931, the *New York Times* reported the "fatal shooting late Tuesday of Winslow Elliott, 12 year old son of a Montclair banker, by a playmate, illustrating a film scene the chum had seen a short time before." This led to the call of the Lion's Club for a crusade banning gangster films. A Warner Brothers official, who asked that his name not be revealed in apparent fear of reprisal, made immediate concessions. "There will be no more gangster pictures shown in Montclair in 1931," he pledged.[49]

The industry, nevertheless, had not finished their run. The film *Scarface*, slated for release in 1932 by Howard Hughes, led to all sorts of problems in foreign relations. After seeing the film in a prescreening, Colonel Joy expressed initial enthusiasm in a letter to Hays on 30 September 1931: "[Director Howard] Hawks has shown the picture, at various times to such men as Fairbanks, Thalberg, Harold Lloyd and others. They have each hailed it as the greatest picture of its kind ever made. . . ."[50] *Variety* later declared: "Presumably the last of the gangster films, on a promise, it is going to make people sorry that there won't be any more." James Shelley Hamilton proclaimed it "more brutal, more cruel, more wholesale than any of its predecessors."[51]

On 9 March 1932, F. L. Herron wrote Hays on the crisis likely to ensue from the release of *Scarface* abroad. He began by citing a review of the film: "Most of the names in the cast are indicative of Italian nationality; Tony speaks with an Italian accent and his mother and other members of his family are definitely of that race." Herron then asked Hays:

Just what answer can I give the Italian Ambassador when he asks us about this, after having promised him to stop the use of Italians as gangsters in our pictures; also, of course, SCARFACE, is going to cause bad publicity in foreign markets where the papers have been very vicious in their attacks on American gangster films.[52]

Italy's ambassador to the United States Giacomo de Martino soon thereafter sent a blistering letter to Colonel Herron:

This film has produced a very vivacious reaction on the part of Italian Americans. . . . In fact, an American official is heard to pronounce the words "Take them Back to Italy."

[C]riminality is considered something coming from outside and not as an internal national problem such as every nation has to contend with, as a desease [*sic*] imported from Italy and not, as it is instead, a plague which every civilization, even the best, cannot entirely eliminate. . . .[53]

After confirming with Jason Joy that in no part of the film does a U.S. official declare "Take them back to Italy," Herron otherwise realized the hopelessness of his case with the Italians. Temporarily willing to scuttle Hays's long-avowed goal of selling America to the world, he admitted to Joy:

My one hope on the picture from the United Artists standpoint is that when Mussolini sees it, as he already has asked to see it, that he may look at it from the angle that it is a good lesson to the Italians who leave their native country.[54]

Evidently not amused, Mussolini and his government imposed a ban on *Scarface*.[55] (Hollywood's leadership later made efforts at patching up differences with Il Duce. Just before joining United Artists in the summer of 1936, Hollywood's first Ivy League producer, Walter Wanger, met Mussolini and then pronounced the conqueror of Ethiopia to be "a marvelous man.")[56]

The problem with *Scarface* exposed some of the limits of the doctrine of "compensating values." There are many cases in which its logic might induce a producer to make a film more transgressive. As early as 11 September 1931, Lamar Trotti had contacted Joy about ways of accentuating compensating values in *Scarface*. In his memo, Trotti had observed:

[E. B.] Derr, [production executive] of Caddo [Company], telephoned Friday with a new suggestion. He said in view of the fact that Scarface is quite a hero, he thought it might help to insert a scene of *children being shot*. This, he said, would certainly make people dislike him. I told him that I thought this would only add further danger and that it ought to be avoided by all means, that so far from helping the situation, it would add to the problem. . . .[57]

Into the breach leapt Hays, according to playwright and syndicated columnist Robert E. Sherwood. Hays had his own ideas about how compensating values might rescue virtue from the otherwise wicked heroism of Scarface. As Sherwood explained, Hughes had originally shown

the chief criminal being shot down in the gutter by the police – which would seem to be a sufficiently idealistic conclusion. (Practically everyone who can read knows that the really Big Shots are not put to death by the law but by the Bigger Shots. The law gets them when they neglect to give the government its legitimate share of their illegitimate gains.)

However, the death in the gutter was not drastic enough to suit Gen. Hays. He proclaimed that the arch-criminal on *Scarface* must be brought to trial, convicted and sentenced, and that the picture must end with the public hanging. Public indignation would never be satisfied by anything less in the way of punishment![58]

Noting that it has been a long time "since public indignation has been satisfied by the hanging of an Al Capone, a Dion O'Bannion, a Frankie

Uale, or a Legs Diamond," Sherwood thought Hays pushed the story beyond the boundaries of realism.

When Howard Hughes protested that Paul Muni, the star of *Scarface*, had already left Hollywood for a run on the Broadway stage, Hays would not retreat and instead commanded, "Use a double!" Sherwood noted that Hughes eventually carried out these orders, though without convincing results. "It isn't easy to photograph a big trial scene, followed by a hanging scene, in which everyone is present except the victim."

Traveling to Hollywood with U.S. Vice-President Charles Curtis, Hays still felt confident enough in his enterprise to broadcast the view that "censorship is un-American." Hughes, following months of struggle with the MPPDA, finally knuckled under and sent the Hays version of *Scarface* to New York. "Packed with uplifting messages devoid of all suggestion that the criminal can ever gain an advantage in the battle with law and order," wrote Sherwood, *Scarface* went before New York state's board of film censors, who witnessed Hays in exhilaration over the insertion of the appropriate compensating values. Unmoved, the New York State Board of Censorship rejected *Scarface* outright.

"Which was a fortunate development," gloated Sherwood, for it finally prompted Hughes to rise up against this "medieval muzzling." Hughes decided to release *Scarface* in its original version in those states lacking political censorship. "In New York and other states," concluded Sherwood, "he will take the picture into court in an effort to prove that *Scarface* is not injurious to public morals and might even be beneficial in stimulating public protest against what is surely the sorest evil of our day."

Abroad *Scarface* ran into bans before five of the eight provincial censorship boards of Canada, as well as in Trinidad and Australia; but many European countries declined strict censorship of the film. Similar to Herron's observation about Mussolini, the British Board of Film Censors tended to approve U.S. crime films precisely because these works, by distasteful counterexample, ratified the superiority of British civilization. Occasionally it seemed salutary to remind their national audience of the many failings of U.S. society. The BBFC, meanwhile, cracked down hard on British films depicting criminality in the United Kingdom, a policy that ironically led to charges that European censorship boards aided and abetted Hollywood's conquering of the domestic market.[59] The MPPDA, in its zeal to return to its earlier stated mission of selling America to the world, finally persuaded its members to curtail the production of gangster films. As late as 1953, the body placed strict conditions on the granting of certificates to Warner Brothers permitting them to show *Little Caesar* (1930) and *The Public*

Enemy (1931). According to a memorandum dated 13 August 1953, the Production Code Administration (PCA), since 1934 the successor to the MPPDA's Studio Relations Committee, explained the need to sacrifice immediate film profits to the demands of U.S. foreign policy:

[W]hile this office had no fear about releasing these pictures in this country, there was a very considerable concern about giving them world-wide release. People in large parts of Europe and throughout the majority of Asia would have no appreciation of the fact that there was a twenty-year time differential involved, and would consider these pictures as *current* rather than contemporary. It seemed to us that we might be playing directly into the hands of the Communists, offering them material which they could use to assault the American culture, were these pictures to be released abroad. We told the studio that we would be happy to send the certificates immediately if we were to get an assurance that their plans were for release only in this country.[60]

Though the gangster cycle of films came to an end in 1932, Hollywood unleashed a horror cycle that antagonized censors, in particular *Frankenstein*, a film banned in 1932 in Sweden, Belfast, Ireland, Australia, and in 1935 in Italy and Czechoslovakia. "Because of gruesome scenes," wrote the Czech authorities, *Frankenstein* was thoroughly repugnant to national sensibilities. *Dr. Jekyll* and *Murders in the Rue Morgue* also stirred controversy, with Joy admitting that despite the latter "lack[ing] the punch of *Frankenstein*," the scene of "the ape pursuing the girl is sufficiently disturbing."[61] Films of an erotic or perhaps suggestive nature appeared on the upswing during 1932–4, as Hays himself cited quasi-scientific estimates that 24 out of 111 films in production during the autumn of 1932 took up illicit sexual relations.[62] With the ban on gangster pictures, Jason Joy wrote Joseph Breen on 15 December 1931, and forecast this increase:

[W]ith crime practically denied them, with box office figures down, with high pressure methods being employed back home to spur the studios on to get a little more cash, it was almost inevitable that sex, as the nearest thing at hand, and pretty generally sure-fire, should be seized upon. It was.[63]

The debut of stage star Mae West on celluloid in 1932 excited spectators and ignited pulpits. West wreaked havoc with the conventional Victorian assumption that solely the male took pleasure in sexuality. "The only girl who has satisfied more patrons than Chesterfields," as she was characterized in the soon-to-be censored script of *I'm No Angel*. (West, with her lusty delight in sensuality, represented a standing repudiation to Victoria's own reputed advice on lovemaking: "Close your eyes and think of the Empire.") Moralists delivered themselves of fiery oratory on the depravity of her films, though in retrospect her role as singlehandedly energizing a national crusade is somewhat exaggerated.[64] Another genre of films that attracted inordinate attention, the fallen-woman picture, sometimes depicted "compensating values," but in others the woman who adopts the fast life gains from gold digging a little too much for the guardians of morality. Throughout 1932–5, amid much press coverage and dissemination among elite opinion makers, a series of academic studies carried out by the secular Motion Picture Research Council (MPRC) identified these films as destroying moral standards among young women.

While the arrival of the MPRC's Payne Fund studies and Hays's subsequent reconstruction of events has contributed to the sense that 1932–4 represented a conjuncture of heightened sexual danger, the problem stretched well beyond these contours. The MPPDA enjoyed mixed success in eliminating past movies that had enraged the industry's critics. The Fox film *Hot for Paris* (1929), which in its negative portrayal of Frenchmen provoked rioting by French soldiers stationed in China, also faced a wave of complaints in the United States. In vain, the MPPDA tried to clean up the picture. In a letter of 31 January 1930, Marion MacCoy of the New York State Federation of Women's Clubs told MPPDA Secretary (and former governor of Maine) Carl E. Milliken that it was "quite the rawest talking picture which I have personally seen and it seems impossible that any others could have been produced which equalled it in undesirable qualities." Among the lines in its original script are the following: "Tonight I'll get you more women than you can shake a stick at," "No – the girls in Havre always give me something," and "I've eaten my breadfruit in the South Seas, where it's as hot as a bride's breath."[65]

The inability of the MPPDA to secure fuller cooperation from the industry in the rerelease of films such as *Hot for Paris* and regarding the repeated use of double entendres and sexual innuendos in the work of Mae West made Hays aware that his precensorship mechanism required a boost in regulatory powers. Unfortunately, his chief guardian of morals, James Wingate, who succeeded Jason Joy in 1932, seemed too preoccupied with narrow censorship of offensive words – notably the term "lousy," which gave offense to British censors – and not enough with broader conceptual issues, such as reconstructing narratives and creating values. The impetus for change came from the Catholics, though (as is often forgotten) with important support from Protestant and secular authorities. Noting his dissatisfaction with Wingate and later registering the controversy swirling from the largely WASP Payne Fund studies, the MPPDA's Joseph Breen, a conservative Catholic, worked in his spare time on mobilizing his church against the moguls, a hobby that would soon redound to his own leap in influence over the industry. As early as 29 August 1931, Breen wrote Hays an eight-page, single-spaced letter venting outrage at industry executives for their absence of moral probity. He presented among his allegations a recent birthday party that "one executive of a large studio . . . gave to another executive of the same studio." During this festive occasion, "The *name cards* of the dinner were *condrums* [sic] for the men and *cotex* [sic], on which was a dash of ketchup for the women." Insinuating that this was by no means an isolated episode, Breen continued that

One very prominent lady star told *a group of correspondents who were interviewing her* that she is a lesbian. Down at the Los Angeles TIMES they told me the most amazing story of sexual perversion, sexual irregularity, etc., that I have ever heard. Recently, the head of a prominent studio was caught in bed, fornicating with his neighbor's wife, by his own wife who came into the room, revolver in hand and failed to kill both of the bed-fellows simply because, in her excitement, she failed to quickly unfasten the lock on the pistol. A studio head whom you and I know *personally* very well is just now the laugh of the town because of his conspicuous and public liason [sic] with a star who is reputed to be the most notorious pervert in all Hollywood. And so it goes.[66]

While more restrained in his public pronouncements and in his letters to Hays, Breen sometimes exploded with volleys of seething anti-Semitism in correspondence with his Catholic colleagues. Writing Martin Quigley on 1 May 1932, he despaired:

I hate like hell to admit it, but really the Code to which you and I have given so much, is of no consequence whatever. Much of the talk you hear about it from Hays, or Joy, is bunk. Joy means well. So does the boss, for that matter. But the fact is that these dam [sic] Jews are a dirty, filthy lot. Their only standard is the standard of the box-office. To attempt to talk ethical values to them is time worse than wasted.[67]

Breen had indeed lost faith in Hays's ability to impose moral order on the studio heads. Declaring that "Hays is not strong in qualities of leadership," Breen suggested that he stands "in abject fear of certain of the executives of our member companies," a condition apparently confirmed in the *Scarface* episode: "Howard Hughes and Joe Schenck . . . have just given him the trimming of his life on the advertising and exploitation of *Scarface*."[68]

Writing the Jesuit Wilfrid Parsons on 10 October 1932, Breen declared that "Hays . . . sold us all a first-class bill of goods when he put over the Code on us." While conceding that Hays "may not have done this knowingly or with malice afterthought," Breen argued that perhaps "Hays thought these lousy Jews out here would abide by the Code's provisions but if he did then he should be censured for his lack of proper knowledge of the breed." He told Father Parsons that "Sexual perversion is rampant. . . . Any number of our directors and stars are perverts of the strangest kind. . . . These Jews seem to think of nothing but money making and sexual indulgence. . . . Ninety-five percent of these folks are Jews of an Eastern European lineage. They are, probably, the scum of the scum of the earth." As for his close friend Quigley, the coauthor of the code, Breen repeated his astonishment that "Martin . . . ever thought the Code could be made to work." Calling Quigley's knowledge of Hollywood "purely superficial," Breen concluded: "How else explain his confidence that these dirty lice would entertain, even for an instant, any such procedure as that suggested by a Code of Ethics?"[69]

After a year of frenetic correspondence among Catholics Breen, Quigley, and Fathers Parsons and Lord, they pressed Bishop Cantwell of Los Angeles and other high clergy into action. Parsons wrote Breen on 25 August 1933 that there should be "a National Protest Week . . . in which the whole country led by our people join."[70] Though Father Lord admitted "the worst of the gangster orgy is over," he compared the film moguls to those "who sold rotten beef to the soldiers during the Spanish–American War; or . . . the manufacturers who sell poisonous canned goods in defiance of the Pure Food Act. . . ." All embraced the doctrine that if "to make money, it had to be rotten, then it would be rotten." The Catholic masses, Lord thought, had to disrupt this economic logic.[71]

In October 1933, Archbishop A. G. Cicognani fired what Hays called "the opening gun" against celluloid purveyors of smut and criminality. As apostolic delegate to the United States, he thundered in anger before the National Conference of Catholic Charities held at the Metropolitan Opera House in New York: "What a massacre of innocent youth is taking place hour by hour! How shall the crimes that have their direst source in motion pictures be measured?" In November 1933, Bishop John J. Cantwell of Los Angeles appealed to the Knights of Columbus to begin a movement to clean up films, then followed up later that month in Washington before the annual meeting of U.S. Catholic bishops. Concerning the erosion of the Production Code, Cantwell observed that:

Steadily during the past two or three years the regulations of the Code have been "honored more in the breach than in the observance," [*sic*] with the result that a new and complete overhauling is imperative if the motion picture industry is to survive unhampered by additional state censorship bodies or a federal censorship law.[72]

Spurred by Cantwell, the bishops immediately appointed a committee on films. In an announcement from Washington, D.C., on 28 April 1934, this committee unveiled the Legion of Decency, a body designed to mobilize the Catholic laity against depravity in films. Requesting that Catholics take a pledge not to patronize filthy films, the Legion in the opening weeks received hundreds of thousands of signatures, later reaching 7–9 million adherents, according to the church sociologist Father Paul Facey.[73] In many dioceses, the Legion also asked Protestant leaders for support to clean up films, in a spirit of ecumenism atypical of pre–Vatican II Catholicism.

The movie moguls had sometimes stood complacent amid other moral panics about film, but this time they took immediate notice. "Scared by the specter of a possible boycott . . . that could easily extend around the earth, the moguls who make America's motion-pictures have once more taken a vow to purify their products . . . ," wrote the *Literary Digest* (New York, 7 July 1934). Only this time, their vow proved to be no temporary ploy, no public relations palliative. "What scared them as they had never been scared before . . . was . . . that the Catholic Church, like the American film, is universal. . . . Catholic Bishops can make shots which will be heard around the world," concluded the *Literary Digest*.

THE LEGION'S ARMY OF NON-CATHOLIC ALLIES

The Catholics soon benefited from a stampede of allies:

Protestants. The Federal Council of Churches of Christ in America, the largest Protestant organization in the United States – representing leading Presbyterians, Southern Methodists, Lutherans, Baptists, Methodists, Moravians, Episcopalians, Dutch and German Reformed sects – passed a resolution on 22 June 1934 supporting the work of the Legion of Decency. The council recommended:

that members of the Protestant Churches, their families and citizens generally, cooperate with the objectives of the Legion of Decency by refusing to patronize objectionable films. The binding pledge of the Legion may or may not be signed, according to the individual conscience, but its purpose should be kept.[74]

Several major metropolitan areas witnessed Catholic, Protestant, and Jewish cooperation against offensive films. On 13 June 1934, the Chicago City Council officially endorsed the nationwide crusade and demanded cooperation among the Federation of Protestant Churches, the Catholics, and Jewish synagogues in buttressing Legion of Decency efforts.[75]

Jews. Attending a conference of rabbis in mid-1934, Solomon Goldman, the spiritual leader of Temple Anshe Emet, hailed the development, declaring that

Jewish leaders from all over the United States have pleaded from the pulpit for some means of cleaning up the movies. I am sure that throngs of our people now not only heard with pleasure of the formation of a concerted movement against smut, but also will sign the pledge to boycott suggestive photoplays.[76]

Convening in Wernersville, Pennsylvania, the Central Conference of Jewish Rabbis passed a resolution praising the Legion's efforts and setting up a committee to coordinate action with Protestants and Catholics.[77]

Overseas Support. The development of Catholic organizations on film in France and Belgium proceeded apace (see Part III on these countries). The moguls naturally worried about the Legion's overseas Catholic allies, but the movement also received a boost from much of the non-Catholic world. "China, Japan, Turkey, and several European countries have complained with increasing bitterness against some of Hollywood's portrayals of American life," reported the *Literary Digest* (27 June 1934). The Rochester *Times-Union* (6 July 1934) enthusiastically noted that reports flocking "from England are to the effect that the Catholic campaign in the United States, with which Protestants and Jews are linked, had found a marked reaction there." The enrollment of Americans in the Legion of Decency "is paralleled by the enrollment of 'Councils of Action' in the larger British districts. In South Wales, nonconformists are reported joining with Catholics in the movement to purge the movies of obscenity," it noted. The Dayton, Ohio, *News-Week* (7 July 1934) declared that "in Hollywood last week the sun did not shine" because from Rome "came a prophecy that the Pope would launch a world crusade to combat immoral films. In Germany *The Kid* and *Tarzan* were banned because of their 'absurd and brutalizing' themes. In Canada, England, and Wales groups of movie-goers organized to boycott indecent pictures."[78] With receipts from abroad representing 40 percent of the box-office total, Hollywood film producers could hardly dismiss such disquiet; but as will be seen, the foreign film monitors often found greater immorality in the works of their domestic producers and thus inadvertently legitimated Hollywood productions as wholesome family fare.

Secular Organizations. The Motion Picture Research Council emerged as the single most important secular organization in the United States to support the crusade against Hollywood-generated moral decay. Founded in

September 1927 (as the National Committee for Study of Social Values in Motion Pictures) by Dr. William Short, himself a Congregationalist minister, the MPRC featured an array of university leaders, establishment intellectuals, and social scientists dedicated to studying the effects of film on criminality, juvenile delinquency, and the mental hygiene of the nation. University of Chicago sociologist E. W. Burgess hailed Short for developing "a well thought out program of disinterested and scientific research as a preliminary to a program of social control."[79] Harvard University economic historian Edwin F. Gay, one of the founders of the Council on Foreign Relations; Ray Lyman Wilbur, the president of Stanford; Mrs. James Roosevelt, mother of FDR (then governor of New York); Mrs. August Belmont, formerly known as the acclaimed actress Eleanor Robson; and public-relations pioneer Ivy L. Lee were among the early membership, the latter three eventually resigning. Former Princeton president John Grier Hibbeen accepted its chairmanship in July 1932, followed in August 1933 by Harvard president A. Lawrence Lowell, who exclaimed: "I want to do some good for the rest of my life . . . the investigation has been thoroughly scientific . . . I do not see how I could decline."[80] Ray Lyman Wilbur became Short's successor as the director of the MPRC and moved its headquarters from New York to San Francisco, allegedly to be closer to Hollywood. Supported by grants from the Payne Fund of Ohio and the Social Science Research Council, the MPRC turned to the new psychology to demonstrate the dangers of film. Its research identified film as the culprit in the unleashing of a wild eroticism among youth. Sociologist Edward A. Ross of the University of Wisconsin proclaimed that contemporary youth are more "sex wise, sex excited, and sex absorbed than of any generation which we have knowledge." Moreover, Ross threw down the gauntlet: "If we wish to become the most erotic people in the civilized world we have only to continue to yield up our children to the demands of the motion picture industry." More ominous was the revelation by sociologists Herbert Blumer and Philip Hauser of the University of Chicago that their research on motion pictures in penal institutions indicated that "Several pictures in institutions seem to have increased homosexual practices, especially between white and colored girls. Whenever a fairly romantic love picture is displayed in the institution, the amount of note-passing between white and colored girls increases until it becomes a discipline problem." According to the MPRC's Payne Fund studies on delinquency:

Forty-one percent of 252 delinquent girls said it was the movie-made urge that inclined them to wild parties and which ultimately landed them in trouble. Rightly or wrongly, they attributed to the movies a leading place in stimulating cravings for an easy life, for luxury, for cabarets, road-houses, and wild parties, and for having men make love to them and, ultimately for their particular delinquency. Nearly forty percent said they were moved to invite men to make love to them after seeing passionate sex pictures. Fourteen percent said they acquired ideas from the movies for making money by "gold-digging" men; 25 percent by living with and being supported by a man.

Male delinquents, likewise, testified to using certain types of movies as excitants for arousing and stimulating the passions of girls.[81]

With the support of Hays, Raymond Moley denounced the MPRC's work: "Despite the absurdity of the New Psychology, it is being made the basis of a vast amount of pseudo-scientific literature . . . dealing with the supposed effects of movies on our children. . . ." While not every MPRC project ratified the dominant views of its social science leadership, the organization adopted a posture of suspicion and cultural Cassandraism toward the film industry. When not clothed in the arid language of the social sciences, their memoranda suggest an agenda more draconian than many of the religious crusaders in their midst. In one of the MPRC's main documents used for fund-raising and attracting establishment support, they wrote: "The men who control the film industry are mostly foreign born or of foreign blood. These men came out of the foreign colonies and have grown up with the industry."[82] An enthusiastic supporter of the MPRC who soon emerged as director of the National Committee on Education by Radio, Armstrong Perry wrote William Short in 1929 and alleged that just as the typhus epidemic had been spread by Italian immigrants, the Hollywood foreigners had carried with them the germs of moral pollution. In the former case, the Board of Health "had sense enough to lock up the Italian women who were doing the washing in the town reservoir, and that stopped the epidemic." Perry suggested that "if a group of bakers were producing a type of cake that appealed to children but made them sick . . . [s]ome might be found to be suffering from a type of insanity that led them to put poison into their cakes." He recommended that the

motion picture producers could be analyzed, psychologically. Their daily lives and habits could be known. It could be determined which of them, if any, had erotic mania, which were drug addicts, which were alcoholics, which were cases of arrested mental development and so on. With these facts known, it would be easy to point out the results of mental disease and other weaknesses in the motion pictures which they produce. It might be possible that many of these sources of pollution could be cut off from the stream of motion pictures being produced, by an appeal to laws already in force. The facts concerning persons mentally diseased, and the carriers of mental germs, could be placed in the hands of competent persons who were in a position to act upon them.[83]

Saluting Perry for "some good suggestions . . . which we may be able to make use of," Short responded that the MPRC still had to produce the studies documenting "whether or not the movies are polluting the social stream."[84]

In the MPRC's secret minutes, opposition to censorship often seemed a mere tactical maneuver. In its official minutes of 31 May 1933, its director and founder Short admitted: "I am not against censorship, so far as I know the members of our group, most of them are not opposed to censorship. But if we should be drawn into the censorship whirlpool, our usefulness as a committee would be ended."[85] The MPRC seized the opportunity to mobilize the elite press and the university intelligentsia behind the Legion boycott.

The Media. The vast majority of the nation's newspapers hailed the ferment against the film industry. According to an MPPDA report on U.S. press editorials, 128 U.S. newspapers strongly supported the Legion of Decency drive, 24 gave it qualified approval, and a mere 20 expressed opposition.[86] Squawks of disapproval could be found in the *New York World–Telegram* (26 June 1934), which feared that the nation's propensity for crusades led to the abysmal episode of Prohibition. In contrast to its view, William Randolph Hearst typified the spirit of the Depression-era press baron. Despite regularly delivering illicit love to a Hollywood starlet at the château San Simeon, Hearst hurled an editorial thunderbolt (*New York American*, 8 July 1934) that resounded from his Pacific Coast hacienda to the Eastern seaboard:

God bless the churches! They are performing their holiest function in preserving the moral standards of the people. . . .

Our screen is definitely not as degenerate as our drama, our art and our letters, but its demoralization is more dangerous. . . .

It has been faithless to its responsibility, indifferent to its obligation, and it is incurring today the penalty of its negligence and faithlessness. . . .

My papers . . . have often told the producers of their profligacy, warned them of the inevitable consequences. . . .

. . . The era of cheap indecency is over.[87]

The relative absence of dissent from the film crusade alarmed civil libertarians, who thought filmmakers to be stalked and terror-stricken by the now rampaging movement. Editorializing that the movie moguls planned to spend $2 million in order to present their side of the story, Massachusetts's *Fall River Herald–News* (8 June 1934) egged on its readers to step up the pressure:

Thoroughly frightened . . . the producers . . . are digging up some of the millions gleaned by pandering to morons and degenerates in a desperate effort to persuade an outraged public that they have turned over a new leaf. . . .
    If Hollywood hucksters of filth find themselves eventually hampered and harassed by restrictions that are too drastic, actually unreasonable . . . they will have only their own greedy stupidity to thank.

The issue of children often became raised by those who thought the claims of censorship outweigh those of freedom of expression. In a letter to the *Boston Post* (17 May 1934), Charles Hooper of Coeur d'Alene, Idaho, explained that he finds

movies rotten to the core, a succession of scenes of women smoking, drinking, painting themselves, and doing worse . . . eye-blinding light flicker, deafening noises . . . men and women in a mad whirl like an insane dance macabre; loud, coarse, slangy, vulgar language full of double meanings; gross materialism without a trace of spirituality or refinement, and frequent scenes or obscenes of nearly nude women and lewd gestures.
    And I saw what grieved me to the heart: Children, unchaperoned, laughing at nasty words and scenes.

The fear of film's effects on children sometimes elicited extreme proposals. The *West Tulsa News* (24 May 1934) seemed unabashed in holding up Nazi Germany as a model for reform:

Will America do as much for her children in the motion picture field as Germany? "By a Nazi decree, German children will not be permitted to see sensational or crime films." Will Tulsa give her children the motion picture protection comparable to Vienna [*sic*]? . . .
    From all that can be determined, Tulsa has done as much or more in this field than any other city of the United States, for which due credit should be given the Tulsa Council of Parent–Teacher Associations.[88]

There were less savory elements in the U.S. political landscape hoping to exploit such bumbling endorsement of authoritarianism. William Dudley Pelley, who founded the Silver Shirt movement in 1933, made Hollywood a central focus in galvanizing support for home-grown American fascism. In articles during 1933 and 1934 for his journal *Liberation,* carrying such titles as "Are You Revolutionary-Minded Through Jewish Entertainment?" "Has Your Child Learned to Applaud Murder Yet?" and "Sugar Coated Communism for American Movie Audiences," the former Hollywood screenwriter turned aspiring führer decried

[t]he fleshpots of Hollywood, Oriental custodians of adolescent entertainment. One short word for all of it – JEWS! Do you think me unduly incensed about them! I've

seen too many Gentile maidens ravished and been unable to do anything about it. They have a concupiscent slogan in screendom: "Don't hire until you see the whites of their thighs!"[89]

In deciding to intervene against Hollywood, the mainstream churches may have denied more dangerous political elements such as Pelley an exclusive forum for rallying new adherents. However, such a generous view of church action does not absolve these institutions from a disturbing asymmetry in response to the societal "menaces" at hand: that is, repeated crusades against Hollywood's alleged crimes and a rather half-hearted willingness to endorse vigilance against the ravages of fascism. An article in the *New York Times* (20 June 1934) quietly called attention to some of the contradictions in the church movement to clean up films. The Protestant directors of the Philadelphia Federation of Churches asked ministers to mobilize their flock against attending degrading motion pictures, but when it came to Nazi Germany they seemed paralyzed in prescribing action against Hitlerism. While passing a statement disapproving of Nazism, they vetoed a proposal to boycott German goods. The federation attached to the resolution on Nazism the proclamation, "We do not feel as a church group that we can approve the principle of boycott."

Others preferred to target individual artists. Under mounting attack, the actress Mae West found her film *It Ain't No Sin* a recipient of the Archdiocese of Chicago's "immoral and indecent" category, the forerunner of the Legion's vaunted "C" rating – "CONDEMNED." The New York State Board of Regents denied *It Ain't No Sin* a license. Shrugging her shoulders, West declared with requisite aplomb, "If they think it's too warm, I'll cool it off."[90] In the years ahead, West would be one of two Hollywood figures whose names were banned from the newspapers and magazines of the vast Hearst media empire, sharing the honor with Orson Welles. In 1936, Hearst proclaimed that West's films "pander to the lewd elements of the community" and called for Hays to begin a renewed crackdown on her work, his campaign and editorial outbursts apparently provoked by the actress's light putdown of his mistress, Marion Davies. (It is said that Welles's fate had been sealed by "Rosebud," the opening line of *Citizen Kane* and Hearst's name for Davies's genitalia.)[91]

While the moral mobilization of U.S. society continued into late 1934 and beyond, the film leadership for all practical purposes surrendered to the demands of the Legion in June 1934. Meeting in Cincinnati, the Catholic Bishops' Committee on Motion Pictures, comprising Archbishop John T. McNicholas, Bishop John J. Cantwell of Los Angeles, Bishop Hugh C.

Boyle of Pittsburgh, and Bishop John Noll of Fort Wayne, issued the following statement on 21 June 1934:

During the past several months the Catholic Bishops' Committee on Motion Pictures, in co-operation with the authorities of all the dioceses of the country, has been waging a campaign of protest against the destructive moral influence of evil motion pictures. There has been no wish to harm nor destroy the motion picture business. . . . But the evil character of portions of many motion pictures, and the low standards of some motion pictures, have forced the Bishops to take direct and aggressive action in safe-guarding the moral well-being of their people. These recent activities against motion pictures which offend decency and morality were launched only after years of vain hope that the producers of these pictures would realize the harm being done and take positive steps to correct the trend. The Committee is not hostile to the entertainment business; in fact, it recognizes entertainment as a virtual necessity in modern life. But such entertainment must be of a wholesome character, and to that objective the Committee has earnestly addressed its efforts.

The Legion of Decency, whose members pledge themselves not to patronize theatres showing offensive films, has gathered to its banner many thousands of adherents wherever it has been introduced. Plans are being developed to extend its membership to every town and city in the United States and to invite all persons in sympathy with its purpose to lend their support.[92]

Calling "purification of the cinema . . . an outstanding moral issue of the day," the bishops met two Catholic lay figures sent by the MPPDA: Martin Quigley of New York and Joseph I. Breen of Hollywood. On 22 June 1934, Will Hays announced that Breen would be given extraordinary powers to regulate the content of films:

At the quarterly meeting of the Board of Directors of the Motion Picture Producers and Distributors of America, Inc., action has been taken to amend its system of self-regulation in order to eliminate appeals from the decisions of the Production Code Administration to the jury of producers in Hollywood.

Additional local authority has been assigned to the Production Code Administration in Hollywood, of which Joseph I. Breen is the Director, and the personnel will be amplified. Any appeal from the decision of the Production Code Administration rests only with the Board of Directors of the Motion Picture Producers and Distributors of America in New York, which assumes final responsibility for the character of the pictures.[93]

Quigley and Breen successfully convinced the bishops that the new effort was in earnest, prompting other moral crusaders to accuse them of selling out the clean-films movement, including their past allies, the Jesuit Daniel Lord and Chicago's George Cardinal Mundelein.[94] The MPPDA representatives at the Cincinnati Bishops Conference reported, in Hays's words, that "the war had been called off. However . . . only conditionally."

This, nevertheless, gave Hays great joy, and Breen's hand became further "strengthened . . . by prescribing a fine of twenty-five thousand dollars to be imposed on any member company which should ever release a picture without the certificate and seal of approval of the PCA." Writing in the early 1950s, Hays added that "I am glad to record that in all the years since the prescription of the fine the Association has never had to invoke it . . . the PCA has never lost an appeal regarding a script and only three or four altogether with respect to finished films."[95]

The last statement may betray a certain propensity for hyperbole on Hays's part, as several directors proved adept at transgressing limits established by Breen. However, the new regime succeeded in containing cycles of raunch and criminality that could gain momentum in those days when the Hollywood producer faced a far less punitive and daunting appeals process.

The isolated civil libertarians quivered and quaked about the relative dearth of dissent from the moral crusade enveloping American life. The New York *Morning Telegraph* (9 July 1934) admitted that: "The amazing spectacle is the sheep-like way in which the industry, the newspapers and presumably intelligent adults have cowered down before the reform forces without a struggle." The *Morning Telegraph* largely blamed its own profession: "The newspapers with one accord have sided with the reform groups." The *Nation* (9 July 1934) took the heterodox view that the reformers had in the past inadvertently fed the aesthetic of "infantile salacity" that characterized much Hollywood production. As they explained it:

The Hays organization – trying desperately to please the international market as well as 10,000 different native women's clubs – has frowned upon anything containing the vestige of an idea because every idea is bound to offend someone.

Thus unable "really [to] interpret morals, manners, economics, or politics," they continued, "What in heaven's name is left them except a kind of brainless, simpering, hypocritical salacity?" The *Nation* also thought the apocalyptic rhetoric about the moguls' depravity had given little insight into the practice of their craft:

The magnates of Hollywood are not emissaries of Satan seeking whom they may destroy. They are . . . business men of rather limited imagination eagerly seeking for a common denominator, and so far unable to find anything except legs, questionable jokes, and bedroom stories which seem to possess the requisite universal appeal.

Swimming against the currents of the reform movement, they concluded that

If the movies were given the freedom now enjoyed by the play and the novel to treat serious things seriously; if the ostensible moral were not always required to be so completely conventional; then the very competition of serious themes might well reduce somewhat the number of merely salacious spectacles.

The National Council on Freedom from Censorship, a unit of the American Civil Liberties Union, met on 15 July 1934 and the following day issued a statement containing the signatures of Barrett H. Clark, playwright and critic; Elmer Rice, playwright and vice-chairman of the National Council; James Rorty, writer; Mary Ware Dennett, sociologist; B. W. Huebsch, publisher; Henry J. Eckstein, attorney; and Dr. Louis I. Harris, former New York Commissioner of Health. Sent to Patrick Cardinal Hayes, the interfaith council of the Legion of Decency, the Motion Picture Research Council, and others, the ACLU unit concluded:

In the absence of any constructive contribution by these self-appointed organizations, we fear they are laying the foundation for a form of censorship either governmental or religious, not only of the movies, but of the stage, the radio, and books, magazines, and the press. To the first class of censorship we are militantly opposed and we believe that any form of religious censorship would be subversive of the religious liberty clauses in our basic law, which guarantees the separation of Church and State.[96]

They called upon these organizations to clarify their views on state and federal censorship of movies.

Many jurists and legislators did not believe that the film industry was entitled to the First Amendment rights of other media. *Mutual Film* v. *Ohio* (1915) served as the landmark decision upholding this view, with the Supreme Court refusing to hear another movie censorship case until the advanced date of 1952. Speaking for a unanimous Court, Justice Joseph McKenna rendered the judgment in 1915 that movies were not speech:

The exhibition of motion pictures is a business pure and simple, originated and conducted for profit . . . not to be regarded, nor intended to be regarded by the Ohio Constitution, we think, as part of the press of the country or as organs of public opinion. They are mere representations of events, of ideas and sentiments published or known; vivid, useful, and entertaining, no doubt, but . . . capable of evil, having power for it, the greater because of their attractiveness and manner of exhibition.[97]

Denied the shield of First Amendment rights, movies remained vulnerable to insurgent campaigns for state and federal legislation. While Hollywood fan magazines became the target of Catholic boycott efforts in 1935 for their alleged specialization in "nudes" and "leg art," their publishers could at least vest greater security in the U.S. Constitution than could the film producers.[98] The Catholic bishops, as well as Hays, declared their desire to avert federal censorship measures. However, Hays in his ritual invocation of the phrase "censorship is un-American" seemed oblivious to the possibility that the shackles he imposed on the industry constituted an assault on liberty. A longtime Hays booster, the Hollywood journalist and historian Terry Ramsaye, sincerely believed that the decision of MGM to scuttle production of Sinclair Lewis's politically biting *It Can't Happen Here* (1936) to have "all of the vast significance that would attach to a decision by . . . Armour and Company to discontinue a brand of ham."[99] At the fateful quarterly meeting of the MPPDA (13 June 1934), Hays carried with him the doctrine of compensating values and the limits it imposed on the makers of films. The range of subjects proscribed extends well beyond celluloid fare for the prurient and devotees of blood-and-thunder. Declaring that the Production Code Administration's doctrine of "[c]ompensating moral values" demands "that in the end the audience feels that evil is wrong and good is right," Hays held a somewhat altered and abbreviated version of the twenty-page Code that listed the following proscriptions:

1. Religion, religious practices, and church authorities must be treated with respect, in the widest sense of the word.
2. Nothing subversive of the fundamental law of the land and of duly constituted authority can be shown. Communistic propaganda, for example, is banned from the screen.
3. High Government officials must not be presented as untrue to their trust, without suffering the proper consequences.
4. The judiciary and the machinery of criminal law must not be presented in such a way as to undermine faith in justice. An individual judge, or district attorney, or jail warden may be shown to be corrupt; but there must be no reflection on the law in general, and the offender must be punished.
5. The police must not be presented as incompetent, corrupt, cruel or ridiculous, in such a way as to belittle law-enforcing officers as a class.
6. Perjury, under any circumstances whatever, is wrong.
7. Riots, and agitation inciting to public violence, can be indicated only to the extent necessary for the purposes of plot development.[100]

The movie moguls' decision to grant Breen's PCA vastly augmented powers supplied Hays the means to infuse films with his vision of American values. Hays often spoke of the PCA code as a triumph for Judeo-Christian morality, though satirists were quick to note that many stories of the Old Testament could not be faithfully recounted on celluloid due to Breen's strictures. As Elliot Paul reflected:

If we accept the theory of divine inspiration, it becomes evident that The Author did not share the ideas of censorship now prevalent throughout the world and virulent in Hollywood. Unpleasant, even the most shocking realities were not glossed over by Him. . . . He did not soft-pedal the sex life of Biblical heroes and heroines or dilute His war stories to spare the nerves of anxious mothers. He did not side-step racial animosities or political controversies. . . . [I]f God wrote the Bible He took it for granted that the human race could face the facts.[101]

And yet, the twentieth century's greatest literature has been produced in a repressive wilderness, under the shadow of death squads in Latin America and Gulags in Eastern Europe; certainly U.S. commercial cinema did not plunge toward the artistic sterility so glibly predicted by the literati and the libertarian. By many measures, the first fifteen years of the code's stricter enforcement represented the golden age of U.S. cinema. Contrary to the Orwellian vision of repression, forms of transgression eventually insert themselves into all regimes of censorship.[102] Euphemism, symbol, and alternative systems of representation allowed filmmakers to speak about the unspeakable. Moreover, trial and error, negotiation, and compromise became inscribed in the process of deliberations with Breen.

THE LEGION MARCHES ON

The work of the Legion of Decency received powerful international endorsement on 29 June 1936 when Pope Pius XI issued to the U.S. Catholic bishops his *Vigilanti Cura: Encyclical Letter on Improper Motion Pictures.* Declaring himself "able to proclaim joyfully that few problems of these latter times have so closely united the Bishops and the people as the one resolved by cooperation in this holy crusade," Pius noted that "Not only Catholics, but also high-minded Protestants, Jews, and many others accepted your lead and joined their efforts with yours in restoring wise standards, both artistic and moral to the cinema." Through "the outstanding success of the crusade," he reported that "crime and vice are portrayed less frequently; sin no longer is so openly approved or acclaimed; false ideas of life are no longer presented in so flagrant a manner to the impressionable minds of youth." Though it was widely "predicted that artistic values of the motion picture would be impaired seriously by the reform insisted upon by the 'Legion of Decency,'" Pius judged that "quite the contrary happened and the 'Legion of Decency' has given no little impetus to the efforts to advance the cinema on the road to noble artistic significance by directing it towards the production of classic masterpieces. . . ."[103]

Pius gave a lift to the efforts of European analogues to the Legion: l'Office Catholique International du Cinéma (OCIC), representing several European nations, and the Centre Catholique d'Action Cinématographique de Belgique. As these organizations labored to deny exhibition time to the loose-moraled film productions of the European avant-garde, they came under assault for abetting Hollywood's global supremacy. The PCA's own reluctance to grant certificates to masterworks of European cinema made it a target for those judging it a tool of the moguls in securing monopolistic control of the U.S. market. Naturally the PCA thought that claim a shabby distortion of its earnest efforts in the policing of morals. Moreover, the moguls and their marketing experts remained convinced that only in rare circumstances did foreign films succeed outside big cities and university towns, the habitat of those scarce species the urban sophisticate and the cosmopolitan intellectual.

Ultimately the PCA succeeded in reducing the clamor against films as a source of reckless immorality and unbridled wickedness. Partisans of the Belgian-based OCIC estimated that 65 percent of U.S. movies in 1930 received either a morally questionable or rejected rating; in the late 1940s, they placed only 15 percent of films in these categories.[104] In 1934, the Archdiocese of Chicago approved 52 films as "suitable" and 41 as "offensive in spots," while rejecting 31 as "immoral and indecent." On 17 November 1941, Archbishop John T. McNicholas of Cincinnati, chairman of the Episcopal Committee on Motion Pictures, reported that of 521 films observed by the Legion of Decency during the review year of 1940–1 ending 31 October, only 7 had been placed in the condemned class, 3 fewer than in 1939–40. According to the archbishop's breakdown, 267 pictures or 51.25 percent belonged in Class A1 as totally acceptable, 197 or 37.81 percent in Class A2 as unobjectionable for adults, and 50 or 9.6 percent in Class B as objectionable in part. While the Chicago archdiocese had a reputation for standards more stringent than the Legion of Decency's, there can be little doubt that the PCA had accomplished a major renovation in the content of films with only 1 percent of the Legion-viewed films condemned in 1941, compared to 25 percent on the Chicago archdiocese list of 1934.[105] Certain legislators began to direct their wrath toward Hollywood less against immorality on screen and more against activities off screen. As the text of the ill-fated Illinois House Bill no. 445, introduced by Representative William F. Gibbs (Democrat) on 14 March 1939, expressed it:

Whereas the home is the bulwark of this, or any other nation, and the home is being destroyed in our country today because so little attention is being given to the marriage contract, and as a result thereof the divorce evil is gnawing at the vitals of the American Home;

Whereas, to our young boys and girls the marriage contract has become a play-thing, largely because of the examples set them by the stars of Hollywood where divorce and marriage are so common among many of the most luminous stars. . . .
Whereas, through the newspaper and radio, these so-called glamorous stars are held up as idols to young Americans, who believe that anything they do, buy, or wear is the proper thing to do and many of our business firms capitalize on this idea by advertising their goods as the same as those used by the stars of Hollywood, thus inducing the patronage of our young people; and
Whereas, when our youth read or hear of the numerous marriages and divorces among their idols, they think nothing of it and by such attitudes begins the insidious destruction of the American Home – a process more deadly and far-reaching than all the destructive ammunition of the World War, now, therefore,
Be it enacted by the State of Illinois, represented in the General Assembly. . . .
[No theater] . . . shall exhibit or display therein any motion picture in which there appears in the filmed cast of characters therefor, or in any poster, placard, pamphlet or other advertisement relating thereto, the names of any person who has been di-vorced two or more times. . . .[106]

Illinois did not stand alone in looking beyond immediate content on screen. In response to a previous British campaign against alleged Holly-wood cruelty to animals, Joseph Breen reminded them that he was interest-ed only in what was depicted on celluloid and not in the conditions of its creation: "What may have occurred in the actual making of a picture . . . is no specific concern of mine."[107]

CONCLUSION

There are three relevant conclusions to be made about the evolution and development of the Hays Office:

(1) Hays had been in search of avenues for strengthening the structures of industry self-regulation years prior to the Legion of Decency campaign. Rather than regarding it as his enemy, he skillfully maneuvered the Legion's efforts to overcome alternative campaigns, especially those backing federal censorship. Hays had incorporated both Catholic and Protestant moralists onto the payroll of the MPPDA, including Breen. While Breen and Quigley took initiative in developing the Legion of Decency on their own, Hays re-mained close enough to these protagonists that he could hope to steer the movement in support of his larger agenda. On 30 March 1934, Quigley wrote Breen that Hays "tells me, privately, he thinks the campaign is a good thing, but that officially he is telling his people that if it goes on it may de-stroy the business."[108] Contrary to the spontaneist view of history, Breen, Quigley, and the Jesuits Lord and Parsons carried out an extensive corre-

spondence seeking to galvanize Catholic action on film for two years prior to its fruition in the Legion of Decency. Throughout the activism of his lieutenant Breen, Hays seemed complacent, if not complicit, in the eyes of the moguls who, as Joseph Kennedy implied, resented his failure to anticipate and squelch anti-industry agitation.[109] Britain's *Film Daily* referred to Hays as Paul von Hindenburg and Breen as "the Hitler of Hollywood," a formulation that perhaps conveyed the MPPDA chief's loose responsibility for the Philadelphia Catholic's ascension to leadership of the PCA.[110]

(2) The view that Catholics engaged in a reign of moral terror over the industry is often a crude and ahistorical caricature. The historian Arthur Schlesinger Jr. asserted in early 1954: "The plain fact of the matter is that for nearly a generation the movies of this country have been filmed according to the ground rules of a minority religious faith."[111] Schlesinger's blanket condemnation of Catholic power in the industry became the preferred mantra of a revitalized liberalism no longer prone to scapegoating the Jews. Nevertheless, the dominant U.S. Catholic stand on film proved to be less supportive of crushing state intervention than the alternatives among Protestant counterparts. Protestants and Catholics served as censors in many nations; yet, as was the case of the Netherlands in the mid-1920s, some Catholics joined Left politicians at blocking (temporarily) Calvinist efforts to clamp down further on films.[112] U.S. Catholics, Protestants, and Jews all supported stricter moral regulation of film in the 1930s, a cause that fits Gramsci's description of a hegemonic ideology, one that is accepted as the common sense of an epoch and embraced by representatives of otherwise incompatible classes and creeds. Those who fiercely opposed censorship boards usually approved of limitation on speech by other means. In the early twentieth century, the Mayor of New York William J. Gaynor (1848–1913) became the scourge of moral regulators when he dared to veto censorship by the board of education despite a 70–1 vote in its favor by the board of aldermen. Nonetheless, in 1912 even this hero of modern libertarianism challenged "the people who are crying out against the moving-picture shows to give me an instance of an obscene or immoral picture being shown in them, so that the exhibitor may be prosecuted. . . ."[113]

The view that Catholics imposed their beliefs on the industry is vitiated by, among other things, divisions within the Catholic community itself. As Jason Joy pointed out to Breen concerning the film *Private Lives* (1931):

You even thought the lines concerning the Catholic Church were justifiable and inoffensive. . . . In fact I don't seem to find any agreement among you Catholics yourselves. Can't you go into a huddle and find out whether you have been maligned or endorsed?[114]

Those who offended the Catholic Right, for example, by rallying in support of Republican Spain may not have escaped unscathed, as James Cagney
likely lost the title role in *Knute Rockne – All American,* the film saga of
Notre Dame. Still he retained massive fan loyalty among the Catholic working classes. Though approximately a tenth of films in the first decade of
Breen's reign found themselves on the Legion's B or morally "objectionable
in part" list, a hair's breadth from the C or condemned rating, Catholic clerics in any case fulminated against this fare, to little avail. Breen chortled
with glee that the percentage of films treating social issues declined from
23.4 percent in 1935 to 9.2 percent in 1939, though his figures fail to register the findings of modern social scientists: a steady and sometimes increasing number of films during the 1930s that portray "wealthy decadence as
a danger to individuals or society," "big business villains," and "marriage/
romance across class lines."[115] The crusade against such potential class-war
themes came less from the Catholic film movement and more, as will be
seen, from the likes of former U.S. Chamber of Commerce chieftain Eric A.
Johnston, libertarian Ayn Rand, and a whole variety of communist-fighting
members of Congress.

It should also be noted that, in Breen's negotiations with producers over
the content of films, he often surrendered on positions made during the
initial advisory period in a movie's development. In February 1944, Breen
wrote Jack Warner concerning the advance script of *Mildred Pierce,* to star
Joan Crawford, and condemned it for containing "so many sordid and re-
pellent elements. . . ." Recoiling at "the suggestion of a kind of incestuous
love on the part of the man who is willing to marry the mother in the hope
of entering into immoral relations with the daughter," Breen appeared to
quash the film's production: "we respectfully submit that you dismiss this
story from any further consideration."[116] Despite the claim of columnist
Harold Heffernan that if James Cain's novel "ever reached the screen minus
at least a 100 percent whitewashing the fire department would have to be
called out," Warner Brothers made the film, retaining plenty of incestuous
fireworks.[117] At the end of the day, the PCA coughed up the certificate.

The image of Breen as an iron-fisted dictator who always had his way
does not mesh well with his accounts of the process. As he wrote Quigley
on 25 September 1937,

The constant quarrelling, fighting, arguing – the daily evidence that the sincerity of
those I have to contend assays about 10 per cent – the never-ending nervous tension
which brings sleepless nights that are harrowing – is getting the better of me . . .
I am due for a nervous breakdown and an early grave . . . my digestion has gone to
pot. I frequently vomit without any seeming cause at all.[118]

His colleague and successor at the helm, the Episcopalian Geoffrey Shur-lock, admitted that the PCA's goal was always to grant the certificate per-mitting exhibition, a climate that encouraged negotiation, experiment, and compromise, rather than the suppression practiced by a pure censorship regime.[119] When Breen appeared to be too activist in checking films sym-pathetic to Republican Spain in the late 1930s, Hays employed an investi-gator to rein him in, quietly reasserting WASP moral authority. Accusing the producer Walter Wanger of seeking "to convey support to the Red cause in Spain," a frustrated Martin Quigley told Breen that "Hays, as might be expected, is ducking the issue."[120] Hollywood did not, however, begin a cycle of Loyalist Spain films; the moguls sincerely believed that "message pictures do not sell." As Twentieth Century–Fox production chief Darryl F. Zanuck, a man with a penchant for crudeness, expressed it:

Every time I got together with Louie Mayer [of MGM] or Jack Cohn [of Columbia] they used to try to fill me with pious crap about giving the public what they wanted in those troublous times, which was entertainment pure and simple – by which they meant Garbo's grunts and Lana Turner's tits.

In *State Fair* (1933) and *Love Finds Andy Hardy* (1938), he found

nothing to worry about except was Janet Gaynor going to get to the state fair and Andy Hardy get to kiss the girl next door. And meanwhile, out there, the Nazis were on the rampage in Europe and our own country was going through a crisis of hunger and unemployment and upheaval.[121]

Wanger himself repelled Quigley's charges of a Bolshevik or anarchist agenda. He told *Liberty* magazine (September 1938): "I believe in bigger, wetter swimming pools and more polo ponies."[122]

Hollywood, according to Hays, produced entertainment and opposed propaganda, a formulation that shielded the industry from its interwar en-emies but became grounds for renewed anti-industry agitation during the cold war.

(3) Amid the cultural and religious turbulence, economics drove the MPPDA to step up the moral regulation of film.[123] The Jesuit Daniel Lord had advised the MPPDA: "It is agreed among you that *good morals is good business.*"[124] Warning his staff to resist production of sleazy films that ap-parently make a quick buck, MGM's head of production Irving Thalberg had cross words for one director who did otherwise: "You've got a smash hit. A few more like that and you'll smash the industry."[125]

In his corporatist homilies, Hays spoke often about the unscrupulous operator who kills the proverbial golden goose for all by profiteering in foul merchandise. In 1919, the Mexican government politely asked Hollywood producers to refrain from portraying the country as a land of greasers and squalor; they had little success until 1922, when the state called for a total boycott of Hollywood films. Faced with his first crisis at the helm of the MPPDA, Hays swung into action and opened negotiations with Mexico. The fear that Hollywood could lose its foreign markets, essential to the industry's expansion, remained a steady theme of the MPPDA's moral regulators. In a letter of 7 June 1932, F. L. Herron, the head of the MPPDA's foreign division, wrote Jason Joy concerning gangster films: "We are getting into terribly deep water and the first thing we know we are going to have our product barred from Italy, and instructions from the Foreign Office in Rome will be sent to every country in the world. . . ." He added that this cycle of films would deny market share to more profitable lines: "I would not be at all surprised . . . if United Artists [distributors of *Scarface*] were banned from distributing pictures in Italy, which would hurt them more on their Chaplin pictures than any others, as his pictures get splendid distribution there."[126] On 31 December 1935, Herron wrote Breen about a scene in Errol Flynn's *Captain Blood* in which the heroine Arabella (played by Olivia de Havilland) "has her dress pulled down in front until the cleavage is just about that in *Nell Gwyn*" – a previous British film first praised by *The Times* (London) (24 September 1934) for its portrayal of "a merry slut." Directed by Herbert Wilcox and starring his future wife Anna Neagle as the orange seller who pursues an affair with Charles II, *Nell Gwyn* had soon led to a moral panic. Herron reflected on *Captain Blood*: "I think the studio [Warner] ought to be watched because . . . we must keep our eyes on our money markets, and the main money market is England outside of the United States."[127] When *Pygmalion* producer Gabriel Pascal, intervening on behalf of George Bernard Shaw, asked Breen to restore a scene in which the father suggests his daughter is illegitimate, the PCA chief blithely rebuffed arguments about maintaining the work's artistic integrity by declaring: "If I were you, I would not worry too much about it . . . the fact that this particular scene will not be in the picture, will not impair one iota, its box office value."[128] Brandishing rapier wit to stymie the advances of Samuel Goldwyn in London, Shaw knew all too well the industry's priorities. As the playwright remarked to the former glove salesman from Minsk: "The trouble, Mr. Goldwyn, is that you are only interested in art, whereas I am interested in money."[129]

Partisans of the Legion of Decency stressed that its main tactic, the threat of boycott, relied on economics, rather than the state, in enforcing film-industry fidelity to the code. Their conception of the economic was, nevertheless, narrowly circumscribed. Preferring to target individual films, U.S. Catholics retained a suspicion of the WASP-dominated state, a stance that may have vitiated efforts at escalating economic pressure. Though the Catholic Daughters of America, with 760 "courts" (local chapters) in 45 states, Canada, Cuba, Panama, and Puerto Rico, clamored for passage of the Neely–Pettengill Bill, many U.S. Catholics frustrated industry opponents by remaining aloof from such legislative campaigns to ban *block booking*[130] – a practice that required exhibitors to accept films in advance of production. "Strange to say," once wrote John J. Cantwell, Bishop of Los Angeles and San Diego, "some of these vile pictures are forced upon moving picture theatres."[131] Exhibitors at home and abroad, perhaps self-servingly, blamed blind and block booking for compelling them to display allegedly filthy movies. Hays dedicated his lobbying efforts to protecting this restraint of trade, and the Catholics unwittingly helped him in failing to galvanize popular support for antimonopoly legislation. Thus Hays rather preferred their truncated definition of the economic. For Hays, the goal was to remove the moral controversy over film from the sphere of politics.

Though an innovative servant of capitalist interests, he may not have been the first of his kind to understand how Catholic wariness about the Protestant-dominated state could be exploited to sidetrack reform. Prior to World War I, Catholic moralists expressed outrage about the length of the work week and the use of child labor, yet many Roman Catholic leaders in the United States also clipped their words when it came to state intervention against these scourges.[132]

It could not be comfortably stated that the movie magnates had extricated themselves from further crises and suspicions. As representatives of an international business, they found themselves trapped between the sometimes contradictory demands of their critics at home and abroad. Both of these groups were unabashed in alleging the denationalizing quality of Hollywood entertainment. At home, the moguls found themselves pilloried for supposed deficiencies in their Americanism, a charge that proliferated on the eve of the Arbuckle scandal of 1921, found expression among some proponents of stricter film regulation in the 1930s, notably the predominantly WASP Motion Picture Research Council, and received ample airing through three sets of federal hearings during the 1940s: the U.S. Senate's investigation (1941) into Hollywood's incitement of the United States into war and foreign entanglements; the Truman inquiry into cost overruns on military films, with its widespread assumption that Jews used film commissions to get themselves out of front-line military service; and finally the HUAC investigations of 1947 into Hollywood's contribution to internal subversion. Abroad the movie moguls faced the reverse complaint: Hollywood's constant patriotic bleatings and *Yankee Doodle Dandy* celebration of the superiorities of the American way of life became the occasion for Europe's reactionary forces to blame the Jews for sapping national will and love of *patrie*, while more genteel elements decried the egalitarian coloraturas of U.S. productions that threatened natural hierarchy and tradition. The PCA gave Hays the means to excise much material from film that antagonized specific foreign publics; and Breen wielded this ax in some cases with regret, and in others with gusto. Hays's triumphalism about fortifying the PCA in 1934, however, obscured the reality that in a myriad of foreign lands the MPPDA's most contentious battles were yet to come.

CHAPTER TWO

Hollywood and the State Department
OVERSEAS EXPANSION AND AMERICA'S SUBVERSION

WINNING THE WORLD FOR THE AMERICAN WAY

"There are few American industries that are more dependent on foreign markets than the motion picture industry; and there are still fewer industries in which American dominance of world markets has in the past been more dramatic and more complete," observed the *Harvard Business Review* of April 1930.[1]

Despite foreign and domestic tumult against Hollywood films, the U S. government became committed to securing the industry's dominance overseas. Overcoming State Department functionaries appalled by the vulgarity of the entertainment industry, Will Hays successfully cemented alliances between Washington and the MPPDA. This chapter explores the growth of government service to Hollywood's overseas drive, repeatedly threatened but unshaken by several waves of domestic attack on the film industry. Hollywood and the State Department frequently faced common domestic enemies, particularly those regarding internationalism as anathema and foreign entanglements as perilous to the American republic.

Prior to Will Hays's rise to national prominence, the U.S. government established precedents for serving film-industry expansion. During World War I, the Committee on Public Information (CPI) coordinated boycotts against the showing of entertainment produced by the Central Powers. Working through the War Trade Board (WTB), CPI leader George Creel deftly banned export of Hollywood entertainment to those foreign theaters continuing to show German films. He also threatened similar sanctions against those theaters reluctant to show CPI newsreels. Grateful for state intervention against their German competition, the leadership of the U.S. film industry understood that Creel's program entailed costs: in particular, his obstinate denial of export licenses for any thrillers dealing with the desperado Jesse James, the skull-cracking bouncer Harry "Gyp the Blood" Horowitz, and themes of the sordid side of North American life.[2]

Although U.S. government officials exhibited early unease with Hollywood's lapses into the lurid, Washington became convinced that American movies facilitated U.S. preeminence in the global economy. Hays made it his task to reinforce such thinking. During the 1920s, Secretary of Commerce Herbert Hoover engineered a fivefold staff increase in the department's Bureau of Foreign and Domestic Commerce (BFDC) and placed its twenty-five hundred workers under the aegis of Dr. Julius Klein, a Protestant intellectual distinguished as an economic historian of Spain and Latin America. With commercial attachés spanning the globe, Klein brought home the role of Hollywood in accelerating the acceptance of U.S. manufactured wares and the American way of life.[3] Testifying before a congressional committee in January 1926, Klein told a dramatic story of being shipwrecked off Peru a year following World War I and noticing how American products had displaced the prewar dominance of British wares – thanks, in his view, to Hollywood. Moreover, he observed: "I do not think it is any exaggeration to say that the motion picture is perhaps the most potent single contributor to a better understanding of the United States in Latin America."

When asked if film could be of similar help in China, Klein elaborated that the motion picture

is invaluable in all markets where there is a high percentage of illiteracy among the people, for from the pictures they see they get their impressions of how we live, the clothes we wear, and so forth. In fact there has been a complete change in the demand for commodities in dozens of countries. I can cite you instances of the expansion of trade in the Far East, traceable directly to the effects of the motion picture.[4]

In 1926, Klein added a Motion Picture Section to the Department of Commerce, a division headed by Clarence J. North. Admonishing the Department of Commerce's attachés to remain ever vigilant, North asked them to report changes in overseas demand that could be attributed to motion pictures. Writing to Raymond Miller, the U.S. Commercial Attaché in Brussels, North asserted:

You are well aware of the important part that American entertainment films play in selling other lines of American merchandise. We have on record, in some countries, that different styles in furniture, bath room fixtures, wearing apparel, automobiles, etc., shown in American motion pictures has influenced the importers of such commodities so as to satisfy the requests of their clients. . . .

He added that he wanted such information on Belgium because "The Bureau has recently been approached by a number of important elements in the Motion Picture industry with the request that any specific examples that can be furnished as proof of this will be of tremendous value." Some attachés, including the dutiful Miller, pleaded ignorance of film's magical powers in transforming the wants of foreign consumers. Undaunted by the occasional rebuff, North managed to build up a substantial storehouse of cases ready to be unfurled before Hollywood's domestic critics.[5]

With a previous membership in the Republican cabinet and his friendship with Hoover intact, Hays found the Department of Commerce eager to assist the film industry. Having secured the services of Commerce, he labored assiduously at cultivating the Department of State. The State Department remained more central than Commerce in the industry's global strategy: Hays relied on it to carry out negotiations with foreign governments, many actively seeking to stymie Hollywood.

Starting in 1925, Germany established a *Kontingent* system limiting the proportion of foreign films shown in its domestic market, the beginning of a European wave of quotas. Runaway inflation in 1923 had encouraged Hollywood producers to withhold their product; with the ensuing economic stabilization, this massive film backlog came to be viewed as a threat to the recovering German market. The German scheme required that for each import of a foreign film, a similar German production had to be rented for distribution to exhibitors. A British Board of Trade inquiry concluded that exhibitors proved able to escape its provisions: "although the '*kontingent*' was 50 per cent, it was said that approximately 25 per cent of German films was exhibited."[6] In March 1927, the British Parliament erected legislation with a scale of quotas; subsequently amended in committee, it escalated the proportion of British films from 5 percent of the home market in 1928 to over 20 percent by 1936. Through the law of 16 July 1927, Italy set up a contingency system requiring the first-run houses to reserve one day in ten for Italian films. In 1928, France's Herriot government tried to establish a 4 : 1 ratio between U.S. films imported into France and French films exported to the States; but after Hays spearheaded a boycott, the terms were watered down to 7 : 1. Meanwhile, exchange controls became an added weapon in the arsenal of foreign politicians. According to Hays, "Germany was the first nation to set up exchange barriers as early as 1925. By 1933, more than thirty countries were forbidding the exit of any foreign exchange."[7]

The State Department authorized Hays to announce boycotts of selected countries inhospitable to U.S. films. On some occasions, State and Commerce appeared to be in competition over who could render the best service to the industry. Hoover's staff wondered whether the United States should imitate Britain's Department of Overseas Trade, which for part of the 1920s sought to harmonize policy between Britain's Foreign Office and its Board of Trade. Britain soon abandoned this experiment, and the United States chose to keep its State Department *primus inter pares* – first among equals.

A tormented Hays wrote the State Department on 7 January 1926 and requested its help "with the present agitation against American films which is growing worse and rapidly spreading throughout the world." Crediting that "globe-trotting observer the Prince of Wales" with having coined the expression "trade follows the film, rather than the flag," Hays reminded the State Department that the "screen acts as a voiceless salesman for the goods it pictures," and thus carries prosperity to the United States.[8]

The State Department swung into action immediately, directing its foreign officers on 30 January 1926 "to submit a thorough report indicating . . . whether you find evidence of agitation or governmental or other activity directed against American films." Requesting "suggestions for overcoming . . . harmful effects" from such agitation, Assistant Secretary of State Leland Harrison demanded that foreign officers "should in the future report promptly . . . any appearance of or increase in agitation or activity against American films." He concluded that in the event a government considers measures "prejudicial to American motion picture interests, you are authorized, if contemplated actions should appear to be discriminatory or clearly unreasonable . . . to take informally appropriate steps calculated to protect the interests in question."[9]

In the months ahead, reports on anti-Hollywood agitation flowed into Washington. In Germany, the *Tagliche Rundschau* (3 August 1926) declared: "The sentimentality, naiveté and tiring happy-ending principle of the average American film have provoked a defensive movement not only in Germany but in all Europe."[10]

In the 18 May 1926 edition of the *Berliner Zeitung am Mittag*, its film commentator observed, "The world monopoly of the American film first and most completely became evident in London. The British film is wiped out. (Do you hear that, UFA?)" Foreseeing potential doom for UFA, Germany's largest film producer, the newspaper attributed the U.S. success in London to the construction of luxury picture palaces such as the Tivoli in the Strand, the Capital in Haymarket, and the Plaza in Regent Street. Their goal is no longer one of "*'épater le bourgeois'* but 'flabbergasting the farmer,'" claimed its correspondent, who believed that Hollywood flourished through the exploitation of rural idiocy. As the newspaper concluded:

The Americans count on the innocence of the farmer, who is removed from civilization by many days' travel out on his prairie. All these masses of gold, silver, cut-glass chandeliers, thick carpets, pages in fancy costumes, all this carries a farmer into fairyland, while it turns our stomach.[11]

In Norway, the Communal Association of Cinematographers in mid-1926 resolved to raise 100,000 kroner a year to support Norwegian film and "for the purpose of combatting the unfortunate influence of foreign, especially American films." Despite having 90 percent of its screen time occupied by U.S. films, Norway had yet to adopt protective legislation. In the *Morgenbladet* of 10 February 1926, Beggt Berg, a Swedish photographer of African wildlife, warned in an editorial entitled "The American Luxury and Falsehood Film" that, having investigated film production of continental Europe and the United States at "the official request of the Swedish Government,"

I can assure you that this business is animated by no more honorable feelings towards our country's millions of citizens than the English–Indian opium trade bears towards the Chinese. I wish that all European parliament members could see for only half an hour the faces of the half dozen gentlemen of Galician–American mixture who dominate the American film.[12]

He boldly predicted that if they had, "before the end of the year European countries would be surrounded by barriers more effective than any erected at frontiers during the war." For Berg, "the American 'luxury and falsehood' film has made more people unhappy and dissatisfied with life than all the world's cocaine, tobacco, and liquor combined."

Not everyone in Norway stood in accord with Sweden's Berg. Even Henrik Berg (no relation), chairman of the Communal Cinematographers' Association, conceded in a survey on American versus European films conducted by the newspaper *Arbeiderbladet* on 6 March and 13 March 1926:

One cannot very well couple Americanization and poor taste now that almost all the best known European film-makers and actresses have emigrated to America and left their mark on the production of American films.

The Foreign Minister of the Netherlands, H. A. van Karnebeek (Liberal Party), claimed that Dutch efforts to fortify local censorship in 1926 had less to do with anti-Americanism and more with general revulsion against film from all sources [Fig. 5]. Observing that "many of them exhibit scenes of crime and . . . immoral sexual relations and there is a general opinion among Dutch Statesmen that films of such character have a deleterious effect upon the public conscience," van Karnebeek told of a Social Democratic Workers' Party parliamentarian who aimed to reduce the presence of cinema theaters "upon the grounds that wives and children of laboring men are tempted by a passion for these spectacles to extravagance and waste of time." This popular passion for film in the Netherlands may have been news to the U.S. State Department because George E. Anderson, the consul-general in Rotterdam, had reported in 1922 that the Dutch are surprisingly "slow to move in such things; they are inherently conservative and as a race they much prefer cafe life to visiting the cinematograph theatres." Though sometimes regarded as a Germanophile, van Karnebeek seemed determined to show that the Dutch politicians were even-handed in public policy and did not overtly favor Germany's UFA over the Hollywood majors. During the mid-1920s, the artist and writer L. J. Jordaan had carried out a campaign in the weekly *Amsterdammer* favoring German productions over U.S. films, one that too often revealed Americans to be a money-obsessed lot, bereft of the finer sensibilities.[13]

Meanwhile, the American consulate in London reported significant agitation against U.S. films on several grounds:

1. "British picture patrons are becoming 'Americanized'";
2. the decline of British customs and culture, "especially throughout the colonies";
3. "The system of 'block booking,'" which "leads to the showing of poor pictures";
4. the depiction of "crime and immorality generally," sapping the morals of "young persons"; and
5. the belief that "The British industry should be developed on the grounds of national culture and imperial solidarity."[14]

Regarding the last theme, foreign officers commonly believed that anti-Hollywood agitation had been generated by self-serving representatives of local film industries. Walter T. Costello, the U.S. Vice Consul in Australia, indicated that "The commercial criticism of American films emanates from a small body of local producers and is also aggravated and encouraged by English producers who are trying to establish themselves."[15] While warning U.S. producers to curtail the frequent use of the decadent English fop as a stock character in comedies, Costello found his thesis that Anglo–Australian movie interests were at the source of the agitation ratified by other foreign officers. In Spain, the U.S. consulate claimed that Hollywood continued to make Spaniards among the worst of its villains, but little agitation ensued because of the general weakness of the Spanish film industry.[16] Although a strong domestic film lobby often proved an irritant to Hollywood, the

DE BIOSCOOPWET AANGENOMEN.

THE BIOSCOPE BILL PASSED.

VERJAAGD!
DRIVEN OUT

FIGURE 5. Many nations tightened censorship legislation throughout the interwar period. In the spring of 1926, a new coalition government in the Netherlands with a Protestant prime minister heightened the censorship powers of local governments. A Dutch newspaper depicts a scissors- and umbrella-wielding opponent of the film industry who is forcing Chaplin and other familiar stars out of the country.

MPPDA and certain State Department officials likely exaggerated its role, preferring to tar opponents as animated by greed and self-promotion. Often the most active lobbyists against Hollywood appeared to take little interest in cinema as art, craft, or investment, a sensibility rendering opponents ill-equipped to fashion an alternative film strategy.

As consular reports on anti-Hollywood agitation blanketed the State Department in Washington, the MPPDA may have been heartened by the news that in many countries the upheaval appeared minimal or nonexistent. Similar to the situation in Spain, foreign officers gave many nations a clean bill of health, finding no virus of anti-Hollywood fever in such regions as Belgium, Bulgaria, Greece, Ireland, Latvia, Portugal, Switzerland, and Palestine.

Nevertheless, the State Department had some officials who liked to evoke former Secretary of State Charles Evans Hughes's speech on the industry's malevolent influence abroad. They represented a current of thought that Hollywood did not serve the national interest. On 25 March 1929, Henry S. Villard, a senior figure in the State Department's Office of the Economic Adviser, conceded that "Repeated picturization of American automobiles, furniture, wearing apparel, etc. has an undoubted effect in creating a market for such commodities," and yet he declared a certain sympathy with foreign critics of Hollywood:

[T]he French are resentful that their nationals are so often pictured as immoral, the Spanish and Italians that they are so frequently villains, the English that they are snobs, etc. The sensitiveness of the Latin temperament to constant tactless allusions of this kind has found vigorous expression on several occasions in Spain, Brazil, Mexico, and Costa Rica. The latter country in fact has deemed it necessary to legislate against the exhibition of films which might give rise to demonstrations or outbursts of national feeling.

While Villard tried to give constructive suggestions on improving the prospects for Hollywood abroad, he could not suppress his misgivings about the enterprise:

It is debatable whether the present widespread exhibition of American motion pictures is desirable from the viewpoint of the United States. It is obvious that a considerable proportion of the Hollywood product bases its entertainment appeal on cheap emotionalism, sensational or suggestive episodes, or over-emphasized scenes of wealth, fast living or immorality. The unwholesome moral effect of such pictures, especially on certain illiterate or ignorant races of the Far East, is in itself a serious responsibility for this country. . . . The many pictures of "wild west" shootings, the exaggerations of fashionable life (with such scenes as intoxication in a country claiming prohibition), and lately the "underworld" and "gangster" themes, certainly do not tend to establish a favorable conception of American manners and morals. That the standards of American films shown abroad is harmful to the country's reputation was pointed out by Secretary Hughes. . . . Although false propaganda of this sort is of course entirely unconscious on the part of the American producers, who are concerned only with the commercial aspects of the industry, it is largely responsible for spreading the notion that the United States if not peopled principally by bandits and bootleggers is at any rate the land where every one achieves financial or industrial success. There is the further tendency in the ostentatious depiction of riches and the attributes of wealth to make for unrest and dissatisfaction abroad, which in turn gives impetus to attempted immigration with resulting disillusion and resentment.[17]

EARLY DOMESTIC MOBILIZERS AGAINST HOLLYWOOD

The State Department had been under fire from several domestic groups for the help it gave Hollywood, including the Motion Picture Research Council, the Daughters of the American Revolution, and the Citizens League of Maryland for Better Motion Pictures. In 1922, the State Conference of the DAR asked the State Department to place an embargo on motion pictures that, in the words of Cornelia A. Gibbs of the Citizens League of Maryland, "debauch youth and build up ill will for this country all over the world." Claiming that the State Department declined to reply to this resolution, Gibbs further reproached the department's functionaries for allowing MPPDA Secretary Carl E. Milliken, the former governor of Maine, to represent the United States at the League of Nations Committee for Intellectual Cooperation and on another occasion permitting Will Hays "to send his employer's propaganda . . . in our country's diplomatic mail sacks." Unbeknownst to Gibbs, Hays had at his disposal a set of the State Department's secret cable codes even during the FDR administration, evidence that the Indiana Republican's status as an establishment insider carried over to his political rivals. Speaking for the Citizens League, Gibbs resented the State Department for giving Hays "our government's help in forcing films on reluctant countries that tried to cut down on the films the industry was sending them." Writing elsewhere in the early 1930s in the *Baltimore Catholic Review,* the Episcopalian Gibbs exclaimed that "The good-will of the world toward this country is jeopardized because we are pictured with an overwhelming predominance of debased womanhood, flaunting the technique of the harlot and emphasizing crime and lawlessness." She cited such "smutty" films as the feature *Hot for Paris* and the short *The Dancing Gob.* Father John McLaughlin of Saint Brendan's Church, New Haven, blithely declared the movie producers "a crowd of people who represent the most contemptible element in American life."[18] In a booklet entitled *The Moving Picture Menace* (ca. 1928), the Reverend Clifford Gray Twombly of Lancaster, Pennsylvania, opposed promoting U.S. films abroad: "[I]f we Americans do not realize their danger to our own life and ideals, many other nations like Great Britain and France and Germany and Italy and Japan are realizing the danger to their life and ideals, for they are vehemently protesting against the immoral influence and corruption of such American films and putting the ban upon them." In his five-part series for the *Christian Century*, which was later distributed as the booklet *The Menace of the Movies* (ca. 1930), Professor Fred Eastman of the Chicago Theological Seminary assailed the Department of Commerce in similar terms for its aid to the film industry:

> The Congress of the United States, in its session of 1925–26, appropriated a special fund for the creation of a motion picture section in the bureau of foreign and domestic commerce. . . . We have, therefore, a bureau in Washington whose job is to help American movie producers sell their films abroad, even though those films undermine the good will of our foreign neighbors to us. Why not a bureau to spread smallpox?[19]

Eastman asserted that Washington had caved into the demands of the movie industry because those in the command posts of the state correctly saw that "trade follows the film." However, Eastman urged Americans to reject the logic of the market as the highest recognized value in the society:

> Without doubt our pictures have stimulated foreign people to want to buy certain machines, household conveniences, and other American products, but if, along with these commendable results, they poison the minds of Europeans against American culture and misrepresent our ideals and character, is the net result a liability or an asset? What will it profit the United States to gain the whole world of trade and lose its own soul?

Eastman concluded that the filmmakers had won over the government through the media Svengali, Hays:

> He has given the "right slant" to the news. He has lulled the church people to sleep with his soft speeches. He has staved off censorship. His employers have just renewed his contract. . . . Behind a Presbyterian false front, they have gone merrily on making money out of muck.

Things, of course, were never so smooth for Hays as had been alleged by his frustrated enemies. By the mid-1930s, the Legion of Decency campaign had provoked scolding winds of criticism from the mainstream media about debauchery in the movie medium. Moreover, some moguls dispensed with gratitude to Hays when the political and social climate grew inhospitable to the industry during this renewed time of troubles. The chair of the Securities and Exchange Commission Joseph P. Kennedy, at one time a major player in the industry, wrote Raymond Moley on 17 July 1934 indicating disgust with those possibly contemplating the scuttling of the Hays regime at the MPPDA. "I am for him [Hays] because I think he is getting a rotten deal," asserted Kennedy. "He saved the motion picture industry at least five times in the past ten years and his efforts always were for decency. He just couldn't be one hundred places at once to keep his eye on them. Another good fellow getting a rotten break."[20]

The period from 1930 to 1945, enshrined as the golden age of Hollywood, brought with it innumerable stresses for Hollywood. From an economic standpoint, the movie industry received an incredible 83 cents out of every dollar spent on leisure activities in the United States.[21] Nevertheless, profits underwent wild fluctuations, as costs soared rapidly for the new talking-film technology and the luxurious picture palaces that represented for millions their respite from looming Depression squalor. Individual blockbuster films carried expenses exceeding those for the construction of large apartment complexes, with star and executive receiving rewards more lavish than most other capitalist enterprises. (See the tables on the following page.)

Five major companies underwent reorganizations during the 1930s, as the Morgan and Rockefeller financial interests assumed financial control of the industry's commanding heights. Proving themselves inept at reviving the industry, they sought to promote the efficiency expert and austerity over the extravagance and glamor that distinguished the Hollywood product. The bankers soon retreated, ceding further control to a corporate managerial stratum well anchored in Hollywood's production values and alien to Wall Street. Meanwhile, a federal antitrust suit of 1938 hung over the industry like the proverbial sword of Damocles, the weapon of choice in a battle that ushered in the breakup of the great studio empires a full decade later. After an approach by the MPPDA, Secretary of Commerce Harry Hopkins (1938–40) tried to shield the movie corporations from this litigation by proposing his own investigation and a mild restructuring of the industry. The Department of Justice may have accepted a temporary retreat, but it remained determined not to abandon the case for a capitalist order more hospitable to competition outside the MPPDA.

Hollywood's Total Production Costs,
Biennially, 1921–37

Year	Cost of production	% change
1921	$ 77,397,000	—
1923	86,418,000	+11.7
1925	93,636,000	+8.4
1927	134,343,000	+43.5
1929	184,102,000	+37.0
1931	154,436,000	−16.1
1933	119,343,000	−22.7
1935	161,865,000	+35.6
1937	197,741,000	+22.2

Sources (both tables): Leo Rosten, *Hollywood: The Movie Colony, the Movie Makers* (1941), and SEC data.

Executive Remuneration as a
Percentage of Net Profits, 1937

1.	Department stores	32.10%
2.	Motion pictures	18.96
3.	Meat packers	16.11
4.	Chain grocery (food)	15.58
5.	Cement	14.18
6.	Rubber tires	9.31
7.	Office machinery	7.99
8.	Sugar refiners (cane)	7.65
9.	Containers and closures	6.65
10.	Sugar refiners (beet)	5.18
11.	Chain stores (variety)	4.77
12.	Steel	3.66
13.	Cigarettes	3.63
14.	Chemicals and fertilizers	3.60
15.	Agricultural machinery	3.46
16.	Mail-order houses	2.97
17.	Oil refiners	1.67
18.	Automobiles	1.52

Net Earnings, Seven Major Motion Picture Companies, 1935–9

Company	Net earnings ($ thousands)				
	1935	1936	1937	1938	1939
Loew's	$7,626	$10,584	$14,334	$9,918	$9,538
Paramount	653	6,012	6,045	2,866	2,758
20th C.–Fox	3,090	7,723	8,617	7,252	4,147
Warner Bros.	674	3,177	5,876	1,930	1,741
Columbia	1,815	1,569	1,318	183	2
RKO	685	2,486	1,821	19	−229
Universal	−677	−1,835	−1,085	−591	1,153

	% change			
	1935–6	1936–7	1937–8	1938–9
Loew's	+38.8	+35.4	−30.8	−3.8
Paramount	+820.7	+0.5	−52.6	−0.4
20th C.–Fox	+149.9	+11.6	−15.8	−42.8
Warner Bros.	+371.4	+45.9	−67.1	−9.8
Columbia	−13.5	−16.0	−86.1	−98.9
RKO	+262.9	−36.5	−99.0	−110.0
Universal	—	—	—	—

Sources: Leo Rosten, *Hollywood: The Movie Colony, the Movie Makers* (1941), and SEC data.

THE ISOLATIONIST COUNTERATTACK

From the standpoint of politics and foreign policy, the MPPDA had to retain composure in the midst of several unforeseen spasms of hostility. In January 1941, U.S. Senator Burton K. Wheeler claimed that "the motion picture industry is carrying on a violent propaganda campaign intending to incite the American people to the point where they will become involved in war." In a Senate speech of 31 July 1941, he reiterated that "the motion picture industry has been carrying on the most gigantic campaign of propaganda for war that was ever known in the history of the United States." In a Saint Louis speech of 1 August 1941, Senator Gerald Nye declared that "these movie companies have been operating as war propaganda machines almost as if they were directed from a single central bureau." He added that "These men, with the motion picture films in their hands, can address 80,000,000 people a week, cunningly and persistently inoculating them with the virus of war. . . . The movie industry has a stake of millions of dollars annually in Britain winning the war. Are you ready to send your boys to bleed and die in Europe to make the world safe for this industry and its financial backers?" In a speech of 11 September 1941 in Des Moines, Iowa, Charles A. Lindbergh identified the three groups seeking war as "the British, the Jewish, and the Roosevelt Administration." In the event of war, he predicted "the Jewish groups . . . will be among the first to feel its consequences." They had been able to imperil the nation through "their large ownership and influence in our motion pictures, our press, our radio and our Government."[22]

In 1939, in response to Warner Brothers' production of *Confessions of a Nazi Spy*, the German chargé d'affaires Hans Thomsen warned Secretary of State Cordell Hull of Hollywood's "pernicious propaganda poisoning German–American relations." Under German pressure, Italy, Japan, Sweden, and Yugoslavia banned the production, and Goebbels's press department promised a series of films highlighting the blight of gangsterism and other social ills on U.S. society, apparently unaware that these topics had been a staple of Warner Brothers' Depression-era production. The newspaper of the German-American Bund (*Deutscher Weckruf und Beobachter*, 18 May 1939) had called Warner Brothers' anti-Nazi film a "nightmarish concoction" based "on the choicest collection of flubdub that a diseased mind could possibly pick out of the public ashcan."[23]

On 1 August 1941, Senators Nye of North Dakota and Bennett Champ Clark of Missouri had introduced Senate Resolution 152, "authorizing an investigation of war propaganda disseminated by the motion picture industry and of any monopoly in the production, distribution or exhibition of motion pictures." Convened 9–26 September 1941, the subcommittee of the Committee on Interstate Commerce included four isolationists (Senators D. Worth Clark of Idaho, Homer T. Bone of Washington, Charles W. Tobey of New Hampshire, and C. Wayland Brooks of Illinois) and only one nonisolationist (Senator Ernest W. McFarland of Arizona). Clark of Idaho chaired the subcommittee, while Wheeler of Montana viewed the proceedings from his perch as chair of the Senate Committee on Interstate Commerce. Though the specific remedies to be sought were at this point vague, Wheeler had directly warned Will Hays as well as Paramount News back in January: "The propaganda for war that is being waged by the motion picture companies of this country is reaching a point at which I believe legislation will have to be enacted regulating the industry in this respect unless the industry itself displays a more impartial attitude."[24]

Nye began the hearings with an impassioned plea, denying that his efforts were animated by anti-Semitic motives. His oratorical bromide called to mind Hilaire Belloc's observation that many people suspicious of Jews "excuse themselves as a rule at the beginning of their remarks by saying, 'I am no Anti-Semite.'"[25] While the isolationist movement has often been too broadly tarred as an anti-Semitic cause, Nye failed miserably in dispelling the belief that his own politics carried this miasma. He opened his testimony with the apologia:

Those primarily responsible for the propaganda pictures are born abroad. They came to our land and took citizenship here entertaining violent animosities toward certain causes abroad. . . . If they lose sight of what some Americans might call the first interests of America in times like these, I can excuse them. But their prejudices by no means necessitate our closing our eyes to these interests and refraining from any undertaking to correct their error.[26]

Unlike the Legion of Decency campaign of 1934, the majority of the national press rallied to the defense of the film industry in late 1941. Dorothy Thompson in her *New York Post* column of 12 September 1941, entitled "Our Own Dreyfus Case," proclaimed that:

The American Dreyfus case is a much bigger affair, a much more dangerous affair, and involves many more basic questions than the French affair at the end of the last century.
    . . . Through this case, Senator Nye and associates intend to awaken an anti-Semitic movement in the United States, stop all attacks on Hitler and Hitlerism on the ground that criticism of the Nazi regime is war-mongering, . . . and pave the way for a collaborationist regime in America. . . .
    It is the greatest Nazi propaganda stunt ever pulled off in the United States.

Thompson's rhetorical flourishes and Dreyfus analogies in retrospect seem strained and hyperbolic. While Nazi sympathizers such as the Irish-American director Russell Mack and the radio commentator G. Allison Phelps encouraged the inquisition, Nye and Wheeler appeared much of the time to be defensive about claims they harbored anti-Semitic views; and one of the most aggressive producer of anti-Nazi movies to testify, Harry M. Warner, found himself saluted by Senator Clark of Idaho as a person whom "no one on this committee questions [as to] either your Americanism or your sincerity."[27] One would be hard pressed to find an anti-Dreyfusard ready to declare the framed officer a sincere French patriot, save for Charles Maurras rhapsodizing in tones sarcastic.

Hays soon organized the defense of the industry. He relied on the ardent internationalist Wendell Willkie, a Hoosier native as well as graduate of Indiana University college and law school, to provide its legal counsel. Paid a handsome $100,000, Willkie proved adept at undermining the committee's claim to be free of racial animosity and divisive tactics, his legal advocacy aided in the public arena by a sympathetic media corps. Hays liked to disseminate the claim that of 530 pictures produced in the previous year, a meager 7 dealt with anti-Nazi themes. Upon seeing this statistic, many newspapers declared that the film leadership instead deserves rebuke for showing such timidity in an era of fascist menace. Columnist Archer Winsten of the *New York Post* (21 January 1941) remarked that Nazism has produced "the most world-shattering events of our day and age. Only seven pictures dealing with them! . . . To put it bluntly, the Hays apology should have been turned about. The industry might well apologize for not having made more such films. . . ."[28] Astonishingly Louis B. Mayer, the president of the era's wealthiest studio, MGM, attacked director William Wyler for the anti-German bias of *Mrs. Miniver,* a film in preproduction during 1941 and released in 1942. Mayer warned Wyler: "This is a big corporation. I'm responsible to my stockholders. We have theatres all over the world, including a couple in Berlin. We don't make hate pictures. We don't hate anybody. We're not at war."[29] The MGM leader's panicky tone may have represented a retreat from his Anglophile pronouncements at a lavish dinner of Hollywood moguls in late autumn 1940 organized by Alexander Korda, who in Churchill's closest circles was regarded as Britain's unofficial ambassador to Hollywood. Commander A. W. Jarratt happily reported to the director general of Britain's Ministry of Information: "Mr. Mayer . . . stated that, speaking for everyone present that evening, we could rely on the producers of Hollywood doing everything to help the Great Cause for which the British Empire was fighting. . . ."[30] Ultimately, Mayer probably believed that

Hollywood could deliver a pro-British film without attacking Germans directly.

Despite Mayer's burst of sensitivity about not offending German sensibilities, Hays probably understated the number of films with anti-Nazi themes. He furnished an analysis for Wheeler that, although "no appreciable fraction of even these small percentages of the total can be said to show an intention to incite to war," his office found that "Exactly 27 of the 530 features or 5 percent pertained in any way whatsoever to international politics, or current events in Europe."[31] Less inclined to diplomatic niceties, Willkie argued that 50 of the 1,100 films since the start of World War II carried war-related themes, and "some of these fifty, we are glad to admit, do portray Nazism for what it is – a cruel, lustful, ruthless, and cynical force."[32] Moreover, the allegorical message of Warner Brothers' *Sea Hawk* (1940), which championed English freedom under Elizabeth I against the rampaging tyranny of Habsburg Spain, may have merited condemnation as shallow Whig history, but it could not be viewed by the sophisticated as innocent of contemporary politics.[33] In sprucing up the script for Warner Brothers' production of *Juarez* (1939), about Mexico's Liberal president of the mid-nineteenth century, Wolfgang Reinhardt desired that "every child must be able to realize that Napoleon, in his Mexican adventure, is none other than Mussolini plus Hitler in their Spanish adventure."[34] *The Hunchback of Notre Dame* (1939) establishes a loose analogy between the oppression of medieval Gypsies and the plight of European Jewry. The Senate subcommittee proved inept at making such connections, as Senator Clark himself confessed that "I do not think I have seen over one moving picture in six years."[35] Senator Gerald Nye spoke of a list of seventeen films inciting America to war, yet he too displayed little familiarity with the movies, despite an extravagant assertion that the seventeen thousand U.S. cinemas provide "17,000 daily and nightly mass meetings for war."[36]

President Roosevelt had been informed that Will Hays's "idea is to prove that pictures are not being used for defense," even though "The other representatives of the Industry don't want that" and "the best men in the Industry are ready to go into these hearings fighting. . . ."[37] Hays had initially adopted the posture that Hollywood films were "pure entertainment" and thus innocent of politics. He may have worried that Hollywood would otherwise struggle if asked to name any recent films articulating the isolationist point of view, even though this happened to be a strong current in U.S. public opinion.[38]

Soon Willkie and a few moguls (Warner and Zanuck) departed from the "pure entertainment" strategy by arguing that historical accuracy required the depiction of tyranny. In contrast to the caution of both mogul Mayer and that of Hays with his strategy of downplaying the number of anti-Nazi films, Harry M. Warner stood defiant, proudly defending his studio's production of anti-Nazi films: "I am opposed to Nazi-ism. . . . I am ready to give myself and all my personal resources to aid in the defeat of the Nazi menace to the American people." However, he did not believe the few anti-Nazi films produced by Warner Brothers represented propaganda, but rather saw them as works of artistic realism. "I deny that the pictures produced by my company are 'propaganda,' as has been alleged," he stated. He then underlined the committee's failure to view those films judged as reprehensible among Hollywood's recent production:

Senator Nye has said that our picture *Sergeant York* is designed to create war hysteria. Senator Clark has added *Confessions of a Nazi Spy* to the isolationist blacklist. John T. Flynn, in turn, has added *Underground*. These witnesses have not seen these pictures, so I cannot imagine how they can judge them.

Sergeant York is a factual portrait of the life of one of the great heroes of the last war. If that is propaganda, we plead guilty. *Confessions of a Nazi Spy* is a factual portrayal of a Nazi spy ring that actually operated in New York City. If that is propaganda, we plead guilty.[39]

Already under fire from most of the elite press, the isolationist bloc in the Senate had particular trouble handling Willkie and the testimony of Darryl F. Zanuck. As we shall soon see, Senator Ernest McFarland (Democrat, Arizona) thought so much of the latter that it may well have encouraged him to recommend that the Dies Committee turn the tables and step up investigating the isolationists. Zanuck would later funnel another $100,000 to Willkie for the screen rights to *One World* (1943), the former Republican presidential candidate's blueprint for postwar order and a book the Twentieth Century–Fox founder sincerely believed supplied an invincible plan for international harmony: "If ever the world needed a picture with the theories of Wendell L. Willkie, it certainly needs it now." In Zanuck's vision for the eventually shelved screenplay:

[W]hen we lose our loved ones, instead of walking around with a patriotic halo on our heads, we should be damned mad about it and ready to strangle the first jerk who gets up at the peace table and starts yammering about Isolationism or the preservation of the British Empire or anything that does not guarantee equality of opportunity for all. . . .[40]

With an indefinite suspension of hearings by Thanksgiving, the immediate crisis for the industry appeared over. The congressional isolationists faced further ridicule for the campaign against war propaganda when the

Japanese bombed Pearl Harbor on 7 December 1941. The investigation seems to have reached a final crashing halt. In particular, Alexander Korda and Charlie Chaplin could cheer that they had been rescued from subpoenas seeking their testimony.

Nonetheless, these efforts produced lingering aftershocks, leaving certain film-industry personnel in trauma. Nye's suggestion that American boys would be sent "to bleed and die in Europe to make the world safe for this industry" did not go away, as could be seen in the testimony during 1942 and 1943 before the U.S. Army's Inspector General on cost overruns and army commissions. The producer Milton Sperling explained why he felt compelled to resign his army commission in a unit helping to produce propaganda films for Washington:

[W]hen I joined the Service many people began discussing the seemingly obvious connotations of that entry. . . . They said that the rich and powerful members of the industry were protecting their own by securing commissions for them, that if you went down the list of officers in the affiliated unit you would find that three out of four of them were, first, related to the heads of the business, second, that they were Jewish.[41]

Because of this, Colonel Darryl F. Zanuck, vice-president of Twentieth Century–Fox, Major Sam Briskin, who worked with Frank Capra for most of World War II, and Mendel Silberg, a lawyer representing Columbia, RKO, Hal Roach Studios, and Korda Productions, called a meeting with Lieutenant Sperling and others. Sperling observed: "There was great fear that the newspapers would take it up, particularly the Hearst press . . . a New York columnist named Ed Sullivan was shortly going to publish a column exposing the unit."[42]

The columnist and radio personality Jimmie Fidler, who testified against the industry during the Nye hearings, was especially feared, added Sperling. "That the motion picture business and the Jews in Hollywood were on the spot anyhow – the anti-Semites, the isolationists, the critics of the movies would fasten on this as an example of typical Jewish Hollywood procedure." He called this "a grim and dangerous situation."[43]

Receiving a letter from Colonel Zanuck, one of the highest-ranking Gentiles in the industry, Sperling recalled the following lines from that epistle:

"Criticism is growing – we are sitting on dynamite – this is liable to be the most dangerous thing that has ever happened to the picture business. We have gone through one Senate investigation and you can never tell when they will start asking questions again. The Jewish question has been raised very strongly." – "I, personally," said Zanuck in the letter, "will tell them all to go to hell if they bring the Jewish question into this, but you can't stop people from talking."[44]

Zanuck had previously shut down Wheeler and Nye in late 1941 by testifying about his Methodist background and small-town roots in Wahoo, Nebraska. Noting that Hollywood produced "pictures so strong and powerful that they sold the American way of life not only to America but to the entire world," Zanuck observed that when "Hitler and his flunky Mussolini" took over Germany and Italy, "The first thing they did was ban our pictures, throw us out. They wanted no part of the American way of life." Senator Ernest McFarland declared the speech "the best I ever heard." With new political trouble now brewing for the industry, however, Zanuck raised doubts that his oratorical talents could stem the tide of potentially hostile oversight.[45]

At the same time as the U.S. Army Inspector General carried out his investigation, Senator Harry S. Truman (Missouri) ran the U.S. Senate Special Committee Investigating the National Defense Program.[46] Congressional elements thought the industry might be overcharging the army on contracts for training films, and all too hastily judged Colonel Zanuck to be a double-dipper who remained on his company's payroll while using his military position to steer business to Twentieth Century–Fox. Suspicious of Hollywood, the Truman committee found its effort frustrated by the refusal of the army's Inspector General to turn over to the Congress the testimony of Sperling and dozens of others. Lieutenant Colonel John Harlan Amen declared that to do so would be a betrayal of trust to those who gave testimony under a pledge of confidentiality. Threatening the Inspector General with contempt of Congress charges, Truman ultimately failed in his quest to recover these documents. After some mild reforms in the procurement process and the insinuation of various senators that Hollywood used its power to shirk duties in time of war, Truman folded his tent and let the industry proceed in the production of propaganda films. While Hollywood generated impressive profits on its feature productions, Zanuck resented the charges of cost overruns on training films, as the studios on occasion donated equipment and the services of fabulously remunerated stars and executives for free or cut rates. Indeed the army testified favorably about the quality and pricing policies of the major film producers. The astronomical costs of the Hollywood production system, nevertheless, rendered the industry prey to attacks from the outside efficiency expert. Truman for one did not share the complacent posture of Secretary of War Henry Stimson (1940–5) on war production under capitalism. "If you are going to try to go to war, or to prepare for war, in a capitalist country," wrote Stimson in his diary entry of 26 August 1940, "you have got to let business make money out of the process or business won't work." In 1943, the U.S. Congress decided to trim the budget of the film bureau of the domestic Office of War Information (OWI) from $1,222,904 to $50,000, a decision that likely did not anger an industry hoping to reduce government interference and competition.

In slashing the film budget, noted Wyoming Senator Joseph C. O'Mahoney, "The action of the committee was based upon the contention . . . that the Government should not make any pictures at all; that such pictures should be made by the established motion picture companies at Hollywood and elsewhere." Earlier Senator Kenneth McKellar of Tennessee had called the motion picture "the best means of aiding the war effort of which I know . . . ," and Massachusetts Senator Henry Cabot Lodge Jr. observed that "it is much better to have the motion pictures made in Hollywood by moving picture professionals, under a Government precept, if you will, rather than have the Government itself try to make moving pictures. . . ."[47] Although some of this political rhetoric was sincere, many members of Congress wanted Hollywood's government support slashed largely because of partisan resentment that certain films favored the New Deal.

For themselves, the Inspector General's documents provide testimony of an industry alarmed by the prospects for populist anti-Semitic backlash. The setback for Wheeler and Nye in 1941 hardly exorcised this threat in the eyes of the moguls.

THE SPECTRE OF JUDEO-BOLSHEVISM

This can be seen most dramatically in the outcry against Left propaganda in film, in the conflation of Judaism with communism, what European fascist ideologues had labeled the dangers of Judeo-Bolshevism. In 1943, Warner Brothers made a film, *Mission to Moscow*, designed to solidify the friendship of the American and Soviet peoples in a time of war. Whether Jack Warner produced the film because of urgings from President Franklin D. Roosevelt during a special meeting, as he claimed in his memoirs, or because he was asked by the U.S. ambassador to the USSR, Joseph Davies, as he testified under oath before the House Un-American Activities Committee (HUAC) in 1947, *Mission to Moscow* provided a warm portrayal of Soviet Russia that rankled critics of the industry.[48] Opponents of FDR already had moaned that this movie studio had too cozy a relationship with New Dealism. "If there is an exception worth taking," interjected *Time* (16 August 1943), "it is to Warner Bros.' continued public rumbleseating with the President of the United States. . . . [I]n two pictures so close together as *Mission to Moscow* and *This Is the Army*, the President is referred to with such breath-catching reverence, it seems only decent that the audience should dim the lights, steal out softly, and leave them alone together." Despite frequent letters of support from Jack and Harry Warner, FDR seemed rather aloof from the making of *Mission to Moscow* and often courteously rebuffed Jack Warner's offers of showing up at the White House with exclusive movie showings for the commander-in-chief. "Will you tell Jack Warner there isn't a prayer of my going into the movies until 1945!?" declared Roosevelt in November 1942 when asked by the movie executive if he could narrate a documentary dramatizing the U.S. war effort.[49]

Anti-Stalinist liberals such as John Dewey soon decried the inaccuracies of *Mission to Moscow* concerning the purges and liquidations of the 1930s; patriotic organizations including the American Legion attacked the film for giving approval to godless communism. Oddly to some, the Catholic Legion of Decency granted it a seal for adult audiences. More lethal venom came from those willing to associate the film's lax attitude about Stalinism to Jewish betrayal of Americanism. On 21 May 1943, W. F. Flowers of Encino, California, wrote to Warner Brothers concerning *Mission to Moscow*:

Allow me to congratulate you on a very open faced piece of communistic propaganda. I believe you have done a good job from the standpoint of propaganda work, but a work that is going to backfire not only on Warner Bros but on the Jewish race as well.[50]

Industry leaders found themselves so defensive about charges of Jewish favoritism that, even when the gravity of the Holocaust collapsed upon them, they often hesitated in depicting on celluloid the Nazi attempt to exterminate their people. Postwar propaganda reels, such as the English-language version of *Death Mills*, avoided references to the Jews in its narration of the death camps, instead declaring that victims came from "all religious faiths, of all political beliefs."[51] Orson Welles's film *The Stranger* (1946) is a surprising exception to this gingerliness about the Holocaust in its fictional portrayal of a fiendish SS officer called Franz Kindler who escapes to Connecticut and, posing as Charles Rankin, a charming instructor of history, marries a paragon of WASP wholesomeness (played by Loretta Young). While it came under attack for failing to vindicate the genius credentials of Welles, the film possessed one substantive virtue: its rare willingness to allow Edward G. Robinson, as the anti-Nazi investigator Wilson, to show footage of death camps. "This is a gas chamber. . . . This is a lime pit," described Robinson, abandoning the staccato diction of his gangster roles. The investigator becomes suspicious of the seemingly irreproachable Rankin/Kindler after a dinner discussion in which the SS man hides his identity by warning Americans of the warlike character innate to Germans. But did not the German Marx write about peace and brotherhood? counters one American. Marx was a Jew, not a German, explains the historian – an observation seemingly approved by the Americans present. A day later, however, Wilson thinks about it again: Perhaps only a Nazi would be so confident in declaring Marx not to be German. The inverstigor's flash of insight, in most likelihood, failed to resonate with his U.S. audience.[52]

Inclined to think otherwise, Hollywood producer David O. Selznick lost a large bet when he proved unable to refute Ben Hecht's claim that most Americans thought of the genius behind *Gone with the Wind* and *The Wizard of Oz* as a Jew first and an American second, if at all.[53]

Hollywood did tackle anti-Semitism in films such as RKO's *Crossfire* (1947) and Twentieth Century–Fox's *Gentleman's Agreement* (1947), the latter a project of Darryl F. Zanuck, who thought America was now ready for more mature themes. As Zanuck explained his thinking toward the end of World War II,

[W]hen the boys come from home from the battlefields overseas, you will find they have changed. They have learned things in Europe and the Far East. . . . The war has made Americans think, and they aren't going to be so interested in trivial, trashy movies anymore. Oh yes, I recognize that there'll always be a market for Betty Grable and Lana Turner and all that tit stuff. But they're coming back with new thoughts, new ideas, new hungers . . . we at Fox have got to plan to measure up to their new maturity.[54]

Hence, he went ahead with *Gentleman's Agreement,* in which a Gentile masquerades as a Jew and is confronted with petty discrimination on a regular basis. The movie elicited this observation from Ring Lardner on its moral: Don't be mean to a Jew, because he might just turn out to be a Gentile. Its director, Elia Kazan, noted that "It was repeatedly pointed out that here the word 'Jew' was used for the first time in a major Hollywood film. . . . As I see it now the film is patronizing. We seem to have been doing a favor to people who we considered needed a favor of understanding. Noblesse oblige." James Agee cited it as an example of Hollywood's "safe fearlessness" against racism.[55]

Safe fearlessness or not, Hollywood quickly found itself on the defensive after World War II. *Mission to Moscow, Song of Russia,* and *North Star,* films sympathetic to the Soviet Union that were made with the active encouragement of Washington during the war, proved to be ideological boomerangs, clobbering the industry with congressional investigations and surveillance by the Federal Bureau of Investigation. Though the internationalist wing of the establishment had shielded the film industry from the fury of the isolationists in 1941, this time many moderate liberals joined the cold-war clamor for loyalty oaths and vigilance against subversive propaganda emanating from the culture industries. The cold-war fervor of the internationalists, moreover, led them to turn the tables with treachery charges on the isolationists. Secretary of the Navy James Forrestal declared that the Nye committee of the mid-1930s "staffed by Communist attorneys . . . had much to do with the curtailment of our own armaments industry."[56]

Underappreciated today is how much the initial HUAC assault on Hollywood returned to the anti-Semitic subtext of the Senate inquiry of 1941 in its allegations of industry disloyalty to American values. When HUAC began its hearings on Hollywood in the fall of 1947, a group of celebrity civil libertarians arrived to support those screenwriters under accusation of engaging in subversive activities. Among the celebrities present for the early proceeding were John Huston, Phillip Dunne, Ira Gershwin, Danny Kaye, Gene Kelly, Paul Henreid, June Havoc, and Evelyn Keyes. HUAC graciously placed them in the front row of audience seats. Soon afterward Representative John Rankin, a powerful Democrat from Mississippi, stood up and delivered the following analysis of the celebrities present:

I want to read you some of these names. One of the names is June Havoc. We found out from the Motion Picture Almanac that her real name is June Hovick. Another one was Danny Kaye, and we found out his real name was David Daniel Kaminsky. Another one here is . . . Eddie Cantor, whose real name is Eddie Iskowitz. There is one who calls himself Edward Robinson. His real name is Emmanuel Goldberg [actually, Goldenberg]. There is another who calls himself Melvyn Douglas, whose real name is Melvyn Hesselberg. There are others too numerous to mention. They are attacking the committee for doing its duty to protect the country and save the American people from the horrible fate the Communists have meted out to the unfortunate Christian people of Europe.[57]

In resurrecting the spectre of Judeo-Bolshevism eviscerating Christian civilization, Rankin found far less of an outcry than that which had greeted Wheeler, Nye, and Lindbergh a few years earlier. When Rankin took control of HUAC in 1944 after the retirement of the ailing Martin Dies, he declared that his investigations into Hollywood would uncover "the greatest hotbed of subversive activities in the United States" and "one of the most dangerous plots ever instigated for the overthrow of the government."[58]

In judging the artistic production of Hollywood, the HUAC leadership curiously returned to the terrain of artistic realism, a construct developed by Harry M. Warner in his defense of the anti-Nazi films produced by his studio. On 20 October 1947 they interviewed Soviet expatriate Ayn Rand, a popular novelist, occasional Hollywood screenwriter, developer of objectivist philosophy, and a self-appointed expert on the Soviet Union. They demanded to know whether MGM's *Song of Russia* (1944) conformed to accepted standards of historical veracity. The film stars Robert Taylor as a conductor who is urged by a young Russian woman (Susan Peters) to play a concert in her village. They fall in love, but most inconveniently the Germans then invade Russia. Operation Barbarosa thus frustrates the lovers' quest for eternal happiness. MGM's Louis B. Mayer blamed the film on pressure from a government coordinator, and then sheepishly explained that, except for the music of Tchaikovsky, the story could have taken place in Switzerland for all he cared. Rand judged such apologetics as most unacceptable, though she at least believed Mayer that he himself had no intention of fomenting Red propaganda. In her testimony before the committee, she excoriated the film for its inaccuracies, most of them aesthetic: The sets and costumes did not reflect Moscow as she recalled it. Most galling, however, was the prominence of smiling Russians in the film. In one scene, Robert Taylor speaks admiringly of a symphony crowd at a grand restaurant: "I can't get over it. Everyone seems to be having such a good time. I always thought Russians were sad and melancholy people – you know, sitting around brooding about their souls."[59] For Rand, under Stalinism the Russians were indeed brooding, a people so profoundly unhappy that to portray them smiling was reckless artistic license. Representative John McDowell, a Republican from Pennsylvania, responded: "You paint a very dismal picture of Russia. You made a great point about the number of children who were unhappy. Doesn't anybody smile in Russia any more?"[60]

"Well, if you ask me literally, pretty much no," declared Rand.

"They don't smile?" again followed an astonished McDowell.

"Not quite that way, no," affirmed Rand, unwilling to concede any territory. "If they do, it is privately and accidentally." When Democratic Congressman John Wood of Georgia asked her if it at least made sense to keep Russia fighting the Germans, Rand remained defiant: "I think we could have used the lend–lease supplies that we sent there to much better advantage ourselves." Those so drunk with hubris that they thought it proper to deceive the American public with misleading films such as *Song of Russia* further proved themselves inebriated with totalitarian values. "If it is to deceive the American people," she said, ". . . then that sort of attitude is nothing but the theory of the Nazi elite, that a choice group of intellectual or other leaders will tell the people lies for their own good." At the time of the film's release, most serious critics found the film's liberties with reality

to be a cause for mild amusement, not the opium of the intellectuals so beloved of Rand and her HUAC minions. As Richard Winnington said shortly
after the release of *Song of Russia:* "Film makers have evolved a new tongue
– the broken accent deriving from no known language to be used by foreigners on all occasions."[61] For a Rand, Hollywood's shoddy production
values had their roots in intellectual flabbiness confirming the triumph of
the totalitarian cast of mind. (It was not a question of "high" art versus
"low" art: She would later condemn Shakespeare's plays for limiting the
role of free will in human affairs and Beethoven's melodies for a malevolent
attitude to life, whereas she celebrated Mickey Spillane and Ian Fleming as
the age's Romantic literary heroes, the majestic inheritors of Sir Walter Scott
and Alexandre Dumas *père*.)[62]

In the end, members of Congress failed to be impressed by the Orthodox priests who consecrate the couple's union, a marriage that could be seen
as a repudiation of the atheistic tenets of Bolshevism. *Song of Russia* did
have a few genuine leftists work on its production, notably the screenwriter
Paul Jarrico – denounced as a communist by Richard Collins, his cowriter
on the picture, and called before HUAC in 1951. Jarrico later helped create *Salt of the Earth* (1954), a film about mining strikes in New Mexico
that HUAC stalwarts on the floor of the U.S. Congress condemned as
racialist incitement and a Red assault on U.S. liberty.

The Austrian thinker Ludwig von Mises, mentor of the classical liberal
scholar Friedrich A. Hayek and described as "the world's foremost libertarian economist," would later carp that "Popular actors and playwrights.
. . . live in palatial houses with butlers and swimming pools. . . . Yet, Hollywood and Broadway are hotbeds of communism. Authors and performers
are to be found among the most bigoted supporters of Sovietism."[63] However, the explanation of journalist and cultural historian Otto Friedrich for
Song of Russia's inaccuracies appears more to the point:

> What Miss Rand could not seem to understand, what the House committee could
> not seem to understand, was that *Song of Russia* was rubbish not because of any
> political purpose, subversive or otherwise, but because M-G-M was in the business
> of producing rubbish. That was its function, its nature, its mission. . . . M-G-M was
> the home of Andy Hardy, of Judy Garland, and Esther Williams, and no Commu-
> nist ideology could ever penetrate or take root in such a playland. When Louis B.
> Mayer of Minsk decided to make a movie about Russia, he would inevitably make
> it the Russia of Andy Hardy, accompanied by Tchaichovsky.[64]

As for the political climate of filmmaking, Darryl Zanuck explained the
pattern set during the interwar years:

I guess I was apolitical, because whereas Louie [Mayer] and Jack [Cohn] threw up
their hands and said "Red propaganda" whenever I mentioned them [films on the
Depression and Nazism], I kept on thinking that every single happening I was reading about in the newspapers and newsmagazines was the stuff of moving pictures.
But they kept warning me to stay away from such things. "Give 'em cowboys, tits
and gangsters," said Jack Cohn. "That's the way to keep 'em happy." Louie Mayer
put it more pompously. "Give them glamour," he said. Glamour! In 1939, when
the world was going to pieces![65]

Jack and Harry Warner, who had adopted an aggressive posture toward
Senator Nye in 1941, first quivered and then folded before the HUAC onslaught. Unable to hide behind the principle of artistic realism, Jack tried
to explain away the making of *Mission to Moscow* as his foolish willingness to succumb to Washington. Portraying himself as locked in battle with
communist termites who had bored their way into Warner Brothers' screenwriting corps, he had taken steps to smoke them out.

Despite HUAC's stern accusations about Hollywood's service to Soviet
expansionism, the State Department did not scuttle its policy of helping the
film industry spread its influence abroad. The department itself then came
under persistent assault from HUAC. While less frequently attacked with
the anti-Semitic innuendo flung at Hollywood, the WASP-dominated State
Department found itself portrayed in increasingly unsavory images: weak,
effeminate men, wearing striped pants and speaking in phony British ac-
cents, as Joe McCarthy later said of Dean Acheson. Nebraska Senator Hugh
Butler expressed the hatred for Acheson this way: "I watch his smart-aleck
manner and his British clothes, and that New Dealism, and I want to shout,
'Get out. Get out. You stand for everything that has been wrong with this
country for years.'"[66] The Hollywood Jew and the State Department WASP
had one common feature: They were said to be internationalists who put
grandiose foreign interests above the national interest. Both Hollywood and
the State Department had similar responses to HUAC's campaign: The former adopted the blacklist of suspected leftists, the latter removed from sensitive posts those judged "soft" on communism. (Naturally the burden of
HUAC's crusade fell harder on the Jews than WASPs; the latter ran the society. The HUAC reinforcement of images of disloyalty probably helped
postpone Jewish assimilation in many elite institutions for two decades, until the late 1960s: According to a study of the nation's fifty largest commercial banks in 1972, a meager 1.3 percent of the senior officers and 0.9 percent of the junior executives came from Jewish backgrounds. In New York,
a city where 50 percent of the college graduates were Jewish, its nine largest
banks had only one Jew among their 173 senior officers.)[67]

Though prepared to apply modifications to its interwar strategy, the Department of State again aggressively promoted the U.S. film industry abroad. After confidential conversations with the MPPDA, Assistant Secretary of State A. A. Berle issued the memorandum dated 22 February 1944, "American Motion Pictures in the Postwar World," sent to most of the U.S. diplomatic corps. In it, he asserted that "American motion pictures act as salesmen for American products, salesmen that are readily welcomed by the public." He elaborated:

The Department feels . . . that it is particularly important at this time that you should fully understand the value of the American motion picture to the national welfare and the importance that the government attaches to the unrestricted distribution of American motion pictures abroad, especially in the postwar period. The Department desires to cooperate fully in the protection of the American motion picture industry abroad.[68]

Berle added that the State Department "expects in return that the industry will cooperate wholeheartedly with the Government with a view to insuring that the pictures distributed abroad will reflect credit on the good name and reputation of this country and its institutions." He therefore told diplomatic officers "that the Department is requesting your comments and suggestions concerning the pictures themselves."[69]

Will Hays responded favorably to this initiative. He noted that after World War I it had been difficult to restore global order. Now, heading toward the postwar world, the film industry would have to meet this central challenge. For all of HUAC's enmity toward Hollywood, Hays agreed that arresting the forces of disarray and subversion should serve as the principle animating postwar culture. Recognizing that "difficulties . . . will have to be faced in regaining a fair proportion of our foreign markets in a war-devastated world," Hays placed the industry on guard in a report delivered to the MPPDA's annual meeting in New York on 29 March 1945. He warned against "the ever present problem of self-discipline which we may expect to be increased by the war's effects on moral standards. We shall need to maintain an unbroken front of self-regulation."[70]

Opening foreign markets and maintaining discipline in an unruly world order became passions for leaders at both the MPPDA and the State Department. Too anxious to seize the fruits of victory, however, the film industry soon had to be restrained by a State Department aware that its faithful service to one sector of the capitalist class might imperil the interests of the whole. Will Hays, elected to his twenty-fourth term as MPPDA president in March 1945, stepped down shortly thereafter in favor of Eric A. Johnston, the president of the U.S. Chamber of Commerce and a Republican widely held to have U.S. presidential aspirations in his own right. "If ever humankind and geography have been brought together under the most propitious circumstances, it is here in the United States of America," wrote Johnston in his book *America Unlimited* (1944). "One feels almost that this kindly Providence which contrived this miracle is watching . . . to see how the epic test of man's capacity for grandeur is working out," elaborated the former Marine captain and bayonet instructor, who could not resist adding two questions: "Can man, thus richly dowered with all the prerequisites of greatness, live up to his magnificent opportunity? Can we temper his spirit and lift his mind to new and unprecedented levels?" In essays such as "Utopia Is Production" (1946), he cheered that "the motion picture industry sets the styles for half the world." Thus he told those who wield control over "the most powerful medium for influencing people which man has ever built" to get cracking, so that "We can set new styles in living," and that "The doctrine of production must be made completely popular."[71] The leatherneck Johnston arrived with a belligerent tone toward European social democrats and all those so foolhardy as to propose limits on the market dominance of Hollywood films. At first eager to serve, the U.S. State Department had the unenviable task of acquainting Johnston with the realities of diplomacy.

CHAPTER THREE

The MPAA and the State Department
ORDER AND AUTONOMY IN THE POSTWAR WORLD

BREAKING DOWN BARRIERS

Shortly before A. A. Berle prepared his memorandum "American Motion Pictures in the Postwar World," Will H. Hays of the MPPDA gave Secretary of State Cordell Hull a briefing on the basic aims of the industry in the postwar world. On 18 October 1943, Hays called "the motion picture industry . . . unique in the export field . . . because some forty percent of its product serves foreign fields." He claimed that "no other American business of size . . . even approaches this percentage." Unfortunately, noted Hays, "That so large a portion of industry earnings must accrue abroad, renders the industry peculiarly susceptible to foreign governmental discrimination. . . ."

Mounting discrimination could have catastrophic results, for:

The approximately forty percent of motion picture revenue which is foreign, *is the margin by which supremacy of United States pictures is financed and maintained.* . . .

It is, therefore, cumulatively emphasized that loss of *foreign market means lessening of domestic market* because that which created and sustains both is the ability, financially and artistically, *to produce better pictures.* . . .

To maintain foreign markets, Washington must renew attentive service to the film corporations:

We do . . . recognize that, as an industry we are virtually without effect in dealing with foreign government. Just as we have dealt, and can deal, with foreign industry, we ask that our government deal with foreign governments. . . .

The imposition of discriminatory taxes, restrictive orders, quotas and regulations in limitation of United States' distribution, are matters clearly beyond our industry's effective province. . . .

Lest the State Department prefer vacillation to renewed support, Hays sang a familiar refrain touting film's promotion of U.S. industry:

It must never be forgotten that foreign governments are wholly aware of the power of film in creating markets *for other products*. The record of this power is so clear as to warrant on their part energized attempts to use home-produced film to broaden world consumption of *all their other exportable merchandise*.

Attempting appraisals of our problem solely from the standpoint of films is accordingly profound error. The cake is much larger than that. It is, in truth, frosted with the greatest single factor in world commerce. Efforts to control it may be anticipated in kind and degree.[1]

In addressing specific nations and potential trouble spots, Hays believed that the Russian film industry would emerge as "a competitor of mettle" due to "its huge population, its fine artistic tradition, its dawning industrial appreciation and the inevitable development of its natural resources." His flourish of praise for Soviet capabilities may have been a case of taking too seriously the uplifting forecast of Frank Capra's *Battle of Russia* newsreel and Warner Brothers' feature *Mission to Moscow*. A more cataclysmic tone surrounded his warnings about "the vast and capable *British Empire*," which in his margin annotation is proclaimed "a potential Goliath. . . ." Without naming Yorkshire miller J. Arthur Rank, Hays warned the secretary of State that "A capable motion picture magnate of England has indulged the most laudable frankness in announcing his determination to control the British motion picture industry and drive for dominance in the world markets." He had progressed so far that a fearful British government decided "to announce restriction of his monopolistic tendencies." Of particular concern to Hays remained the market of South America. Britain's Rank talked of plans for expansion there, while other European countries had designs on this precious asset for Hollywood.[2]

As diplomatic officers scrambled to respond to Berle's demand for information on overseas markets, F. W. Allport, the European manager of the MPPDA's International Department, prepared a new memorandum on 14 July 1944 identifying the main restrictions on Hollywood films that needed to be lifted in the coming postwar settlement. Dividing the world into four groupings – Axis countries, countries occupied under duress, other countries participating in the war, and neutral countries – Allport regretted that even nations holding trade agreements with the United States showed little hesitation in constructing ramparts full of restrictions against film. His full cataloging makes for tedious reading, but the sampling below is a representative one:

Allport memorandum on film restrictions
I. Axis countries
    Germany
    Requirement of domestic production in order to release or to obtain permits
        for the importation and release of American films.
    Requirement that dubbing, if any, be done within the country.
    Definite limitation of the number of American films which may be imported
        and/or released.
    Requirement to obtain import licenses.
    Discrimination against American films in favor of films of other countries.
    Political or pre-censorship, in conjunction with or in addition to normal
        censorship, under dictation of Minister of Propaganda.
    Existence of *Reichsfilmkammer*, controlling the operation of the motion
        picture trade.
    Dubbing tax.
    Prohibition or limitation of remittances in payment for American films.
    Domination of International Film Chamber, whose influence in favor of
        German films extends to the 17 member countries.
II. Countries Occupied under Duress
    a) Countries with Trade Treaty with U.S.
    France
    Prohibition or limitation of remittances in payment for American film.
    Requirement that films be dubbed within the country into the language of the
        country.
    Definite limitations of the number of American films which may be imported
        and/or released. (dubbed films)
    Limitation on release of American films. (original version)
    The Netherlands
    Excessive censorship fees.
    Control of entire film industry by Nederlandsche Bioscope Bond, preventing
        American companies from opening own offices or distributing newsreels,
        for example.
    b) Countries without Trade Treaty with U.S.
    Norway
    Discriminatory tax measures which reduce taxes on theatres when domestic
        films are shown.
    Government or municipal operation of motion picture theatres.
    Fixed minimum prices which distributors may charge exhibitors for film.
    Denmark
    High customs duties.
    Discriminatory tax measures which reduce taxes on theatres when domestic
        films are shown.
    Massive censorship fees.
    License required for importation of film and export of proceeds from
        distribution if super-imposed titles added outside Denmark.
    Control of entire film industry by Film Board, Denmark controlling State
        Distributing Company. Decides which films are exempt from taxation.

Requirement that local managers of branch offices of American companies be nationals of the country and be licensed by their government.

III. Others Participating in the War
a) Countries with Trade Agreement with U.S.

United Kingdom

High Customs Duties.

Imperial Preferential Tariff favoring films and or advertising accessories from other countries.

Differential between import duties on negatives and positives which force American companies to print films domestically.

High import duties on film accessories such as advertising material.

Excessive censorship fees.

Requirement of domestic production in order to release or to obtain permits for the importation and release of American films. (Distribution quota has the effect of forcing distributors of American films to buy or produce domestic films.)

Exhibition quotas and other measures requiring theatres to show domestic films.

Canada

Discriminatory tariffs favoring French and Polish films in addition to British films.

Differential between import duties on negatives and positives which force American companies to print films domestically.

Remittance taxes in form of income tax, royalty tax, etc.

Exhibition quotas and other measures requiring theatres to show domestic films. (some Provinces – newsreels)

Fixed minimum prices which distributors may charge exhibitors for film.[3]

Heading into the postwar period, the State Department continued to stand by its ideological rationale for helping the movie industry abroad, the belief that "trade follows the film." The State Department also sought to reward the film industry for its service in World War II, a declaration that stoked up resistance from such circles as the Citizens League of Maryland for Better Motion Pictures. "We were disturbed to read a statement . . . which said that the motion picture industry had been such a help in the war that there would be no restraints placed upon it in the future," wrote Cornelia A. Gibbs, chair of its vigilance committee, in a letter to the Department of State. Soon contacting Undersecretary of State Joseph C. Grew on 28 June 1945, she assailed one of the central works of U.S. war propaganda, Walt Disney's *The Three Caballeros*, and cited a letter to the *New York Times* as evidence of its perfidious nature: "'Here is a film which in plain words is a 'girlie' show, and the fact that the girls are from South America could hardly matter.'"[4] For a film seeking solidarity among the peoples of the Americas, *The Three Caballeros* – which combined live-action and animated sequences – offered conflicting counsel: Male homosocial bonding gives way to an anarchic individualism in frenzied pursuit of the sexually wild Latina. As the film's title track boldly rhapsodizes,

> We're three caballeros,
> Three gay caballeros . . .
> Like brother to brother,
> We're all for each other,
> Like three caballeros
> Together we'll stay.
> Through fair or stormy weather
> We stand close together,
> Like books on a shelf
> and friends though we may be
> When some Latin baby
> Says yes, no or maybe,
> Each man is for himself!

John Mason Brown in *The Saturday Review* termed "*The Three Caballeros* one of the most unfortunate experiments since Prohibition," and Barbara Deming in the *Partisan Review* (1945) observed that "Walt indeed has wrought something monstrous," though it "is not Disney's private mon-ster, his personal nightmare. It is a nightmare of these times."[5]

In the early postwar juncture, the State Department did not seem terribly moved by moral and aesthetic attacks on Hollywood from domestic sources. Nevertheless, its functionaries repeatedly voiced two lingering fears about its relationship to the U.S. film industry:

1. film and its destabilizing effects on global order; and
2. the autonomy of the State Department from the MPPDA.

The resolution of these issues sheds light on State Department strategy for balancing the needs of U.S. corporations with the overall health of global capitalism.

FILM AND ITS DESTABILIZING EFFECTS ON GLOBAL ORDER

The State Department found in its ranks many diplomatic officers insecure about Hollywood's reliability in the battle of ideas. Moreover, they worried that the film industry's appetite for economic dominance could set a bad precedent in occupation zones. If certain U.S. industries proved too overwhelming to a war-damaged European bourgeoisie, this class would be hampered in seeing prospects for recovery. In a worst-case scenario, certain capitalist sectors could tumble into terminal decay, rendering Western Europe susceptible to radical contagion.

Meanwhile, in the battle of ideas, many films encoded with doctrines of manifest conservatism became decoded in a seemingly radical manner, a phenomenon thought peculiarly salient among poorer European and Third World audiences. Bertrand Russell in his *History of Western Philosophy* (1945) remarked that "a philosophy, developed in a politically and economically advanced country, which is, in its birthplace, little more than a clarification and systematization of prevalent opinion, may become elsewhere a source of revolutionary ardour and, ultimately, of actual revolution." During the interwar years, Poland's rightist government banned Universal's *Show Boat* because the song "Ol' Man River" was judged "proletarian propaganda" apt to foment revolution.[6] Many critics contended that Hollywood wreaked havoc with gender relations in traditional societies. Reporting on the conclusions of his son during a trip to Latin America in 1929, S. J. Duggan of the New York–based Institute of International Education warned that

the movies have had a profound effect upon the lives of the South Americans themselves. . . . The freedom which North American girls have has created a great deal of restlessness among the girls of the younger generation. They are insisting on the right to go on the streets unchaperoned, to drive automobiles . . . things which, although all right in the United States, are revolutionary in Latin America.[7]

Ulyses Petit de Murat, film critic for South America's largest afternoon newspaper, *Critica*, declared that:

The Argentine is . . . concerned with the domination of women in North American films. It seems ridiculous to see men managed by their secretaries and gain the will to struggle, create and almost live because of a woman.[8]

Paramount's 1932 production of *Madame Butterfly* (based on the Belasco play, not Puccini's opera) brought fierce condemnation in Japan because during a scene of Cho-Cho San (Sylvia Sidney) kissing Lieutenant Pinkerton (Cary Grant), she inadvertently exposes her bare elbow, a gesture thought equivalent to nudity. Though handled "with pathetic caution," reported the Hollywood writer Leo Rosten in 1941, the scene became a symbol representing Hollywood's desire to destroy respect for Japan's ancient moral codes.[9]

When Berle sent out his directive, diplomatic officers proved sensitive to such occasions for international incident. Elbert G. Matthews, the chargé d'affaires for the U.S. legation in Kabul, Afghanistan, warned the secretary of State that

Not all films suitable for Iran should be released for exhibition in Afghanistan. The Iranians are on the whole more worldly than the Afghans, and they do not, as the Afghans do, belong to the puritanical and fanatical Sunni sect of Islam. The picture best suited for Afghanistan are, on the one hand, comedies, 'Westerns,' and light entertainment generally, and, on the other hand, historical and biographical dramas.[10]

After warning that "Religious pictures should . . . be eschewed," Matthews called attention to the risks involved in depicting women on screen in Afghanistan:

Films with too great an emphasis on feminine undress might also be omitted from Afghan distribution lists, as Afghan standards with respect to semi-nudity are even more rigorous than those of the Hays Organization.

While suggesting that many Afghans might enjoy this fare, perhaps contradicting his construct of a wildly puritanical nation, Matthews concluded that these films in the end "do not contribute to a better understanding of American morals and customs." James W. Gantenbein, the American chargé d'affaires in Quito, Ecuador, responded to Berle's directive by writing:

[O]ur motion pictures should avoid the distorted views of American life conveyed in films stressing gangsters, cheap luxury, high-speed, gaudy living and shallow sophistication. They should correct the current overemphasis on bigness, power and mechanized energy and the underemphasis on good taste, and the quality and fineness of our material and non-material products. They should see to it that the information that they convey about the average American is as accurate as their historical props usually are, and so help to break down the traditionally adverse stereotypes of these people concerning American life, stereotypes which have been reinforced by the distortions of the typical commercial film.[11]

Gantenbein proposed that "some of these values may be secured by the continuation of our educational and cultural 16mm. films, one of the important functions of which is serving as continuous antidotes to many of our commercial motion pictures." Boaz Long, reporting to the State Department from Guatemala on 28 September 1944, wondered whether the unbridled free market encouraged the sort of film able to win respect for the United States from Latin American audiences: "Since profit is the motive of the motion picture industry, if it cannot produce a high grade type of film which will make money in Latin America, then some way can perhaps be found to subsidize such films."[12] Others seemed less enthralled with the State Department's track record in obtaining noncommercial films. In a memorandum on the "Display of 35mm and 16mm Non-Theatrical Motion Pictures," the historian Carlton J. H. Hayes, serving as U.S. ambassador to Spain, declared that "Some films are excellent . . . but a large percentage are not suitable for adult Spanish audiences." He demanded: "we must have material of a higher standard." Among the films scorned by Hayes were *Americans All*, which he called "Tactless to show . . . to Spaniards because the maps show how South America was 'chained' to Spain for centuries"; *Andy Hardy's Dilemma*, termed "Utterly useless here"; *Mr. Blabbermouth*, only "Made for U.S.A. consumption"; and *Sail Ho*, deplored as "Stupid and in bad taste." Ambassador Hayes still retained hope that more could be done with films inspired by the State Department and outside the control of the movie majors.[13]

As the Allied armies liberated Western Europe, the U.S. occupation forces shut down German films and soon replaced them with Hollywood fare. The reactions these films received often left both Hollywood and the occupation authorities in a state of bewilderment. One of the early films put on display in Germany was *The Maltese Falcon*, revered as one of Hollywood's masterpieces. According to the *Military Government Bulletin* (22 December 1945), an angry viewer from Karlsruhe denounced its showing "on the ground that it portrayed Americans as gangsters, à la Goebbels!"[14] In the United States, Hollywood had received much praise during the war for reducing the display of gangsters, who became replaced by Nazis as the typical film heavy. The *Cleveland News* (17 May 1943) stated that one of

the most salutary effects of the war on Hollywood production has been the almost total disappearance of the gangster picture – a type which once not only paid large dividends but gave the United States an international reputation as a hot bed of gangsterism . . . so now that the cycle of American gangster pictures is over, the cycle of Hitler gangster pictures has begun.[15]

In enforcing the PCA code during 1942, Joseph Breen at first sought to restrain the industry from depicting the murder of German agents in anti-Nazi films. "The function of the Code is not to be patriotic," he wrote; "it is to be moral."[16] But even Breen relented when Hollywood producers reminded him that the United States, after all, was at war. As the cold war heated up, or froze down as it were, communist heavies quickly replaced Nazis as villains, though James Cagney in *White Heat* made a valiant effort at reviving the traditional gangster movie. Playing a gangster in *Key Largo* (1948), Edward G. Robinson registered the communist's enhanced villainy in his complaint of being deported from the United States "like I was a dirty Red or something."[17] As noted in Chapter 1, the PCA resisted granting export permits to gangster films for fear that they played into the hands of an expansionist communism eager to discredit U.S. society.

Of major distress to the State Department came the realization that many Germans acutely disliked U.S. films, or at least the ones permitted by the occupation authorities. The belief of many social scientists and cultural critics that Hollywood created passive, homogenized audiences appeared falsified by the vivacious and varied response of publics not only in Germany but in other nations as well. In contrast to the Hays (and Johnston) Office's propaganda that U.S. film had universal appeal, the foreign officers reporting back to Berle demonstrated considerable variation by nationality in audience approval of films and genres. For obvious reasons, the State Department took special interest in the progress of German audiences toward approving the American way of life. In a memorandum of 26 February 1947, James R. Wilkinson, the American consul general, reported the distressing news that

Since the occupation of Germany by the American army, American motion pictures have been shown throughout Bavaria. It is generally agreed by observers here that the German reaction to these films has been unsatisfactory, although attendance at theatres continues to increase.[18]

According to Wilkinson, Germans had several grievances:

1. the lack of films dubbed or spoken in German;
2. Hollywood's targeting of the twelve- to twenty-year-old audience, leading to less mature themes – "In Germany . . . going to motion pictures is an adult matter and films in Germany prior to the war were produced primarily for adult patrons";
3. a German preference for realism and documentary over the American tendency toward fantasy and improbable plots;
4. the occupation regime's erroneous belief that

motion pictures showing the military strength of the United States should be exhibited to the Germans so that they would be impressed with our power. Instead of having this result, however, the militaristic pictures were received with disapproval by the Germans. The Germans apparently were already sufficiently impressed with American military accomplishments and did not need to be reminded of it.

The State Department collected many German reactions to U.S. films from interrogations conducted by the Information Control Division. They are sprinkled throughout Wilkinson's memorandum:

From Eichstatt: "The local population is greatly dissatisfied with the type of films supplied in local theatres. . . . Many American films appear not to make sense, they seem stupidly conceived and are very superficial. The American film stars are pretty, beautifully groomed and dressed but are not actors and have no talent except their physical beauty."

From Landshut: ". . . During the past five months, ten American films were presented, of which only four were well received, four moderately liked, and two not appreciated at all."

From Deggendorf: "People in the Kreis who have seen the film *Going My Way* enjoyed it very much and are still talking about it. . . . We think that there should be more films of this calibre."

On Newsreels: "The newsreel should not confine itself to football matches or natural disasters, but should include more pictures showing significant political and historic events as well as films illustrating the customs and way of life of other peoples."

On Pictures of the Nürnberg Trials: "The average German is given a chance to view for some time, not a defendant guilty of heinous crimes, but one of the leaders of the Third Reich, the Herr Reichsmarschall."

The Civil Censorship Division regularly intercepted letters by German citizens and searched them for insight on films. Among a sampling of comments from German letters include the following:

". . . saw an American movie . . . *Sun Valley Serenade* [*Adoptiertes Glueck*]. It was quite nice for a change. Otherwise it is very rare that a movie from over there is liked. . . ." "They are mostly sloppy love stories."

" . . *Gaslight* [*Gaslicht und Schatten*] . . . was quite nice, but generally the American films do not appeal to us particularly."

". . . American films . . . they should send more of them over, because there is a lot of rubbish amongst them. . . ."

". . . It was a pleasure to see *The Men in Her Life* [*Roman einer Taenzerin*] . . . on the whole . . . I am not enthusiastic over the American movies . . . the rubbish they show here. . . ."

". . . last night we saw the movie starring Sonja Henie: *Sun Valley Serenade* . . . quite nice, only we did not like that horrible jazz music. . . ."

". . . it was a relief . . . after the usual American war movies *Henry the Fifth*, *Going My Way* are the only two movies out of thirty that I liked. I do not mind a good musical film with jazz and a revue, but nearly every movie glorifies Pearl Harbor, the 'GI' and the 'Pin-up Girl.' All the world knows that America won the war. . . ."

". . . saw an American movie *Going My Way* . . . a Catholic film . . . I liked it very much."

". . . Movies . . . I am a regular customer there, that is if they show a decent picture. The things they often show us now are atrocious. But that is also the general opinion. We are not used to such trash. . . ."

"We see from time to time an American moving picture. . . . They are much better than the German pictures."

Obviously German views on U.S. films were hardly uniform, and it is apparent that the impressive resonance of *Going My Way* starring Bing Crosby as a priest had something to do with Catholic predominance in Bavaria and the Rhineland. Even so, according to the *Norddeutsche Zeitung* (Hanover, 26 June 1950), Berliner Protestants clamored for Bing Crosby films, while *The Song of Bernadette* stood as one of the most popular films throughout Germany.[19] Judging by the editorials in such papers as the *Münchner Mittag*, the fledgling postwar German press still resented (1) the childish singing and didacticism of U.S. films, (2) the dated, decade-old quality of many movies given permission for release, and (3) the absence of cultural and cinematic diversity. According to the *Mittag* (21 February 1947): "When shall we people of the U.S. Zone be promoted from the lowest sort of elementary object lessons to the higher classes of U.S. films?" Commenting on Paramount's *Union Pacific* (1939), a Western filmed in black and white by Cecil B. DeMille, they complained: "it should not be concealed . . . that this picture is at least ten years old [*sic*]." A week earlier, this newspaper had thought that specific older films deserved presentation, but classics of world cinema and not insipid escapism. As its correspondent explained:

I don't like to see a historical picture which emphasizes nationalism, dripping morals and "unshakeable love of country" (and I don't care whose country is involved). There are too many pictures which show pleasure in playing war! . . .
What I want to see is the entire scale of world humanity. . . .

Worried by *Gone with the Wind*'s portrayal of master–slave relations and a benighted racism, the U.S. occupation authorities blocked its showing in Germany. The *Mittag* pleaded for them to relent:

America should not withhold her great triumphs as she has *Gone with the Wind*. . . . Russia should thrill us again with such a picture as . . . *Potemkin*. . . . France should mix charm with jokes again. We know England probably better than any country when we think of *Bengali* [i.e., *Lives of a Bengal Lancer*] but we want to learn more about her.
    And I want to see German pictures, not committing the mistake of following the old methods or complying with the instructions of a "new" Propaganda Ministry. We ought to remember the high standard of our first sound films . . . and realize what we have to live up to.[20]

The State Department and the U.S. occupation government did seek to resuscitate the German film industry, in the process angering a few Hollywood film moguls. On 30 January 1946, Paramount Pictures made an ambitious proposal to acquire a large number of German theaters where they

planned to expand the presentation of U.S. films. In a secret office memorandum of 7 February 1946, Eugene Anderson of the State Department's
Occupied Areas Division (ADO) wrote John Begg, a department policymaker on media issues, with a fierce rejection of the proposal as naked "economic imperialism." Unless Paramount had been owed reparations or had
lost theaters "to the Nazi regime by some kind of forced sale," its representatives were otherwise out of line, argued Anderson. As he explained to
Begg:

> Paramount's proposal amounts to economic imperialism under the guise of wishing
> to assist in the reeducation of Germany by assuring that American films will be wide-
> ly shown in Germany. I think that the distribution and showing of American films
> could be arranged in some other way, and that the effect of them upon the German
> people would be far greater if unaccompanied by the loss of ownership of movie
> theatres to the German nation.

Anderson raised the specter that giving in to the film industry would set
a precedent for other U.S. capitalists to demand ownership rights in Germany and thus destroy the capacity of the German bourgeoisie for economic revival:

> This utilization of the German defeat to acquire control of their movies by borrow-
> ing Reichsmarks might be imitated in every other line, so that in the end Germany
> might have provided the money through loans of its blocked currency for the sale
> of all its property to foreigners. This kind of policy might well destroy the possibil-
> ity of Germany ever reviving as a prosperous and independent nation. It would un-
> dermine the basis for our reeducation policy, and would supply an excellent foun-
> dation for the revival of some kind of Nazism.

He added that Germany needed to have some control over its future cultural life:

> If we hope, as we do, ever to bring Germany back into the international family of
> nations, we have to prepare her for resuming at some future date the responsibility
> for her own cultural life. This policy includes the protection of those basic facilities
> for her cultural life such as the continued ownership by Germans of her movie the-
> atres. It includes the protection against the alienation of these to foreign firms during
> this present period of control.[21]

John Kenneth Galbraith, director of the Office of Economic Security
Policy, formally rejected Paramount's proposal. In a letter of 27 March 1946
to Bernard Bernstein, the film corporation's legal representative, Galbraith
noted that neither normal economic life as stipulated in the Potsdam Declaration nor "Quadripartite agreement in the Allied Control Council . . . as
to the conditions under which extensions of foreign enterprise in Germany

are to be permitted" had yet to be achieved. "It is appreciated that there
are other aspects of your client's proposal than the purely economic ones,"
Galbraith concluded, "but it is not felt that the possible cultural or propaganda values deriving from extensive American ownership of German motion picture theatres outweigh the economic undesirability at this time of
such an extension of American property interests in Germany." While Anderson had judged Paramount's maneuver to be foolhardy from the standpoint of economic and cultural policy, Galbraith and the State Department
downplayed culture, instead justifying their rebuff on economic and political grounds.[22]

Opposition to film-industry ambitions in Germany had been enunciated
during the war itself. In a secret memorandum of 8 January 1944, John J.
McCloy, the future high commissioner of Germany, warned former Secretary of Commerce Harry Hopkins (still an FDR adviser on foreign affairs)
to reject the proposal for U.S. control of Germany's film industry proffered
by Colonel Darryl Zanuck, the powerful Twentieth Century–Fox executive.
While modestly conceding that his "views on the future of German motion
pictures are not worth much," McCloy urged Hopkins to resist Zanuck:

> The Zanuck proposal to abolish the German industry and to encourage private film
> companies of Allied nations (particularly the U.S.) to establish subsidiary units in
> Germany would also be a concern to the State Department. I should like to note,
> however, that that proposal is . . . subject to considerable objection. Offhand I do
> not see why they should not have their own movies if they want to make them, as
> well as their own books. The logical outcome of this almost amounts to continu-
> ous Allied control of all their industry and culture and I think that approaches non-
> sense.[23]

Rather than blindly promoting the interests of U.S. capitalists over German rivals, McCloy held the view that a European bourgeoisie kept pros-
trate could portend economic unrest and social decay.

German politicians, intellectuals of the Left and Right, and, later, students of U.S. cultural imperialism claimed that the occupation regime intentionally sought to destroy the German film industry. They identified Washington's pursuit of decartelization and initial breakup of the interwar movie
goliath UFA. In a report of 15 March 1951 entitled "Crisis in the Bavarian
Film Industry," Vice Consul Richard H. Donald admitted that Bavarian film
producers had grown disenchanted with the industry's "fragmentation into
small and what is termed 'economically unfeasible units.' . . ." He added
that when the breakup of the UFA monopoly is completed, the Bavarians
hope that some of the properties "will result in the fusing together of the
present small producers into larger units."[24] The Motion Picture Export As-

sociation of American (MPEAA) resisted efforts at strengthening the German film industry, as its representative Theodore Smith wrote Isaiah Frank at the State Department concerning the German government's proposal of a *Bundesfilmkammer,* a federal film chamber. Smith observed:

This instantly evokes the memory of the infamous *Reichsfilmkammer* created by the late unlamented Dr. Goebbels during the Third Reich. It is not intended to draw too close a parallel between Goebbels' obsequious organization and the proposed organization, but the very suggestion seems to be symptomatic of the "cartel mindedness" and of the disposition to the pre-war bond of industry and state that demonstrated their inherent dangers only too well.[25]

While continuing to press for German compliance with the General Agreement on Tariffs and Trade (GATT, 1947), the Department of State no longer responded impulsively to such dire predictions of gloom. The MPEAA did not stand alone, however. Eberhard Klagemann, the owner of the Munich-based Klagemann Film Company and president of the West German Film Producers' Association, worried in a statement from March 1952 that "the German industry is practically in a state of bankruptcy because of decentralization, the production of films by 'artisan methods,' and lack of capital." He noted plans for (1) "voluntarily raising film rentals . . . from which production would be partially financed," and (2) "the foundation of a Federal Film Bank, the existence of which would automatically expose the industry to strong governmental influence."[26] While noting his industry's hostility to the latter proposal and opposition in the Bundestag, he feared that the measure would command passionate trade-union support. In a subsequent meeting with the State Department in Washington, he warned them in uncompromising terms:

Mr. Klagemann replied that both the Federal and Länder governments are aware of the political advantages obtainable through state ownership of the film industry; that the public has little concern with the problem and, if anything, takes the attitude that German films were better under Goebbels so why not revert to the old system; and that in the absence of some effective organized resistance, the German film industry will revert to a state monopoly.[27]

Klagemann urged the State Department to block any move toward nationalization, but George W. Baker, speaking for Washington, informed him that the United States no longer had the authority to do so. He had only moral suasion at his disposal in influencing Germans on the virtues of free enterprise.

Proponents of a narrow instrumentalist version of U.S. cultural policy, the view that Washington intentionally sought to destroy Germany's culture industries in favor of Hollywood, run into several problems:

1. The U.S. Federal government had, after all, rebuffed Hollywood plans for conquering Germany in the Zanuck and Paramount proposals elaborated above.

2. Decartelization undoubtedly did weaken the German film industry, but in 1948 Hollywood itself was subject to decartelization in the form of a federal ruling engineering the breakup of a U.S. film industry that had previously featured significant vertical integration of production, distribution, and exhibition.

3. The decline of the German industry had many elements beyond the immediate control of Washington: the loss of the German-language market east of the Elbe, the Bohemian Forest, and those territories previously under the Axis boot during World War II. Such massive shrinkage in market size ensured convulsions in the industry, if not dramatic reorganization.

There is little doubt that the State Department would have defended Hollywood's interests more aggressively if postwar Germany had quickly proved a formidable rival of the U.S. culture industry. Its very weakness, however, allowed Washington to take the high road, and even Acheson on 13 September 1951 wondered: "Is there any possible way in which U.S. film producers might be willing to use their blocked accounts to help the German industry?" He quickly conceded: "Admittedly, American producers are not expected to be enthusiastic about helping to build competition for themselves in the German market." In spite of this, "some top-level leaders in U.S. industry have claimed they are eager to be of help in re-establishing a healthy West German industry."[28] Hollywood, seeking to escape the unions and high labor costs in Los Angeles, had proven more amenable to overseas production in the postwar world, a trend exacerbated by blocked exchange. Despite the desires of the State Department, in October 1951 an official in Frankfurt working for the U.S. High Commission in Germany (HICOG) threw cold water on the idea of expanding Hollywood coproduction arrangements in Germany because of fears that this sensitive market would be the one apt to provoke a U.S. labor uprising.[29]

Acheson concluded by supplying ammunition to those attributing to him motives of cultural imperialism: "Dr. Rudolf Vogel has been in the United States, interviewing motion picture producers concerning plans for coproduction by German and U.S. firms of anti-communist films." Previously, on 8 August 1951, Acheson had explained that Vogel, chairman of the Bundestag Committee on Press, Radio, and Films, had met State Department officers in hopes of having the U.S. government "enter into the arrangements between the German film industry and United States produc-

ers." Acheson reported that the departmental officers present "explained to
Dr. Vogel that the American industry is independent and that the United
States Government would hardly be a partner to any arrangement which
American producers might make with German films." Acheson, nonetheless, seemed enthusiastic about Vogel because his proposal adopted the principles that films "should be successful at the box office as well as being
ideologically correct."[30]

The new German government did not make life easy for the Motion
Picture Association of America (as the MPPDA had been renamed in 1946,
early in Eric Johnston's presidency): It increasingly labored to restrict the
number of U.S. films imported into Germany. There had been no restrictive
measures from the capitulation until January 1950, but the MPAA companies in 1949 voluntarily agreed to limit imports to 150 films (15 each for
its 10 companies), and non-MPAA companies brought in an additional 10
in total. Though the MPAA pressed the leading film organization in Germany, the SPIO (Spitzenorganisation der Filmwirtschaft), and the Federal
Ministry of Economics for 180 MPAA licenses and 20 for the independents
in the following year, the Germans resisted for 1950 and 1951. They wanted 150 U.S. licenses but then reluctantly conceded 160 (135 for the MPAA,
20 for the companies in SIMPP [Society of Independent Motion Picture
Producers], and 5 for other independents in 1951). The MPAA resented
the State Department and the HICOG for treating the German position as
reasonable and for apparently acceding to the creeping restrictions.[31]

The State Department relied on GATT to limit the extent of German
quotas by noting the treaty's prohibition of their use either to protect the
domestic film industry or as a bargaining weapon to heighten exports. As
Acheson noted, "import quotas are permitted only for balance-of-payment
reasons and are required to be progressively relaxed as balance-of-payment
situation of country improves."[32] He argued that a screen quota allocating
a percentage of playing time to films of domestic origin was preferable to
numerical import quotas. McCloy soon whittled the German proportion of
play time from 35 percent to 27 percent in screen quota negotiations. Despite these victories, the MPAA expressed mounting disgust with Washington's conciliatory posture toward Bonn. The previous rejection of the earlier Zanuck and Paramount proposals, the timidity in snuffing out improper
German state subsidies to the film industry, and claims in September 1951
that Washington gave lucrative newsreels to German exhibitors had led
individual MPAA companies to express disenchantment with the State
Department and the HICOG. Richard G. Leonard, a representative of
the Finance Division for the High Commission in Germany, reported that

MPAA rage against German quotas had spilled over to allegations of ineffectual backing from Washington. Leonard warned, "MPAA representative
here has voiced strongly his dissatisfaction with agreement and indicated
refusal to cooperate in the future with HICOG on projects, such as Berlin
film festival."[33]

For the State Department, issues of postwar order took priority over the
immediate economic needs of Hollywood. Theodore Kaghan, chief of the
Information Services Division in the Office of Public Affairs, HICOG Frankfurt, explained to the State Department its aims:

HICOG welcomes the opportunity to discuss various measures that might be taken
to assist the German film industry in attaining a sound financial basis with a view
to preventing further inroads by Communists in the Hamburg area and precluding
the possibility of former UFA management recreating a German monopoly.[34]

The State Department feared infiltration of the film industry by East
German leftists on the one hand and reconstitution of UFA by far-Right
Hugenberg interests based in Düsseldorf on the other.[35] In the interwar period, former Krupp managing director Alfred Hugenberg had been a feared
enemy of Hollywood. His campaign against the Universal film *All Quiet
on the Western Front* (1930) inspired Goebbels and others to call for a quarantine against Jewish ideological contagion. The postwar MPAA agreed
that the German film industry needed protection against these dangers, but
its leadership could not happily accept State Department willingness to sell
its own companies short. The State Department recognized that the narrow
interests of individual sectors of the business community sometimes had to
be sacrificed for the long-term survival of capitalism as a whole. The High
Commissioner for Germany, John J. McCloy, understood this role of the
state more consciously than other corporate brethren. Later recognized by
mainstream and Marxist journalistic wags as the chairman incarnate of the
executive committee of the ruling class, he did not flinch at moderating
Hollywood's ravenous appetite for expansion.

Having been promised the world in the heady days at the end of World
War II – much to the distress of such U.S. opponents of the film industry
as the indefatigable Cornelia A. Gibbs – the MPAA would have to rest content with domination in a mere three of the globe's four corners.

THE AUTONOMY OF THE STATE DEPARTMENT FROM THE MPAA

During the bright days of the New Deal, Josephus Daniels, the embattled
U.S. ambassador to Mexico, proposed that Washington make a momentous

change in the conduct of foreign policy. He called on the Roosevelt Administration to abandon the traditional "messenger boy" relationship of the
foreign policy apparatus to major U.S. corporations. In one of the more
colorful philippics against U.S. foreign policy, Major General Smedley D.
Butler claimed in 1935 that he was indeed more than a messenger boy:

> I spent most of my time being a high-class muscle man for Big Business, for Wall
> Street and for the bankers. . . . I helped make Haiti and Cuba a decent place for the
> National City Bank boys to collect revenues in. . . . I helped purify Nicaragua for
> the international banking house of Brown Brothers in 1909–1912. I brought light
> to the Dominican Republic for American sugar interests in 1916. I helped make
> Honduras "right" for American fruit companies in 1903. . . .[36]

Fully cognizant of the strength of corporate power in the U.S. political
order, the State and Commerce departments found it difficult not to revert
to patterns of serving individual corporations and industries as clients requiring swift and responsive support. The film industry took ample advantage of its client status, thus meriting aggressive intervention on behalf of
its interests abroad.

Even at the height of state–corporate cooperation during the Republican administrations of the 1920s, however, State and Commerce recognized
that too faithful an obedience to the demands of the business community
sometimes imperiled long-term corporate expansion abroad. When the tidal
wave of quota legislation swept over western Europe in the latter half of
the 1920s, Clarence North of the Department of Commerce had to remind
the industry that nations had legitimate cultural reasons for protecting their
domestic film industries. This would not go away, even though the industry pinned extravagant hopes on the League of Nations Conference on the
Abolition of Import and Export Prohibitions and Restrictions, conducted in Geneva during 1928, to rid them of quotas once and for all. Telling
George E. Canty and later the MPPDA's foreign manager Frederick Herron
that "such European countries as feel that they want to have film restriction
are going to have it irrespective of Geneva or any other conference," North
had to acquaint the moguls with the realities of diplomacy, that nations le-
gitimately feared for their culture and were not just looking for an angle to
squeeze them out of wealth. As he explained to Canty,

> I honestly do think that the cultural argument is one which can honestly be advanced
> in good faith and which must be legitimately met. England, for example, I believe,
> was stampeded into their film legislation almost entirely through their patriotic so-
> cieties who believed that English customs and traditions were in danger. (I am not
> overlooking the fact either in the case of England that the fact that she was losing
> trade through the influence of American films had a considerable amount to do with
> her adoption of legislation.)[37]

Frederick Herron had argued to Julius Klein that censorship of individual films should be the proper domain of foreign-state intervention against Hollywood's cultural threat, not the imposition of rigid quotas. After many governments signed the Geneva agreement on removing barriers, they later stepped up censorship measures, a major weapon against Hollywood in the fascist world. Seemingly forgetting the views enunciated in the memorandum to Klein, Herron and the MPPDA found themselves fighting a rearguard action against the tightening vise of censorship regimes abroad. Subsequent developments confirmed North in his sober warning that Geneva and similar accords would not free Hollywood from its special status in the world of goods; more than just a commodity, film sold dreams, culture, and an entire way of life. Governments would not treat trade in film the same as deliveries of toasters, ball bearings, and lead pipe.

The State Department in the interwar years had several officials willing to challenge the film industry even more aggressively than their colleagues at Commerce. The Villard memorandum from the late 1920s, condemning Hollywood's portrayal of foreigners, was discussed in Chapter 2. In 1939, Assistant Secretary of State Francis B. Sayre called on his department to resist

backing to a large degree the complaints of the motion picture industry. I do not have too great confidence in the leaders of the moving picture industry and would regret to see the State Department too thoroughly committed to battle for the claims of the industry.[38]

Despite these outbursts of unease throughout the interwar period, both State and Commerce placed themselves in the position of serving the film industry as clients. Commerce regularly collected data on the global industry, monitored restrictive legislation, and kept foreign states and corporations aware of U.S. films, particularly those of use to industrial and agricultural concerns. The last activity admittedly proved to be of higher value to industrial corporations and advertising firms than to the MPPDA companies.

As noted earlier, the State Department handled direct negotiations with many foreign governments on quota issues at the behest of the MPPDA. During that fateful first wave of quotas in the 1920s, the MPPDA initially annoyed the State Department by the organization's sort of false insiderism, its claim to have such powerful contacts in each country that they would triumph over the forces of protectionism. The repeated defeats of the 1920s, and especially the protectionist 1930s, helped Hays and his lieutenants realize their vulnerability, encouraging a cooperative ethos. On the eve of the Second World War, the Treasury Department stood up to the MPPDA more defiantly than State and Commerce, as it warned foreign officers that the film industry could not expect extraordinary state intervention to free currency in accounts blocked because of mounting balance-of-payments problems, particularly in the United Kingdom, a country by then furiously in the midst of rearmament.

By the time of Berle's memorandum "American Motion Pictures in the Postwar World" and the early months of victory, the MPPDA had probably reached the apex of State Department–industry cooperation. While Berle excised from his preliminary draft the most dramatic phrases about film's role in the American century to come, he fully expected foreign officers to pave the way for Hollywood in the years ahead. Most officers proved compliant, though a few tarried in their response and others punctuated their analyses with snarling contempt for Hollywood's imbecilities. Cultural diplomacy designed to provide a showcase for contemporary artists, classical musicians, and literary sophisticates inspired these malcontents, who thought Jackson Pollock, Aaron Copland, and Archibald Macleish a more worthy trio to impress Europeans than Humphrey Bogart, Clark Gable, and Rita Hayworth.

The close embrace of the State Department and the MPPDA came partially undone in the early postwar years (by which time the latter had become the MPAA). As tempting as it is to blame the culture-vulture element within the State Department for such an outcome, there are other historical agents who pried apart this alliance. The State Department decided that asserting greater autonomy from the newly renamed association would set a precedent ultimately better for the interests of U.S. capitalism and the vitality of the film industry itself.

The main sites leading to this reconceptualization of state–industry relations were postwar Britain, France, and Germany. In the latter two nations, attempts to establish an absolute numerical limit on U.S. film imports led to charges that the State Department had sold out the interests of independents, the non-MPAA companies. In a few cases, these independents promoted themselves as more significant in commercial and artistic terms than the laggards among the film majors. The crushing defeat of the MPAA member companies in the Justice Department's antitrust case in 1948 reinforced the State Department's leadership in demanding greater independence from the MPAA.

During the late 1940s, negotiations with France represented the first great mobilization of the independents against State Department favoritism toward the MPAA. (See Chapter 10.) The German case fell into place in 1950 when Ellis Arnall, the president of the Society of Independent Motion

Picture Producers, took issue with a routine notification "from the Office of the United States High Commissioner for Germany to the effect that the German Economics Ministry has agreed to issue import licences for ten (10) films produced by U.S. independents during 1950." As Arnall elaborated in his initial response of 10 March 1950:

[W]e are very concerned to learn of the discrimination being practiced against independent producers. It is our information that each of the ten Motion Picture Association members has been allotted fifteen (15) permits. Any system that allots to the independents only ten permits and to the major group one hundred fifty permits is grossly unfair and unjust and has no relationship to the quality of the pictures involved.

As a matter of fact, the permit system is vicious and restrictive and should not be countenanced by the High Commissioner. If an import license permit system is employed, the licenses should be justly allotted and the Society of Independent Motion Picture Producers and its members feel that the discriminatory regulations now in effect should be altered, modified and changed.[39]

When the German Ministry of Economics reduced the MPAA total from 150 to 135 and doubled the SIMPP allocation from 10 to 20 for 1951, the MPAA thought themselves deserted by the U.S. occupation authorities and the State Department. On 20 October 1950, *Film Daily* produced an article that played in the well-worn record grooves of cozy MPAA–State Department relations. Emblazoned with the headline "Government Backs MPAA's German Import Fight," the article proclaimed that "Full State Department support of the American companies' position was assured last weekend when Eric A. Johnston and John McCarthy, MPAA president and vice-president, conferred quietly in Washington with the Director of the Bureau of German Affairs in the Department." An unremarkable story just a few years earlier, this claim brought swift denunciation and denial from the HICOG and State Department. Dean Acheson on 7 November 1950 clarified: "At that meeting *no* commitment was made to 'back the MPAA German import fight.'" He concluded that policy changes "would be explored with HICOG"; however, "the Department has no wish or intention to force more U.S. films upon the German market in support of American motion picture distributors."[40] The State Department in harmony with GATT repeatedly voiced its preference for a screen quota setting aside a percentage for German films over absolute numerical limits on U.S. films. Still, Alfred V. Roemer, chief of the Plans and Policy Unit, Office of Public Affairs, HICOG Frankfurt, insisted that "we are not 'battling' the Germans nor are we backing up 'MPAA's German import fight' . . . no commitment was made to 'back up' the MPAA fight."[41]

The State Department's posture of independence did not sit well with some film majors. During the following year, their representatives made a variety of accusations against the Department of State that caused exasperation among foreign officers. On 24 September 1951, F. McCracken Fisher of the State Department's Informational Media Guaranty Program sent a memorandum to his IMG colleague Herbert T. Edwards entitled "Report on Meeting of Board of Directors of United Newsreel Co., Inc., September 21, 1951." At this corporate meeting, Murray Silverstone, foreign manager of Twentieth Century–Fox, unleashed a volley of attacks on the State Department. According to Fisher, "He [Silverstone] said that 20th Century Fox feels that the Department has treated it most shabbily, has in fact treated the industry with a lack of good faith."[42]

Claiming that the State Department had agreed to cancel its newsreel, *Welt im Film*, once U.S. companies were permitted to operate in Germany again, Silverstone believed that, in Fisher's words, "the Department's reel, produced at taxpayer's expense and furnished free, continued to be distributed despite the earlier agreement to cease when an American reel was started." Silverstone had tolerated the situation, but asked "if and when *Welt im Film* was discontinued Fox be allowed to make an offer for its assets." Instead *Welt im Film* allegedly had been placed in the hands of a German firm, Allianz Films, which was given distribution rights. Fisher said, if true,

This means that a U.S. Government subsidized newsreel is competing with a commercial American newsreel in Germany. Moreover, it means that a newsreel, produced exclusively with U.S. taxpayers' money and therefore an American asset, is turned over free and without charge to a local German firm to distribute. He [Silverstone] said that this will shortly drive Fox out of business in Germany.

Several times Mr. Silverstone remarked . . . that any morning the firms might wake up to find that Indian, Indonesian or other firms had been given the business they had sacrificed so much to build up for the Department.

As those present began foaming with rage, Silverstone pulled out "all propaganda stops on such themes as 'free enterprise,' 'monopoly,' anti-Germanism, Government driving private industry out of business, and 'patriotism,' . . . creating the emotional climate he desired among his hearers." Without the notable intervention of Michael Clofine of Loew's, who "refused to be stampeded," in Fisher's account, the gathering otherwise would have approved "the passage of several hastily worded motions."

The State Department soon provided its own version of events, noting that any company could bid on distributing *Welt im Film* and that, contrary to giving the Germans U.S. government assets for free, these contracts had strict limitations: namely, short durations and specific regions. They did not mention two other relevant considerations:

1. reports on certain German audiences, particularly in Berlin, indicating that Fox newsreels had low appeal,[43] and
2. the British possessing a stake in the making of *Welt im Film* productions until the beginning of 1950, and thus possibly objecting to any undue favoritism by the State Department toward U.S. companies.

For all the fretting and fuming about State Department and HICOG abandonment, the MPAA companies failed to register the U.S. government's willingness to overlook the film majors' absence of good faith with the Germans. For instance, the German's much-decried import limitation system remained predicated on "voluntary quotas," and the majors routinely exceeded their limits. According to a study by Henry Pilgert released by the HICOG's historical division,

voluntary restriction agreeable to both sides . . . was not successful and the number of foreign films continued to increase. . . . Foreign competition continued to plague the German motion picture industry throughout the HICOG period since many of the companies did not adhere to their self-imposed quotas as is indicated by the . . . table:[44]

Proportion of German and Foreign Films . . . in West Germany

Rental year	pre-1948	1948/49	1949/50	1950/51	1951/52
Germany	16	33	65	75	64
Austria	15	18	29	32	22
U.S.A.	131	64	145	202	226
France	203	47	50	31	44
England	148	42	50	28	21
Italy	0	5	4	33	24
Other	21	6	31	34	37
Total	534	215	374	435	438

When the State Department requested in 1950 that Spyros B. Skouras, the president of Twentieth Century–Fox, drop plans for a movie about Field Marshal Rommel, the company instead went ahead with production. Geoffrey Lewis, acting director of the State Department's Bureau of German Affairs, declared Rommel "an unfortunate subject for a motion picture" that "would almost certainly be misrepresented abroad." Instead of punishing Twentieth Century–Fox, McCloy in early 1952 caved into Skouras's ensuing pleas to release *The Desert Fox* in Germany. An elated Skouras left, agreeing that the Rommel film would be withheld from distribution in Germany until "after the elections" and until certain changes in the script had been made. . . . Later discussion revealed that by the phrase "after the elections" Mr. Skouras had meant after the Germans had taken a decision with respect to participation in European defense. . . .[45]

As part of the Economic Cooperation Administration's efforts to promote European recovery (i.e., the Marshall Plan), the Informational Media Guaranty Program continued to convert weak and blocked currencies into dollars at generous rates so long as the film companies produced works promoting the American way of life. From its formation in 1948 to its termination in 1955, the IMG transferred over $7 million in payments concerning the German market, 70 percent of which went to U.S. film companies. As the U.S. government continued payments to the film companies throughout the 1950s via the USIA and other vehicles, Congressman H. R. Gross (Republican, Iowa) declared that the "Motion Picture Export Association has been given a pretty good ride on the informational media gravy train."[46]

For the future, the State Department made it clear that it did not want to represent the MPAA directly in negotiations with foreign governments. In January 1954, Secretary of State John Foster Dulles gave a full elaboration on why it was adopting this break from interwar and early postwar policy:

The Department is opposed to HICOG participation in the proposed negotiations in such a way as to either indirectly or directly imply that any resulting agreement is approved by this Government. Recent experience with the French agreement – formerly a government-to-government arrangement – has led to the conclusion that the disadvantages of participation by this Government outweigh the advantages.

In the first place, the peculiarities of the motion picture industry – the adamant attitude of foreign countries in severely limiting the number of American films shown, for cultural as well as commercial reasons, and the existence or probability of blocked balance – leads to provisions in MPAA agreements which are inconsistent with our general policy. Because the provisions are largely forced on the MPAA by the foreign governments, we feel there is little we can do about them, but we could not accept them as negotiator or signatory. For example, it would certainly be inappropriate for the Department to underwrite an agreement containing a provision that part of the transferred dollar earnings be utilized for the promotion in the United States of German film imports. In the second place, despite the unique character of motion picture trade problems, it appears unwise to handle these problems in a special government-to-government agreement when no other products are similarly treated. The precedent established would be difficult to overlook if other industries came to us for assistance in this manner. Bilateral government-to-government agreements on specific commodities are open to criticism in that they tend to replace private trading to a varied extent with state trading, a trend which the Department does not wish to encourage. Finally, such agreements would make it necessary for the Department, in the last analysis, to resolve disputes between different segments of American industry – a task the Department is not in a position to undertake.[47]

Dulles's stern instruction might be regarded as a defeat for the MPAA; but that would be a misreading of a transformation in state–corporate relations. The early years of the change led to misunderstandings and dismay with the State Department, but once these were ironed out, the MPAA continued to flourish. Its problems lay elsewhere: The rise of television proved to be the primary culprit in diminishing film theater attendance worldwide. The need to lure audiences from their bland TV comedies and vapid variety shows led major film companies to press the limits of PCA control in the 1950s and early 1960s, ultimately weakening the vaunted moral authority of the MPAA. Soon the Legion of Decency began clashing regularly with the latitudinarian MPAA. Such an outcome suggests that the victory of the Hays Office in the 1930s had important commercial underpinnings. When television removed millions of families from regular cinema viewing, it altered the moral economy of cinema. Even the Legion of Decency began to surrender ground, culminating in its decision to grant Warner Brothers' lewd-language rendition of *Who's Afraid of Virginia Woolf?* (1966) a qualified approval for adult audiences. The MPAA's role as a regulator of morals and definer of American values came to an end in the cultural revolution of the 1960s.

The MPAA's role as a trade organization, however, continued to be of powerful global impact. The MPPDA's reorganization at the end of World War II into the MPAA and the MPEAA allowed the movie majors to weather the storms of an impending antitrust defeat and the new era of greater State Department autonomy. The MPEAA, a trade cartel permitted under special guidelines of the Webb–Pomerene Export Trust Act (1918), gave the film corporations the means to collude abroad in ways forbidden them at home. No longer counting on the State Department to handle its negotiations with foreign regimes, the MPEAA began to regard the new order as a form of progress. As former LBJ advisor and long-term MPEAA/MPAA president Jack Valenti declared in 1968: "To my knowledge, the motion picture is the only U.S. enterprise that negotiates on its own with foreign governments." While Will Hays called the MPPDA "almost an adjunct of our State Department," the MPEAA relished its nickname as "the little State Department."[48]

The postwar State Department called for a major shift in tactics, and some in the film industry prematurely thought they had been abandoned.

In fact, however, the State Department and the MPAA shared similar goals: the promotion of U.S. ideas and the expansion of U.S. capitalism abroad. Having applied previous GATT agreements and implied withdrawal of Marshall Plan aid to moderate restrictions on Hollywood expansion, particularly in Great Britain and France, the State Department continued to use international trade forums as an arena for demanding greater access for U.S. cultural exports. Echoing Will Hays's last testament as MPPDA president, U.S. Secretary of State John Foster Dulles – whose brother Allen in his legal duties for Sullivan and Cromwell represented the film industry – regularly enunciated the principle of "free flow of information" as a cornerstone of U.S. foreign policy. Europeans and later Third World nationalists under the aegis of UNESCO condemned this doctrine as spelling for their societies cultural despoliation and ruin.

The history of resistance to Hollywood and the construction of alternative centers of cultural power are the subjects of subsequent chapters. The sites of these struggles are Great Britain, Hollywood's most important overseas market; France, a nation that in the early years of film dominated the global industry and only with belatedness responded with protectionism; and Belgium, a small nation overwhelmed by cultural production from several formidable powers. Popular culture became the sphere in which the United States most nearly fulfilled Henry Luce's exorbitant prophecy of the American Century. The response to that cultural force therefore remains central to comprehending not only the contemporary age but also the shape of history to come.

PART TWO

GREAT BRITAIN

CHAPTER FOUR

Grierson, the Documentary Spirit, and the Projection of Britain

"WHERE CAN I SEE A BRITISH FILM?"

Owen D. Young, the General Electric executive and chairman of the board of RCA, spoke vividly of a self-awareness among America's interwar leadership that the United States should supplant Great Britain as the preeminent global power. He pointed to his conversations with naval officers who recounted that U.S. President Woodrow Wilson

> had reached the conclusion, as a result of his experience in Paris, that there were three dominating factors in international relations – international transportation, international communication, and petroleum – and that the influence which a country exercised in international affairs would be largely dependent upon their position of dominance in these three activities. . . .[1]

According to Young's confidants, Wilson gave the United States "the edge in petroleum, Britain in shipping, with communications divided – cable to Britain and wireless to the U.S." In his calculus of power, the U.S. president conspicuously neglected cinema as a force to be reckoned with in international communications. Neither his Republican successors nor overseas parliamentarians would do likewise, as the visual arts came to be assigned mythic powers in shaping the fortunes of empire. Indeed Neville Kearney, the head of the films division of the influential Federation of British Industries, admonished Britain's Foreign Office:

> It used to be said – and rightly – in pre-war days that Germany successfully enhanced her mercantile position by the development of "Kultur" and the inculcation of the teutonic spirit in overseas communities by means of "circles" and "turnvereinen." The film is for America a much more potent pacific weapon than any that Germany was ever in a position to wield, and it is at the same time a weapon that enables America to derive important revenues from overseas . . . comparable in many ways, although not in financial magnitude, with that enjoyed by this

country through the carrying capacity of British ships – and a much more spectacular one.[2]

In the British press of the interwar years, Will Hays's brash speech in
1923 enunciating his aim of Americanizing the world appeared to be on its
way toward fulfillment. Among the most passionate newspapers decrying
this state of affairs, the *Daily Express* (18 March 1927) asserted:

The plain truth about the film situation is that the bulk of our picturegoers are
Americanized to an extent that makes them regard a British film as a foreign film,
and an interesting but more frequently irritating interlude to their favorite entertainment. They go to see American stars; they have been brought up on American publicity. They talk America, think America, and dream America. We have several million people, mostly women, who, to all intent and purpose, are temporary American
citizens.

Inserting this text into the heart of his remarks before the House of
Commons, Lieutenant Colonel R. V. K. Applin (Conservative, Enfield) observed, "There is the greatest indictment . . . yet of the system under which
films are shown in this country."[3]

At the height of the crisis in domestic film output in 1925, the sole British picture under production for one part of the year was *Satan's Sister,* a
Betty Balfour vehicle shot mainly in Jamaica and based on a novel of H. de
Vere Stacpoole.[4] Perhaps prematurely, the British trade journal *Bioscope*
(6 March 1924) had carried the caption "Lights Out" when it could find
no British films under production for that week.[5] In 1924, the British produced 58 feature films, sliding to 34 in 1925 and then 26 in 1926. "There
was in fact some danger of production in this country ceasing altogether,"
explained a future Board of Trade memorandum. The United States had
flooded Britain with 620 films in 1926. In 1927, British legislation supported by the likes of Applin soon produced an upswing in national production:
128 long films in 1929 and 189 in 1935.[6] Nonetheless, the *Evening Standard* (28 February 1937) later drew attention to its limits by featuring an
American woman helplessly pleading before a West End cinema: "Where
can I see a British film? I am tired of American films; I see them in America,
and that's all I see here."[7]

Many elite Britons more than shared her sentiments. "Let every part of
Merry England be merry in its own way. Death to Hollywood!" declared
John Maynard Keynes, temporarily drunk with hopes for aggressive policy
intervention on behalf of British culture. As an economist, he carried the
additional anxiety of knowing that costly film imports would render his
nation less able to meet its balance of payments. Keynes's call for cultural
cleansing came in a BBC broadcast at the end of World War II and proved

ephemeral. Under attack from the U.S. film industry and perhaps aware that the U.S. State Department would take note of his oratorical Molotov, he issued an apology, albeit one laced with a dash of sardonic Keynesian wit. "[F]orgive me my eccentricity," he explained, claiming no hostile intent.[8]

The British government generated several successive waves of legislation that many hoped would revive national film production: in the latter half of the 1920s, the formation of a modest Empire Marketing Board and then the imposition of quotas compelling the display of British films; in the 1930s, the reinforcement of quotas and the establishment of a "cost" standard for inclusion; and in the aftermath of World War II the riveting of a harsh 75 percent ad valorem tax on foreign film and further ratcheting up of quotas. These legislative interventions provided part of the scaffolding upon which the dominant forces in the construction of a British film industry sought expansion of the nation's capabilities in the cinematic arts. This chapter and the two that follow indeed focus on the strategies of three of the preeminent figures in developing British film: the documentarist John Grierson, the Hungarian producer-director Alexander Korda, and the mill owner-turned-film magnate J. Arthur Rank. Piloting British film during the apex of Hollywood's global supremacy, they encountered a state not always welcoming to their various programs and panaceas for fortifying local film production. Korda and Rank represented a commercial challenge to Hollywood, both seeking success in the capitalist world market. In contrast, Grierson adopted horizons decidedly local: The modest documentary and British state subsidy were avenues for reinforcing national and regional ways of life. Though promoting international emulation of his model, Grierson saw film as preserving local community otherwise eroded by the onslaughts of modernity.

For those resisting incipient Americanization, state intervention on behalf of British film began in earnest during the latter half of the 1920s. Largely private efforts, such as a film league formed by Lord Beaverbrook and A. C. Bromhead, had borne little fruit. Another initiative, the British Films Week project of 1924, also quickly sputtered, earning the wrath of a youthful Paul Rotha.[9] The Federation of British Industries, with the participation of Bromhead, continued to press the government on film policy, as its members feared further loss of manufacturing trade to the United States if Westminster stuck with its ostrichlike posture.

The apparent turning point came in June 1925 as a parliamentary furor erupted over a fraternity-style prank gone awry by the British subsidiary of Universal Films. Claimed to be producing an army recruitment film, the Universal operatives tricked soldiers from the Hampshire Heavy Brigade,

Royal Artillery, into providing a guard of honor and a band to perform
"The British Grenadiers":

> Some talk of Alexander and some of Herakles
> Of Conon and Lysander, and some Miltiades;
> But of all the world's brave heroes, there's none that can compare,
> With a tow, row, row, row, row, to the British Grenadiers. . . .
> None of those ancient heroes e'er saw a cannon ball,
> Or knew the force of powder to slay their foes withal;
> But our brave boys do know it, and banish all their fears,
> With a tow, row, row, row, row, to the British Grenadiers. . . .

In reality, Universal had been using the hapless troops to escort the new
movie *The Phantom of the Opera* to the site of its London premiere. Calling the commanding officer "the victim of a clever and humiliating hoax,"
the Secretary of State for War Sir Laming Worthington-Evans told the Parliament that "the company had previously applied to the War Office for
soldiers to appear in scenes at the arrival of their film and had been told
that permission could not be given. . . ."[10] The company's agents had then
quickly cooked up a subterfuge. Though Universal apologized and subsequently returned the ill-gotten footage to Whitehall, the brouhaha had done
its damage. In a parliamentary address of 29 June 1925, Prime Minister
Stanley Baldwin weighed in for greater controls over Hollywood, as he
wondered whether

> the time has come . . . to see that the larger proportion of the films exhibited in this
> country are British – *(cheers)* – having regard . . . to the enormous power which the
> film is developing for propaganda purposes, and the danger to which we in this
> country and our Empire are in if we allow that method of propaganda to be entirely
> in the hands of foreign countries.[11]

In the previous week, major British newspapers including *The Times*,
Daily Telegraph, *Morning Post*, and *Manchester Guardian* ran an appeal
signed by poet laureate Thomas Hardy, composer Sir Edward Elgar, actress
Lena Ashwell, and Lord Carson and Lord Newton. Calling for "the Prime
Minister to institute an inquiry" that would seek "measures . . . to establish
a film industry in this country on a sound foundation," they asserted that

> high national and patriotic interests are involved. . . . These films are shown in our
> Dominions, colonies, and dependencies, and in all of the world outside the British
> Commonwealth of Nations. Many of them are inferior productions, neither healthy
> nor patriotic in tone, while the psychological influence which they convey may have
> far-reaching consequences.
>   What is the explanation of this state of things, which we venture to describe as
> deplorable?[12]

Lord Newton may have been the catalyst moving this galaxy of elite luminaries to action. Having previously pressed the government in May 1925 to appoint a committee in order "to make recommendations as to the best means of re-establishing this industry, having regard to the industrial, commercial, educational, and Imperial interests involved," Newton pondered:

Imagine what the effect must be upon millions of our coloured fellow citizens in remote parts of the world who perpetually have American films thrust upon them which frequently present the white man under the most unfavourable conditions.[13]

A few important proponents of an activist films policy had direct economic stakes in the industry, though allies could be found in disparate walks of life. Speaking before the shareholders of Stoll Picture Productions Ltd. on 3 June 1925, Sir Oswald Stoll proposed a license fee on U.S. films that would be used to support the home industry. According to the paraphrase of his speech by the *Manchester Guardian,* Stoll said:

The British Empire would soon be completely Americanised simply because we were allowing British life and ideas to be gratuitously wiped off the screen.[14]

Despite the outcry from Stoll, Lord Newton, and Prime Minister Baldwin, action on film policy crept forward at an agonizingly slow pace. The Moyne committee report of 1936 later explained that Baldwin's cabinet exhorted the producers, distributors, and exhibitors to try one last effort at voluntary cooperation. Despite repeated calls for a British version of the Hays Office, these sectors could not muster unity. Exhibitors, who registered the lion's share of their profits from U.S. films, looked askance at producer schemes for quotas, voluntary or otherwise, designed to stem the flow of foreign pictures. Under pressure from the Overseas Committee of the Federation of British Industries, Sir Philip Cunliffe-Lister, the president of the Board of Trade, then reignited government efforts in this domain, making cinema a central issue at the Imperial Conference of November 1926. This spawned public inquiries on cinema throughout the colonies and Dominions.[15]

THE EMB, JOHN GRIERSON, AND THE RISE OF BRITISH DOCUMENTARY

The formation of the Empire Marketing Board in May 1926 is sometimes regarded as the first concrete state action on behalf of film, though its provision for cinema stood at threadbare levels for much of its existence: £1,217 out of a total budget of £134,804 in 1926, £17,748 out of £226,361 in 1929. Rotha regarded the budgets of the official EMB Films Unit formed in January 1930 as "absurdly small" and called its equipment "ludicrously inadequate," consisting of a DeVry, an Eyemo, and a hand-cranked silent Debrie, the first two scratching negative like housecats greeting virgin furniture. The EMB had as its mission the goal "to further the marketing in the UK of Empire products, including home agriculture produce." The Colonial Secretary L. S. Amery told the House of Commons that the EMB's chief target was foodstuffs, notably "to increase the consumption of Empire fruit in this country." By pursuing scientific research in entomology, animal husbandry, and botany, as well as economic inquiry into foreign markets, the EMB sought, he said, "to suggest methods both of increasing the production of fruit within the Empire and of improving the conditions under which it is packed, transported and marketed." Publicity campaigns relying on posters and press advertising occupied its early efforts in marketing.[16]

The story of the EMB and British film usually begins with a fish story. In 1929, John Grierson directed the first and most famous of the EMB's feature-length movies, *Drifters,* a story of the herring industry based in Scotland's Shetland Islands. The topic had been chosen in part to outwit the tightfisted guardians of Britain's Treasury who did not regard film production as a fiscally sound enterprise. The Secretary of the EMB Stephen Tallents, more prone than Grierson to express horror at Hollywood's commanding position in Great Britain, latched on to the herring industry because he knew the financial secretary to the Treasury, Arthur Michael Samuel, had produced a book on the subject, *The Herring: Its Effect on the History of Britain* (1918). When Treasury began muttering its usual appeals to the imperatives of fiscal probity, the Colonial Secretary and Chairman of the EMB L. S. Amery recalled how Samuel's "weighty official objections to the whole fantastic idea of our film project were successfully countered by the judicious suggestion that his personal expert knowledge might be invaluable to us for the particular film." In Tallents's account, Samuel began by stressing how his experience as director of the soft drink firm Apollinaris gave him intimate knowledge of the advertising trade and film's ineffectual quality. After the Chairman of the EMB's Film Committee Walter Elliot and Amery rebuffed him by calling the proposal "a background film, not advertising," Tallents recounted that quickly, then, "we dangled our herring bait in front of the Financial Secretary." Samuel bit, "genially offering to help us with his deep knowledge of the herring industry and ourselves warmly welcoming his offer."[17] Wonderful anecdotes as these may be, it is nevertheless likely that resort to such extraordinary contrivance may not have been a favorable omen for establishing lasting victories. Moreover, the attitude of Grierson and Tallents that Treasury had in its leadership ranks un-sophisticated chumps who could be outwitted in the arts of bureaucratic legerdemain did not endear them to this department. Unbeknownst to Grierson and his allies, Treasury officials often saw through their ruses and privately left interdepartmental correspondence saying so.[18]

Born near Stirling, Scotland, in 1898 and educated at Glasgow University, Grierson took a winding path toward film production, influenced by his admiration of local Clydeside labor, whose struggles went undocument-ed, and the writings of American moral philosophers on modern media in the shaping of mass opinion. A recipient of a Rockefeller Foundation grant, Grierson studied at the University of Chicago from 1924 to 1927. He came to venerate the writings of the two Walts, Whitman and Lippmann, the for-mer for asserting the need for a democratic arts and literature, the latter for confronting the problem of mass opinion in the new conditions of moder-nity. For democracy to triumph, Whitman asserted that "it will be at least as much (I think likely double as much) the result of democratic literature and arts (if we get them) as of democratic parties." According to Grierson, he and his Chicago cohort especially "noted the conclusion of such men as Walter Lippmann, that because the citizen, under modern conditions, could not know everything about everything all the time, democratic citizenship was impossible." Seeking to "solve the problem," Grierson thought that ra-dio and cinema might become "necessary instruments in both the practice of government and the enjoyment of citizenship." He indeed credited Lipp-mann's direct intervention for this turn in his life's mission. While studying at "the Political Science School in Chicago," Grierson readily admitted that, despite reading Lippmann, "I must confess that we did not think so much about the film or about the radio. We were concerned with the influence of modern newspapers." He then revealed:

It was Mr. Lippmann himself who turned this educational research in the direction of the film. I talked to him one day of the labor involved in following developments of the Yellow Press. . . . He mentioned that we would do better to follow the dra-matic patterns of the film through the changing character of our time, and the box-office records of success and failure which were on file.[19]

Grierson found the necessary files for such research by contacting yet another Walter, Walter Wanger, who had served with Lippmann during World War I as an officer in U.S. Army Intelligence and as a member of Woodrow Wilson's staff at the Paris Peace Conference. A producer for Para-mount during the 1920s, the Dartmouth-educated Wanger later became one of Hollywood's leading production chiefs at Paramount, Columbia, and

MGM. Grierson pronounced this research responsible for his theory of "the directive use of films . . . based on two essential factors: the observation of the ordinary or the actual, and the discovery within the actual of the patterns which gave it significance for civic education." Paul Rotha pounced on this statement as "the mainspring of documentary thinking and development." Grierson himself coined the term "documentary" in 1926, as he rebuffed the sneers of leading British film critic Caroline A. Lejeune toward its neologistic crudity. In response to Lejeune's taunts that the movement should dump "this gruesome word 'documentary,'" Grierson noted that "I said at the time, 'Well, I think we'd better hang on to this word because if it's so ugly nobody will steal it.' And that, of course, is what happened. It was so ugly that nobody would steal it."[20]

Grierson made dramatic claims for Britain's contribution to the rise of documentary. "The documentary film was . . . an essentially British development," he declared in 1938. He identified "three good reasons" why documentary film "came to develop in England." First, "It permitted the national talent for emotional understatement to operate in a medium not given to understatement." Second, "It allowed an adventure in arts to assume the respectability of a public service. The third reason was the Empire Marketing Board and a man called Tallents." He claimed that "Tallents's contribution at that time deserves to go down among the more curious feats of Civil Service bravery."[21]

Tallents, who earlier had pronounced it "horrible to think that the British Empire is receiving its education from a place called Hollywood," scrupulously avoided the term "propaganda" to describe the work of the EMB. In his book *The Projection of Britain* (1932), he called for an organization "in the borderland which lies between Government and private enterprise, a school of national projection" that would build ties with a variety of organs: advertising agencies, the BBC, Fleet Street, and international news agencies. In 1933, the Imperial Committee on Economic Consultation and Co-operation recommended what appeared to be a devastating blow to Tallents's vision, as it successfully jettisoned the Empire Marketing Board, a body eliminated on the grounds of Depression-era fiscal belt tightening. During the Ottawa Imperial Economic Conference of 1932, South Africa, the Irish Free State, and Canada had rejected plans for a general customs union, a blow to EMB visionaries already scapegoated for failing to rescue Britain from deepening economic crisis. Still, in 1933, the recently knighted Tallents landed safely back on his feet at the General Post Office (GPO) public relations department, where he convinced Postmaster General Sir Kingsley Wood to take over the EMB Film Unit and its celluloid library. In

1935, the creation of the British Council, the nation's first peacetime propaganda agency, owed much to Tallents's philosophical blueprint. Though
the EMB had emerged from anxieties about American cultural colonization
and supremacy in trade, the British Council sprouted as a response to the
propaganda onslaughts emanating from fascist Italy and Nazi Germany.
According to British Foreign Secretary Samuel Hoare, commenting in 1935:

In all, the danger of German cultural and commercial penetration, which may be
expected to increase as the power and wealth of Germany revives, makes it particularly desirable for British cultural propaganda to secure as firm a hold as possible
on the minds and interests of the population, and particularly the younger generation, before the counter-attraction becomes too strong.[22]

Notably less squeamish than Tallents about calling British productions
"propaganda," Hoare encountered critics decrying the council's work as
"nationalisation of thought." Early yelps of opposition gave way, however,
as Goebbels's unrelenting barrage of Aryan supremacist film and broadcasts
only magnified support for the British Council, which began with a £5,000
budget that escalated to £160,000 by 1938–9. The BBC also sought a greater foreign presence, establishing an Empire Service in 1932 and later in the
decade accepting an infusion of new funds for broadcasting in several European languages. The British Council retained two Achilles heels, however:
a focus on elite rather than popular audiences and a failure to develop a
program for the United States, where anti-British ideology pulsated among
isolationists and non–Anglo-Saxon immigrants.[23] In fairness to British policymakers, too overt and concerted a drive in the United States risked spark-
ing isolationist wrath, as Hollywood discovered in 1941 when segments of
the U.S. Congress set up an investigation into British propaganda on the
silver screen.

The EMB-cum-GPO Film Unit soon produced an identifiable body of
work that won it accolades as an alternative to the Hollywood product.
Dominated by a trio of public-school- and Cambridge-educated directors,
Basil Wright, Arthur Elton, and Stuart Legg, the GPO unit broadened its
resource base often with sponsorship by governmental, semipublic, and private bodies. Basil Wright's *Song of Ceylon,* supported in 1934 by the Ceylon Tea Propaganda Board and produced by Grierson, received tributes
from the novelist and film critic Graham Greene, who was otherwise quick
to lambaste British cinema for its lack of imagination. He instead called
Wright's depiction of a bird startled by a bell and then crossing mountain-
side, forest, and plain as "one of the loveliest visual metaphors I have ever
seen on any screen." Regarding *Song of Ceylon* as an "example to all direc-

tors of perfect construction and the perfect application of montage," Greene
tended to overlook the film's shallow engagement with South Asian labor
history as well as its reliance on an assortment of Orientalist tropes and
clichés.[24]

Harry Watt, another Scotsman at the GPO and later a distinguished feature filmmaker at Ealing Studios, declared that the GPO's work underwent
renewal with Grierson's hiring in 1934 of the Brazilian-born Alberto Cavalcanti. After expulsion from a Brazilian law school and then training as an
architect in Geneva, he had become a force in the French cinematic avant-
garde. His surrealist heritage found reinforcement with the arrival of the
most poetic of British documentarists, Humphrey Jennings, who, despite
continued hostility from Grierson, joined André Breton, Herbert Read, and
Roland Penrose on the Organising Committee of the 1936 International
Surrealist Exhibition.[25] According to Watt, "the arrival of Cavalcanti in the
GPO film unit was the turning point of British documentary because . . .
we really were pretty amateur and a lot of the films were second rate. . . ."
Cavalcanti corrected the GPO's utter ineptitude in the use of sound. In an
odd aesthetic conservatism, Rotha thought the talkie breakthrough to be
the emphasis of glitzy Hollywood and alien to documentary. Working outside the GPO, Rotha made the film *Contact* for Bruce Woolfe's British Instructional Pictures in 1932–3 at the behest of Imperial Airways and Shell.
Today maligned for its parsimonious use of sound, *Contact* is regarded as
a throwback to the silent era. With Cavalcanti, sound became engaged with
the poetry of Auden and the majestic music of Britten. W. H. Auden and
Benjamin Britten collaborated on Cavalcanti's study of miners *Coal Face*
(1936) and Wright and Watt's "film poem" to the postal train *Night Mail*
(1936). Although the experimental sound track on *Coal Face* backfired,
sound showed its possibilities in *Night Mail*, a film that Lord Carrington,
High Commissioner in Australia in 1957, later claimed that "After 29 years
. . . is still in the widest popular demand from our Film Library in Australia." Even *Night Mail*, though, suffered from the GPO's cheap equipment,
a British Visatone sound recording system.[26]

When the Moyne committee assembled testimony and evidence on the
future of British film, it found much of the elite press and film journals ready
to anoint documentary as the standard-bearer of British culture, what Robert Herring in the *Manchester Guardian* (11 February 1936) termed the nation's "chief contribution to the cinema." *The Times* (23 November 1935)
proclaimed that "A great public has now been won for films of the Documentary kind, in which the British school is preeminent." While countering
that documentary remains "much ignored in this country," the *Morning*

Post (27 January 1936) said it "nevertheless contains more claims to recognition and to greatness than all the super-productions of the commercial studios." In the *Daily Telegraph* (31 January 1936), Harold Nicolson adjudged the genre "more educative, intellectual, more aesthetic" than Hollywood films and "therefore more durable." Professor Lancelot Hogben in the film journal *Sight and Sound* seconded this sentiment and proclaimed that "a man or woman who does not realise" documentary's contribution to human welfare "belongs to the political past and has no place in the political future." In the triumphant view of the trade paper *The Cinema* (13 February 1936), documentary has "contributed more to social advancement and thought than the entertainment film has done in thirty years."[27]

Notwithstanding such ringing endorsement, documentary still could not escape its place at the periphery of the film industry. Its marginalized status had several sources worth exploration if its historical trajectory is to be understood.

First, despite much sympathetic commentary on the cultural pages of the prestige press, documentary had assembled powerful enemies: one bloc in the film trade, the other among the Tory Right. Britain's film corporations resented the GPO unit and routinely noted that its producers received state subsidies and thus could underprice the efforts of private enterprise in this domain. Grierson had been offered £350,000 to surrender the GPO's film library to the firm Gaumont–British, and his resistance did not endear him to Britain's minimoguls.[28] At the same time, exhibitors thought efforts at educating the popular classes to be foolhardy and, fearful of an ensuing decline in audience, sought to forestall the Moyne committee's endorsement of a short-films quota that would immediately benefit documentary. The rise of the double feature in the 1930s threatened the death knell for the short film, as exhibitors shunned the latter for newsreels. Short films held over 6 percent of screen time in the year ending 1934, then began an ominous descent to 4.21 percent by September 1935 and, by 1939, a microscopic 2.25 percent.[29] In the Moyne committee's own summary of the oral evidence of the Cinematograph Exhibitors Association, the theater owners explained "that the public come to the cinemas to be amused, not to be educated." A witness identified the GPO film *BBC: The Voice of Britain* (1934–5) as a production he "himself had been prepared to book if the price were lower," but "the public would not have it." This was the grim reality, even though the CEA itself "marked the film high in their report."[30]

Thus the major base for viewing documentaries remained the film societies and cinema clubs scattered throughout Britain. Launched in France during the early 1920s, the international cinema club movement gained momentum in Britain when Ivor Montagu founded the London Film Society in 1925. Permitting Britons a "private" venue for viewing films denied a certificate by the British Board of Film Censors, the Film Society featured the works of Soviet and continental European directors. "There were about forty British film societies in operation by 1939," estimated film commentator Roger Manvell; a decade later, "the number approaches 200."[31]

Unhappy about Britain's deepening exposure to Soviet film craft, the Tory Right suspected the political sympathies of the documentary movement. The former press officer of the Conservative Office Oliver Bell told the Manchester Press Club that leading members of the documentary unit were on the payroll of the Soviet Union. His ideological craftsmanship left a patina of authority due to Bell's service as a director of the British Film Institute, even though this body had fallen under the control of the private film trade during the interwar years.[32] Bell and his friends had not taken notice that the most brain-spattering and windpipe-slitting practitioners of anti-Bolshevism also admired the Soviet filmmaker Sergei Eisenstein – notably, Joseph Goebbels. (An alarmed Eisenstein told the Nazi propagandist to refrain from praising his cinematic art.)[33]

Rotha later wrote that the documentarists decided to forgo a libel case; but the Red accusation dogged Grierson and his movement. After 1938, Grierson left Great Britain for Canada, where he built up the National Film Board. On 6 September 1945, Igor Gouzenko, a code clerk in the USSR embassy in Ottawa, revealed a network of Soviet spies in Canada, and among those implicated was a woman who had done a stint as Grierson's secretary. Royal Canadian Mounted Police and parliamentary investigators grilled Grierson constantly, as Prime Minister Mackenzie King gloomily wrote in his diaries: "Canada is more or less honeycombed with Communist leaders. . . ." Of Grierson, King recorded in his diary on 20 February 1946: "I have been suspicious of his sympathies with communism, etc." Fond of bird and bee metaphors, he also referred to "a Communist nest" at the National Film Board. A Royal Commission – better known as the Taschereau–Kellock Commission, after Supreme Court Justices Robert Taschereau and R. L. Kellock – called up numerous witnesses, including Grierson during April and May 1946. Grierson rebuffed the prosecution's lob, "First of all, are you a communist or communistically inclined?" by stating that, having been trained as a public servant for eighteen years in "the classical Whitehall school," "that meant . . . you have no political affiliations." Grierson's denials notwithstanding, King refused to follow his recommendations for his successor at the NFB. Meanwhile, when Grierson left to take a post in February 1947 as a mass media and public information advisor to Julian

Huxley at UNESCO, the Federal Bureau of Investigation and J. Edgar Hoover continued to bark constantly of his service to treachery. Grierson eventually resigned in February 1948, unable to fulfill his global plans for an alternative media policy. The headline of the *New York World-Telegram* screamed: "UN Fires Canadian Atom Spy Case Figure." Grierson reflected that Washington's meddling with UNESCO initiatives ensured that the agency would be unable to challenge what he called the U.S. "stranglehold" on world communications.[34]

Most commentators treat the communist-mole accusations against Grierson as silliness and paranoia, an indictment of the tactics of the Red-baiting Right. Doggedly sniffing about for evidence of Irish and Bolshevik subversion, the Special Branch, Scotland Yard's counterespionage unit, dispatched Arthur Cain to monitor Grierson during part of 1936 and 1937. Harry Watt used to tease the Special Branch "shadow" with preposterous intrigues. "All right for tonight, Joe? Got the bomb? The job is on," he would say.[35] It should be recalled, however, that Grierson's left-leaning colleagues in film criticism and the documentary movement may not have aided his self-image as a Whitehall public servant above the fray of party politics. Writing to Paul Rotha from Capetown, South Africa, on 11 July 1934, cinema theorist David Schrire denounced film critic C. A. Lejeune for calling Grierson "the most considerable voice in all departments of modern cinema in England." Declaring "Whatever that bitch says is always wrong," Schrire went on a trash-talking binge that insinuated Stalinist loyalties in Grierson and lifted Rotha up as an artistic genius superior to the overly lauded Scotsman. In a private rant that could have baleful consequences if it fell into the hands of documentary's enemies, Schrire observed:

THE ONLY ALTERNATIVE FOR PEOPLE IN OUR ECONOMIC POSITION IS TO BECOME PROFESSIONAL FULL TIME REVOLUTIONARIES. And what if we disagree with the Stalintern? Will J. G. and his support us? Like hell they will![36]

Perhaps referring to Grierson's hiring of leftist Ralph Bond, Schrire wondered:

[W]hat has Grierson done except mouth radical claptrap and take lessons in elementary Stalinism from some,fishy looking simp in the party's panel of "intellectual" pimps. . . . It is about time that the myth that is Grierson is exploded. . . . What has he done in pictures except organise the ultimate refuges of a decadent finance capital.[37]

The last vague remark may touch on a second area of vulnerability for the documentary movement: sponsorship. Documentary relied heavily on

sponsorship from government bodies and private corporations. "Among
many social growths in the 1930s in the Western world a new kind of animal was born: not a Press officer nor an advertising manager, but a highly
respectable figure, the Public Relations Man," proclaimed Rotha. Jack Bed-
dington of Shell-Mex and BP, Frank Pick of London Transport, Snowden
Gamble of Imperial Airways, Colonel Medlicott of Anglo-Iranian Oil, Tom-
mie Tallents of the Orient Shipping Line, S. C. Leslie and A. P. Ryan representing the gas industry, and Alexander Wolcough for oil, exemplified this
new breed willing to unleash the power of film.[38]

Despite all the charges of leftism swirling against the documentarists,
Tory governments and the corporate PR operatives put their talents to use.
The Labour Party proved lethargic in pursuing the new medium, and when
it finally achieved power in 1945, new Board of Trade President Stafford
Cripps found his plans for a more ambitious information policy snuffed out
by the formidable figures of Foreign Minister Ernest Bevin and the Home
Office's Herbert Morrison.

The corporate sponsorship, coupled with the Oxbridge background of
the documentarists, earned the movement suspicions from the Left. The Oxonian Auden had collaborated with the documentarists, but even he did not
approve of the social aroma and the wheels of commerce animating many
of its projects. According to the first issue of *World Film News*, a leading
organ of the documentarists:

Auden says that British documentary directors are upper middle class and never likely to understand workers. He says that sponsorship by Government Departments
and industrial companies will never permit a truthful account of their people.[39]

World Film News rebuffed Auden's critique by claiming that, through
the trials and tribulations of filmmaking, the documentarist develops an
identity and empathy with the beleaguered proletariat. "What is more important than paternities is that documentary forces its serfs to live and learn
with workmen under working conditions," the journal asserted.[40] Contra
such claims, this goal of bonding the film crew with the proletariat could
have been hampered by peculiarities of the Grierson aesthetic: The Scotsman put near total focus on the world of work to the exclusion of the community and leisure activities of the workers. At one point, he expressed a
bellyful of repugnance for Humphrey Jennings, who portrayed a kazoo-
playing band of workers in his film *Spare Time* (1939). Presenting workers
goofing off and in moments of levity apparently clashed with the Griersonian preference for proles to be in postures of heroic stature and dignity.[41]

Meanwhile, the place of the public-relations operative in this enterprise almost certainly posed problems for the British documentary movement's oft-stated goal of deepening democracy. Walter Lippmann, the inspiration for Grierson's life project, spoke of "the manufacture of consent," necessary in the face of the erratic and irresponsible mass man. Declaring that "knowledge of how to create consent will alter every political calculation and modify every political premise," Lippmann previously noted that "the manipulation of masses through symbols may be the only quick way of having a critical thing done." Moreover, "representative government . . . cannot be worked successfully . . . unless there is an independent, expert organization for making the unseen facts intelligible to those who have to make the decisions."[42] Lippmann, along with the University of Chicago's chief expert on propaganda, Harold Lasswell, and the father of public relations, Edward Bernays, set out to refine the mechanisms for achieving the manufacture of consent. The new public-relations operatives seized upon film as one of the tools for remolding opinion.

H. L. Mencken once reflected that Lippmann had "started out life with high hopes for democracy and an almost mystical belief in the congenital wisdom of the masses," which he surrendered to the conviction that most people are "ignorant and unteachable." Although Mencken erroneously believed that Lippmann's socialist phase as a Harvard undergraduate had been one of fervent devotion to the common man, he may have identified an area in which Grierson broke with Lippmann.[43] Grierson's optimism about film's ability to teach and educate the public differed from Lippmann's cold pessimism about the capabilities of the so-called masses. Still, the documentary makers had to furnish a product that did not offend corporate and government sponsors – those constraints ensuring that Oliver Bell's specter of a Red fraternity was a phantom and one defanged of revolutionary bite. Stephen Tallents himself constructed a list stipulating appropriate topics and the proper depiction of reality in EMB films:

The monarchy (with its growing scarcity value)
Parliamentary institutions (with all the value of a first edition)
The British Navy
The English Bible, Shakespeare, and Dickens
In international affairs – a reputation for disinterestedness
In national affairs – a tradition of justice, law, and order
In national character – a reputation for coolness
In commerce – a reputation for fair dealing
In manufacture – a reputation for quality
In sport – a reputation for fair play.[44]

While there were later breaches, Harry Watt, who believed that "we were left-wing to a man," admitted that "I never knew of a Party member amongst us." He then sheepishly conceded:

The truth is that if we had indulged in real social criticism to any extent, we would have immediately been without sponsorship and our whole experiment, which was artistically a fine one, would have finished. So we compromised.[45]

Rotha ratified this stark judgment:

Few of the famous documentaries of the '30s were actually concerned with attacks on social problems. To take six "classics" of the period – *Drifters, Song of Ceylon, Night Mail, North Sea, Aero-Engine, Pett and Pott* – only Wright's Ceylon film had any remote connection with the exposure of social problems. No film made officially by either the E.M.B. or G.P.O. Film Units (under a Tory Government recall) did anything whatsoever to hasten "the process of socialization." Of the main films that did attack social problems – *Housing Problems, Enough to Eat?, Today We Live, Eastern Valley, Children at School,* and *Face of Britain* – only one was produced under Grierson's aegis. . . . It is interesting that the record shows so few of the films in the '30s to have been socially attentive.[46]

The documentarists' devotion to portraying social reality too often participated in a naïve empiricism ratifying things as they are and not as they ought to be. In resolving the is/ought problematic of Western philosophy, British documentary stayed safely on the "is" side of the equation and, as Watt confessed, employed few tools to unhinge the panels of dominant ideology. In Grierson's *Drifters*, the work of the fishermen follows immutable rhythms, appearing to be part of nature rather than inserted in a social order constructed and reconstructed on behalf of the powerful. David Schrire proved to be one of the more acute critics of the *Drifters* aesthetic, comparing it to the anthropological romanticism of the American Robert Flaherty, director of the legendary film of Eskimo life *Nanook of the North* (1922) and later a collaborator with the EMB/GPO unit:

Remember the contempt Grierson had for the actual marketing of the fish, the regret he appeared to express that the fish, the fruits of the glorious adventurous fishermen, was bought and sold for money. Shouldn't his protest have been that the fish was often thrown back into the sea, or used as manure, because of the economic system which did not allow people to afford to buy it? . . . Flaherty ran away into the anthropological present; Grierson dealt with actual industry or occupation but ran away from its social meaning. He said, as it were, I like the adventure, the joy of the catch, but when I see that it is sold just like a pair of trousers in Petticoat Lane, my soul revolts and I would rather no fish were caught.[47]

British documentary's sometimes complacent view of the camera as a mirror recording social reality led to a third danger for the movement: lackluster approval at the box office. The celebration of the ordinary in documentary did not always sit well with audiences, who in polls indicated that cinema represented for them an escape from the ennui and misery of work and daily life. In his enterprise, Grierson undoubtedly came under the influence of the Soviet filmmakers Victor Turin and, to a lesser extent, Eisenstein, who allegedly carped at the presentation of *Drifters* before the showing of his *Potemkin* in London because the techniques used in the herring spectacle gave away the plot in his revolutionary saga. While Grierson increasingly came to deny Russian influences on British documentary art, and Rotha condemned "the cult for Soviet films" that "has become slightly hysterical and more than a little tedious in its parrot-like cry," both British and Soviet filmmakers had checkered success at box offices home and abroad. Eisenstein, nevertheless, credited Hollywood's D. W. Griffith with influencing his film craft, and, despite a growing propensity toward vitriolic denunciations of the U.S. film industry, he chose topics with a majesty and drama alien to the British documentarists. In the celebration of the ordinary and ordinary lives, the Russian Revolution provides a backdrop of titanic, global proportions – unlike the herring saga, which conveys just another day living in working-class paradise.[48]

A central element of the British documentary aesthetic was the rejection of the Hollywood star system. The commercial film producer Herbert Wilcox worried in 1932 that British film's lack of "virility" resulted from a failure to create larger-than-life stars. The celebration of the ordinary meant eschewal of the hero in history. Hollywood had built up audiences and product loyalty by glorification of individual stars and heroic personalities in history. British documentary rejected this as crass commercialism and false promotion of bourgeois individualism. The French political philosopher and social critic Régis Debray observes that, for the Left, "History is made by the masses," while "the Right" holds "that a flock without a shepherd is a stampeding mob." He adds that in the portrayal of the past: "The history of the Right is a portrait gallery, that of the Left a succession of crowd movements. French Revolution, the June days of 1848, Commune, Popular Front: these uprisings have no face or several." In contrast to the thirteen-volume history of the French workers movement by the Left's Jean Maîtron, the Right produces "a succession of hagiographies": Saint Louis, Richelieu, Louis XIV, and others.[49] Though Britain has a tradition of right-wing people's history (Chesterton, Belloc, and, more recently, Laslett), it is again the Left that dominates this genre. One of its founders, J. R. Green, in his *Short History of the English People* (1877), declared his intention "to pass lightly and briefly over . . . the personal adventures of kings and nobles, the pomp of courts or the intrigues of favourites, and to dwell at length on . . . the history of the nation itself."

In the case of British documentary, its presentation became less a celebration of the crowd, as depicted by Green, and sometimes a flight from people. The American critic Harry Alan Potamkin suggested that Grierson takes less delight in the herring workers and much more in the fish themselves. "Where are the people in his film?" Potamkin pleaded. "He is more engrossed with the independent graces of fish in the water."[50] Graham Greene's reference to the bird in the *Song of Ceylon* and Alexander Korda's claim to Paul Rotha that his proudest accomplishment was helping Huxley complete the documentary *The Private Life of the Gannets* (1934) are exhibits of a film craft that displaces human agency in favor of nature, a refuge from the ever-mutable worlds of commerce and politics. In some films, nature itself becomes the adversary, displacing blame for the human predicament from tyrannical institutions or a class of oppressors. In searching for models for the work of the EMB, Tallents shared Grierson's admiration of Victor Turin's film on the construction of the Turkistan–Siberian Railroad, *Turksib* (1929). Claiming to have witnessed the reception of *Turksib* "by a selected audience of English businessmen and labour representatives" who judged it "finer . . . than any other they had viewed," Tallents marveled: "It has no personal story, and no individual actors. Its hero is the slowly advancing railway, its villain the forces of drought and storm, of ice and rock and flood."[51]

Turin's deployment of the humanity-versus-nature trope proved much more influential to Grierson's British documentary movement than the usually cited Soviet suspects Eisenstein and Pudovkin. Grierson appeared to make a distinction between what he called (1) *human documentary*, film dealing with the inevitable aspects of existence, *la condition humaine* – labor, death, and the caprices of nature – and (2) *social documentary*, which focuses on conditions of injustice at a specific time and place, the miseries of war, the ravages of unemployment, and the truncheon-wielding brutality of the police. The former deals with the natural, the latter with more human-made tragedy.[52] For the most part, the British movement preferred human to social documentary, even while claiming its own hallmark to be "social realism." Critics took it at its word. Brecht aptly warned that the portrayal of realism in art is a construct relying on a variety of symbols and conventions. "[R]ealism . . . is an old concept which has been much used by many men and many purposes," he wrote in the late 1930s, "and before it can be applied we must spring-clean it. . . ." Pointing out that "Literary works cannot be taken over like factories, or literary forms of expression like industrial methods," he suggested that "Reality alters; to represent it the means of representation must alter too." Brecht's riposte against convention and formalism is a salutary caution against the documentarists who uncritically believed in the timelessness of their representations of reality. He termed it "a mistake to treat" realism as "fully explained, unsullied, unambiguous and without a past."[53]

Now to give Grierson his due, he clearly recognized that his brand of realism relied on deployment of a specific symbolic universe, which he opposed to the conventions of, say, newsreels. Documentary, reasserted Grierson, is "the creative treatment of actuality." He also began to assert some distance between himself and advocates of the humanity-versus-nature trope, notably Turin and Flaherty. Of *Turksib,* he admitted that the film "gave every impression of building a railway, but the approach was too detached to appreciate just how precisely or humanly it was built."[54] Of Flaherty, he gave himself pause over *Man of Aran* (1934), a film depicting poverty-racked fishermen dwelling in an island off Northern Ireland. The film's climax featured a shark hunt designed to obtain oil desperately needed for the men's lamps. In point of fact, this was a dramatic ruse hatched by Flaherty: These islanders had not hunted shark in over three generations. Grierson's alarm may have been heightened after the film received Italy's coveted Mussolini Cup in September 1934, and when Goebbels regularly lavished praise on Flaherty for showing heroism in the face of hostile nature.[55] Grierson himself had saluted Flaherty in 1926 for not flinching in portraying "a cruel procedure" of tattooing inflicted on Polynesian youth "before they take their place beside manhood." "[L]et us reflect," Grierson had enthused, "that perhaps it summons a bravery that is healthful for the race."[56] For all of his later retreats, Grierson failed to engage with the Brechtian insight that the conventions of realism must change as reality alters; in concrete terms, the late-nineteenth-century realism of a Tolstoy had grown outmoded in the 1930s. During the 1970s and 1980s, British documentarists and film critics turned on Grierson by claiming that his methods had bequeathed to British cinema an artistic straitjacket. Unbeknownst to these latter-day anti-Griersonians, C. A. Lejeune as early as 1932 had feared that Grierson had already obstructed alternative film currents in developing what she called a "rather tiresome tradition."[57]

It did not appear to be Grierson's intention to enforce artistic closure on the documentary movement. More elastic in aesthetic judgment than

some of his documentarist colleagues, he proved appreciative of Hollywood's artistic gifts and dominance of world screens. Such bursts of ecu-
menicalism could potentially inflame documentary's squabble-hungry protagonists. Of the reception of the U.S. film industry in Great Britain, Paul
Rotha later decried the postwar growth of "a young generation of film addicts" who have "sprouted to adulate a hung-over era in cinema that they
did not experience at first hand." Referring to "the glorification of the
Hollywood years of the 1920s–40s," Rotha said, "I find it almost as nauseating as when I see partly-educated teenagers flashing Swastika badges and
cloth Iron Crosses when I see this salivating over the Hollywood years of
whoredom." Saluting Stroheim for telling a BBC-TV audience in 1954 that
"Hollywood is just a whore" and Flaherty for declaring after the filming of
Moana (1926) that "Hollywood is like floating over an open sewer in a flat-
bottomed glass boat," Rotha then turned to condemning:

the Fox's, the Laemmles, the Zukors, the Schencks, the Mayers, the Cohns, the Warners, the Selznicks and all their countless hangers-on . . . as parasitic to society as
their counterparts in banking, insurance, accountancy, real estate, property development, alcohol trading and, of course, politics. They dealt in entertainment in
terms of flesh as others dealt in drugs, drink and property. I find it slightly revolting
that servile adulation should be given to such gangsters. . . .[58]

In contrast to the simmering vitriol of Rotha, Grierson advised Britain's
cultural Cassandras to moderate their anti-Hollywood fervor. Calling attention to the Imperial Conferences of 1926 and 1930 that demanded "'more
British films,'" Grierson cautioned "the amateurs of the breakfast-table"
who "either complain wildly of the cheapness and vulgarity of all things
American, or they say again and yet again, that English cinema has only
to go to English literature and English scenery to conquer the world." The
Cardiff-based *South Wales News* (25/26 February 1926) echoed this theme
with tedious regularity, as its editorial writers declared of America:

In every branch of art – in the drama, music, and literature – she lags far behind us;
and this being so it is obviously a very serious matter that she should be dominant
in the British cinema. It is simply incredible that British enterprise is powerless to
check this mischief. . . . All that is needed is the application of brains, enterprise,
and capital.[59]

Noting that "the path of cinematic conquest is a little more difficult,"
Grierson judged that Britons:

rather foolishly underestimate the task when we deny the quality of American films.
They represent a command of invention, a mastery of technique and a courage of
dramatic effect which our own films only rarely approach. The United States itself,

by its very medley of strange races and swift happenings, is almost bound to prosper in the more inventive aspect of story-telling.[60]

Indeed in the early years of World War II Grierson urged his old GPO comrades to turn to Hollywood for the creation of pro-British propaganda. He told Arthur Elton that

England's selfishness and England's self-concentration have been deeply abhorrent to the rest of the world. Its decadent social structure remains a puzzle to younger and more vital peoples; and no sooner do they hear the bright word about the rising spirit of the people in England, than their hopes are dashed to the ground by some wandering snob.[61]

He then called on Elton to "Make the Americans do your propaganda for you. They know the style and the tempo and where films fit. England doesn't and it is too late to learn."

Grierson's lapse into pessimism may have sold his nation's capabilities short, as the war provided a unity of purpose that ignited British film production. His lugubrious tone made some wonder if he had lost faith in Britain's documentary movement. At the war's end, David Schrire speculated that "Grierson must be getting worn out. He should sell himself to Hollywood which . . . is beginning to take an interest in the possibilities of doc[umentary]."[62] While fighting in vain for a 20 percent short-film quota in the mid-1930s, Grierson had already made the damaging concession to the Moyne committee:

Shorts do not, in any theatres, except in very special circumstances, pull on the audience. . . . I might cite the notorious case . . . from Birmingham, of a man who ordered 24 of the worst shorts because he maintained they cleared his audience quickly![63]

Grierson's skepticism that his alternative film vision might ever supplant Hollywood left partisans of documentary cold. He threw additional chilled lager on Alexander Korda's and J. Arthur Rank's visions of a Hollywood-on-the-Thames, the creation of a British rival to the U.S. film industry.

In the midst of Grierson's nattering negativism, there could be found in him an underlying optimism about documentary and alternatives to Hollywood. Grierson maintained that documentary and the short film would play several roles in the future of Great Britain:

1. educating the public about issues and institutions central to democracy;
2. countering the American universe of Hollywood and what he called the West London bias of British film by introducing audiences to life in Scotland, Northern Ireland, Ceylon, and distant outposts of the Empire; and
3. supplying the new medium of television.

In testimony before the Moyne committee and in leading organs of the doc-
umentary movement such as *World Film News*, Grierson alerted fellow
Scotsman Sir John Reith, the director-general of the BBC, to the possibilities
of documentary and short films for the emergent technology of television.
Long after the British state packed up the last remnants of his film unit,
Grierson and his cohorts became staple figures on the BBC of the 1950s.
        British feature film also owed a modest debt to Grierson's movement.
Ealing Studios, perhaps the most successful British film enterprise of the
1940s and 1950s, developed its signature style of realism and local community under the influence of documentary. The GPO's Cavalcanti and Watt
both joined Ealing. Cavalcanti temporarily returned to his surrealist roots
with his "Ventriloquist's Dummy" segment of the anthology picture *Dead
of Night* (1945), among the most chilling and macabre of British films.
While Watt's *The Overlanders* (1946) and *Eureka Stockade* (1948) are not
the most treasured films of Ealing's output, they are still appreciated in Australia, where the studio made a short but determined break from its Little
Englander horizons.
        For those prepared to deny the legacy of the documentary movement,
it is only fitting that Grierson closed with a fish story to justify its future.
"The analogy between films and fish should not be lightly dismissed," he
maintained. "I could cite the case of the people of London, whose taste has
been so perverted over the years that if they ever tasted a fresh fish, which
is beyond the realm of possibility, they would certainly reject it as rotten."[64]
In retaining a space for the artisan of film against the industrial machinery
of Hollywood, Grierson hoped to reacquaint Britons, if ever so briefly, with
the taste of fresh fish, the life of a palpable community at work, and the art
animating the marching triumph of democracy.

CHAPTER FIVE

The Korda Road to Riches, Recovery, and Ruin

THE FEDERATION SEARCHES FOR A FILM SAVIOR

The leading representative of British capitalism, the Federation of British Industries, never regarded documentary as a serious alternative to a successful feature film industry. In 1926, they had mounted the heavy guns designed to stanch the inpouring of Hollywood films throughout the empire. The Federation's report indeed set the agenda for the Imperial Conference of 1926. As Lord Newton once said of this private body's influence in the corridors of Whitehall: "This Government, like the previous Government, has a sort of superstitious reverence for the Federation of British Industries."[1] Labour MP Philip Snowden attacked Sir Philip Cunliffe-Lister, the president of the Board of Trade, as "simply a tool in the hands of the Federation of British Industries."[2]

In 1931, the Federation initiated renewed pressure on the Foreign Office and the Board of Trade to fortify British film. Federation memoranda made no mention of *Drifters*, and its strategy showed that the documentary movement had not swept over those members of the elite best placed to invest in the industry.

The Federation of British Industries based its renewed campaign on two underlying fears:

1. Hollywood preeminence would continue to hurt demand for British goods and services, and the revival of British industry depended on support from the silver screen.
2. The rise of the talking film now imperiled the Queen's English as Americanisms infiltrated the language with unprecedented force.

Angus Fletcher of the British Library of Information later told the Foreign Office that he preferred early films because they were "mercifully silent."[3]

The Federation of British Industries proposed two strategies for over-coming this perilous state of affairs. First, the body argued that control of the exhibition sector was the key to Hollywood's global power. While this had plausibility for the U.S. domestic market, it did not fully explain how the United States managed to dominate most overseas markets where it lacked any substantial ownership stake. The Federation appeared to have grounds insofar as vertical integration had assisted the film majors in rais-ing capital and ensuring a base of theaters granting immediate screen time for new releases.

Second, the Federation of British Industries called on the Board of Trade and the Foreign Office to get behind a movement for a British blockbuster film, a colossal success that would trigger the growth of a vibrant film in-dustry, what some economists might call the "multiplier effect," vaudeville style.

The Foreign Office initially liked the idea, and it backed the idea of a movie produced by an international heavyweight, perhaps Charlie Chaplin [Fig. 6]. The Foreign Office wondered "whether Chaplin could be persuad-ed to give the 'Old Country' a leg up."[4] Foreign Office staff and Federation officials began tracking Chaplin throughout the spring of 1931 in hopes of landing a meeting with the man whom Neville Kearney, the head of the Fed-eration's film division, called "our wandering comedian." Chaplin proved adept at eluding the civil servants of the world's greatest empire. When he finally heard that the proposed screenplay involved a story of the romance of John Smith and Pocahontas, thought to be of special transatlantic ap-peal, Chaplin told a newspaper that he had no interest in such a vehicle. The ill-starred Foreign Office and the Federation of British Industries said such a rebuff would not deter them, as Chaplin had yet to see the script. Eventually they surrendered the idea of winning over the charming Tramp, though they thought the project would eventually come to fruition. Soon their blockbuster dreams went by the wayside.[5]

In the previous months, the Foreign Office had busied itself with inves-tigation of Hollywood-generated incidents and named two general sources: (1) those Hollywood films giving offense to British sensibilities and (2) those shown in foreign lands that brought diplomatic protests to Whitehall, with overseas governments thus demanding that Britain join action against un-savory forces in the cinema industry. Curiously, British Foreign Office staff found themselves unable to locate many files of such complaints, and they could not recall themselves details of past crises. The Foreign Office appar-ently did not attract avid cinephiles to its ranks. Eventually it turned to rep-resentatives of the MPPDA, the Hays Office, to attempt augmenting its list

FIGURE 6. On 21 February 1931, Charlie Chaplin takes a stroll with Prime Minister Ramsay MacDonald, a frequent critic of Hollywood's dangers to the British Empire. In the early 1930s, some members of His Majesty's government sought to convince Chaplin to make a film about Pocahontas, a production that they hoped would become a blockbuster and revive British cinema. The actor ignored their overtures. *Source:* Public Record Office, PRO 30/69/1666.

of diplomatic affronts at the hands of Hollywood. Hays's eagerness to meet aggrieved foreign representatives may have rendered him vulnerable on this occasion. Of the incidents in the Foreign Office's files, they were relatively few and far between:[6]

1. In 1921, Britain's ambassador to Paris approached the Quai d'Orsay (i.e., French Ministry of Foreign Affairs), requesting that the film *How Lord Kitchener Was Betrayed* not be displayed in France. The director

of the Sûreté Générale told British officials he would be on special guard if it entered the country. The film made the wild accusation that a War Office functionary seduced by a German-born woman spilled details of the journey of the *HMS Hampshire*, a vessel subsequently blown up in 1916. In contrast, the British government maintained that Kitchener's ship traveled off course because of fog and thus hit the fatal mine field without German foreknowledge of its destination.

In 1922, Britain's ambassador to Washington, Sir Auckland Geddes, met State Department functionaries "unofficially" in hopes of stopping its display. "The State Department replied that they had no legal ground for prohibiting its exhibition," claimed the Foreign Office minute, "but suggested a direct approach to Mr. Will Hays . . . who subsequently informed the Embassy that he had received assurances that American producers would refuse to distribute it."

2. In 1923, Hays embraced a similar posture when asked to block the exhibition of *Birth of a Nation* in South Africa, a potential racial powderkeg.

3. In 1924, another D. W. Griffith film, *America* (discussed in Chapter 1), mobilized Britain's ambassador to the United States to demand excisions of content deemed hostile to His Majesty's government.

   In 1925, the British Embassy in Paris staged a presentation of the French version of Griffith's spectacle, called *Pour Indépendance,* and "proposed certain deletions, which were accepted."

4. In early 1930, British authorities judged that the U.S. film *Green Goddess* treated India "in an offensive manner," "but our Ambassador decided that to protest would only advertise it."

The Foreign Office also listed demands in 1927 by Britain's ambassador to Switzerland for a German production company to trim offensive passages from its film *La Prisonnière de Changhai* (*Gefangene von Shanghai*). Fears in 1929 that *Storm over Asia* (*Potomok Chingis-Khana*), a Soviet film displaying "British soldiers attacking Orientals," might provoke anticolonialist rage met a cooler diplomatic response; the British ambassador in Berlin "decided not to protest against its being shown in Berlin."

In 1931, the British government tried to establish an informal mechanism whereby Hollywood could consult an official with loose ties to the British Embassy in Los Angeles on films dealing with the nation or the empire. High hopes for the scheme evaporated when the designated functionary, R. L. Nosworthy, received a transfer from Los Angeles during late 1931. In reality, the Hays Office under Joseph Breen subsequently pressured the studios to consult the British government, but compliance could be erratic as Breen discovered during rows over *Gunga Din* and *The Prince and the Pauper*.[7]

As the 1930s opened, the Foreign Office retained a sunshiny veneer of hope for British film, despite inauspicious horizons: Documentary commanded only a small sliver of the domestic market, the scheme for monitoring Hollywood films met an ill-fated start, and plans for a blockbuster proved abortive. In 1932, the producer Herbert Wilcox, a cofounder of Elstree Studios, bemoaned the dearth of stars, the lack of a Gary Cooper or a Clark Gable: "Britain has no leading man with the standard of virility which cinema audiences of today demand of their film heroes." Bernard Charman, the London correspondent for the *Motion Picture Herald*, echoed his sentiment: "Britain has got to find he-men if she is to struggle for a place in the world markets."[8]

The Foreign Office's sincere desire to advance the flow of British film appeared clumsy and clogged by tired anti-Semitic reflexes toward the best known of British film producers, Gaumont–British Ltd., which was led by the Jewish Ostrer family. The British Library of Information (BLI) in 1934 informed the Foreign Office that "we were not wildly enthusiastic about the British character of Gaumont–British." For good measure, the BLI functionary added that the New York–based British Film Society of America, an organ to promote the nation's film exports, was unacceptable because of behind-the-scenes Gaumont–British manipulation and the likelihood that "an English community in a very un-American city [New York], are not the best judges of what is good publicity (as we would regard it)." After subsequently learning that Gaumont–British "is not at all in favour of the Society," an apparent Foreign Office official still minuted that "Gaumont–British is, like any other film company essentially commercial" and "is known in the trade as Gaumont–Yiddish." J. G. Ward, when told that the company had made a "bad impression . . . with the trade press and with publicity people" in the United States, advised: "The racial origin of the Gaumont–British people is unlikely to have produced much modesty."[9]

ALEXANDER KORDA: THE LION HAS WINGS

Neverthless, in late 1933 British film found its blockbuster and for most of the decade its anointed savior, a Jewish director, long exiled from Hungary, who called himself Alexander Korda. The name Korda came from the young Hungarian's favorite part of the Catholic mass, the Latin incantation "Sursum corda"; that is to say, "Lift up your hearts!" Korda's flamboyant emergence has probably led most historians to underplay the role of other

commercial successes in reviving British film, including Herbert Wilcox's
U.K. box-office hit of 1934, *Nell Gwyn*.[10] However, in weaving patriotic
themes with intrigues in the private life of Charles II, Wilcox would consciously imitate the Hungarian's model for success.

Korda's own magical rise to the apex of British film did come through
a circuitous transatlantic route. In October 1933, Korda's company, London Films, chose to have the premiere of his film *The Private Life of Henry
VIII* in New York rather than London. The wizards of Wardour Street, the
location of the largest British film companies, had spurned his project. "The
public would never stand for it," said the executives of Gaumont–British.
The British branches of Fox, Paramount, and even United Artists rejected
it for distribution, the last company changing its mind after U.S. executive
Murray Silverstone consulted a report bubbling with praise penned by UA's
chief of British production, Richard Norton (later Lord Grantley). Opening
on 12 October 1933 at Radio City Music Hall, New York, Korda's film
became an instant media sensation, a box-office triumph, and an Oscar
winner for Charles Laughton, whose rambunctious wrestling and turkey-
chomping poses produced the most memorable of screen portraits of the
Tudor prince. In its first week the film missed the record for the most revenue at a single theater by £100. For a film costing £50,000–80,000, it eventually grossed over £500,000 worldwide. Its arrival in Britain two weeks
after the New York premiere met similar accolades. "Greatest British Film
Triumph!" screamed the *Daily Mail* in a four-column headline; the *Daily
Telegraph* called it "A picture in a thousand," and the *Sunday Express*
judged that "Korda deserves all the congratulations that have been show-
ered on him."[11]

The popular legend treats *The Private Life of Henry VIII* as Korda's first
British film. In reality, he had been toiling in the field of *quota quickies*,
movies made on cheap budgets and short shooting schedules so that British exhibitors and American film companies could meet the terms of Parliament's 1927 Quota Act. In the early 1930s, Korda had made seven quota
quickies before his blockbuster triumph. The *Motion Picture Herald* (New
York) saluted Korda's quota production *Reserved for Ladies* (1932) and
noted that "good pictures, wherever they may be produced, reflect benefits
upon the whole industry of the motion picture."[12] For the most part, however, quota quickies had earned the wrath of British politicians and the public. Though they gave needed experience to aspiring directors, and some
repudiated the materialism of U.S. culture, these films would come under
fierce assault during the Moyne committee inquiry into cinema of 1934–6.
Women employed to clean out the debris and foul grime left by theater au-

diences became known as the only viewers of these movies. In an article entitled "Charwomen and Quota Films: Drama and Dust," G. A. Atkinson
declared in *The Era* (10 July 1935) that "Cinema charwomen are the real
– almost the only – public experts on Quota films." In "Film Without an
Audience: Quota Farce at the Adelphi," C. M. Ashton followed up in *The
Era* (6 November 1935) with an account of the quota quickie *Hello Sweetheart*:

Out of interest and amusement I attended a performance, arriving at the theatre at
six o'clock. Naturally, at 6:20 the whole of the remaining audience left the theatre,
and I remained on to the end, till 7:30, having an entire screening to myself, while
the theatre was being dusted out by the attendants.[13]

Wild accusations flew that the British affiliates of Hollywood companies
created these movies with the express purpose of damaging Britain's reputation for cinema artistry. Following the Moyne hearings, Parliament enacted a cost threshold, forcing companies to expend a certain level of resources
before a movie could receive quota credit. It also granted up to triple weight
for films that had blockbuster-level budgets. The parliamentarians rejected
the Moyne committee's call for a body to monitor the quality of movies,
subsequently seen as cumbersome and a potential affront to liberty of expression. Pure economics triumphed over subjective qualitative measures.

Korda assumed the mission of transforming Wardour Street from producers of slapdash quota quickies to an industry geared for churning out
films for the global market. He became an articulate defender of the British
imperial ideal and a spokesperson for legislative efforts to support British
film. As a young filmmaker and editor of a film journal in Hungary, he had
decried German dominance of the screens of Mitteleuropa during World
War I. In an interview in late 1917 in the Korda-edited weekly *Mozihet*
(Cine-Weekly), he had proclaimed that:

I have a deep faith in Hungarian films. . . . I do not expect Hungarian film production to vegetate among the many other national film industries; I believe unflinch-
ingly and have been shouting it at the top of my voice for four or five years: we
Hungarians will soon get to the top. . . .[14]

Referring to the Nordisk Company, under siege from a boycott unleashed by the Allied Powers, as "the paramount film power in Germany
today," Korda believed this firm would seek "a monopoly in Germany, Austria, and Hungary -- if the latter two countries are given a share in the world
markets." Predicting that "It will be a great battle," he foresaw failure for
Nordisk's ambitions:

In the future battles for the world markets of films the decision won't be brought about by millions of marks but by good films. And in this respect I consider the German mammoth enterprise far weaker than the studios of the Western powers. That is why I do not believe that the coming film-war will bring a victory for Germany or turn Hungarian film-production into a servile appendage of the Germans.

Korda's Hungarian friend and biographer Paul Tabori remarked, "It is a striking fact that if one substituted 'British' for 'Hungarian' and 'American' for 'German,' these statements would be completely valid today."[15] Notwithstanding the sheer brazenness of Korda's frequent prediction of German defeat on the actual battlefields of World War I, he often had to be more diplomatic with Hollywood and the Americans. Dependent on Hollywood for distribution in the largest cinema market in the world, he chose his fighting words more carefully and, on many occasions, adopted flattery to win over U.S. allies for his production company, London Films. Korda practiced what is today known as one of Lapham's Rules of Influence: "Comparable to suntan lotion or moisturizing cream, also to furniture polish and ski wax," flattery "cannot be too often or too recklessly applied."[16] In 1932, Korda wrote the U.S. film trade editor Martin Quigley with the observation that "the idea which prevailed here and in Europe sometime ago . . . that the American did not want European pictures, is nothing but a silly invention of those who do not know the business or who are not able to produce pictures of a standard recognized thruout [sic] the world." He elaborated that "the British motion picture industry is not a rival but a partner." Korda approvingly quoted Quigley's words that the Hungarian's "film more nearly resembles Hollywood products than anything previously done over here and that this fact should not be despised because Hollywood has without question established a standard to which the public the world over looks."[17]

In constructing Denham Studios for London Films, Korda saw himself as an architect of a Hollywood-on-the-Thames; yet he should not be regarded as slavishly devoted to Hollywood or as one who owed primary loyalties to U.S. interests. Such charges resounded during World War II, when Korda spent substantial time in the United States on film projects. A close ally of Churchill, who rewarded him with a knighthood in 1942, Korda had to endure taunts that he sold out Britain when he in fact had duties to help the spread of pro-Allied and pro-British film. Both Michael Balcon and J. B. Priestley railed against the British colony in Hollywood, as the former spoke of "deserters," "cowards," and those living it up, including the "plump young technician" Hitchcock.[18] Unable to defend himself, lest he then offend Americans suspicious of foreign operatives in the United States, Korda politely ignored his British detractors.

Korda became a devoted British patriot, so much so that his films embrace an antiquated, nineteenth-century glorification of the empire. His high-Tory sentiments put him at odds with many of his artists and likely his heterodox brothers, who still gave devoted service to London Films. Korda was not the only "outsider" who built film success in Britain through faithful flag-waving. Perhaps his main rival in Britain's commercial cinema, the producer-director Herbert Wilcox liked to boast of his Irish parentage and devotion to Roman Catholicism; yet he won English audiences with patriotic spectacle glorifying British monarchy and empire. Commenting on Wilcox's sequence of Queen Victoria films of the late 1930s (*Victoria the Great; Sixty Glorious Years*), Robert Vansittart of the Foreign Office hailed him: "You've made a film that is a warm tribute to the British Empire and at a time when the first step has been shamefully taken to bring about its disintegration."[19] One of Korda's tormenters, the novelist Graham Greene, begged to differ about Wilcox's "applauded course." Now "well protected as a steam-roller," in Greene's view, Wilcox "irons out opposition. . . . Instead, we have flags, anthems, leading articles, a tombstone reticence." With Wilcox joining Hollywood for a production of *Nurse Edith Cavell* (1939), Greene regretted that "when the drums of propaganda begin to beat again we can hardly expect a popular film producer to stand aloof seeking the tragic values in Miss Cavell's story. . . . [T]he English creative spirit has never risen higher in her commemoration than a statue cut in soap and an emotional melodrama."[20]

Korda's own loyalty to traditional Britain may have grown from gratitude to a nation that had adopted him as its cinematic Messiah after Hollywood had treated him with utter contempt. While Korda evidently did not harbor grudges, the studio bosses during his stint there in the late 1920s and early 1930s ran him out of town with a blend of ruthlessness and cruelty which the Hollywood executive class too often meted out with gusto. When Korda first greeted Joseph P. Kennedy, film financier and patriarch of what would become America's leading political family, the Irish-American owner of First National Films had only scorn for the Hungarian's courteous demeanor and formal decorum: "Who does that guy think he is, some kind of fucking baron or something?" Korda later referred to Kennedy's brief control of First National as "a four week reign of terror." After switching to Fox Studios, recently wrested away from its founder, William Fox, by Winfield Sheehan, Korda soon judged the crudities of Kennedy to be mild in comparison. Sheehan and his production chief Sol Wurtzel, wrote Korda's nephew Michael, "combined sadism and stupidity to an extraordinary degree. The one was tall, thin and humorless, like an Irish cop out of uniform; the other a cigar-chewing vulgarian, who was reputed to make

Harry Cohn look like a gentleman by comparison."[21] ("King" Cohn, the chief of Columbia Pictures, was known as the "bastard's bastard" and "His Crudeness," a man who gave the reason why he constantly drove his work force so hard: "So my sons won't have to sleep with their grandmother." Not apt to mention his Jewish heritage, Cohn once snapped: "Around this studio the only Jews we put into pictures play Indians." When others objected to his harsh demeanor, he shot back: "I am the king here. Whoever eats my bread sings my song.")[22]

Naturally Wurtzel detested Korda for having intellectual pretensions, and he took delight in assigning the Hungarian to films of unmatched insipidness. Putting Korda in charge of Fox's production of *The Princess and the Plumber,* Wurtzel gave a series of erratic and capricious orders and then hectored his director for not obeying his daily diktats. On 15 October 1930, he wrote Korda: "You are hereby notified that . . . in disregarding and disobeying instructions . . . in the motion picture you have directed entitled *The Princess and the Plumber,* said contract and the employment thereby created is hereby terminated." In a letter of the same day, Korda desperately pleaded: "I appeal to your sense of fairness. . . . I emphatically deny that I ever disregarded or disobeyed given instructions." Wurtzel refused to see him, and his aides thoroughly enjoyed the hazing of Korda. Executive Alfred Wright wrote Wurtzel on Korda: "This 'bird' certainly writes a swell letter which makes me think it might be a good idea for you to talk to him. However, use your own judgment."[23] He subjected Korda to the final indignity of a Sunday viewing of *The Princess and the Plumber* with Wurtzel's twelve-year-old son designated the film critic of choice. Yanking the cigar out of his snout, Wurtzel *père* demanded the youngster's reaction: "What do you think of it?" "It stinks," proclaimed the supercilious brat. Wurtzel then gave Korda the wave of his cigar: "You heard the kid. It stinks. You're through."[24]

Thrown $14,000 in severance pay, Korda settled his divorce, sold his house on North Rodeo Drive, socked away his belongings in storage, and then headed to the nearest travel agency. When asked by the travel agent for his destination, the wandering Hungarian requested, "Just out of here."[25]

He ruled out Hungary, whence he had fled the White Terror in 1919, and now Berlin because of the menace of Brown Shirts. Choosing Paris as a civilized antidote to the parched cultural Gobi Desert of Los Angeles, he landed a post with Paramount's continental European division. Korda ran a French cast through a production of *Marius* and then reshot the same film with a troupe of German actors, thus supplying two markets in one stroke.

His efficiency impressed the studio so much that Paramount named him chief of its London operation. There he began his output of quota quickies, and afterward his first "independent" production in Britain, *The Private Life of Henry VIII.*

Korda thrived in London and championed the cause of his newly adopted nation. Screenwriter Herman J. Mankiewicz in the mid-1920s had beckoned the Chicago journalist Ben Hecht to come to Hollywood because "your only competition are idiots," and Korda found a similar situation in Britain of the 1930s, where few had truly mastered the craft of feature-film production. Accorded a respect absent from the foul-mouthed Kennedys, Wurtzels, and assorted hangers-on, he also realized that the British environment best fulfilled a deep need to be his own boss. In 1935, he joined Charlie Chaplin, Mary Pickford, Douglas Fairbanks, and D. W. Griffith as a full partner in United Artists in order to ensure distribution of his films in North America. Given a testimonial dinner at the American Academy of Arts and Sciences during the summer of 1935, Korda denied that Britain and Hollywood were in conflict: "In France, Germany, and England, when a picture is finished the first thing they want to know is what Hollywood thinks of it. It is not the aim of England to raid Hollywood." Yet he relished his welcome as a victorious titan, notably the speech of Twentieth Century–Fox executive Darryl F. Zanuck, who apologized for the shabby treatment of five years earlier. "[F]or the first time since his disgrace," wrote *Collier's*, ". . . there were genuflections by the greatest and hosannas from the highest," while "the lesser rajahs could not get close enough to catch his eye." Nevertheless, the flattery may have been animated by lingering fears that Korda might succeed in constructing a Hollywood-on-the-Thames, with strong links to continental Europe, a transnational film operation able to compete with the moguls. As one anonymous executive bitterly revealed to *Collier's:*

Alexander Korda can stand on the corner of Hollywood Boulevard and Vine Street and wave a checkbook and all our actors and actresses, stars and featured players, and cameramen and technicians and writers and directors would desert our studios and pour around him from all over town and follow him just like the way the rats of Hamelin (he said Hamburg, so help me) ran after the Pied Piper. They're calling this fellow Alexander the Great – but he's Napoleon, too, if you ask me. He's just about the czar of the international film business today.[26]

Such a specter probably gripped the smaller Hollywood majors, "the lesser rajahs," more seriously than wealthy studios such as MGM. Still, Hollywood executives judged it wise to cooperate with Korda, rather than risk his turning to a posture of hand-to-hand combat against their global preeminence. In 1929, Britain's *Morning Post* had indeed proposed a British "home market that might be the whole of Europe: if not too Wellsian a dream, a United States of Europe in films which would deal a very shrewd blow to the American world ascendancy."27

Korda had several qualities that rendered him confident in his mission of reviving a British film industry. From the outset he had to overcome enemies who thought a Hungarian Jew had no business representing the English character to the rest of the world. When the British government granted him naturalized citizenship in 1936, Korda, amid a toast from Charles Laughton and a descending Union Jack in the background, proudly swaggered: "I have only one thing to say – to hell with the bloody foreigner."28 Korda turned what many thought to be an Achilles heel into the foundation of his film philosophy. He asserted that popular film relies heavily on national stereotype and that the outsider is much better equipped to notice the more pronounced features of local character than the native. The native filmmaker is too drawn to subtleties and nuances that are difficult to decipher by a global audience. As Korda explained:

An outsider often makes the best job of a national film. He is not encumbered with excessively detailed knowledge and associations. He gets a fresh slant on things. For instance, I should hate to try to make a Hungarian film, while I would love to make one about the Highlands that would be a really national Scottish film and indeed I plan to do so.29

Declaring "the best Hungarian film I have ever seen" to be one made by the Belgian Jacques Feyder and that France's René Clair "could make a better London picture than any of the English directors," Korda rebuffed those "who think it odd that a Hungarian from Hollywood should direct an English historical film."30

In 1934, London Films released a production revered as the quintessence of Englishness, *The Scarlet Pimpernel*. Its leading lights – the producer Korda, the screenwriter Lajos Biró, and the actor Leslie Howard as the hero Sir Percy Blakeney – are all Hungarians. *Pimpernel Smith*, a modernized version of the story also starring Howard, became a staple of viewers during World War II. Korda's productions endear themselves to the British by a stress on certain qualities in national character, specifically the superior sense of humor deployed by Blakeney and then Pimpernel Smith in outwitting, respectively, the tyrannical French Jacobins and the Nazi officers. The reigning syllogism is as follows: We British are free and hence clever, the most humorous people on the planet; they (Jacobins and Nazis) are totalitarian and devoid of wit. The actor and comedian John Cleese later put it another way: "An Englishman would rather be told he is a bad lover than that he has no sense of humor."

In other films, Korda employs national stereotypes to show a different side of the French than the killjoy Jacobin. In *The Rise of Catherine the Great* (1934), Russian Grand Duke Peter turns to his aide Lecocq, played by Gerald du Maurier, who is supposed to be an expert on love because he is French. The French aide orders the prince's staff to deliver a wine "of a vintage to make up a woman's mind." When Peter cheats on Catherine on their wedding night, he turns to Lecocq and says that he should not be scandalized, as he is French. Peter demands to know if Lecocq himself has been married, and the Frenchman deftly replies, "Not officially. But I have dabbled in it."

Korda never seeks to challenge monarchy and hierarchical institutions. Rather, his characteristic technique is to employ paradox and light cynicism to challenge the pretensions of the powerful, to chop them down a few notches from their lofty perches. Henry VIII is a once-mighty king humbled by the whims of his wives; the pauper in his version of Twain's *Prince and the Pauper* proves to be more of a prince than the actual prince; Helen of Troy is stronger than the male rulers; Don Juan is regarded by the women as a sexual dud and an impostor [Fig. 7]; and, in the exception that proves the rule, Catherine the Great ascends to the throne but is portrayed as a model of chastity who concocted a lascivious reputation only as a means of gaining attention from her power-mad husband.[31] His movies tend to display warm relations between aristocrats and proletarians, quite different from Michael Balcon's British films of the 1930s that contrast middle-class virtue with the rakish proclivities of the aristocracy. Korda has been accused of anti-middle-class bias in portraying the bourgeoisie as prudish and avaricious. Aristocracy and proletarians are guilty of excess, but there is an aristocratic code that, once followed, can restore dignity and honor.[32] While the Frankfurt School, Brecht, and many radical intellectuals flocked to the United States, Britain welcomed a cohort of so-called White Revolutionaries, émigrés devoted to aristocracy and the charms of the ancien régime.[33]

Korda's wit is light and rarely lacerating. He does not seek to upset tradition. Again, his commitment to the status quo is most aggressively displayed in his empire cycle of films, which revert to a nineteenth-century sensibility in their approval of British rule. Indian nationalists indeed greeted Korda's productions with riot and threat of generalized unrest.

In terms of upgrading British film art, Korda regularly purchased the rights to the novels of the nation's leading writers. Previously Grierson had rejected the frequent British claim that, because the nation produced the greatest playwrights and storytellers in world literature, its cinema should eventually outperform the U.S. competition. Korda, however, liked to surround himself with the literary set, and yet dozens of works he obtained never underwent production. More than a few he sold back to Hollywood. His use of star literary talent in any case did not prove to be a panacea for British film. The futuristic *Things to Come* (1936) is one of Korda's outstanding films, and yet it remains marred by the heavy-handed stamp of H. G. Wells in its finale. The speeches are too wooden and high-minded to be believable, and viewers in the age of ecology are apt to regard the prophet of progress at film's end as a totalitarian zealot leading the planet to a brave new enslavement. Graham Greene in the 1930s repeatedly attacked Korda for his screenwriting style, notably the work of his Hungarian sidekick, Lajos Biró. The Biró stamp can be found on two Charles Laughton vehicles, *The Private Life of Henry VIII* (1933) and *Rembrandt* (1936), films that are based on vignettes, tableaux, rather than a seamless narrative. Greene objected to the lack of a coherent story line in many Korda films, the heavy reliance on chopped-up, disemboweled glimpses into the lives of his subjects. Instead of fretting about Greene's astringent criticism of "the Denham style," Korda decided to hire him as a writer. His magnanimous gesture initially yielded few productions, but after World War II Greene came up with a story that is one of the masterworks of the Korda stable, *The Third Man* (1949). Greene's work undoubtedly benefited from the inspiration of Orson Welles, who nonchalantly added one of the greatest flourishes of dialogue in screen history:

In Italy for thirty years under the Borgias, they had warfare, terror, murder, bloodshed – they produced Michelangelo, Leonardo da Vinci, and the Renaissance. In Switzerland they had brotherly love, five hundred years of democracy and peace, and what did that produce? The cuckoo clock.

Korda's economic triumph with *The Private Life of Henry VIII* brought with it explosive expansion of the British film industry, the beginning of a "boom-and-bust" cycle that exposed the fragility of his enterprise. In 1928, the total cost of British film production stood at £500,000; by 1937, it had ballooned to £7 million, with financing ensured by a combination of insurance underwriters and banking interests. Korda's construction of Denham Studios and expanded production cycle had been carried out with the backing of Prudential. Testifying for the Westminster Bank in 1939, Sir Stafford Cripps discussed the euphoria in the City of London (the financial district) after Korda's *The Private Life of Henry VIII* and producer Max Schach's formation of the Capitol Group of production companies in 1935:

FIGURE 7. On the night of the premiere of *The Private Life of Don Juan* (1934), the Bombay-born film star Merle Oberon and Alexander Korda, whom she would marry in 1939, greet admirers at the new London Pavilion. Enabling Korda to poke fun at the legend of Don Juan, the film failed to win the accolades of the previous year's blockbuster, *The Private Life of Henry VIII*. Less than a decade later, Korda became the first film director to be knighted in Britain. *Source:* Hulton|Archive.

[T]here was a good deal of talk about encouraging British film production as against American production. Everybody apparently thought that it was the easiest way in the world to make money, and that it did not matter how much was spent, as the inexhaustible resources of the people who went to see the films would be sufficient reimbursement of whatever money was spent.[34]

The sluggishness of the marine insurance market in the 1930s encouraged companies to seek new fields of investment. Cripps explained how a team of London brokers seduced insurance underwriters and banking interests into incredible leaps of investment in a high-risk industry. They began by snaring marine underwriters into issuing "guarantee policies for some share of the total amount of 50,000 pounds":

> Relying on the security of the guarantee given by the marine underwriters, the bank would advance the cash. After the first few dealings in that way it appeared that it became nearly automatic for these companies to adopt this procedure and get as much money as they wanted. . . .
>
> Out of the sums advanced were taken the premiums which had to be paid to the underwriters and commission which was to be paid to the Brokers, and a further sum was set aside into a reserve account to guarantee the payment of the interest to the bank on the loan. . . .
>
> At that time no one seemed to think why this delightful state of affairs should ever come to an end. . . . The companies got as much money as they wanted, and that enabled them to give the distributing companies a very favourable deal.
>
> The actors were able to charge most fabulous fees. The underwriters got a great deal of what appeared to be most lucrative business at a time when the marine market was very dull. The Brokers were doing very well indeed by reason of their commission. And the banks were finding a sufficient use for their money at a decent rate of interest with the guarantee of the insurance companies behind them.[35]

At the end of fiscal 1934–5, Korda's London Films carried £30,000 in debts; by May 1936 the firm had been spilling prodigious sums of red ink, now exceeding £330,000. In October 1936, Britain's sixteen new production companies, with London Films lumped in, possessed £875,000 in working capital and owed nearly £4.2 million in debentures, mortgages, and short-term loans. The entire industry had amassed loans and mortgages exceeding £12.5 million. Throughout 1936, bankers swooped down on the Hungarian and demanded austerities. Amid profuse apologies and mobilization of the famous Korda charm, he convinced them that Denham Studios would be run in a less extravagant manner and that one of his upcoming productions should yield staggering profits.[36] General recognition of the crisis came from an unlikely quarter, John Grierson, leader of the Film Council, "a small research group" seeking to "look behind the gossip, rumours, hunches, and half-truths of Wardour Street." He claimed that it had grown "dangerous to muddle along in an industry in which the difference between showmanship and racketeering is often slight." *World Film News* in January 1937 reproduced the findings of the Film Council that financial hemorrhaging continued unabated, and this issue became a staple in the hands of London financiers seeking to rein in the wizards of Wardour Street. After "the intelligence section of one of the bigger banks" perused the January *WFN*, reported Grierson, "Within a week came the news that the lavish credits till now advanced to the film industry, were to be brought under review."[37] Crisis and retrenchment began in rapid order: the calling in of loans, studios put under receivership, and London Films itself having to resort to salary slashing. "[U]nless we can get a bigger return from the American market for British pictures Gaumont–British will be compelled to abandon production," pronounced its president, Isidore Ostrer, who soon shut down its studio at Shepherd's Bush. In April 1937 the underwriters appointed a committee of investigation that, according to a PEP study, "caused the investors to bring to an end this part of the production boom, and by its repercussions made a slump inevitable."[38] The freewheeling days were over for Korda, at least for now. The Yorkshire miller J. Arthur Rank swallowed up much of the industry, and in his hands rested the fate of British film.

Korda's failure to achieve a sustained British film renaissance and an institution on a par with the successful Hollywood film majors has been the source of subsequent retrospection and analysis. His model for sustaining a world-class film industry had several points of vulnerability:

(1) Korda's backers believed that *The Private Life of Henry VIII* proved that U.S. audiences no longer possessed antipathy to British subjects and in many cases actively welcomed them. The empire cycle of the film majors reinforced such thinking. Nevertheless, the Hollywood majors realized that they had to step gingerly when approaching British topics, a lesson Korda's people learned all too late. As Gradwell Sears, the general sales manager of Warner Brothers, New York, explained to Jack Warner concerning *The Private Lives of Elizabeth and Essex* (WB, 1939), starring Bette Davis and Errol Flynn:

The reaction to the title *The Private Lives of Elizabeth and Essex* is extremely bad. I am getting letters of protest from every part of the country and my own people tell me that wherever they go exhibitors are objecting to the title. They say that it smacks of Alexander Korda and that in the south, mid-west and small towns particularly, it will be confused with an English picture, which as you know do very little business especially in small towns.[39]

On this occasion, Warner resisted Sears, who counseled that:

I recognize the value of the title *The Private Lives of Elizabeth and Essex* for the foreign market, but I implore you Jack, not to use this title for American consumption, because it will cost us hundreds of thousands of dollars. *The Lady and the Knight, The Knight and the Lady* or any other title which suggests romance and adventure will serve far better than the present title which positively identifies this material as an English historical drama.[40]

Earlier Warner had protested that it would be a violation of manners to call "a Queen a lady," and then maintained that the superstardom of Bette Davis and Errol Flynn would ensure that this picture "will do just as much business as it would under any other title."[41] Flynn himself sought to change the title to *The Knight and the Lady*, but Davis balked at the

Tasmanian's insolent maneuver. In the end, the film's anemic box-office performance vindicated Sears's view that small-town America had weak desire for productions carrying too heavy an English aroma. After a torrent of costume dramas followed *The Private Life of Henry VIII*, one Kansas City theater owner issued a refusal to display any future films "in which men wrote with feathers."[42]

Korda's decision to obtain an ownership stake in United Artists ended up frustrating his efforts to penetrate North American markets. Unlike the leading Hollywood majors, United Artists owned no theaters and therefore could not ensure exhibition of his productions. Denied first-run status by the big-city circuits, he searched for openings among independents in the hinterlands. Once small-town exhibitors turned cold on Korda he had little means of showing product that broke new ground. Isolated to quasi-sophisticated pockets in large U.S. cities and in the Canadian market, he then saw his operation trampled on the European continent, where fascism rode high in the saddle. Whether in the advocacy of peace in *Things to Come* (1936) or in the parody of European dictators in *Storm in a Teacup* (1937), London Films did not endear itself to the stormtrooper caste poised to chart Europe's destiny.

(2) The desire to achieve rapid expansion and global-scale production compelled Korda to dependence on the City of London for huge infusions of investment. The British industry thus remained at the mercy of a relative handful of firms inclined to chafe at the unorthodox business practices of movie's minimoguls. Korda himself regretted overbuilding at Denham, its seven sound stages ensuring that he regularly had to rent out space to industry operators able to elude his supervisory capacity. Korda's mania for blockbusters led to wasteful extravagance and opulences that made his enterprise appear to be run on the principles of the aristocratic court and the Monte Carlo gambler, rather than the accounting techniques of Britain's button-down banking establishment.

Film hardly stood alone as vulnerable to the whims of the banking elite. The *Financial Times* (26 September 1921) had demanded of a British cabinet minister whether he realized that "'half a dozen men' at top of the five big banks could upset the whole fabric of Government finance by refraining from renewing Treasury bills?" Yet Korda should have recognized that bankers were more likely to bring down a maverick capitalist than a national government, and a Tory regime at that.

When the magnitude of Korda's debts spilled into the open, the City men privately retreated into a rebarbative anti-Semitism that complicated prospects for the renewal of investment. According to the diary of Sir Robert Bruce Lockhart (23 August 1938):

Last night Bayliss-Smith, who is a leading chartered accountant and represents the creditors in some of the big cinema financial messes in this country, says the cinema industry here has cost the banks and insurance companies about 4,000,000 pounds. Most of this lost by Jews – like Korda and Max Schacht [sic]. Latter already lost a packet for German government before Hitler. Has now done same here, in Bayliss-Smith's opinion, and he would not say so lightly, Korda is a much worse man than Schacht. Schacht is just a slick Jew who sees financial moves ahead of the other fellow. Korda is a crook and, according to Bayliss-Smith, an evil man.[43]

The renowned British producer Michael Balcon pointed out that, because of the Hungarian's breakthrough in late 1933, the City investors eagerly flocked toward continental European filmmakers fleeing Nazism or Italian fascism, "flamboyant figures who had meteoric careers in film production, most of them pale imitations of Alex Korda." They then unfairly blamed Korda for their ill-fated investments, as they discovered all too late that "Latin charm and *gemutlichkeit* are no permanent substitute for professional experience and training."[44] In response to the refugee invasion, MGM posted a sign that is often attributed to Korda: "IT'S NOT ENOUGH TO BE HUNGARIAN; YOU HAVE TO HAVE TALENT TOO."[45] Basil Wright of the GPO unit likened the post–*Henry VIII* surge of investment and the crisis of 1937 to the South Sea Bubble of 1720. Nevertheless, he made a distinction between crass financial manipulators, among whom he included Schach, those who "never built a studio, never added anything to the sum of things for the industry," and Korda. Noting that Korda had "the princely quality of the Renaissance," Wright told his biographer Karol Kulick in 1973 that despite "numerous mistakes . . . he left us with a lot of bricks and mortar and some laboratories," as well as many "good films, don't forget that."[46]

In an article that appeared in the French paper *Cinématographe*, Marcel Ermans condemned Korda for taking

it upon himself to address a "message" to the world, to the confusion of the Americans. . . . To illustrate the philosophy of Papa Wells and to produce at the cost of millions, such films as *Shape of Things to Come, Man Who Could Work Miracles, Don Juan,* it was not necessary to possess sumptuous studios.[47]

Yet he also reflected:

In our time, as we all know, the spiritual is obscured by the intellectual, and the intellectual by the technical. One should not be surprised to see palaces thrown up to shelter gigantic machines placed at the service of shallow ideas and making ephemeral and artificial productions. But one day perhaps some genius will arise to make use of the marvelous instrument which lies at Denham.

On that day a brilliant director, a poet, a creator, a lion like Stroheim, or a magician like Murnau, will reign upon one or more of the floors at Denham, and we shall wink at each other and say, "Old Korda knew what he was doing after all."[48]

The editors of *World Film News* issued a powerful retort to Ermans's philippic:

Korda has been ambitious and his ambition has at least been the means of giving scale for the first time to British production. He has made it think of big things and has pointed, like Cortez, to the horizon. The results have been sometimes disappointing and more often than not his films have been more expensive than they should have been. All this because Korda has not succeeded in making organisation keep in step with that ambition. . . .

But this need not blind anyone to the fact that Korda's quality has been of historic importance in the development of British cinema. . . . He is still, to-day, the only fighting figure in the British cinema independent enough and tough enough in the cause of the British film to match swords with the American bosses. . . . One may doubt, and many do, that he is the best leader for British cinema; for he is on the one hand not a native, nor is he a born leader who knows how to keep strong people with him. But he is the only imaginative figure one sees in a bunch of dimwits and the only courageous figure in a bunch of lily-livers. And that will do for now.[49]

Alexander Korda would continue to hold a prominent part in the future of British film. He never relinquished the habits of extravagance, encapsulated in his famous advice to his son upon giving him a £5 note for his birthday: "Don't spend it. Waste it!" He insisted that Paulette Goddard wear genuine emeralds in *An Ideal Husband* "Because it makes her feel better." Shortly after World War II, Korda gambled almost everything on the Scottish historical drama he once prophesied would be the best of its genre, a film called *Bonnie Prince Charlie*. It was not even a contender for such an accolade, and it became one of the greatest money losers in British cinema history, a film that helped plunge Britain into the down side of the "boom-and-bust" cycle. Korda pronounced the statement that some regard as his epitaph, that his mistakes were rare, but "if I make one, it's a beauty." Director Anthony Kimmins reported in 1958 that the popularity of *Bonnie Prince Charlie* in Scotland recouped most of its cost in what Paul Tabori called "the very long run."[50] However, as Keynes cruelly reminded us about capitalist economics, "in the long run" we are all dead, and indeed Korda had perished by the time Kimmins could announce his happy news. From the late 1930s through the 1950s, the destiny of British film slipped from Korda's grasp into the hands of a man cast in a different mold: the teetotaling Methodist J. Arthur Rank.

THE CINEMATOGRAPH FILMS ACT OF 1938

Before the transition to the Age of Rank, the British Parliament had to confront the state of the nation's film industry, a situation made urgent by the impending expiration of the decade-long Cinematograph Films Act of 1927 and the swirling financial crisis. Oliver Stanley, the president of the Board of Trade, rose before the Parliament on 4 November 1937 and gave an impassioned defense of retaining quotas in the proposed Cinematograph Films Act of 1938. Noting that "in 1926 . . . British production had fallen under 5 per cent," Stanley observed that

The Act was passed in 1927. By 1932 British production was 24 per cent. of the films being shown, and in 1936 it had risen to 29.45 per cent.; in other words, in 1926 the industry was on the point of death, but to-day, in spite of its difficulties, many of which are not the fault of any legislation, it is quite an important industry.[51]

Yet this "important industry" had no doubt been rendered vulnerable by its lifeline, the 1927 act. Viscount Swinton (Phillip Cunliffe-Lister), who had introduced the 1927 legislation, told the House of Lords in March 1938 that the sixfold leap in Britain's share of its domestic market had been heavily padded by quota quickies, films "cheap and nasty. That brought British films into disrepute." He charged that the largely U.S.-dominated distributors had quota quickies "produced with a certain intention that they should not only be nasty and inferior but so appear, and so deprecate the genuine British film. That . . . occasioned great embarrassment to exhibitors."[52] Speaking for the Board of Trade's Stanley, Captain Wallace declared quota quickies to be "the curse of the British film industry, and the destruction of that horrible abortion . . . is a major object of the present Bill."[53]

While Lord Strabolgi cautioned British parliamentarians to refrain from incendiary claims that Americans "deliberately made bad" British films, he called attention to a second area of crisis for British cinema, the disarray in finance. Strabolgi declared that "financial interests in the City of London . . . burned their fingers badly, and when once these gentry burn their fingers in a particular industry they leave that industry and go elsewhere." Because of the volatility of this gentry element, he regretted that Stanley had spurned the Moyne committee's recommendation of a "semi-official finance corporation."[54] One of the most disquieting developments had been the recent prospectus for Odeon Theatres, which sought to raise £6 million in capital by pledging, according to one parliamentarian, "that it would not in any shape or form, or in any circumstances, directly or indirectly, indulge in the production of British films."[55] At this point, the gentry element could be successfully pitched to invest in exhibition with a promised quarantine against production, an ominous horizon for those seeking to lift British cinema on to the next plateau.

The parliamentary debate of the 1920s had been more heavily marked by forecasts of imperial decline at the hands of Hollywood than the deliberations on the 1938 act. Nevertheless, leading parliamentarians punctuated the 1937–8 round with condemnations of British cultural malaise and Hollywood's aim to destroy the nation's civilization. Oliver Stanley interrupted his matter-of-fact Board of Trade presentation of legislative detail with a dramatic peroration:

We are on our defense as Westerners and as democrats. The decadence of the West is just as much the talk of the bazaars of the East as the decay of democracy is the stock leader of the newspapers of the dictators. Wherever in the world a film by its lack of taste or lack of character, by showing an exotic and eccentric minority as a national element, by showing the fantastic in the guise of the normal, gives colour to either of these beliefs, then it is weakening our defences. I do not want our defences to be made in Hollywood.[56]

Preoccupied with the politics of leisure, Stanley months earlier had proclaimed that

we shall see an era of shorter and shorter working hours and of more and more real leisure. . . . What use are we going to make of leisure of that kind? We know what use the Greeks made of it. Over 2000 years later we are still acting Greek plays and admiring Greek art and we still imitate Greek games.[57]

Stanley added: "I believe that our ability to solve this problem of the use of leisure, more perhaps than on anything else, is going to depend the future of this country and of this civilization."[58]

Harkening back to Stanley's words, Sir Arnold Wilson (Conservative, Hitchin), a key member of the Moyne committee, wondered whether British civilization could meet the standards of its classical ancestors. He turned to the words of Lord Baden-Powell, founder of the Boy Scouts, who condemned the mass man and woman for polluting the temple of leisure [Fig. 8]. Baden-Powell proclaimed in a current Boy Scout magazine that "our young people, like those of other countries, are becoming imbued with the herd instinct." In particular, he observed:

Because a well-advertised film actor arrived at Waterloo the other day 3,000 young women fought their way to look at him – and these are expected to have the balance of mind to be responsible for electing our rulers.

Mass-suggestion is robbing men and women of their individual self-control and the power of initiative.[59]

Hailing an English film journal for producing "a straight, honest but restrained truth about the American film industry in this country," Wilson

FIGURE 8. Lord Robert Baden-Powell (1857–1941), the founder of the Boy Scouts, condemned cinema for contributing to the herd mentality that imperiled Western civilization. *Source:* Public Record Office, INF 9/1276.

inserted its words into his address: "America . . . has stifled every national screen aspiration in a blanket of cosmopolitan vulgarity, as innocent of formative expression as of social integrity." He then spun verse from Milton's "Lycidas" (1637), using it to embroider his conclusion that American values were worse in many measures than the leading totalitarian ideologies of the epoch:

> "The hungry sheep look up and are not fed. . . .
> "Rot inwardly and foul contagion spread. . . ."
> Not the contagion of Communism or Fascism, which, good or bad, represents ideals not primarily selfish, but of the worship of money, and of violence, and the acceptance of the lowest motives as natural and inevitable.[60]

Wilson's belief that fascism occupied a higher moral plane than American values may have rendered him pliable to Mussolini's demand that Brit-

ain leave the fate of Abyssinia to the marauding Italians. "I had the honor
to be received by Signor Mussolini," he wrote the *Times* (24 September
1935), "All I have heard and seen in Rome and elsewhere convinces me,
that having done our utmost to fulfil our obligations, we should now stand
aside." He also maintained, "I have met Hitler repeatedly. I believe him to
be a great instrument of peace in the world." Even after the Czech invasion
and the Munich Accord, he politely suggested that Britain "be prepared to
consider the return to Germany of some of her former colonies as part of
a general settlement." Earlier in 1938, he had proclaimed, "I hope to God
Franco wins in Spain, and the sooner the better."[61]

Some of Wilson's other allies in the film debate thought the American
challenge to be more menacing to British national survival than fascism.
Decrying the "mixture of glucose, chewing gum, leaden bullets and nasal
noises" emanating from the modern movie palaces, Reginald William Sorensen (Labour, West Leyton) "rather assumed that the chief function of the
cinema in this country was to accomplish what I am sure will never be accomplished, or even attempted, in any other way – the annexation of this
country by the United States of America." Horrified by the spread of popular expressions including "OK, Chief" and "Sez you," Sorensen admitted:
"As it is, the United States have already advanced far towards that annexation. . . ." Unless Britain could rescue cinema from the hands of those in
which "it becomes merely an opiate," he believed "this country will be
conquered, not by the sword, but by the invasion of American finance and
American thought."[62]

Shortly after Sorensen's outbursts, MP Tom Smith (Labour, Normanton)
took umbrage at indiscriminate use of the American actress in British films,
as these pampered stars commanded exorbitant salaries and a retinue of foreign staff. "Otherwise, she may, I am told, refuse to play," he noted. "It
seems to me that a jolly good spanking would do some of them good."[63]

Considering the fury of these oratorical interventions, the legislation
of 1938 instead proved to be moderate and restrained. First, it established
lighter quotas for long film, trimmed from the 1937 level of 20 percent for
exhibitors and renters (i.e., distributors) to 12.5 percent for exhibitors and
15 percent for renters. The Board of Trade opted for a gap requiring more
films from renters in order to placate exhibitors, who complained of little
choice when the quota schedules stood congruent between these two sectors. Producers grimaced at the decision to lighten quotas, as many thought
they should be raised to reflect a British proportion of screen time exceeding
29 percent in 1936. Small independent cinema owners responded that those
in the provinces encountered difficulty meeting the 20 percent quota since
they were routinely denied access to British films caught in the maw of the

large first-run cinema chains of the metropolis. In the fiscal year ending September 1935, 147 out of approximately 4,000 cinemas stood in default on the quota; in September 1936, this leapt to 350.[64] The legislation also imposed a new quota on short film, set at 7.5 percent for exhibitors and 10 percent for renters. Expressing the view that documentary is Britain's greatest contribution to world cinema, several parliamentarians angrily faulted the Board of Trade for not seeking a higher short quota. The Board of Trade responded that the 1927 act had had *no* short quota and that the critics overestimated British capacity for producing short films. They found it harder to admit that exhibitors loathed shorts as having little box-office appeal, and working-class audiences experiencing the Depression appeared to shun realist treatments that plunged them back into conditions of unrelieved drudgery.

Second, the legislation attacked the quota quickie by imposing a cost test of approximately £7,500 for labor expenditures on long films and by granting up to triple quota credit for films costing several times more than the minimum. The cost test represented a partial repudiation of the Moyne committee demands for a quality test, rejected because financiers might balk at funding an expensive film that could then be rejected by a capricious committee. Others worried that considerations of quality might lead to accusations of state censorship against unwelcome or innovative film projects. Still the Board of Trade allowed an appeals process for films not meeting the cost threshold, a minor concession to the "quality" yardstick.

Despite regularly delivering dissent against the quota legislation, particularly its escalating levels till 1948, the MPPDA of Will Hays won a mild victory with the 1938 act. Its immediate reduction of quotas and the provision for a triple counting of expensive films provided a modicum of relief from those demanding intensified protection of British film. Hays remained disappointed, as he had hoped that forthcoming talks on behalf of free trade between Britain and the United States led by Cordell Hull would give the Americans a free hand in lands flying the Union Jack. In the late 1920s, Hays had banked on the multilateral Geneva conference to compel countries to remove barriers to unfettered film imports; now he counted on the liberalizing Cordell Hull to deliver relief. On both occasions, victories for freer trade did not yield Hays the open market he relished. As Board of Trade President Oliver Stanley, oblivious to the influence of foreign footwear on the artistic imagination of Van Gogh and Magritte, expressed it:

You may complain about the imports of foreign boots, but . . . although foreign boots may give a man a corn, they cannot give him an idea, whereas a permanent and unrelieved diet of foreign films can give their audiences not only ideas but ideals.[65]

The third feature of the 1938 act was the appointment of an advisory panel to the Board of Trade, the Cinematograph Films Council. Comprising twenty-one members, ten from the industry and eleven independents, the body had vested in it powers of consultation on major policy decisions and revisions of quota, as well as the duty of furnishing an annual report to the Board of Trade and Parliament. This proposal became a ferociously disputed bone of contention, as parliamentarians chafed at its departure from the Moyne committee's recommendation of a powerful commission with a chairman and two to four members independent of the industry. Designed to administer the forthcoming 1938 act, the commission proposal represented an oblique response to the specter of Will Hays: the apparent unity of the U.S. film industry and its absence among competing British factions. Throughout the 1920s and 1930s, British critics cried out for a Hays figure or organization to impose unity on the warring British industry. In February and March 1929, a "special investigation" in the *Morning Post* called on Colonel A. C. Bromhead, chairman of Gaumont–British, to become "the 'Tsar' of the British industry," though "it may be that what the industry requires is a Napoleon rather than a Tsar." The newspaper added that Bromhead exudes "administrative ability not unworthy of the Corsican, but not the least important side of Napoleon's genius was his choice of Marshals." In vain, the *Morning Post* sought out "the ideal type of leader" for the film industry, "a former Viceroy, Lord Chancellor, or an admiral or a general."[66] During his address of March 1938 to the House of Lords, Lord Moyne bitterly complained of British film's "various conflicting interests," noting "that they are not merely divided between" exhibitors, renters (distributors), and producers, "but that each section has got very considerable cross-interests within its own group."[67] Small independent exhibitors often clashed with the first-run cinema circuits possessing easy access to new releases, British renters worried about their U.S.-owned counterparts, and producers of expensive British feature movies resented the lamentable wares of the quota-quickie bloc.

An independent commission, thought Moyne, could impose the necessary unity to face the American challenge. Notwithstanding, as Viscount Swinton observed, "It is quite true that the industry itself is in disagreement. Indeed there are very few things it is able to agree upon, but the one thing that it did agree upon was that none of them wanted a completely independent Films Council."[68] Despite similar arrangements for the sugar and livestock industries, the film interests resisted the proposal. Across the Atlantic, Will Hays's MPPDA disparaged the Moyne committee for its lèse majesté:

The sine qua non of membership on the Commission is that the commissioners shall have "absolute independence from professional or any other pecuniary connection with any branch of the film industry." In other words, apparently, that they should know little or nothing of the vast and complicated mechanism whose destiny is to be placed in their hands.[69]

Facing ideological grapeshot fired at home and from abroad, the Board of Trade quickly ran from the idea of an independent commission. It was not true that all in the film industry had opposed Moyne's vision; Grierson's small circle of documentarists gave vocal support for the body. Dissident parliamentarians (Tom Williams, Lord Strabolgi, J. J. Lawson) peppered Oliver Stanley with volleys of criticism for his retreat, to no avail. The British Foreign Office and Treasury undoubtedly would have resisted an institution that could complicate trade negotiations with U.S. Secretary of State Hull. Unable to find unity from within through a trade organization or from without through the imposition of the state, the British film industry soon found a capitalist of gargantuan wealth ready to tackle the task: J. Arthur Rank.

CHAPTER SIX

The Age of Rank

THE METHODIST, LADY YULE, AND THE LEAGUE OF GENTLEMEN

In the early 1930s, the Federation of British Industries regularly claimed that dominance over the exhibition sector was the key to the United States' global control of cinema. In 1927, MP Philip Snowden predicted that quotas would destroy the exhibition sector; instead it flourished throughout the 1930s, a lesson learned by J. Arthur Rank. He would not allow his destiny to be shaped by other exhibitors, those once christened "the illiterate masters of Wardour Street."[1] Korda had an international strategy, yet remained handicapped by meager access to exhibition outlets. Rank pledged to marry an ambitious production program with absorption of exhibition units throughout the United Kingdom and in parts of North America. While modestly proclaiming ignorance of the ways of the film world – "like some benevolent but rather stupid Renaissance despot," observed a less charitable historian – Rank became the self-appointed shepherd of Britain's resurgence in the global entertainment industry.[2]

Like that of John Grierson, J. Arthur Rank's involvement in the film industry, oddly enough, also begins with a fish story. A devout Methodist, Rank hoped to fund modest films with moral fiber, and he had early enthusiasm about a story surrounding a fishing community. Rank teamed up with Lady Yule, the teetotaling widow of a Calcutta jute merchant worth an estimated £15 million and a woman for whom life "was a perpetual battle against boredom," wrote Rank's biographer Alan Wood.[3] The Rank–Yule alliance of 1934 led to the creation of a film company called British National, which quickly churned out *Turn of the Tide*, a drama about family rivalries in a Yorkshire fishing village. Filmed at Robin's Hood Bay near Whitby, the fish saga took third place at the 1935 Venice Film Festival, and Rank eagerly anticipated the reaping of box-office rewards through its distributor, Gaumont–British. Instead Gaumont–British did little to promote the film, and it languished in warehouses. When he sent John Corfield to confront Mark Ostrer, head of Gaumont's exhibition sector, the theater chief rudely cut down Rank, the novice film financier: "I've never heard of him, and I don't want to hear of him." Prior to this incident, Rank had been investing in General Film Distributors (GFD) run by C. M. Woolf, who had resigned as Managing Director of Gaumont–British in early 1935. Some have speculated that the Ostrers gave Rank such horrible service when they realized he had been in cahoots with their talented but disenchanted sales chief. Son of Britain's wealthiest flour magnate, Rank appeared to respond to Ostrer's taunt like the millionaire, observed Wood, "who, piqued at being refused a room in a crowded hotel, promptly bought the hotel itself." In the aftermath of Ostrer's insolence, Rank reflected, "I decided that the film business had got into the hands of the wrong people."[4]

Rank sought out the right people. In 1936, he formed the General Cinema Finance Corporation (GCFC) with Lord Luke, chairman of Bovril, Ltd., which owned large tracts of land in Australia and Argentina; Paul Lindenburg, an international banker, chairman of the Amsterdam-based Hugo Kauffmann and Company Bank, N.V., and Warsaw's Fabrique de Soie Artificielle de Tomaszow, as well as a director of the Roumanian Banking Corporation; Leslie William Farrow, a chartered accountant and chairman of Associated Paper Mills, Ford Paper Mills, British Sudac, and Indeuron, Ltd., as well as deputy chairman of three firms and director of seventeen others; and Lord Portal of Laverstoke, chairman of Wiggins, Teape, and Co., Ltd., a manufacturer of elite paper used for the printing of money in Great Britain and abroad.[5]

Rank's strategy of taking the film business out of "the hands of the wrong people" did not easily win converts. When GCFC set out to seize a 25 percent stake in the financially ailing U.S. film major Universal, Lord Portal approached his close friend Montagu Norman, the powerful governor of the Bank of England. Norman expressed horror that pillars of the establishment would seek involvement with such an unsavory element as film producers. As the producer and publicist Herbert Wilcox recalls the encounter:

Introductions over, Portal started to outline the Universal deal when Norman broke in with: "Wyndham, you're surely not going to interest yourself in that awful film industry?" Portal caught my eye and tried to make out a case, but Norman was adamant: "It's no good, Wyndham, it's unsound. And those dreadful people are not your class. Keep out of it!"[6]

In spite of Norman's blistering outrage, Rank's "league of gentlemen" successfully wired the Universal deal. As Portal explained to Wilcox about Montagu Norman, "Don't take the Governor too seriously. He has a bee in his bonnet about the British film industry." Similar to Stanley Melbourne Bruce, prime minister of Australia during 1923–9 and high commissioner in London during 1933–45, Norman rejected the growing view that cinema was a basic industry and one essential to success in the global economy. When Prudential, backer of Korda and his massive Denham Studios, unsuccessfully clamored in 1937 for a Film Bank that would provide finance to responsible elements of the cinema industry, Norman resisted giving the Bank of England's blessing to the scheme. The crash of 1937 vindicated for him the view that the movie producers were a swinish and odious lot spelling ruin for the City of London.[7]

If Norman's assumption that simple economic prudence militated against investment in the film industry, many wondered why Rank did not join others in abandoning the sinking ship of 1937. The Labour Left and Communist Party theoreticians argued that, behind a facade of religious and civic high-mindedness, Rank was a ruthless capitalist, obtaining assets at bargain basement prices. After Rank's absorption of Gaumont–British and Odeon, Stewart Gillies in Beaverbrook's *Daily Express* (4 March 1945) estimated that, for an outlay of £1.7 million, the flour magnate had gained control of assets worth £50 million. The tension between Rank's economic drives and his religious devotion would become the centerpiece of debates on his life's motivation.[8]

Rank firmly declared that Methodism animated his entry into cinema production. He told the *Methodist Recorder* (26 March 1942): "If I could relate to you some of my various adventures and experiences in the larger film world, you would not only be astonished, but, it would, I think, be as plain to you as it is to me that I was being led by God." Hailing the founder of Methodism, the renegade Oxonian John Wesley, for having "saved us from revolution," Rank found himself attacked on similar grounds as the eighteenth-century religious reformer: the contradiction between advocacy of an austere religion and the promotion of emotion-laden entertainment. Wesley's dramatic appeal to mass sentiment, embodied in the famous image of him preaching to coal miners with faces black and eyes ringed by tears, brought charges that he unleashed the flames of "enthusiasm"; one enemy complained that "he sinks the House of God into a playhouse." Yet Wesley alienated some poor and laboring elements by his campaigns against the people's fun, dancing and drinking, bull-baiting and cock-fighting. He provided little license for children to have games, his belief being that "he who plays when he is a child, will play when he is a man." Though recognizing cheerfulness as a virtue, he decried levity and laughter. "Be serious, avoid all lightness as you would avoid hell-fire and laughing as you would cursing and swearing." Responding to those latter-day Methodists who thought film to be Satan's work, Rank instead invoked the words of Salvation Army founder "General" William Booth: "Why should the Devil have all the best tunes?"[9]

Ordinarily Wesley had little faith that the upper classes could lead a moral regeneration in society. He believed "that all religious movements for reform began among the poor, moving slowly up the social ladder until finally, in the millennial day, they touched the nobility." Wesley said, "to speak the rough truth, I do not desire any intercourse with any persons of quality in England," and he directed Methodist clerics to "not affect the gentleman. You have no more to do with this character than with that of a dancing master."[10] He fondly evoked the biblical injunction "Ye cannot serve God and mammon," and chastised "a true servant of mammon" who will say: "No! Why not? Why cannot we serve both?" Wesley reasserted: "I remind all of you that are of this number, that have the conveniences of life, and something over, that ye walk upon slippery ground. Ye continually on snares and deaths. Ye are every moment on the verge of hell!" The Lord did not hold in high regard those "wearing gorgeous, that is splendid apparel. . . ."[11] Among Methodism's small upper-class following, most preferred the preaching of George Whitefield to Wesley, the former a Calvinist who appealed to the rich with his concept of the Elect, the latter an Arminian committed to the doctrine that all could achieve salvation. Rank clearly allied himself with Wesley's view; moreover, despite his complaints about film falling into the hands of "the wrong people" and his "league of gentlemen," he carried himself as a simple person who surrounded himself with those from ordinary walks of life. An arrogant American journalist demanded of him, "Is it true, Mr. Rank, that you're dumb?" The magnate gave it some thought, "No, just dull."[12] He lacked the equestrian class's Oxbridge pedigree; after attending a private secondary school, Rank had gone to work for his father's flour firm, where he'd swept floors and sweated with the grunts on the milling machines. During the First World War, he had served as a sergeant, a lowly rank in the eyes of the privileged castes, as the much-ridiculed Joe Lampton would later discover in *Room at the Top*. A teacher of Sunday school for most of his adult life, Rank spoke without condescension to the children of the lowbred, the linen-draper and the candlestick maker. *Time* magazine described him as someone who "resembles General de Gaulle, except that he does not share the look of a supercilious camel."

Its sister publication in the Luce stable, *Life*, shared in the mammal metaphors and reflected that the Yorkshire miller "has a nose of generous size
which terminates in a soft downward curve, so that in profile Rank looks
rather like a hungry anteater snuffing at an ants' nest."[13]

Rank's belief that "I am doing this work for God and my country" had
modest beginnings. In 1925, he grabbed an ownership stake in the *Methodist Times*, the main press outlet for his faith and an organ that gave him
contact with critics of immorality in film. Its film commentator, G. A. Atkinson, who later inflamed Indian opinion with his denunciation of miscegenation in film, warned that Hollywood employed a retinue of scientific
marketing experts and "trained psychologists" diabolically studying youth,

ascertaining their pulse, salivary and glandular reactions while they are watching a
drama of erotic emotion. There is nothing haphazard about it. What you see on the
screen is the factory principle in the commercialization of sex.[14]

"Hollywood," he wrote on another occasion, "is engaged in the mass-
production of sex."[15] In the autumn of 1931, the *Bristol Evening Times and
Echo* discussed "three clean British pictures and a different American one,"
of which its critic plainly stated: "I think the Americans have succeeded in
getting past our censor with as glaring an example of undiluted dirt as they
can ever hope to get."[16]

In an editorial entitled "The Demand for Clean Films," the *Methodist
Times* (1 October 1931) responded:

What is the British Board of Film Censors doing to allow this sort of thing to be
produced?
. . . The latest information from the United States is that Hollywood is going even
further in its cynical pandering to depraved imaginations. The films imported from
America are likely to be worse rather than better.[17]

The *Methodist Times* lost faith that the upsurge of British production
generated by the recent quota law could arrest this loathsome trend:

Unfortunately . . . the fact that a film is produced in England is no longer any guarantee that it is English in conception or outlook. Elstree is rapidly becoming a mere
outpost of Hollywood. Not only are the Americans producing over here in an attempt to evade Quota regulations, but the so-called British companies are too often
dominated by international Jews. . . .

R. J. Burnett, the biographer of J. Arthur's father, Joseph Rank, published with E. D. Martell a new study, *The Devil's Camera: Menace of a
Film-Ridden World* (1932), dedicated to the "ultimate sanity of the white
races." It pointed to "a famous critic of the screen" who regards Hollywood

as "the greatest crime-producing agency of this generation," perhaps a reference to Atkinson, who regularly called cinema "the great crime-builder of the age."[18] Laced with Atkinson's testimony that "Talking pictures have stripped woman not only of clothing, but of morals, decency, truth, fidelity, and every civilized quality or virtue," Burnett and Martell's jeremiad observed:

> Most of the actors and actresses seem ready to go to any length in decadence and nakedness to earn the salaries doled out to them by the little group of mainly Jewish promoters who control the greater part of what is now one of the most skilfully organised industries in the world.[19]

In 1933, a religious propaganda organization named "The Guilds of Light" formed the Religious Film Society. An interdenominational body, the Religious Film Society placed Bishop of London A. F. Winnington-Ingram at its helm, but it maintained a weighty Methodist presence. The Reverend Benjamin Gregory, the editor of the *Methodist Times*, R. J. Burnett, and J. Arthur Rank served on its governing committee. Rank became its treasurer, and his interest in film soared, ending his flirtation with the press medium. Financing the supply of projectors to Methodist churches as well as the production of modest religious films, Rank realized that "it was no use giving people in churches cheap, badly made films when they could see up-to-date well-made films at cinemas during the week."[20] Rank's mounting ambition led him to Lady Yule and the production of the fish saga that soon put him at wit's end with Wardour Street.

OTHER CHRISTIAN FILM INITIATIVES

The Methodists did not stand alone in religious activism on British film. The Missionary Societies developed a film committee that sponsored works on the Gospel's spread in the colonies, particularly India, as well as in Africa, China, Japan, and Palestine. In 1934, the Catholic Film Society (CFS), in association with the Catholic Truth Society, established itself and in the years ahead represented on celluloid religious ceremony, monastic life, and the Oberammergau Passion Play. Bishop of Nottingham Francis McNulty served as its president, and Reverend Ferdinand Valentine, O.P., as chairman. Terence McArdle soon produced the CFS film *The Great Awakening* (1934) calling for a youth movement similar to Belgium's Jeunes Ouvriers Catholiques. Seeking to combat "the ever active Communist propaganda," it attempted to give "the young Catholic in factory and workshop a sense of background and support against the all-powerful weapon so difficult for

youth to withstand – ridicule."[21] In July 1934, Catholics also formed the
Westminster Catholic Federation, a body inspired by the triumphs of the
U.S. Legion of Decency against Hollywood. The Archbishop of Cardiff,
working with Catholic Action and several religious societies, stood out as
a mobilizer of Catholic laity for less depiction of criminality and sexuality
on the silver screen. Nevertheless, Catholic efforts in Britain achieved minor
success, and the English Catholic journal *The Month* lambasted its coreli-
gionists. Referring to the failure of the Westminster Catholic Federation's
"Clean Film Campaign" launched in July 1934, T. W. C. Curd despaired
about the inability to replicate the mass mobilization of the U.S.-based Legion of Decency:

The onslaught of paganism call as with a voice of thunder for the mobilization of
our lay forces and the opposing of a united Catholic front to the determined and
well-organized enemies of our Christian civilization. Catholics in other countries are
doing this; why not in England? Are we exempted from action in this matter? Is
there no necessity for it here? Is England, by some sinister and mystifying dispen-
sation of his Satanic Majesty going to be allowed to "contract out" of the consequences of the general scheme of war upon God – perhaps by reason of past services rendered at the time of the Reformation?[22]

Elsewhere, he added that Catholics

are faced with a vigorous, highly-organized and clever opposition, carrying out all
its activities with a single objective – the overthrow of the Christian Social Order,
directed with intelligence and cunning from the devil's own "advanced G.H.Q" at
Moscow. . . .

He berated English Catholics for "fighting half-heartedly" with "neither
unity of purpose, unity of direction nor unity of action." His call to arms
did not revive Catholic forces, and the Catholic Film Society later shut
down with the outbreak of World War II. Its legacy was a series of documentaries and instructional films, including *Sacrament of Baptism, Retreats
for Boys, Dominicans of Woodchester, Franciscans of Guildford,* and *Sacrament of Holy Matrimony,* the last sternly alerting Catholics that the "mixed
marriage and marriage in a registry office" is "Disobedience to God."[23]
    Meanwhile, the Religious Film Society continued to flourish, amalga-
mating in 1939 with the Christian Cinema Council, previously established
in 1935. Although the Archbishop of Canterbury had served as president
of the Christian Cinema Council, the Church of England did not receive
plaudits as the motor of the Religious Film Society's success. A study by
The Arts Enquiry, published by PEP (Political and Economic Planning)
in 1947, concluded that "The financial resources of the Society are rela-

tively large, 'mainly through the generous financial assistance of Mr. J. A. Rank.'"[24]

The Catholic Film Society and the Protestant-based Religious Film Society proceeded on different artistic paths. British Catholics had a dispute that spilled from aesthetics to high theology, as Catholics resisted the depiction of God on celluloid during church services. Methodist preachers thought that film could appear on the altar where it would illustrate Gospel, particularly during sermons. Already the British Board of Film Censors had strictures against portrayals of God on film, as the body cautioned against potential sacrilege and vulgarity. The Methodist eagerness to represent Christ on the altar brought a surprising reproach from the Presbyterian John Grierson, who called it a reversal of the quarrel over transubstantiation: "The Roman Catholic Church will hold that you cannot turn the life of Christ into the substance of film. The Methodists will have no such compunction in giving us the reality. . . . I hope the Church of Scotland will take its stand with Rome. . . ."[25] After viewing pictures of Jesus years earlier, Grierson recalled writing "one of the rudest" reviews of his life. The visual richness of Catholic art and architecture, in remarkable contrast to the whitewashed austerity of most Protestant Dissenting sects, might have suggested that the respective Christian faiths would take inverse positions on the question of celluloid depictions over the altar. Still, some Catholic aesthetes thought it one thing to allow a Michelangelo at the Sistine Chapel or a Van Eyck at Ghent's St. Baaf's Cathedral to paint God in all His Glory; it was quite another to entrust God's celestial aura to the lensmiths and entertainers, modern monuments to the coarse and the low-camp. In the battle between kitsch and Catholicism, the Roman Church thwarted cinema's advance upon the Christian altar, a final sanctuary from this omnipresent medium.

RANK AS PYTHON

In spite of such theological storm and strife, Rank proceeded with the expansion of his film empire. "Like a monopolistic python," later claimed *Time* (19 May 1947), "Rank swallowed up one company after another, digesting or (as he called it) 'rationalizing' the wildly irrational industry."[26] From his base of General Film Distributors and the General Cinema Finance Corporation, he quickly constructed Pinewood Studios in 1936, its five studios a generous expansion over the cramped, single-stage quarters of Elstree Studios, where he and Lady Yule had made *Turn of the Tide*. In 1937, Rank bought out Lady Yule's shares in Pinewood, an action that pleased his lieutenant, C. M. Woolf, who objected to her pestering him about the need to feed the deer she placed on the studio's lavish estate. (Yule regularly expounded on the virtues of kindness to animals, and she forbade jockeys to use the whip on her stable of racehorses.) Next, in 1938 Rank took over Denham Studios from Alexander Korda, whose inability to reproduce the success of *The Private Life of Henry VIII* had led to gushers of red ink, over a million pounds at the time of his studio's surrender. The flour magnate's possession of two King Kong–size studios posed risks at a time of film-industry collapse; yet pressure to fill empty stages became eased as the war forced the government to requisition space from his companies.

Finally, Rank swooped down on the sector that would provide the profits feeding his production strategy: exhibition. In 1938, he bought seven thousand preferred and four thousand ordinary shares in Odeon, which in January 1939 landed him on its board. Most of the Odeon corporate board remained determined to keep Rank at minority status.

Founded in the early 1930s by a Hungarian-Jewish scrap-metal dealer based in Birmingham, Odeon stood for "Oscar Deutsch Entertains Our Nation." In December 1941 Oscar Deutsch, the owner, perished from cancer at age forty-eight, and Lily Deutsch, his wife, decided to sell out to the Yorkshire miller. The organization fit in well with Rank's conception of community-oriented theater, though he did not consider himself bound by Deutsch's cautious pledge to shun film production. While averse to high-stakes gambling, Odeon could sometimes be accused of concocting ruses similar to those of the production companies: For instance, Deutsch convinced contractors to provide several thousand pounds of labor for "free." With the promises of services in hand, he then grabbed financing from banks and other institutions, enabling him to reimburse his contractors. Unlike the producers, however, Deutsch typically made a strong return on the investment, and Rank's participation squelched rumors that the chain had become dangerously overextended. Located in cities and the growing suburban fringe of interwar England, Odeon repudiated the "flea pit" model of theater and endeared itself to Rank for trying to respond to the needs of the local community. With a giant exterior face that seemed to shout of coming attractions, the Odeon featured art deco touches from Lily Deutsch – "Gilded by the Lily," as contemporaries had it. The theater's interior directed all eyes to the screen in contrast to the riot of onion domes and kitsch, the cacophony of clouds and stars found on the ceilings of many rival picture palaces. Rank appreciated Odeon's cleanliness, and he expected his other theaters to meet its standards. Indeed he once made a buffoonish gaffe when stopping his car at a filth-laden theater in Plymouth. Only later, after bellowing at the manager about wanting the place to be in "ship-shape" condition and hectoring him into frenzied efforts at swabbing the decks did Rank realize that the theater belonged to his chief competitor, the ABC chain.[27]

By May 1937, nearly 250 theaters carried the Odeon banner. With standardized facades and decor, Odeon came to be regarded as the Woolworth's of the cinema circuits, a place customers could feel at home whether in their neighborhood or away on vacation. While Rank saw virtues in standardization, he sought to reinforce the chain's response to the needs of particular communities by sponsoring local events and children's matinees.

In the months preceding Oscar Deutsch's death, Rank nailed down his biggest coup of all, control over Gaumont–British. Gaumont–British belonged to the Ostrer family, sons of a Polish-Jewish shoemaker who had joined the exodus away from czarist pogroms. Settling in Bow, located in London's East End, the Ostrers flourished, despite enduring the inflammatory rhetoric of local MP Major William Evans Gordon (Tory, Stepney), who told Parliament that "English families are ruthlessly turned out to make room for foreign invaders. Out they go to make room for Rumanians, Russians, and Poles."[28] Perhaps family memories of such nativist rant inspired Gaumont to make the historical satire *Jew Süss* (1934), a film with anti-Nazi overtones that starred Pamela Ostrer as the ingenue.

Soon, at the helm of this clan, the eldest Ostrer son, Isidore, became an investment banker, a practicing poet, and an economist who published *The Conquest of Gold* in 1932. Counting John Maynard Keynes among his associates, Isidore Ostrer combined a passion for culture with economics. During the 1920s, the Ostrers had become the dominant force at Gaumont–British, confirmed by the resignation in 1929 of its chairman, Colonel A. C. Bromhead. Bromhead had represented the firm since its inception in 1898 as the London branch of the larger and more prestigious parent company based in Paris. Since then, Gaumont–British had gone from being a distributor of French films to the builder of the first major British studio in 1914, to ownership of one of the three largest circuits of British theaters.[29] In other words, it had become the British film corporation furthest on the road to vertical integration. Gaumont–British had run into difficulties in the latter half of the 1930s; most notably, the U.S. market continued to resist its productions. At the same time, the increasing illness of Isidore Ostrer's wife led the couple to spend more time in the healthful air of Arizona, far from the company's command post. As early as May 1931 Ostrer had offered to sell the controlling shares in Gaumont–British to the national government of Ramsay MacDonald; but the Labour regime, often eager to talk about nationalization and the virtues of its Constitution's Clause 4 ("common ownership of the means of production on behalf of the workers") when conveniently out of power, balked at the proposal. In 1936, John Maxwell of Glasgow, the owner of the production company Associated British Picture Company (ABPC) and the Associated British Cinemas (ABC) chain of theaters, made a determined bid at seizing control of Gaumont–British. He thought he had achieved this end, only to discover that Isidore Ostrer had constructed a complex array of voting and nonvoting stocks that effectively prevented any capitalist predator from taking the reins of power. After buying up £600,000 of what turned out to be nonvoting "B" shares, Maxwell learned that he had been outsmarted, and it gnawed away at him like a tapeworm bent on revenge. The diabetic Maxwell saw his health swiftly wither away, and he collapsed dead in 1940. A once mighty capitalist reduced to mockery on Wardour Street, Maxwell had envisioned a colossal exhibition sector that could support a vibrant production enterprise.

Only J. Arthur Rank would realize this extravagant vision. In late October 1941, he convinced the Ostrers to relinquish control over Gaumont–British, a move apparently motivated by Isidore's long hiatuses in the American Southwest. With his purchase of Odeon, Rank now possessed over six hundred theaters, approximately 15 percent of the nation's total but holding a third of the overall seating capacity. To Denham and Pinewood studios, he added Gaumont–British's Gainsborough Film Studios, founded by Michael Balcon in 1924 and a major source of medium-priced feature films. He also received Gaumont–British's distribution network, a delicious revenge for their half-hearted service on *Turn of the Tide* in 1935. "Now I'll find out how much those projectors you sold me *really* cost," he growled to Gaumont–British's Ian Cremieu-Javal, who handled sales of equipment to churches affiliated with the Religious Film Society.[30]

With the deaths of Maxwell, Deutsch, and Rank's chief lieutenant C. M. Woolf in late 1942, as well as the retreats from production of Alexander Korda, Isidore Ostrer, and Lady Yule, Rank had the entire field to himself. The sudden collapse of all competition may have seemed as eerily improbable as the scenario in *Kind Hearts and Coronets,* in which eight relatives perish one by one to pave the way for the tenth Duke of Chalfont; yet Rank explained it as the mysterious unfolding of Divine Plan. The death of Woolf, who had advised Rank on his many moves, may have been the most significant; for Woolf, distrustful of extravagant artistes, would likely have restrained Rank in the field of production. Instead the flour magnate embarked on a production feast, leading to the greatest burst of spending in British cinema history.

Rank's own pythonlike digestive system immediately drew the attention of pathologists at the Board of Trade, which began an inquiry. Fearful of cinemonopoly, Board of Trade President Hugh Dalton exacted a pledge from Rank that he would acquire no additional theaters. By most indications, the Yorkshireman was relatively sated, but he would have preferred to add to his empire perhaps a hundred theaters in select locations.

On the one hand, Rank's possession of six hundred theaters gave him leverage against Hollywood firms whose theaters otherwise denied British films screen time in the United States. On the other hand, he gained enemies among those Britons fearful he would use his clout first to deny British independent producers access to screen time, and then to stanch the flow of his films to non-Rank theaters. Exhibitors had to meet quotas, and if Rank horded British films, he could make life miserable for competitors seeking to comply with provisions of the 1938 Cinematograph Films Act. Enemies of Rank spun a whole web of conspiratorial scenarios that he might employ against surviving small fry.

THE CHILDREN'S CRUSADE AND THE INTELLECTUALS

In April 1943, Rank began his largest initiative for the moral regeneration of British society, his Odeon and Gaumont–British Children's Cinema Clubs, starting with 150 cinemas and an estimated 150,000 children. With participation soon growing to 400 theaters and over 400,000 member children aged 7–14, Rank could claim the affiliation of "roughly one in ten in this age group," declared Mary Field, the director of Gaumont–British's Children's Educational Films (CEF), founded in May 1944.[31] Assembling every Saturday morning from 9:30 until 11:45, the clubs began with a quarter hour of community singing, frequently led by a trained choir or "local music-master." After a delightful cartoon, the members had to recite in unison the Club Promise, stressing "the principles of good citizenship":

I will be truthful and honourable and will always try to make myself a good and honourable young citizen. I will obey my elders and help the aged, the helpless and children smaller than myself. I will always be kind to animals.[32]

Rank apparently adopted this oath from the cinema clubs started in 1937 by his predecessor at the helm of Odeon, Oscar Deutsch. Having affirmed the oath, most clubs listened to a suitably wholesome talk, typically from "a nurse, a clergyman, an explorer, a scientist, the Education Officer or the Medical Officer of Health, a popular figure in the sports world, or a member of the local Corporation who will encourage interest in civic affairs." The Royal Society for the Prevention of Accidents (RSPA) and for the Prevention of Cruelty to Animals (RSPCA) had a special place in the clubs' presentations. In addition, cartoons and slide shows infused children with knowledge of proper hygiene.[33]

Field spoke of art and literary competitions that "have produced a number of extremely encouraging results." She hailed "one ambitious club" for publishing its own newspaper, and numerous others for establishing "stamp clubs, swimming sections, football clubs, camera clubs, physical training classes, libraries, riding and dancing classes." Pantomime and plays were performed both at club functions and then "for entertaining troops in hospital, the old and the infirm." Rivalries developed among clubs through soccer games, swimming races, and spelling bees.[34]

Field held especially high hopes for reaching children in foreign countries. Hailing an Anglo–Soviet "pen pal" scheme, she closed with a boilerplate observation about "the importance of international friendship between children," which "cannot be over-estimated since the world's future lies in their hands." She later served as president of UNESCO's International Centre of Films for Children and Young People (CIFEJ) and became a pioneer of children's programming on the new electronic medium as a supervisor for England's ABC Television during 1958–63. Field wondered "whether Britain, which leads the world in documentary, will be the pioneer and acknowledged leader in the field of children's films."[35]

With large audiences, Rank's Children's Cinema Clubs attracted their share of British critics. Some charged that he was training children to be unquestioning and loyal patrons of commercial cinema, a sort of strategy for maximizing profits. In reality, Rank lost money on the program because, despite packed houses on Saturdays, he could show this fare only one day a week in most markets. The intellectuals engaged in Hegelian meditations on his enterprise's impact on British civilization. The sociologist J. P. Mayer quoted liberally from the original German texts of the Swiss historian Jacob Burckhardt who had despaired about "unsere dummen Basler-Kollossal-Kinderfeste!" ("our dumb, colossal childrens' festivals in Basle!"). This nineteenth-century thinker noted: "Whoever as a child has now and then felt true joy, knows that the latter cannot be felt in the presence of crowds." Burckhardt feared that with the rise of the mass man, people were trained to take special pleasure in "mass meetings" (*Massenversammlungen*) and that soon they "shall weep, when there are not at least a hundred of them, crowded together." Approving Burckhardt's sentiments as prescient wisdom, Mayer observed: "It is extremely doubtful whether Burckhardt would have changed his view, had he been able to witness Mr. Rank's Children's Cinema Clubs." This highbrow sociologist sat for weeks among the children and took notes, ultimately condemning the Rank-inspired decay of civilization. He closed his book with the text of Seneca's "On Roman Games," which warned: "To consort with the crowd is harmful. . . . Certainly, the greater the mob with which we mingle, the greater the danger." Indeed, concluded Seneca, "nothing is so damaging to good character as the habit of lounging at the games; for then it is that vice steals subtly upon one through the avenue of pleasure." Seneca believed that "Even Socrates, Cato, and Laelius might have shaken in their moral strength by a crowd that was unlike them; . . . none of us . . . can withstand the shock of faults that approach . . . with so great a retinue." As a student of French philosophy, Mayer reinforced Seneca with Pascal's *Pensée* no. 139: "I have discovered that all the unhappiness of men arises from one single fact, that they cannot stay quietly in their own room."[36]

Mayer mordantly intoned about its meaning for contemporary Britain: "Must the fate of our civilization be similar to that of the Roman Empire?" He delivered a pessimistic verdict, one enforced by the philosopher and historian of ideas R. G. Collingwood: "The parallel, so far as it has yet developed, is alarmingly close." As Collingwood underlined: "Then came the cinema and the wireless; and the poor, throughout the country, went amusement mad." In blaming all of the masses for this predicament, Mayer departed from Collingwood's belief that the unemployed were most vulnerable to cinema's ravages, those the historian of ideas identified as "functionless and aimless in the community, living only to accept *panem et circenses,* the dole and the films."

For Mayer, Rank's attempt to infuse films with moral values offended against the tradition of "European ethical reflection." Arguing that many people have embraced "the value patterns of the Hays Code-*pur-sang,*" he produced the testimony of a twenty-five-year-old correspondent who reflected that

[T]he films had built a conception of life, which life itself, tended to contradict. . . . But instead of making me disbelieve in and dislike film-life, it made me bitter towards real life. . . . I try to live my life as films would have us believe, and they have helped me to get a great deal out of life, though it is "tough" going.[37]

Condemning this "confession de foi" as an endorsement of the view that "Life should be like film," Mayer responded:

It is a long and depressing journey from Aristotle's *Nicomachean Ethics* to this document, but it may well be that our young author . . . who so sincerely strives to formulate his *Weltanschauung* is not less representative for our contemporary moral conception of life than the great Greek philosopher was for his age.[38]

Under fire from the intelligentsia for naïvely mixing morals and cinema, Rank gained new enemies among those who believed that commercialism had led him to scuttle standards of probity. In 1946, *The Wicked Lady,* produced by the Rank-owned Gainsborough Film Studios, became the year's top-selling British film. Premiering in December 1945, the film soon received attention for plunging necklines and evil behavior that appeared worthy of the title. According to Breen, Universal Pictures, Rank's U.S. distributor, "argued that these costumes with the woman's breasts partially exposed are 'typical of the period' of the picture and that if the costumes were not so constructed – and the breasts so exposed – some artistic integrity would be sacrificed."[39] When the Johnston Office in the U.S. assailed the excess of "cleavage" in his studio's films, Rank tartly responded: "But in England, bosoms aren't sexy!"[40] Moreover, he held that *The Wicked Lady* had powerful moral lessons, as the central malefactor, the aristocratic Lady Skelton (Margaret Lockwood), is gunned down accidentally by her lover, the highwayman Capt. Jerry Jackson (James Mason). Queen Mary attended the premiere at the age of seventy-eight and saluted the flour magnate, "A very good film, Mr. Rank, and a fine moral." Perhaps unaware that a projectionist turned down the sound to spare the Queen's virgin ears from a few moments of salacious dialogue, she delighted Rank with her insight. "Queen Mary," he said, "is the only person to see in the film what I see myself. I only agreed to it because there's a moral in it. You have two pretty girls, Margaret Lockwood and Pat Roc. One of them falls to temptation, and gets shot in the end; the other lives happily. That's the moral."[41]

The film's condemnation of aristocratic excess and its ratification of middle-class restraint did not fully win over Joseph Breen at the Johnston Office, and shots overly revealing of décolletage had to be retaken for the U.S. market. Breen warned that probably "the industry will be denounced in Parliament," and the PCA's refusal of a seal will be called "part of the American 'conspiracy,'" ". . . the desire of the 'monopoly' in this country to deny play dates for the picture."[42] He countered that "We have persistently over a long period of years, refused to approve such 'breast shots.' . . . It was principally because of several unacceptable breast shots that we withheld our approval of Howard Hughes' THE OUTLAW."[43] Rank himself vetoed plans of director Leslie Arliss for a sequel, *The Wicked Lady's Daughter,* an indication that money had not quite bested his religious instinct.

Critics continued to condemn him all the same. The *Manchester Guardian* termed it "A mixture of hot passion and cold suet." Simon Harcourt-Smith of the Labourite *Tribune* appeared out of step with its working-class audience, who flocked to the film, as he paused to remark:

There exists, of course, no reason why J. Arthur Rank should not sanction the inflicting on us of whatever dowdy fancy-dress inanity he will. Lines that issue from a mouth imprisoned between a cotton-wool wig and a machine-made lace cravat appear to please the average audience where they would be intolerable in a modern melodrama. And certainly *The Wicked Lady* is infused with a nonsense of period so authentically Hollywood that it should almost qualify for one of those American releases that must, we gather, be the yardstick of excellence. . . .

But *The Wicked Lady* arouses in me a nausea out of all proportion to the subject.[44]

Evoking "the classical witnesses of Roman decadence, for instance Seneca or Petronius," J. P. Mayer declared that "Circus, pantomime, feast, spectacle, public baths had in Rome probably the same social function as films of today like *Gilda, Madonna of the Seven Moons, Scarlet Street, The Wicked Lady,* and many others." In contrast to social critic Lewis Mumford, who "blames the commercial cinema for this development," Mayer suggested: "We should rather blame State and society, which tolerate the usurpation of a realm of culture which under contemporary circumstances should never be left to the law of *laissez-faire.*"[45]

FROM *OBJECTIVE BURMA* TO THE U.S.–U.K. FILM WAR

Those Britons opposed to the rule of laissez-faire over cinema had already seized upon an incident in the immediate aftermath of World War II: Warner Brothers' failure to portray the heroics of British soldiers in the movie *Objective Burma,* starring Errol Flynn. On 24 September 1945, MP W. S. Shepherd, a lieutenant in the Royal Sussex Regiment, wrote Warner Brothers/London and cast a slur on it as "an insult to the British forces who sacrificed so much" in the Burma campaign. If "this travesty of a film" receives general release, Shepherd said, "I propose to press for the establishment of an organisation which will prevent a repetition, and this would involve the film industry in additional restriction." Warner Brothers received numerous hostile letters from anonymous British sources. "In view of the distortion of true facts, may I humbly suggest that you stuff this film down the lavatory pan, along with some of the other American rubbish that you flood our market with," said a correspondent who adopted the nom de plume "Advance British Films." A self-identified trade unionist calling him- or herself "Disgusted" threatened Warner with a libel action and added for good measure that "We just had about enough of Hollywood bunk and now this stinking piece of film making. . . ." The activist warned that: "The day is not far off when our own studios will be run by the State with the best of our National Artists – so why not go back to the land of Ballyhoo now." "Disgusted" concluded that Britain shall "get along respectably with our Dominions and the Soviet Union. Great nations are not made on whisky drinking seduction and superficial Bunk, and Warners and the U.S.A. are soon going to find this out."[46]

While many of the outcries against *Objective Burma* exude resentment about the vulgarian United States supplanting cultured Britain as the pre-eminent global power, the critics were quick to pinpoint their grievance as one of anger at a distortion of the Burma campaign that "ignores the British effort," stated the *Daily Sketch* (25 September 1945). War Office figures identified six hundred and seventy thousand British, Indian, and African combat troops in the India–Burma Theater (IBT) and only seven thousand Americans. In air strength, the British supplied forty-three thousand personnel; the Americans, thirty thousand. Line-of-communication troops included one hundred and thirty-eight thousand British, Indians, and Africans, and a hundred and twenty thousand Americans. In charge of reporting on the *Objective Burma* affair for the War Office, Major A. E. Sykes of the South East Asia Command (SEAC) claimed that "When the film was shown in Calcutta about five months ago it nearly caused riots. Service men who were on leave from forward jungle areas were furious." Sykes joined many British newspapers in identifying U.S. soldiers also enraged at what Lieutenant-Colonel William H. Taylor of the U.S. Air Force termed "a meretricious hodge-podge." The *Daily Mail* (21 September 1945) called the film "a staggering bit of international bad taste," though "it does the American people credit that the fiercest protests against the pretence that Burma was an American sphere of operations have come from American fighting men in the Pacific."[47]

The *Times* of London declared that *Objective Burma* could have dangerous reverberations:

Because the history of the 1914–1918 war was twisted and obscured by German propagandists, the way was opened for 1939, and it is hardly less important that the nations should know and appreciate the efforts other countries than their own made to the common cause.[48]

French, British, Canadian, and Australian opinion had filed frequent complaints after World War I concerning Hollywood's tendency to give all the credit for triumph to U.S. forces. The *Times* resented those dismissing the flap over *Objective Burma* as "only a film," and the editors reminded elite Britons that "misrepresentation on the screen can do very much more harm than an article in a newspaper."

The *News Chronicle* (22 September 1945) carried the headline "Flynn-flam," and *Reynolds News* (23 September 1945) ran with "Film Insult to Troops." The latter called the performance comparable to "Hamlet without the Prince? This is an invasion of Burma without the Fourteenth Army." Hollywood "besmirches the real thing with tinsel." Ernest Betts in Beaverbrook's *Daily Express* entitled his column, "Why Pay to See This Fake?" Max Milder, representing Warner Brothers in London, believed that the *Daily Express* bore special responsibility for the *Objective Burma* agitation, and in frustration he desperately sought to untangle a conspiracy of sorts: "I think the whole thing has been promoted by someone. . . . Bernstein is very friendly with the Editor of *The Daily Express* – a man by the name of [Arthur] Christiansen." He pointed to a headline in the *Daily Sketch* (26 September 1945) entitled "We Have the True Film on Burma," and claimed "that a lot of this agitation could probably be traced to certain influences at work to boost this 'true film' which they hope to get out real soon."[49]

The British film, entitled *Burma Victory*, became heralded as a model of British fair play compared to Hollywood greed and self-celebration. In contrast to *Objective Burma*, *Burma Victory*, wrote Major E.W. Sheppard in the *Daily Herald*, ensures that "all nationalities are given their full share of credit," from "General Stilwell's feat in building the Ledo highway" down to "the intensive roadmaking by native women and children."[50]

Fearful that the crusade against *Objective Burma* would imperil Warner Brothers' films in Britain, as well as Allied unity, the company halted display of the movie in late September. In October 1945, the *Daily Mirror* called attention to a new Twentieth Century–Fox feature, *The House on 92nd Street*, that gave the distinct impression "that the atomic bomb was discovered, developed and guarded by America, without any help from Britain." According to its film critic, Reg Whitley, "the Hollywood tendency, which reached its climax with the *Objective Burma* film, to belittle by implication the work of our Services in their efforts for victory" has made urgent the strengthening of British movie production. In hopes of averting a repeat of the *Objective Burma* affair, Twentieth Century–Fox sent the film for a quick editing designed to soothe British audiences. "Everything controversial has gone," reported Whitley. "It is now nothing more than a melodramatic documentary describing the FBI's work in spy catching."[51]

U.S. opinion tended to greet wounded British sensibilities as hypersensitive to the point of danger for Allied unity. In an editorial called "Uncle Shylock Again?" New York City's *Liberty* magazine argued that "British–American relations, no matter how tranquil they may look officially, have worsened steadily since the end of the war" and pronounced that:

Some of the British complaints are ludicrous and laughable. For instance, their reaction to the showing of the film *Objective Burma*. . . . In it, a group of Americans drop by parachute to demolish a Jap radar station. . . . This hardly adds up to an attempt by Americans to take credit for the conquest of Burma singlehanded. However, the British seem to think it does, though the more vocal of the objectors obviously have not seen the film.[52]

The commentator counseled "The present British government . . . to take its political courage in hand and actively combat anti-American feeling. Political diffidence and pussyfooting will not do in these times. . . ."

Instead of pursuing this course, the British government sought "Preferential treatment for British films" as "part of an accelerating *national crusade*," charged F. W. Allport, the London representative of the MPAA. In a memorandum to MPAA chief Eric Johnston, who supplied the document to the U.S. Department of State, Allport pronounced that the "Government, Parliament, press, radio (BBC) and public are allied with the industry in this crusade." He blamed "the press, and particularly the film critics, by a continued campaign against American films, in which the BBC takes an active part on occasion."[53] Allport respectfully declined mention of Keynes's "Death to Hollywood" broadcast on the BBC in midsummer 1945.

Declaring that "the Companies are *deeply concerned* over . . . the progressive diversion of screen time to British films," he identified two culprits:

1. Sir Stafford Cripps, president of the Board of Trade, who on 18 March 1946 requested the three leading circuits to add six British films each to the annual 17.5 percent film quota; and
2. the major British circuits, which Allport alleged are "giving British films preferred playing time, key positions and longer initial bookings." For the circuits, "Relative merit is secondary, the policy being to give every possible advantage to British films."[54]

Despite his ownership of two of the three major circuits, J. Arthur Rank escaped direct sniping from the MPAA leadership in the initial postwar period. The MPAA believed that "The Cripps Plan" of 18 March 1946 had been designed to aid independent British producers, who complained that the Rank circuits should be more generous to their creations. Though Allport feared that "the Rank Organisation . . . is in a position to refuse screen time in Great Britain unless it is given screen time in the United States," he had saluted the flour magnate in the past for eschewing state intervention on behalf of his economic empire. Hollywood delighted in Rank's attacks on Britain's Entertainments Tax (ET), which stood at 38 percent of box-office receipts, the highest in Western Europe. In fiscal 1945, the ET raised

£45,936,000 for the British Exchequer, with £39,530,000 coming from cinema (85 percent or £33,600,000 of that figure generated by U.S. movies).[55]

At the war's end, Will Hays hosted a banquet on Rank's behalf at the Waldorf-Astoria, where the film moguls slurped down turtle soup with their chief overseas competitor. The U.S. moguls sent presents to Rank's daughter after the birth of her child. She recalled that such hospitality and niceties came to an abrupt halt in the fall of 1947.

British Treasury officials and the Board of Trade had been under intense pressure throughout 1946 and 1947 to relieve the hemorrhaging of British wealth overseas via the trade deficit with the United States. Generated in part by the import of so-called frivolities, most notably cigarettes and Hollywood films, the balance-of-payments crisis elicited new slogans from the political class: "Grub before Grable," "Bacon before Bogart," and "Food before Fags [Cigarettes]."

Throughout 1946 and 1947, Treasury and the Board of Trade plotted ways of shutting off this financial outflow. However, as early as 11 July 1946, A. G. White of the Board of Trade cautioned his colleagues that they could not hope to follow the example of neighbors such as France. Even though "the American companies will not be allowed to take out of France in dollars more than between 2–3 million dollars a year . . ." or one-fifth of what they earn in the French market, they "would never acquiesce in our blocking anything like four-fifths of their U.K. revenue. . . ."[56] The Board of Trade's "Palache Report" on *Tendencies to Monopoly in the Cinematograph Film Industry* (London: HMSO, 1944) had pointed out that "Prior to the war, American companies . . . obtained $135 million of their annual total film rentals, or 35 percent from foreign sources; $101.2 millions accruing from the British Empire."[57] With the vast majority of their overseas revenues coming from the British Empire, White suggested that the U.S. companies would fight like tigers should Britain try to trap these earnings.

The Board of Trade did not stick to this position for long. Previously it had been skeptical of U.S. will in boycotting the British market. A successful boycott against France in 1928 and a threatened one against Belgium in the mid-1930s grew distant in the minds of the policy elite. As a report of 25 September 1940 expressed the Board of Trade's views, rendered after consultation with film statistician Simon Rowson and exhibitors Oscar Deutsch and Arthur Jarratt:

[I]t is most unlikely that the American companies would in practice boycott this market. . . .

This, however, will not necessarily prevent the bluff from being made and if we are to be in a position to call it, we must have ministerial authority, including the

Foreign Office and Treasury, and also plans to meet the situation if unexpectedly the boycott were brought into force.[58]

As 1947 progressed, British policymakers expressed renewed skepticism about a U.S. boycott, only this time they seemed less concerned than was the case in 1940 about advance preparation. In a top-secret draft to Chancellor of the Exchequer Hugh Dalton (appointed July 1945), Ernest Rowe-Dutton of Treasury proclaimed that "On the whole the Board of Trade consider that the American film interests are unlikely to take reprisals at the expense of British films in America." They had too much to lose in terms of British "goodwill," and such a step would only increase pressure for higher duties on U.S. films. However, he observed:

A more serious danger is that they might all combine and send no more films for exhibition in British cinemas. This, of course, would completely dislocate the circulation of films in this country. . . . Such a boycott would not be unprecedented, for there have recently been at least three or four cases where all the principal U.S. companies withheld their new films from particular European markets. . . . On the other hand, the companies could much less well afford to boycott our important market than, say, Holland or Scandinavia, and the Board of Trade are inclined to think that, rather than do that – especially at the present time, when they are already believed to be hard up for cash – the companies would still carry on and make the best of a bad job.[59]

The "bad job" Rowe-Dutton referred to was a Treasury scheme for a stiff ad valorem tax on foreign films. "The Customs will . . . have recourse to the method of taking duty on deposit at the time of importation," he wrote, "on the basis of a provisional valuation to be adjusted subsequently in the light of the profits actually earned from the exhibition of the film." He observed that since the McKenna duty of 1915 motorcars had been subjected to an ad valorem rate of 33.33 percent. Treasury soon settled on an ad valorem rate of 75 percent for films, a duty frequently called a 300 percent tax by the U.S. film industry (because for every £25 the industry could take out of Britain, they paid £75 in taxes). "The American companies will not like it," forecasted Rowe-Dutton, "but the Board of Trade do not fear that they will refuse to supply films."[60]

On 6 August 1947, Hugh Dalton announced Britain's imposition of a 75 percent ad valorem tax on foreign films. Following a three-hour meeting of the MPAA in New York on 8 August, Eric Johnston proclaimed that they would rivet in place the same weapon adopted against the tariff walls of Australia and the Scandinavian nations: boycott. Falsifying the British cabinet's wishful thinking that the U.S. companies would feel desperate and therefore be willing to accept a truncated portion of British revenue, Johnston pledged resistance. "If the British do not want American pictures," he declared, "that is one thing; if they do, they should not expect to get a dollar's worth of film for 25 cents."[61]

Hollywood found strong support against Britain's action from many old enemies, particularly the newspapers of the old isolationist Right. In an editorial, the *Washington Times Herald* (18 August 1947) called on Americans to rally behind the besieged moguls:

Taking back nothing we've said in the past about Communist propaganda needled into some Hollywood motion pictures and about excessive Hollywood fondness for internationalism as against Americanism, we nevertheless find our sympathies on the U.S. side in the battle which the British Labor Government recently started against American films.[62]

The newspaper targeted the head of the Board of Trade as the ogre of the piece:

Back of all this, according to one story which sounds reasonable to us, is the skinny, puritanical figure of Sir Stafford Cripps. . . .
   Sir Stafford is notoriously one of those gents who hate pleasure for themselves and therefore hate to see other people have a good time. Rather like our prohibitionists. In addition, he is a fanatical Socialist, an admirer of Communist Russia, and an ill-wisher of the United States.

From the standpoint of Britain's Foreign Office, renewed anti-British campaigning among the former isolationist camp spelled potential danger. In early 1947, F. B. A. Rundall of the North America Department expressed alarm about an editorial in the *Cleveland Plain-Dealer* advocating that the United States let the British Empire go down the toilet. Contrasting this with the supposedly responsible view of elite journalists such as Walter Lippmann, who urged rescue of the United Kingdom in his article "The British Problem," Rundall told the Foreign Office that Britain must escalate cold-war tension:

[A]ny marked rapprochement between the U.S.A. and Russia would make our own survival less of a vital national interest. Yet we must allow time for the implications of our collapse to be appreciated, especially among the small-town Republicans who set the tone in the lower house of Congress.[63]

Rather than fearing British collapse, isolationists turned nasty about Whitehall's intervention against a U.S. industry, and they received new encouragement from a wounded Hollywood. The trade newspaper *Variety* (7 January 1948) called on Washington to:

tackle this problem. . . . The very industry which . . . has brought much-needed business and a dream of better things to come into the hearts of millions of men and
women abroad, now is being kicked around like a football.

From the early days of Dalton's announcement, the U.S. State Department looked for avenues to resolve the crisis. Representing the MPAA, Allen
Dulles, a lawyer for Sullivan and Cromwell, asked Undersecretary of State
Robert Lovett on 12 August "whether Congressional action was necessary
for any change in the British loan," the postwar aid package of the United
States to the United Kingdom. Lovett informed Dulles that Congress would
have to be consulted, thus making the MPAA's legal eagle aware that any
scheme seeking to manipulate the loan would require the intrusion of politics. The future CIA chief quickly retreated for the time being. Lovett then
alarmed Dulles by raising the possibility that the boycott was itself a violation of U.S. antitrust law. The undersecretary of State soon lifted the specter of collusion, however, as he subsequently received a memorandum in-
forming him that the Justice Department, despite ongoing antitrust action
against the industry, would not intervene against the boycott. With the dex-
terity of a lawyer, Dulles told Lovett that the boycott was not an action of
the MPAA but rather of the Webb–Pomerene Corporation, which had several of the film majors as members. The British hoped that some non-MPAA
companies, the U.S. independents, would cross the boycott, despite themselves being subject to the 75 percent levy. Often otherwise at loggerheads
with the MPAA, the independents nonetheless rejected their new opportunity in Britain.[64]

After a meeting with Eric Johnston on 23 August 1947, Joint Second
Secretary of the Treasury Sir Wilfrid Eady admitted that Britain had a tremendous challenge ahead, as the U.S. film industry might pose an obstacle
to the European Recovery Program (Marshall Plan). He made the following observations about Britain's response and the nature of the MPAA:

1. It is an extremely powerful lobby in the State Department and capable of very
   considerable malice.
2. Our primary tactical objective with the United States Administration is to re-
   gain early access to the frozen United States credit. It is scarcely conceivable that
   the United States will release the credit without making some conditions to meet
   American interests, e.g. either reductions or repeal of the film tax.
3. Behind all this lies the Marshall Plan and what we may hope to get out of it.
   Here again one must expect this powerful lobby to be exercised against us in
   the discussions that will take place on the Marshall Plan.[65]

Eady believed that by making "some unimportant modification," as an
example of which he included trimming the tax from 300 percent to 240

or 200 percent, the MPAA shall find that "we have . . . spiked their guns."[66] In December, Stafford Cripps took over as Chancellor of the Exchequer, and Harold Wilson replaced him as Board of Trade president. Both Cripps and Wilson resisted retreat. In February, the British ambassador to the United States was told by Eric Johnston that

He disclaimed any attempt to influence us with threats about E.R.P. or our own position of priority in E.R.P., but he did want us to know that some members of the Motion Picture Association (he mentioned Mr. Balaban by name) wanted to placard some extracts from Mr. Wilson's speech [before the House of Commons, 21 January] all over the U.S.A. in theatres and in newspapers as evidence of an intention to socialise the film industry.[67]

Johnston portrayed himself as a moderating force, who could only for so long restrain "this school of thought in the Motion Picture Association." He saw their mounting rage as

fuel added to the fire of opposition to further aid to Britain under E.R.P. or anything else. He said that he had recently been to the White House and had told the whole story to President Truman. The President had commented that if the films tax procedure persisted and spread to other things and to other countries, the U.S.A. and the United Kingdom might as well throw their Havana Charter into the waste paper basket. . . .[68]

Johnston identified Australia and Argentina as two countries that quickly followed Britain's malevolent example.[69]

All of this turbulence placed J. Arthur Rank in a delicate situation, a bit of a sticky wicket. U.S. movie moguls regarded Rank as the British equivalent of Will Hays or Eric Johnston, and they assumed he consulted regularly with the British state on matters of film foreign policy. Part of the misperception had been Rank's fault; in the United States during July 1947, he had reassured his American counterparts that the British government would not take rash and hostile measures against Hollywood.[70] Rank in reality had been caught by surprise at Labour's ad valorem gambit. At first concerned that the British action might undo cooperation with the dominant forces in the U.S. film industry, Rank then bristled at Hollywood's arrogance in holding him responsible for Labour's betrayal. British Treasury's Eady worried that Rank would now be denied U.S. screen time. When the Hollywood boycott showed little sign of cracking, Labour put pressure on Rank to begin a massive increase in domestic film production. Fancying himself a patriot first and a capitalist second, the Methodist millionaire accepted this chalice of peril. Agreeing to embark on extravagant sponsorship of new British films, Rank believed that God had led him to this moment

of destiny. In October 1947, he set out to spend £9,250,000 in order to pro-
duce forty-three feature films, an unprecedented expansion in the 1940s.
Eric Johnston engaged in a rhetoric of disbelief at Rank's actions, what
might be called the MPAA chairman's rat-down-the-gangplank posture.
After all he, Johnston, had done for Britain and its film industry, John Bull
insisted on casting him aside [Fig. 9]. During July, Johnston had boasted to
Rank that virtually every American schoolteacher received a letter from the
U.S. industry advising them to send students to the Rank productions of
Henry V and *Great Expectations*.[71] Rank followed up on the smash success of *Great Expectations* with another Dickens classic, *Oliver Twist*. Part
of his 1947–8 expansion, *Oliver Twist* came under ferocious attack from
Jewish organizations objecting to its portrayal of Fagin, monstrously inhu-
mane in Dickens's novel and now alleged to be dripping with anti-Semitism
in Alec Guinness's performance. Picketed in major cities and unassisted by
a school campaign, it became an orphan of sorts as "the distributing company has given up all thought of distributing the picture in this country,"
wrote Joseph Breen on 14 September 1948.[72]
    Breen, who in the preproduction phase had suggested to the Rank Orga-
nization on 13 May 1947 "the advisability of omitting from the portrayal
of Fagin any elements or inference that would be offensive to any specific
racial group or religion," later found himself denying a PCA seal "because
of the element, in the picture, which definitely suggests a highly offensive
characterization of a Jew."[73] The Anti-Defamation League (ADL) called the
portrayal of Fagin a "grotesque Jewish caricature . . . which Streicher Nazis
tried [to] impose on [the] world," and the New York–based *Independent
Film Journal*, in an editorial headlined "Black Eye for Brotherhood," regarded it as "a faithful reproduction of the Cruickshank drawings used so
extensively by Hitler in fanning religious hatred."[74] Breen held his ground,
despite anger from columnist Bill Gordon, who asked, "Who is more powerful than the Johnston Office?" His readers "all said the same thing – the
Anti-Defamation League." Dorothy E. Hogan (244 E. 86th St., NY, NY)
wrote the MPAA and termed "it a personal disgrace that the city of my birth
would in the true Hitler manner bar the showing of this wonderful classic
. . . because of a powerful minority. This is definitely not the 'American
way'. . . ." With a panel of "six members of its professional staff, 4 Christians, 2 Jews," the National Conference on Christians and Jews called for
a reversal of Breen's edict:

The gang of wretched individuals of which Fagin and Sykes were the villainous leaders, was a criminal gang without regard to any religious or racial description that
would lead to generalization about Jewish villainy . . . the conniving of Mr. Monks

FIGURE 9. With a map showing the global ambitions of his film organization, British movie mogul J. Arthur Rank confers in May 1947 with Eric Johnston, the president of the Motion Picture Association of America (MPAA). Occurring just a few months before Britain slapped a 75 percent ad valorem tax on Hollywood films, the meeting was supposed to solidify cooperation between the U.S. and British film industries. *Source:* Hulton|Archive.

and the cunning cruelty of Sykes overshadow the influence of Fagin insofar as the audience dislike is concerned. The makeup of Guinness presents a Fagin so far removed from twentieth century Jews in appearance and in occupation that we see no likelihood of a widespread transfer in the minds of American audiences to their Jewish neighbors. . . . Fagin is never called a Jew and . . . his speech, for the most part, is that of a definitely English accent. . . .[75]

Breen finally granted the picture a seal in early 1951, but not before requiring sixty-nine cuts representing an incredible 749 feet of footage. Eliminating the "avaricious hand gesture of Fagin asking for money," director

David Lean even offered to insert "a short scene wherein [a] respectable Jewish leader offers services of his community to police when [the] hunt for Fagin is on." Alas Breen had called off the dogs. He resented those previously accusing him of caving into Jewish pressure, as he recalled forbidding films showing "a typical 'silly ass' type of Englishman and the 'oh-la-la' type of Frenchman."[76]

Prior to the flap over *Oliver Twist*, Rank also stood shocked at Christian outcries against *Black Narcissus*, referred to by *Variety* (8 July 1950) as "a grim story, lavishly mounted in Technicolor, of sex-starved nuns." Calling the film "a perverted specimen of bad taste, vicious inaccuracies and ludicrous improbabilities," the Roman Catholic journalist Virginia S. Tomlinson accused Rank of playing "directly into the hands of those subversives who seek today to discredit all religions." Eleanor Lewis, sparked to action by Tomlinson's attack, believed that

we CATHOLICS should gang up on this picture – and with Mr. Breen's help see that the stinky thing is stopped . . . we ought to let Rank keep his "rank" pictures and take them back to England – and stay there.[77]

An admirer of the directors Powell and Pressburger, in spite of the sensuality of their cinema craft, Joseph Breen approved the film, apparently buying the explanation that these were, after all, Protestant nuns representing the Church of England. A conference of Roman Catholic clerics and nuns at the University of Notre Dame wrote a formal plea to Rank:

We hope that your explanation will not be that these are Anglican nuns and, therefore, Roman Catholics should not be offended. Such a reply would be in bad taste, ungallant and derogatory to the religion of many of your countrymen . . . as you well know, the average moviegoer will make no such distinction.[78]

This would not be the last time that Rank the arch-Methodist offended Christian audiences. Breen in 1949 prevented Ealing Studios from referring to the vicar played by Alec Guinness in *Kind Hearts and Coronets* as "a boring old ass." The *Sunday Express* (8 January 1950) explained that Guinness, who had played "an outstanding Fagin," was "stupidly attacked because 'it was anti-Semitic.' . . . His recent success *Kind Hearts and Coronets* has been held up in America because the censor has objected to one line." Rank's problems with U.S. Christians and Jews unexpectedly complicated his organization's ability to prevail in the Anglo–U.S. film wars.

Meanwhile, President of the Board of Trade Harold Wilson repeated over and over like a mantra: Britain would not back down to a Hollywood-engineered film boycott. Abhorring the rawhide values espoused by Johnston and his followers, Wilson initially could not see himself capitulating to an MPAA chief who in 1947 boasted to the House Un-American Activities Committee that "films are serving capitalism effectively as a propaganda medium," so much so that there was "an ugly scuffle among the major companies to be first with the titles 'Soviet Spies' and 'Iron Curtain,' etc." Johnston shared concern with HUAC about "Britain's American diet," which consisted of *Strange Incident* (as *The Ox-Bow Incident* was called in England), "an anti-lynching film," and *Hitler's Children*, "so anti-Nazi that it must have been inspired by Communists."[79] In contrast to the 1930s, the sheer paucity of films during the Johnston era (1945–63) that portray businessmen as villains or the wealthy as decadent would seem a victory for Ayn Rand's cardinal rules for good filmmaking in her "Screen Guide for Americans" (1947): "Don't Smear the Free Enterprise System," "Don't Deify the 'Common Man,'" and "Don't Smear Industrialists."[80] A jovial Johnston had already delivered the news in 1947: "We'll have no more *Grapes of Wrath*, we'll have no more *Tobacco Roads*." The Randian axiom "Don't Glorify Failure" also received the MPAA chief's swift ratification: "We'll have no more films that show the seamy side of American life. We'll have no pictures that deal with labor strikes. We'll have no more pictures that show the banker as a villain."[81] Johnston regularly labeled critics of capitalism "crackpots." Though the Spokane businessman and former vacuum-cleaner salesman admitted there could be "justified criticism of specific practices or policies," he concluded: "In the last analysis, an attack on Big Business . . . is an attack on the American type of civilization."[82]

In his speech of 21 January 1948, Wilson assured the House of Commons: "I am sure that I can say to Hollywood that if they believe they can squeeze us into modifying our attitude on the duty by continuing the embargo, they are backing a loser."[83] But it was Wilson who soon became the loser. Labour had thought their case with the Americans was strengthened by the choice of taxation and an exhibitors quota based on percentages, measures both faithful to the principles of GATT, as opposed to an absolute numerical limit on film imports.

By early 1948, the window open to what Wilfrid Eady had called "unimportant modification of our present stand" seemed thoroughly shut. Exhibitors began to run out of their backlog of American films, and worry spread of empty moviehouses. Neither Whitehall nor the exhibitors came up with any innovative ideas about increasing supply. Some have suggested that the industry accepted too much as an article of faith the view that the masses could not endure films with subtitles; there were several box-office successes available from the Continent that did not cross over the Channel because of this preconception. Rank's assembly line had yet to deliver the bulk of its production.

In the face of British intransigence, the U.S. State Department turned to British Secretary of State for Foreign Affairs Ernest Bevin to rescue the parties from further conflict [Fig. 10]. Former U.S. Secretary of State James Byrnes believed, wrote James Forrestal in his diaries, "that so long as Bevin was in his post as Foreign Minister there would be no possibility of such a breach" between the United States and Great Britain.[84] Bevin thought it preposterous that bickering over movies might sabotage the Marshall Plan. According to U.S. Ambassador Lewis Douglas, commenting on a meeting of 1 March 1948, "Bevin instructed Harold Wilson and Sir Wilfrid Eady of the Treasury to meet with Johnston and [Allen] Dulles with a determination to find a solution rather than with a sceptical and negative approach."[85] His pressure on the cabinet won for him the gratitude of U.S. Secretary of State George Marshall, who saluted Bevin for his "distinctly helpful attitude in making possible an amicable solution to the problem."[86] Bevin received additional reinforcement from Tom O'Brien, general secretary of Britain's National Association of Theatrical and Kine Employees (NATKE), who on 2 March 1948 begged the foreign secretary "to apply your great mind to finding . . . an acceptable solution." He pledged that Bevin "will earn the endearing gratitude of every sane man and woman" in the industry.[87]

Sent back to the negotiating table, Wilson secured a new arrangement with the Americans on 11 March. It produced a formula permitting the U.S. film industry to remove $17 million plus a sum reciprocal to the profits of British films displayed in the United States. As for additional earnings of the U.S. industry, instead of being taxed by Britain, the revenues could be invested in film production and other activities in the United Kingdom. This proved to be a boon for the expansion of the U.S. film industry abroad. Allied with generous tax breaks for overseas investment, provisions maintained by Washington until the Lyndon B. Johnson administration, the U.S. companies so overwhelmed Britain that one of the leading histories of postwar cinema, by the journalist Alexander Walker, calls the British industry "Hollywood, England."[88] Stymied by Red scares and runaway production, the Hollywood trade unions chafed at the further loss of jobs to overseas markets. The *Motion Picture Herald* (15 May 1948) reported "the unencouraging prospect of a flow of films bearing American trademarks which, made in England with English players, settings, etc., will actually be British pictures in all visible respects." The trade newspaper did not know what to make of sorrow-sobbing predictions that Hollywood might achieve "the

FIGURE 10. As foreign minister of Britain in the early postwar period, Ernest Bevin received praise from the U.S. government for helping to settle trade disputes on terms congenial to Hollywood interests. Bevin disappointed those Britons who thought that, with the right public policy, their national film industry might at last tame Hollywood. *Source:* Public Record Office, INF 2/46.

ultimate status of a sort of ghost town where little pictures would be ground out more or less regularly, and sound stages, scarcer than gold two years back, could be leased at bargains by used car dealers."

Wilson tried to claim the agreement a triumph, though the British press failed to share his enthusiasm. The *Financial Times* (15 March 1948) laughed his work out of court:

Had the Marx brothers represented Britain in the negotiations with Mr. Eric John-ston they could hardly have produced a more absurd agreement. . . . Surely our innocent economist-socialist President of the Board of Trade should not have been allowed to play poker with the hard-shelled negotiators from Hollywood.

The hard-Left *Daily Worker* (12 March 1948) decried Wilson's "continuation of the domination of the screen by the propaganda productions of a State which is avowedly out to bring Britain under the sway of the dollar." The *Daily Express* (12 March 1948) was the most mordant, calling it "a dark hour in the history of our land." Only the *News Chronicle* (12 March 1948) mustered enthusiasm, regarding Wilson's work as "a thoroughly good bargain."[89] The *Times* was blandly favorable, taking the neopaternalist tack that the proletariat probably requires some mild opiates to work well otherwise: "Maximum output is not . . . achieved under conditions of maximum austerity. Films, like smoking, are in the practical world of today amenities without which workers would not give their best."[90] The *Manchester Guardian* sought a measured response to Wilson's work, but admitted that it will deliver "more joy in the Californian mansions of American film magnates than in the more modest homes of the colossi who bestride our narrow film world. The fault is not in our stars (for who can resist Miss Lockwood?) but in ourselves that we are underlings."[91] It gave Britons little solace that Hollywood trade journals grumbled about the agreement for making too many concessions to socialism. Although *Variety* (17 March 1948) conceded that most "top execs" believe the agreement "is by far the best that could be expected under the circumstances," others lamented Johnston's actions:

[J]ust by sitting by and waiting the British out, theatre business and production there would have suffered so in eight months to a year from now that the cries of the public, film workers, and exhibs would have forced a capitulation entirely on the American industry's terms.[92]

In *The Great British Picture Show* (1974), George Perry asserted that Wilson "undoubtedly although unwittingly . . . was one of the major destroyers of the film industry."[93] There are two camps in the debate over the British failure to prevail over Hollywood: Many in the industry blamed the government, but another school puts the onus on the film industry. The unions especially thought that the film leadership showed little initiative when given the benefits of protection. In the conclusion of Dickinson and Street:

Before the duty was imposed the government had, on the whole, followed advice from the trade. . . . Once the duty was in operation and the boycott declared, the exhibitors certainly made little effort to help the government . . . the profession collectively adopted a defeatist pose suggesting that there were no alternatives to American films.[94]

The Cinematograph Exhibitors Association (CEA) and NATKE had fired most of their ideological gunpowder at the government, rather than at the MPAA, the source of the embargo.

Nonetheless, there were those who fought valiantly, even tragically so. Harold Wilson could recover from what some saw as a great surrender, the folly of political youth; others may have been less fortunate. It would be a distortion of the record – and an unfeeling calculus – to say that the British film industry comprised a bunch of compradors, full of bluster and noble principles but quick to sell out their nation's interests for the bottom line. As early as 1922, the reputed father of British cinematography, William Friese-Greene, had given an address to British film producers at the Connaught Hotel advising them to take up the struggle against the commanding American supremacy over British screens.[95] While in the midst of his passionate presentation, he fainted; it turned out he was suffering from an acute case of malnutrition, and he soon thereafter died. A generation later, J. Arthur Rank, producer of some of Britain's greatest box-office successes (and flops) imagined himself as following in the footsteps of his father – a flour magnate whose life mission became a battle with Whitehall on behalf of steep tariff walls designed to shut U.S. flour out of the U.K. market. With the film industry, the younger Rank was similarly determined, so much so that he eventually lost much of his considerable wealth. "I am doing this work for my God and my country," he declared, confessing that "the trouble really was that I didn't know anything about producing films. I only took it on because there was nobody else to do the job."[96]

Britain's cinema industry may have seen the threat as Hollywood for many years to come; but in the 1950s, it soon became apparent that the rise of television was causing an irreparable shift and precipitate decline in its audience. Britain went from being the most avid cinemagoers in Western Europe of the 1940s and early 1950s to the worst movie attenders of the region by the late 1970s.

As for the opponents of American cultural dominance of Britain, the battle shifted from cinema to a new front: the war against commercial television.

CHAPTER SEVEN

The U.S.–U.K. Film Conflict

THE FADING DREAM OF MASTERING HOLLYWOOD

The MPAA delivered the British government a stinging defeat during the boycott of 1947–8. For its part, the U.S. State Department had several functionaries inclined to forgive the Board of Trade. Believing that the pasteboard, jerry-built quality of the ad valorem duty came about through sudden economic crisis and not as a form of films policy, Don Bliss, counselor for Economic Affairs in the U.S. Embassy, London, held that the British were indeed "slightly ashamed of it." Bliss became an architect of State Department autonomy from the MPAA, as he thought it better that Johnston, rather than Foggy Bottom, conduct negotiations to settle the crisis. He helped impose the policy, despite initial MPAA resistance:

I have taken the view that negotiations for a compromise in the film controversy should be carried on by the Motion Picture Export Association as far as American interests are concerned. This view is based on the probability that a compromise would involve concessions which only the American companies could be asked to accept on their own responsibility. . . . Pressures are mounting, however, to seek American official intervention and Allport has been recommending this strongly to Eric Johnston.[1]

Bliss added that tobacco and films remain the "two glaring exceptions to the application of austerity" in postwar Britain.

In late 1945, John Maynard Keynes had haggled a $3.75 billion loan from the U.S. Treasury, which granted it in return for a giant concession: British sterling would become a freely convertible currency. This spelled the end of the British Empire as a privileged trading zone. By mid-1947, the enormous loan began to run out. In the opening week of the ad valorem duty, Britain's dollar drain exceeded $30 million per day, totaling $176 million in 10–15 August. As Britain's Treasury feared it might escalate to $300 million per week, the last $700 million of the loan would last only two and

200

a half weeks. Amid such an atmosphere of panic, the British government fastened in place this punitive measure against Hollywood.[2] For Bliss, the loan and the projected Marshall Plan partly served as a subsidy to Hollywood, though he admitted "from the standpoint of morale films are not as unessential as they might on first thought seem."[3]

Still, the British government ultimately deserves to be faulted for a lack of advance planning, as it is evident that throughout 1947 they knew such a drastic measure might soon be necessary. Their miscalculation had several sources:

1. They believed, with some justification, that advance action might tip their hand and alert the U.S. film industry to take defensive measures;
2. They were fancifully confident that Hollywood could not afford to boycott Britain, and, if it did, the action would take the form of a bluff or temporary stalling. The Board of Trade also counted on Hollywood's independents, the non-MPAA firms, to frustrate the MPAA. As the Board of Trade's Rupert Somervell expressed it as late as 11 September 1947,

The weakness of the Americans is the difficulty of keeping their ranks solid especially the independent producers. I gather that some of these are restive even now but a breakaway by them would not necessarily mean that the larger companies would follow.[4]

When the U.S. independents failed Somervell, he bitterly resented them for subsequently complaining to him that J. Arthur Rank did not book their films on his circuit. While supporting an inquiry into Rank's trade practices, Somervell cynically added:

I think it is worthwhile pointing out that these representatives of the great private enterprise country are apparently asking the Government to dictate to private traders where they should buy their goods.[5]

3. The Board of Trade planned to enunciate reforms of the film industry later in 1948, when expiration set in for the 1938 Cinematograph Films Act. In their minds, further inquiry and debate must precede that landmark moment. The currency crisis of 1947, therefore, came a year too early to mesh with their schedule for cinema reform.
4. Britain grew brash and sometimes boastful that during World War II its cinema had finally earned the international prestige and respect that would enable it to compete with Hollywood, especially in the British market. The ideological uplift of fighting fascism had fed Britain's film industry with a unity of purpose that lent a sustained self-confidence and

identifiable stamp to its productions. With many leisure activities restricted during the war, British film attendance had soared. J. Arthur
Rank's investment thus became an important component of cinema's
war revival.

Harold Wilson misjudged the extraordinary circumstances of World
War II, not recognizing that British citizens would soon diversify leisure activities at the expense of cinema. Oddly for a statesman later legendary for
touting the revival of Britain through the white heat of a technological revolution, he long remained oblivious to television's possibilities in altering
the leisure habits of his nation. Meanwhile, postwar British film producers
soon searched for new themes and identity, with Wilson himself expressing discomfort that too many of their films explored themes about what he
called diseased minds: for instance, the hysterical nun (Kathleen Byron) in
Black Narcissus, the mentally disturbed veteran (Kieron Moore) who murders his wife and himself in *Mine Own Executioner*, the sadomasochistic
pianist (Ann Todd) in *The Seventh Veil*, and the misogynistic murderer Pin-
kie Brown (Richard Attenborough) of *Brighton Rock*, who on his wedding
day records the following message to his beloved: "You want me to say I
love you, but I hate you, you little slut."
    Having sailed into troubled waters with faulty navigational equipment,
Wilson made one fateful error in the final showdown with the MPAA. He
and his predecessor egged on Rank to rally production forces, but then Wilson surrendered without trying to get Hollywood to introduce the films
from the nine-month backlog of the boycott at a gradual pace. Thus Rank
came close to completing his productions only to face a tidal wave of Hollywood films. Hollywood's tsunami of cinema made it hard for him to get
screen time at independent theaters and the competing circuits. Though he
controlled over 600 theaters out of Britain's 4,500, Rank needed cooperation from independent exhibitors. They largely snubbed him, many dread-
ing him for in the past having given them limited access to his first-run films
and others simply detesting his hastily slapped together films of the boycott
emergency.
    With the industry spilling prodigious quantities of red ink, fed by Alex-
ander Korda's colossal flop of *Bonnie Prince Charlie*, Wilson intervened
with a quota requiring exhibitors to show 45 percent British films. As Britain's industry for most of the 1940s produced about 25 percent of the films
for its domestic market, this augmented quota enraged both British exhibitors and Eric Johnston at the MPAA. Johnston, who, with the settlement
of the ad valorem crisis, had saluted young Wilson as a man of political

destiny, reverted to designating him a double-dealing charlatan, a greasy polecat not to be trusted. The U.S. State Department, which had some sympathy with Britain's ad valorem plight, now judged that this market would remain a trouble spot until Wilson could be dislodged from office. Bliss and others counseled Johnston to have patience for new elections and the likelihood that the unrealistic targets would collapse of their own accord. Indeed hundreds of exhibitors disobeyed the law. On this occasion, the U.S. State Department refrained from calling on Foreign Minister Ernest Bevin, whose portly presence amid rounds of scotch might mean a new Labour sellout, or what U.S. officials preferred to call redoubled efforts at convivial Anglo–U.S. relations.

As Rank's empire tottered toward economic crisis, Wilson expressed raw contempt for the Methodist Tory. The president of the Board of Trade told Parliament that the industry was just looking for another excuse for one of its periodic crises. When Rank complained that Britain taxed its film enterprises double the rate Hollywood encountered in the United States, Wilson scoffed that he and his fellow producers "found this glorious new alibi under which the Government can be blamed for their misfortunes." Labour MP Michael Foot, a close ally of Rank's frequent nemesis Lord Beaverbrook, dubbed the flour magnate "the Rosenkrantz of the industry."[6] Foot and Wilson did not believe the government had any responsibility for its recent difficulties. In part, Wilson began the process of establishing a state film-financing scheme and regarded himself as the most activist Board of Trade president on cinema policy in Britain's history. In late 1939, E. H. Lever of Prudential, Korda's chief backer, urged formation of a state-supported Film Bank because "if we are at odds with the American Film Industry, or if they cannot get out what they regard as a satisfactory proportion of their takings, they will no doubt cease to finance the production of British films." He regretted that private British banks, Prudential, and other lenders "had already burned their fingers in the Film Industry," and would be unlikely to replenish the wells of cinema finance.[7] Wilson fulfilled Lever's vision, with the National Film Finance Corporation of April 1949 – alas, a year and a half too late for the ad valorem showdown. (Some leaders of film labor unions such as the Association of Cine-Technicians had also made the case for advance preparation as far back as 1941: They added that nationalization or municipalization of cinema circuits might be necessary in order to avert capitulation to Hollywood during a future confrontation.)[8] Fearful of red tape and government intervention in his affairs, Rank shunned Wilson's film-finance program, just as he had opposed earlier versions ventilated by predecessors at the Board of Trade and Prudential.

Korda, by contrast, embraced it with passion and proceeded to squander
£3 million of finance, left in arrears at his death.

The rivers of red ink had their effect on Rank. Having given his artistes
free rein in the 1940s, he now turned to retrenchment and the tightfisted
regime of John Davis. Davis, an executive who came to the Rank Organisation through the acquisition of Odeon, largely avoided talk of Mr. Rank
being on a mission from God and instead coldly counted the prospects for
the bottom line. Unprofitable businesses were quickly shut down: the end
of children's film, the cartoons unit, and Rank's experiment in Independent
Frame, a new projection-based, assembly-line approach to sets pioneered
by art director David Rawnsley (and championed by Michael Powell). Davis, described as a sometimes cruel boss with a visage vaguely reminiscent
of Bob Hope, ran his subordinates ragged. Yelling at one executive who was
wearing a tie and a striped shirt, he told the colleague to change out of his
pajamas. On another occasion, he called an associate on vacation at a Mediterranean beach to report to London immediately. Davis gave him a couple
of minutes of routine orders and then told the hapless employee that was
all, in what amounted to a test of loyalty of a company man.[9]

Davis substantially cut back Rank's film-production schedule, but he
returned the cinema operation to a semblance of profitability, no mean feat
as literally thousands of British theaters closed in the 1950s and early 1960s.
He is most remembered, however, for investing Rank resources into Xerox,
one of the great postwar triumphs of Anglo–American capitalism. While
much of Rank's organization posted lackluster returns, Xerox became one
of the pacesetters of the international business world, with total sales surg-
ing from $33 million in 1959, the year of the first office copier, to $3.6 billion in 1974.[10] According to some accounts, this represented the fastest
growth in revenues for a corporation until Apple introduced its version of
the personal computer in the late 1970s and early 1980s.[11] (In the later decades of the twentieth century, Xerox began to sputter, as Steve Jobs of Apple and other self-styled pirates of Silicon Valley gleefully purloined Xerox
innovations worth billions in revenues.)

In the 1940s, J. Arthur Rank led Britain's popular cinema to its most
sustained period of success; yet, by his own expansive vision of the Rank
Organisation's goals, his enterprise did not succeed in making Britain a serious challenger to Hollywood's global supremacy in the entertainment industry. Rank found himself hampered by several structural weaknesses,
constraints that even the most nimble of capitalist entrepreneurs would have
had trouble surmounting:

(1) Rank depended heavily on profits from U.S. films in his exhibition sector to provide the steady stream of resources for his production strategy. During 1948–9, he gained a reputation for inhospitality toward U.S. productions in an effort to recoup costs on his British films. In most periods, however, Rank believed that to gain exhibition time in the all-important U.S. market, he had to give the Hollywood majors fairly open access to his circuits. Rank's critics urged him to produce fewer high-cost, blockbuster extravaganzas and seek success in the low-cost (Ealing) and middle-cost (Gainsborough) end of the market. The well-crafted "cheap" films could at least be amortized in Great Britain's home market and not depend on pleasing North Americans. Michael Balcon, the leader of Ealing Studios, long opposed the Rank–Korda axis, favoring export over the domestic market. Until John Davis's imposed austerity, Rank resisted this advice, as he firmly believed that Britain should have a global impact in the film industry. Although excoriated in the 1940s for underwriting a cinema of extravagance, the onetime miller still played the pivotal role in financing Ealing's own golden age. Even the low-cost strategy was not invulnerable, and Davis himself sold the declining Ealing operation in the mid-1950s.

(2) Rank's decision to invest heavily in the "little film major" Universal as a means of entry to the North American market proved to be a mixed curse. On the one hand, Universal experienced economic resurgence in the late 1930s and early 1940s, with the wholesome fare of Deanna Durbin and then the wacky antics of Abbott and Costello. Nevertheless, Universal specialized in B-films, *Bride of Frankenstein* horror, and inane comedy. Its distribution network proved to be an awful match for Rank's Shakespearean and prestige productions, with Sir Laurence Olivier unwelcome in theaters catering to the least-refined elements of the North American audience. Korda as well had been hampered in the United States by his link to United Artists, assuredly more highbrow than Universal but largely bereft of an exhibition network.[12] Herbert Wilcox, with his connection to RKO, which by the late 1940s owned 124 U.S. theaters and a share of approximately 75 others, at least could claim a sliver of access to U.S. exhibition outlets.[13]

(3) Rank had to negotiate the difficult tightrope between asserting the British quality of his production and his desire to appeal to the U.S. audience. Both he and Korda faced accusations that the "international style" they aped was creating a bland mid-Atlantic culture. While Rank made concessions to the North American audience, particularly urging his actors to speak in a clearer diction with fewer Britishisms, he still maintained that

his productions had a non-Hollywood aesthetic. He called "realism" the lodestar of the British film and in contrast called Hollywood "Fairyland." Even Korda, second only to Rank's Filippo Del Giudice (cofounder, with Mario Zampi, of Two Cities Films in 1937) as the most glamorous and extravagant of British producers, liked to show obeisance to the documentary movement and the canon of realism, with his peculiar claim that his proudest achievement was support for Huxley's Academy Award–winning *Private Life of the Gannets.* While Rank's prodigal spending on films of fantasy appeared to represent a repudiation of the documentary aesthetic, John Grierson in the end won an important victory in the battle of ideas: Realism became regarded as the hallmark of British film. Despite the many improbable plots in its production line, the Rank-owned Ealing Studios proved the most adept at claiming fidelity to Britain's heritage of realism.[14]

(4) J. Arthur Rank ran into debilitating intracapitalist feuding similar to that experienced by his father the miller. Rank *père* had sworn to take on the U.S.-based grain giants by building a British milling concern of colossal proportions. In so doing, he soon encountered the fury of Britain's smaller, independent milling operations, firms that accused him of crushing their enterprises. In order to compete against global oligopoly capitalism, Joseph Rank felt compelled to overcome pesky competitors in his home market. J. Arthur Rank himself soon faced the anger of independent producers who resented him for dominating studio space and independent exhibitors who believed he frequently gave them last crack at his first-run films. Many openly loathed Rank. Labour politicians, the youthful Michael Foot the most active of his tormenters, charged him with a despicable will to monopoly and power. The revulsion of the independents toward Rank manifested itself in odd rejoicing when the aftermath of Hollywood's boycott inflicted humiliating losses on his film enterprise. British politicians themselves had difficulties negotiating the contradictions of international capitalism: the need for economic units large enough to compete with elephantine U.S. corporations versus the desire to maintain free-market competition in the home market. Britain discovered that a domestic market of 50–55 million citizens might be too small to compete internationally. Rank and much of the political leadership steadfastly looked to trade with the United States and the lands of the British Commonwealth, rather than early incorporation into the fledgling European Economic Community (EEC), as the means of achieving the market scale necessary for maneuvering in the world economy. Britain's small-fry film companies, clinging to a precarious existence, took fright at Rank's explosive growth and did not mind sabotaging him in his darkest hour.

So in the 1950s the apocalyptic Rank yielded to the bottom-line-driven horizons of John Davis. While proud of his many box-office triumphs, Rank blamed his failure to fulfill his mission on the British state and its dependence on the Entertainments Tax (ET). This tax, initiated as a means of raising revenues for the cash-strapped British Exchequer of World War I, grew in the 1940s to onerous levels approaching 38 percent per ticket; yet most British politicians did not mind because they saw it as a levy on Hollywood. Rank begged to differ, noting that in his years of red ink he would have posted profits had he been taxed at the same levels as ordinary businesses. The British state of the interwar years did not use ET revenues for supporting British film production, as the wealth reverted to the general welfare. Under Wilson, Wilfrid Eady hatched what the cabinet called "the Scheme," a program for funneling contributions from the exhibition sector into production. Unlike postwar continental Europe, however, Britain preferred to use these resources for supporting Hollywood-type feature production rather than art-house or documentary works.[15] The market for the latter had grown in the 1950s with the rise of television and the segmentation of the cinema audience into elite and mass markets. The British financing scheme did not leave the United Kingdom well poised to exploit this development. In using Hollywood as their site of competition, Rank, Korda, and latter-day proponents of the Eady Scheme may have set Britain up for failure. If asked to choose between Hollywood and an ersatz Hollywood-on-the-Thames, most foreign audiences preferred the genuine article. The pecksniffian howls of politicians and intellectuals on the shallowness and false glitter of Hollywood made little impact in any case on the tastes of the ordinary cinema patron.

Rank's run on the world market is today regarded as one of ashen defeat; yet his dramatic intervention probably prevented the British industry from being swallowed up by U.S. interests in the aftermath of the collapse of 1937, an economic travesty that scared much of the City from renewed investment. At that historic moment, a popular satire by screenwriter Jeffrey Dell called *Nobody Ordered Wolves* (1939) expressed the predominant sentiment that the British film industry had gone to the dogs. In Dell's novel, Paradox Film Productions run by Napoleon Bott, a character patterned after Alexander Korda, experiences acute financial convulsions. Eventually wolves requisitioned for some vague film extravaganza get loose, marauding the countryside, and causing all kinds of ravenous destruction, including the killing of "eleven cows and a flock of sheep." Toward the end of this incredible farrago, the British Board of Trade is said to be surrendering to Hollywood:

"Well," said Browne, "they've decided to give them the British motion picture industry. . . ."
"I don't believe it," said Benham, who didn't want to believe it.
"Why give them the film business?" demanded Phillip.
Browne raised his eyebrows. "I suppose," he said, "because it was the only thing they could think of that nobody wanted."[16]

The efflorescence of British film during World War II and its immediate aftermath has partial roots in Rank's wondrous ambitions. Britain did not repeat the horror of World War I and *its* aftermath, when the film industry came close to extinction. Michael Balcon, who earlier bore ill-will toward Rank, later conceded that Britons should have given a special thanks to the little-loved but tireless Yorkshire miller. Despite all of their bitter threats of recrimination against Britain, the Hollywood studios themselves had owed much to the British public, whose soaring cinema attendance during the war helped the U.S. industry overcome the Nazi closure of Continental markets. Gratitude, however, is not the foremost impulse of international capitalists, who regard open markets as the natural order of the universe.

Britain had been routed in the MPAA dispute of 1947–8, but not vanquished. It retained a film industry and avenues for national expression. Wounded and then ailing in the early 1950s, the Rank Organisation retreated from its goal of making London a new capital of the global entertainment industry. For those committed to protecting British culture from the onslaughts of Hollywood, the BBC became the last of a long-punctured line of defense.

PART THREE

TWO CONTINENTAL CASE STUDIES: BELGIUM AND FRANCE

CHAPTER EIGHT

Belgium and the Making of an International Catholic Film Movement

BELGIUM UNDER SIEGE

Belgium rarely figures prominently in the annals of cinema history, let alone as a general subject of historical inquiry. The great historian of the French Revolution Jules Michelet (1798–1874) may have set the tone in the mid-nineteenth century when he dismissed Belgium as a mere "English invention":

> There has never been a Belgium and there never shall be. . . . In vain has been created a people of functionaries, who cry constantly: Our nationality! – Alsace, a small strip of territory, has become great, heroic, and morally exemplary since she was united to France. . . . Belgium, incomparably greater and more important, is and will remain sterile so long as she is not with us.[1]

Bismarck in August 1866 gave a Prussian endorsement to the nation's historical irrelevance: "I consider that Belgium, in the long term, will not be able to be a viable state."[2] George Louis Beer, a member of the U.S. delegation at the Versailles Conference, privately expressed contempt for Belgium: "these small nations with intense national feelings bore me."[3] In contrast to Beer's assessment, Belgians themselves have often doubted the very durability of their nationhood, as the Walloon Socialist Jules Destrée (1863–1936), in that most famous plea of Belgian self-abnegation, told the king in 1912:

> Sire, . . . allow me to tell you the truth, the enormous and horrifying truth: there are no Belgians. . . . You are reigning over two different peoples. In Belgium there are Walloons and there are Flemings: there are no Belgians.[4]

For centuries, Belgium has experienced foreign occupation, Burgundian, Spanish, Austrian, French, Dutch, and German – so much so it seems fitting that the most famous film ever directed by a Belgian, Jacques Feyder's French production of *La Kermesse heroïque* (1935), tells the story of Flemish women feasting and lovemaking with the Spanish invaders of 1616. While Feyder declared that he never sought to "deride the heroic resistance against invaders for which the Belgians have always been notable," Belgium can be more forgiven than most for doubting the efficacy of campaigns against foreign domination. In the case of Feyder, Goebbels was not amused by the pacifist frolic of *La Kermesse heroïque*. After summarily banning it, he later hunted the Paris-based director with the Gestapo, egged on by Belgian fascist Léon Degrelle and his Rexist collaborators. Earlier they had condemned the film as a form of French-inspired decadence and waged violent protests in Belgium against the farce.[5] Thus in Belgium, Hollywood did not always face the brunt of demonstrations against cinema's contribution to decaying civilization. According to Val Lorwin, Flemish fear of French cultural subversion remained acute, stemming from eighteenth- and nineteenth-century roots:

> The tide of godlessness which threatened pious Flanders was particularly associated with the French language which oozed crime and demoralization. It was with the French nation, persecution of the church, with French Wallonia, where Flemish immigrants lost their faith and with the francophone . . . bourgeoisie of Flanders itself.[6]

Whereas Flanders has generally been a zone of Hollywood domination, Wallonia in brief periods of the twentieth century has given a plurality to the French film. During 1937, the U.S. Department of Commerce reported that "in the French-speaking territory of Belgium, approximately 40 percent of the films shown are American. This percentage is doubled in the Flemish territory, where fully 80 percent of the films shown are American." In a market requiring over three hundred films, Belgium produced six that year.[7]

If Belgium failed to create a commercial film industry in the first half of the twentieth century, the nation emerged as the European leader in organizing international action against depravity in film. Meanwhile, its documentary film movement achieved recognition for exposing horrifying working conditions and displaying the nation's cultural heritage.[8] Its filmmakers, though, turned often to state bureaucracies and ministries for sponsorship. At its worst, several Belgian documentary practitioners became handmaidens to their nation's imperial mission – an occupational hazard similarly experienced by the founders of Britain's documentary movement. Constantly searching for pacifying exemplars of educational and documentary cinema,

Belgian colonial authorities eventually banned Africans from viewing most commercial feature films, a draconian measure testifying to their fears of exposing *indigènes* (natives) to the untrammeled powers of the *septième art*. Belgium, celebrated as a relative free-trade zone in film by the MPPDA, became the imperial power most willing to follow the logic of Hollywood's bitterest enemies, as they imposed a virtual *cordon sanitaire* against feature film for the black African.

THE INTERNATIONAL CAMPAIGN FOR MORALITY IN FILM

For most of the twentieth century, Belgium has enjoyed a reputation as a leader in international cooperation, a status aided by its frequent neutrality and the perception that the nation poses little threat to the Great Powers. Prior to World War I, Belgians headed perhaps the three most important world peace organizations:

1. the Interparliamentary Union (1889), under the subsequent presidency of Auguste Beernaert, who won the Nobel Peace Prize in 1909 and also led the International League of Catholic Pacifists;
2. the International Peace Bureau (1891), uniting a thousand pacifist societies; and
3. the Socialist International, with its executive commitee headquartered in Brussels and Belgian parliamentarian Émile Vandervelde at its helm.

Between 1901 and 1913, Belgians won three Nobel Peace Prizes. Despite rock-throwing acrimony and noncooperation between Flemings and Walloons, Belgium has emerged in the postwar world as the capital of European union.[9]

In the Catholic Church's international strategy on film, Belgium at times played a more central role than the U.S. Legion of Decency. Though Pope Pius XI in his Encyclical of 1936 (*Vigilanti Cura*) regarded the Legion of Decency as the national model for Catholics, the Belgian church stood out as the international command-and-control center of the movement by heading the Office Catholique International du Cinéma (OCIC), briefly based in Louvain and then Brussels. Organizing international conferences and fostering Catholic ownership and entrepreneurship in the exhibition sector, the OCIC built a films movement well in advance of the Legion of Decency and indeed served to inspire its American cadres. While the pope eventually appeared impatient with European Catholic action on cinema and singled out the U.S. effort for special commendation in 1936, Cardinal Pacelli, the Vatican's secretary of State and the future Pope Pius XII, wrote in 1934 to OCIC president Chanoine (i.e., Canon) Abel Brohée of Louvain that "the Holy Father ardently wishes that in a work so salutary the OCIC finds full understanding and generous collaboration from Catholics of diverse nations. . . ."[10]

Brohée, a close ally of the late Belgian Cardinal Désiré Joseph Mercier (1851–1926), helped with his mission to revive Thomist philosophy in twentieth-century Catholicism. Cardinal Mercier had once told the young Father Fulton Sheen how to confront the media of modernity: "Always keep current: know what the modern world is thinking about, read its poetry, its history, its literature, observe its architecture and its art, hear its music and its theater, and then plunge deeply into St. Thomas and the wisdom of the ancients and you will be able to refute its errors."[11]

The OCIC grew in several steps. In early 1928, Pope Pius XI selected the president of the Union Internationale des Ligues Féminines Catholiques, Petronille Aimee Florentine Steenberghe-Engeringh of the Netherlands, in hopes of galvanizing cooperation on film issues. The union already had plans for its own congress at The Hague. During 23–5 April 1928, the Hague hosted a second venue, what became the first Congrès International Catholique du Cinéma. The pope's early preference for Dutch leadership stemmed from the dynamism and social activism of its woman's organization, in contrast to the rebarbative conservatism of France's Ligue des Femmes Françaises (1901) and the fiercely politicized Ligue Patriotique des Françaises (1902), both too divisive in the mind of the pontiff. Pope Pius XI encouraged women's leadership on film issues, as he believed in their special concern with issues of family and morality. Delegates from fifteen nations participated at The Hague, and a provisional committee set up the OCIC as well as plans for a new congress.[12]

During 17–20 June 1929, the second international Catholic congress on film brought together twenty nations and a definitive constitution, statutes, and administrative bureau for the fledgling OCIC. This conference added to the Catholic agenda the growing medium of radio. The Hague conference had named Dr. Georg Ernst of Munich president of OCIC, while its secretariat had been placed in Paris under Chanoine Joseph Reymond, who in 1932 became editor of France's new Catholic newspaper on radio and film, *Choisir*. The work of the OCIC appeared temporarily stalled in the early 1930s, in part because Ernst and Reymond both remained embroiled in national struggles for moral regulation in Germany and France, respectively. They appeared too ready to use the OCIC to further the aims of their national movements, a situation that hindered coordination of activities on an international scale. Ernst's leadership of the company Leo-films, a specialist in *Gebirgsfilms* (mountain movies), raised additional concerns that his production house distracted focus from the film movement.[13]

The Vatican thus quietly came to support reorganization of the OCIC, and the body turned to Belgium, a country thought to be more hospitable to Catholicism, as well as better situated in promoting internationalism and freedom from Great Power intrigues. Chanoine Abel Brohée, a founder of the organization, took over its presidency in 1933, and its secretariat relocated during the 1930s first to Louvain and then Brussels. President of the Séminaire Léon XIII in Louvain until 1935, Brohée played a central role in Action Catholique and its youth wing, the Association Catholique de la Jeunesse Belge (ACJB).[14] Chanoine Brohée planned the OCIC's third Congress in Brussels from 29 September to 1 October 1933, a conference reuniting nine different countries. On 18 April 1934 the OCIC officially participated in the Congress of the League of Nations' International Institute of Educational Cinema held in Rome. The OCIC's leadership met with Pope Pius; subsequently his secretary of State, Cardinal Pacelli, sent an official letter encouraging the body to redouble its efforts so that members of the Catholic theater network may "tightly coordinate with each other." He called on Catholics to make the "necessary preparation" for "the production of high class films."[15]

During 26–30 April 1935, the OCIC had a delegation at the International Congress of Cinema in Berlin, where the Catholic participants later conducted meetings on their own with Chanoine Brohée. In 1936, Pope Pius XI saluted the Legion of Decency in his aforementioned famous encyclical, and his intervention temporarily raised hopes among OCIC activists of new Catholic initiatives on the international plane. In contrast to those in the United States, European Catholics had succeeded in creating an extensive exhibition circuit, particularly in Belgium, France, Germany, and Italy. In the shaping of public opinion, the OCIC had also given strong encouragement to a Catholic media network, for instance France's *Choisir* edited by Chanoine Joseph Reymond, Germany's *Filmrundschau* under the direction of Father Richard Muckermann, and Belgium's *Persleiding* run by Father Félix Morlion, O.P. The superiority of the European theater and media network over its U.S. counterpart did not alter the reality that the Legion of Decency wielded greater clout over the global film industry. Quite simply, the U.S. industry under oligopoly conditions proved more easily threatened by the prospects of a massive Legion theater boycott, unlike much of Western Europe, where independent companies created single pictures and then routinely folded. Though there were obvious exceptions – UFA-dominated Germany and later J. Arthur Rank stronghold Britain –

Europe had a production structure that was porous and unpredictable, more apt to reward the wildcatter trading on shock value. European independents still had to contend with myriad censorship boards, as well as the unwillingness of Breen's PCA to grant a certificate that would permit widespread display in the United States; but small-fry operators did not have to answer directly to the stratum of corporate executives from the MPPDA companies, predominantly Jewish-Americans who judged obedience to the Catholic Breen as necessary for long-run assurance of stable industry profits. Breen openly bragged that no film successfully submitted by MPPDA companies for a PCA certificate in the second half of the 1930s received the Legion of Decency's C or "Condemned" rating. Only the works of independents and European producers, notably the Czech film *Exstase* (*Ecstasy*, 1936), famous for Hedy Lamarr's nude improvisations, filled the Legion's C rating list.[16] The relative weakness of the European industry created a space for the independent willing to gamble everything on a provocative production that might be a sudden box-office sensation.

Brohée was also confronted with opposition from a different direction: His efforts at fostering internationalism did not sit well with certain architects of European fascism. The Nazis took an aversion to France's *Choisir* for its praise of anti-Hitler films, and upon seizing Paris they had the conservative Catholic cinema weekly shut down. Belgium's Centre Catholique International de Presse et de Cinéma "was occupied, the bank accounts . . . blocked, the funds pillaged, the library and important documentation – perhaps the most remarkable of all Catholic offices in any nation – sold off like scrap paper," recalled Monsignor Louis Picard. "In brief, the result of 20 years of work appeared to be wiped out."[17] Throughout the war, the Belgian Dominican friar Félix Morlion kept a provisional committee of OCIC alive in the United States. Brohée could not deliver a fourth international Catholic cinema congress until 1947. Held in Brussels during July, that congress paid tribute to Brohée, who had suddenly died of a cerebral hemmorhage on 1 May 1947.[18]

Under Brohée, the OCIC adopted as its symbol a drawing of the globe girdled by celluloid with the inscription: "Je suis le maître du monde" (I am the master of the world) [Fig. 11]. Convinced that cinema had become central in the saving of souls and the global battle of ideas, the organization highlighted the communist movement's recognition of the medium's power through Soviet Foreign Minister Maxim Litvinov's declaration that "Le cinéma est le moyen décisif de réaliser les temps révolutionnaires." Father Muckermann of Germany transposed this equation into Catholic terminology by asserting that "Cinema is the great church of modern times."[19]

« Le cinéma est le moyen décisif de réaliser les temps révolutionnaires »

LITVINOFF

Pères et Mères de famille !
Qui aimez vos enfants,
Qui avez le souci de la dignité du foyer.

Industriels et Hommes d'affaires !
Que le désordre social inquiète ;
Que l'avenir de la société et le bien du pays préoccupent.

Catholiques !
Qui croyez à l'Evangile et à sa mission dans le Monde.

Lisez ces lignes

Peut-être alors comprendrez-vous que le CINÉMA est tout de même un peu ... **votre affaire**

FIGURE 11. A globe shrouded in celluloid with the inscription, "I am the master of the world," symbol of the Belgium-based Office Catholique International du Cinéma (OCIC), which sought to galvanize Catholic action on film.

Unfortunately, this "great church of modern times" had been highjacked in the service of evil. "The cinema," observed right-wing ideologue and publishing heir Jean Fayard in the *Revue de Paris* (15 January 1934), "despite censorship – is resolutely engaged in smutty vulgarity." OCIC identified youth and "les Sauvages" of the Third World as the two groups most endangered by this state of affairs. The organization disseminated testimony from several foreign sources about cinema's corrosive effects on Europe's civilizing mission. John Wong-Quincey, rector of the faculty of foreign literature at Beijing University, said that films regularly gave Chinese "a horrible opinion of whites, their morality, their passions, which are out of control without brakes. . . . It is a moral disaster." In Malaysia, a sultan exclaimed, "What a mass of homicides, of traitors, bandits, degenerates, unfaithful spouses, of young women without shame on display in your films. And . . . we had believed for such a long time in the superiority of your civilization."

Reporting at the Rome congress on educational cinema sponsored by the League of Nations and attended by OCIC, a Dr. Porfirio lamented:

It is undeniable that the European may have lost a lot of his prestige in the lands of colored peoples [*les gens de couleur*]. . . . This loss of prestige is due everywhere to cinema . . . an irreperable evil has been done. . . .[20]

To reverse this state of affairs, OCIC appropriated the advice of Monsignor Ladeuze, the Recteur Magnifique of the University of Louvain, who observed: "In order to make their voice heard in the paganized concert, it is necessary that Catholics should have a place in the orchestra." Belgium had already supplied a program for the work ahead. In 1921, a Belgian Catholic distribution firm was established, devoting itself to selling films in accord with Christian morality. The formation of a Catholic cooperative society in 1928 eventually brought together a federation of three hundred theaters in Belgium. Out of the ferment in The Hague and Munich during 1928 and 1929 developed Belgium's Centre Catholique d'Action Cinématographique (CCAC). This organization underwent major expansion inspired by the triumphs of the Legion of Decency in 1934. Among its new arms were

1. the Ligue Catholique du Film/Katholieke Film Liga, dedicated to mobilizing the mass public,
2. a Service de Documentation designed to research developments in cinema,
3. a Commission de Selection de Films seeking to classify films from a Catholic viewpoint, with decisions published on over ten thousand fiches, and
4. a Bureau de Presse called DOCIP (Documentation Cinématographique de la Presse), which collaborated with forty Belgian newspapers.[21]

DOCIP's weekly guide, the *Filmleidung*, classified films as "U" (Universal), "A" (Adults), "Be Careful," and "Forbidden." Its sometimes scathing attacks on films generated hostility from some Antwerp exhibitors, who threatened in 1936 to pull advertising from newspapers that too obligingly ran its denunciations of morally noxious celluloid.[22]

The exhibitors felt aggrieved that their advertisements, oozing with praise of new film releases, were often nullified by adverse DOCIP reviews. Taking a leaf from the U.S. Legion of Decency, DOCIP told malcontented Antwerp exhibitors that the body would organize public meetings, circulars, and press correspondence to begin Catholic boycott of theaters that tried to punish press outlets friendly to its film critique. Though some Catholic circles admitted that "DOCIP is not so strong as it claims and . . . the ecclesiastical authorities dare not lend their support to such violent action," according to Britain's *World Film News,* the threat caused exhibitors to capitulate.[23]

The Reverend Leo Lunders, a member of the Centre Catholique d'Action Cinématographique since 1930, became the CCAC's secretary-general in 1936 and held its leadership post for the next forty years. Born in 1905 in Antwerp, Lunders held professorships in Church History and Patristics at the Maison d'Études Dominicaines in Ghent and Louvain. He became one of the central figures in Belgian cinema, advising Henri Schneider and Henri Storck on their biopic about Father Damien, *Le Pèlerin de l'enfer* (1946), holding memberships in the administrative councils of the Belgian Cinémathèque, the Musée de Cinéma, the Service National des Ciné-clubs, the Centre National du Film pour la Jeunesse, as well as the presidency of the Brussels section of the Association Professionnelle de la Presse Cinématographique Belge. OCIC named him its delegate to UNESCO, and the Vatican did likewise for the Council of Europe. Even Hollywood hired him as a technical advisor, most notably for the background on the Belgian nun in *The Nun's Story,* an Academy Award nominee for Best Picture of 1959. Dramatizing the regimentation of the convent and then the ordeals of missionary work in the Congo, the Warner film has been called "the best study of the religious life ever made in the American cinema" by Albert Johnson in *Film Quarterly* and, by Les and Barbara Keyser in *Hollywood and the Catholic Church,* "the best indication of how the Hollywood catechism trivialized nuns . . . by the one exception to this long tradition . . . the finest film about the Catholic religious life ever made, a masterpiece in its conception and its execution." On this occasion, a Jewish director, Fred Zinnemann, rescued Catholics from vapidity.[24]

It did not take long for Hollywood to return to trivialization, though. Lunders soon plunged from the sublime to the insipid, as his next major consulting opportunity came in MGM's *The Singing Nun* (1966) starring Debbie Reynolds, a film pronounced "icky" by the authoritative Leslie Halliwell.[25]

Lunders's life project stressed two components: (1) improving the consistency of Catholic critical and moral judgment on cinema, and (2) shielding the vulnerable youth population from the medium's lurch into moral decrepitude.

On the first front, Pope Pius XI in *Vigilanti Cura* permitted national Catholic organizations to render varying judgments on films, as he argued that customs and acceptable moral standards, except in the most grave instances of evil, should be compatible with the norms of individual communities. He thought the Vatican should resist universal pronouncements on cinema that failed to weigh the maturity of national audiences. While not seeking to repudiate *Vigilanti Cura*, Lunders worried that the doctrine, sloppily applied, could lead to subversion of Catholic moral doctrine. In 1947, he pointed out that the American film noir *Double Indemnity* received an A2 classification (unobjectionable for adults) by the U.S. Legion of Decency, an "à proscrire" (prohibited) rating in France, and a "nettes réserves" ("definite reservations," but adults admissible) evaluation in Belgium. By his mild distress, Lunders gave evidence that world Catholicism was not the monolith of Protestant and civil libertarian folklore. Thirteen years earlier, France's *Choisir* had pointed an accusatory finger at the Belgian Catholic film organization for its list of "French classics," which included Jean Renoir's *La Chienne* and Jacques Feyder's *Thérèse Raquin*. More shocking to the French Catholics was polite Belgian Catholic praise of the surrealists Epstein and Buñuel. Exasperated, *Choisir* declared itself

surprised to say the least. As much from a Catholic point of view as a French point of view, we can not endorse this . . . and, from a Catholic point of view if there were a ranking to be done among French films, we would not retain *La Chienne* or *Thérèse Raquin*. . . .[26]

Listening to the address of Lunders and proposals previously aired in Rome before the General Council of OCIC during 1946, delegates representing fifteen countries (Austria, Belgium, Canada, Czechoslovakia, France, Great Britain, Hungary, Italy, Luxembourg, Mexico, Netherlands, Peru, Portugal, Spain, Switzerland) of the twenty-four at the OCIC Congress of 1947 in Brussels agreed to standardize the categories for film:

1. ADMISSIBLE POUR TOUS
    éventuellement
    "avec légères réserves"
2. ADMISSIBLE POUR ADULTES
    éventuellement
    "aussi pour adolescents," ou
    "avec réserves," ou
    "avec sérieuses ou nettes réserves"
3. À DECONSEILLER
4. À PROSCRIRE[27]

The U.S. Legion of Decency delegates present did not adopt this system. Having established more uniform categories in most of its member nations, however, OCIC agreed to have the national Catholic organizations send reports and ratings to the Brussels headquarters, where differences and anomalies could undergo further scrutiny, a kind of comparative film studies, Vatican-style.

In the second area of Lunders's life project, juvenile protection, Belgium had already won a Europe-wide reputation for shielding youth from love and crime on celluloid. As far back as 1920, Belgium banned minors under sixteen years of age from viewing films judged only suitable for adults by an appointed censorship panel. Although the Belgian system sometimes showed greater permissiveness on adult films than some European censorship boards, it proved grimly upright and Spartan when it came to approving films for minors. Because many capitalist filmmakers regarded the youth and family audience as crucial for achieving a fair return on their pictures, the companies grudgingly agreed to cuts in footage. According to a report in Belgium's most prestigious newspaper, *Le Soir,* the Commission de Contrôle des Films chopped an enormous quantity of celluloid:[28]

	No. of films submitted	No cuts	Partially cut	Refused
1934	1,198	590	259	289
1935	1,355	749	266	252

Appeals section			
	No. of films submitted	Admitted	Refused
1934	102	34	68
1935	124	64	60

In October 1935, a delegation of the Socialist Cinema Center confronted Belgium's minister of Justice on its tolerance of the board of censors, commonly characterized by the left as "voluntary workers, often cranks." The Socialists rebelled against specific rules, such as the osculation limit forbidding embraces that exceed six yards of film.[29] The *Tarzan* cycle of films starring Johnnie Weismuller was later denied to children's audiences, an action likely provoked by Jane's suggestive cleavage and scenes of carnage visited upon African tribes. Though the Socialists spoke out against Catholic obscurantism, they failed to acknowledge the central role their party's leadership played in establishing the original censorship board. The Belgian Parti Socialiste held the Justice portfolio in the cabinet during 1920, and the minister of Justice, Émile Vandervelde, thundered eloquently on behalf of laws designed to stop "certain films that are not immoral, but which project violent spectacles that can have a suggestive power extremely danger-

ous for weak minds and, everywhere, on the minds of children." Opposing
Vandervelde's Socialist embrace of a censorship board, dissident parliamentarians noted that Belgium had been born of a revolution in 1830 based on
theatrical freedom. On 25 August 1830, young rebels arose at the Théâtre
Royal de la Monnaie in Brussels during a performance of Daniel Auber's
opera *La Muette de Portici*. When Marsaniello launched into a duet with
Pietro calling for courage to fight for freedom of the fatherland, the audience flung off top hats and waved walking sticks, as they headed to the
streets shouting the call to arms against Dutch tyranny. Though later designating himself a "militant socialist" in the title of his memoirs, Vandervelde
stood unmoved by memories of such patriotic bombast and artistic liberty.
He instead commended to Belgian Senators the researches of Judge Paul
Wets, the president of the National and International Federation of Juvenile Judges. Wets called cinema the "father of a new criminality" and the
agent that "has done more for the corruption of youth . . . than any other
secular factor of disorder. . . ."[30]

Both Catholics and Socialists referred often to Wets's testimony throughout the interwar years. Film's endangerment of vulnerable youth would remain a leitmotif of moral regulatory movements for decades to come. In
the postwar years, Lunders assembled for UNESCO a large collection on
cinema legislation on youth, and he paid careful attention to the U.S. hearings on film's contribution to juvenile delinquency during the 1950s. The
Kefauver committee in the U.S. Senate ultimately concluded that film had
a limited or at best mixed responsibility for youth criminality. There were
many others more certain of its dangers. J. Edgar Hoover fulminated
against the film industry's "trash mills which spew out celluloid poison destroying the impressionable minds of youth." According to the FBI's chief,
"In the face of the nation's terrifying juvenile crime wave we are threatened
with a flood of movies and television productions which flaunt indecency
and applaud lawlessness."[31] While the Kefauver committee believed that
films often reflected rather than caused youth criminality, others regarded
the motion picture as an accelerant feeding the fires of juvenile delinquency.
In Ghent, Belgian authorities expressed apprehension about the presentation on 19 June 1958 of Columbia Pictures's *Teen-age Crime Wave* (1955)
[*La Rage du Crime/Drang Naar Misdaad*], a film combining rock 'n' roll,
wild car chases, and slaughter followed by the avenging hail of police bullets.[32] The rise of television kept many adults in the U.S. home, and Hollywood had decided to cultivate the youth market with a raft of teen exploitation films featuring rock, juvenile delinquency, and elsewhere horror and
science fiction: Roger Corman's *Attack of the Crab Monsters* (1957), *The*

Crybaby Killer (1958), *A Bucket of Blood* (1959), American International Pictures' *Hot Rod Girl* (1956), *I Was a Teenage Frankenstein* (1957), *Dragstrip Riot* (1958), Universal's *Monster on the Campus* (1958), the United Artists' release *Riot in Juvenile Prison* (1959), and MGM's *Blackboard Jungle* (1955) – this last film praised by the Kefauver committee for its accuracy but condemned as possibly building sympathy for its reprobate characters. U.S. ambassador to Italy Clare Booth Luce decried the export of *Blackboard Jungle*, a film she thought showed foreigners a pathological turn in U.S. civilization. Causing the film to be removed as an entry in the Venice Film Festival, Luce's action catapulted *Blackboard Jungle* into "the most highly publicized film on the worldwide market," wrote *Variety*.[33]

THE DUBBING AND NUDISM FLAPS

Throughout the interwar and early postwar period, Belgium pursued few initiatives against Hollywood's market dominance, and it relied on the censorship board alone to excise offensive material. In the mid-1930s, the Belgian government sought to require all Hollywood film to be dubbed in Belgium, an action that aimed to create an indigenous movie labor force and technical infrastructure. Belgian artists and musicians whipped up support by extravagant claims that passage of the law would create two thousand jobs.[34] These workers could then be mobilized in the construction of a Belgian film industry. The MPPDA informed its intermediary, the U.S. State Department, to tell the Belgians that such a measure would provoke a strict Hollywood boycott of their nation. France, which had such a law in place, warned the Belgians that French bans on foreign dubbing would be enforced against its neighbor to the north. The MPPDA declared that the Belgian market was Liliputian and thus the most easy upon which to slap economic sanctions. The film-trade organization threatened Belgium-based Gavaerts, Kodak's main competitor in the raw-film industry, with adverse treatment by the Hollywood studios. Belgium soon withdrew the proposal.[35]

For the rest of the decade a flap over a U.S. film extolling the benefits of nudism became the sole occasion for State Department concern with the Belgian film market. On 22 June 1939, Belgian deputy vicomte Charles du Bus de Warnaffe, a member of the Catholic Party and a former minister of Justice, accused the United States of spreading moral rot when an Antwerp exhibitor attempted to show a U.S. independent production called *Nudist Land*. Featuring "an orchestra playing during which time quotations from well-known advocates of nudism are flashed on the screen," the film, reported the New York District office of the Bureau of Foreign and Domestic Commerce, "proceeds to explain the benefits of nudism as evidenced by the healthy bodies of the savages shown" from sub-Saharan Africa, Bali, and Samoa.[36] *Nudist Land* began with a wealth of anthropological footage from around the globe, and then it broke into its narrative drama, the "true-life story" of Betty and Jack Weston from the United States. While Jack Weston is long away on toilsome business trips, his wife finds herself so sick that she enters a hospital. Eventually a friend rescues her by seeking something much more health-enhancing than the conventional routines of Western medicine. Together they sneak off to a nudist camp. When Jack finally locates his wife, he soon recognizes the healing wonders of nudism and is an eager convert to the life-style, a return to natural goodness over the artificial trappings of modern life.[37]

U.S. Secretary of Commerce Harry Hopkins, a longtime confidant of Franklin Roosevelt, appeared alarmed, not because of Belgian pique but upon hearing that the export version of the film cited the U.S. president as an endorser of nudism. FDR supposedly termed the life-style a healthful tonic practiced for centuries by the tribes of Africa. "Nudism will save humanity from the decrepitude towards which it is being precipitated," the U.S. president allegedly said in congratulating the film's producers. "It will revive the race by infusing new blood into it. Your movement is an absolute necessity." The producers conveniently deleted this presidential blessing from the U.S. print of the film.[38]

Leo Lunders and the Centre Catholique d'Action Cinématographique had previously protested the film in a communiqué to the U.S. Embassy in Brussels on 8 May 1939. In his attack on the film in the Belgian Parliament, vicomte du Bus de Warnaffe declared that the majority of its audience was composed of Belgian soldiers, whose moral fiber could be sapped by this "appeal to the basest instincts." He demanded activation of Belgian article 319, which forbids works leading to the "*excitation*" of debauchery, and article 383, which "punishes those who publish or sell obscene images." Invoking King Albert, who held that "a people who defend themselves inspire everyone's respect," du Bus de Warnaffe regretted that once again Belgium is alone, "defending ourselves against a foreign enemy." He implored the state ministry to act with "speed" so that "we may defend ourselves against an outside enemy" and, hence, restore national "self-respect" by "eradicating harmful works which may endanger . . . moral health."[39]

Though staff of the U.S. Consul General in Antwerp subsequently "had seen the film and did not consider it immoral," reported interim chargé d'affaires Orme Wilson, the U.S. State Department showed little desire to muster a fight for the work, least of all one from a non-MPPDA producer.[40] This blowup notwithstanding, Belgium had been an open market for the MPPDA, and the U.S. State Department intended to keep it that way.

The paralysis of the Belgian state in showdowns with Hollywood seriously circumscribed Catholic action in the local market. The determined internationalism of Brohée and Lunders had partial roots in feckless state intervention at home: Belgium supplied only a single-digit percentage of its own feature-film market. However, just when others thought Brussels to be the epitome of inaction against Hollywood and a government frequently celebrated by the MPPDA as a model for the rest of Europe, the Belgian colonial regime took a step that had been only the dream of British and French parliamentarians. In early 1945, Belgium banned black Congolese from the Hollywood picture palace, rendering the commercial cinema theater an all-white oasis in the heart of darkness. (The film studios and the MPAA generated few, if any, squawks of protest until well into the 1950s, a complacency fed by the realization that the vast majority of blacks lived in destitution and simply could not afford attendance at cinema shows.)[41]

In retrospect, there are some who would regard such scorched-earth cultural policy as confirmation of late-twentieth-century Belgian film director Jaco van Dormael's formulation that "Belgium is such a normal country that it is impossible not to be subject to bouts of madness."[42] Most historical accounts of film policy at some point degenerate into narratives of futility, especially for the smallest of nations. Still, Belgium in the postwar period had commercial triumphs in one area of media production: animated cartoons, particularly "Tin Tin" and "Asterix." The spectacular success of the former provoked Charles de Gaulle to remark that the boy detective Tin Tin was his only serious rival on the international scene.

In the Conlusion to this book, there is a brief exploration of the European failure to contest Hollywood's domination of the considerable market for children's films. Europe's cinema avant-garde for the most part did not share the concern of the international Catholic film movement for children's productions. Such a stand, however unconscious, may have been another portent of doom for dreams of restoring European preeminence in the creation of popular culture.

CHAPTER NINE

France and Resistance to Hollywood

EMPIRE, ARTISANS, AND THE STATE

During the decade and a half following the invention of motion pictures in the 1890s, France reigned as the preeminent power in the global film industry. Though data are regarded as unreliable, the French had command of perhaps 70 percent of the global film trade, and indeed boosters for Parisian studios boasted of a 90 percent world market share. Pathé Studios, said to have unleashed "Pathé-mania" across continents, sold twice as many films to North America as the entire U.S. film industry.[1] Jewish owners of nickelodeons came under fire for allegedly allowing the alien French Pathé interests to overwhelm U.S. screens.[2]

The vainglorious brio of Will Hays in the 1920s had had its counterpart a decade earlier among France's leading partisans of the movie medium. French imperialists spoke of conquering slabs of the planet through film in terms as triumphalist as the U.S. Film Czar, who subsequently pledged to sell America to the world through Hollywood motion pictures. In 1914, Colonel Jean-Baptiste Marchand, whose victory at Fashoda, Sudan, in 1898 had been stymied by threats of British intervention against French expansion in Africa, argued that the cinema would bring the more lasting triumph that had otherwise eluded France's warriors and diplomats. In a letter to *Le Film*, he regarded movies as "obviously the weapon which will conquer Africa and many other places."[3] After guerrilla attacks on French soldiers in Fez in 1914, Jules Demaria told a banquet of French cinema organizations how newsreels of French heroics, buttressed by a performance of the "Marseillaise" on a windup gramophone, had quickly pacified the once restless Arabs: "Those very Moroccans who, a few months before, all more or less complicit with an odious massacre, had our soldiers murdered in cold blood, greeted the emblem of France with their applause."[4]

The belief in film's shamanistic power over subaltern races soon seeped beyond France, the leitmotif of Elmer Tracey Barnes's popular American boys' novel *The Motion-Picture Comrades in African Jungles* (1917). For its heroes, the medium had the power of armies, as well as providing an antidote to ennui in permitting the colonizer and adventurer "all sorts of fun frightening the natives with living pictures on a white wall."[5]

If such a magical medium could reach recesses of the irrational, tapping fear and joy that approached the gates of delirium, there were some European elites who did not share Colonel Marchand's enthusiasm about its future role in the fate of empires. Moreover, the French would soon blame the calamity of World War I for allowing the United States to steal mastery over motion pictures. Although the war did spike the guns of French film production, there were also other developments indicating that the days of France's film supremacy were numbered. During 1911–14 the U.S. movie industry had already eroded France's lead in the British Commonwealth and Latin America. Even before, Pathé's control of the U.S. market had been largely thwarted. Charles Pathé, who stood with Louis Lumière as one of the founding giants of the French film industry, later confessed that France had little hope of staving off the American challenge:

In the future, it became necessary to recognize that . . . the United States, with its boundless possibilities, would take possession of the global market probably forever. The war had only hastened a little the achievement of this supremacy. Favored by the magnitude of their interior market which from the standpoint of box office receipts represented 40 to 50 times that of the French market – and may have been around three-fourths of the world market – the Americans could put considerable sums into the execution of their films, completely amortizing on their territory and then come to conquer the export market in all countries, notably those which due to small population would not be allowed the luxury of regular national production.[6]

Pathé's adversaries in France faulted him at war's end for quickly selling off much of his own enterprise to certain Americans and Eastman Kodak. During 1918–20, Pathé and his chief French competitor, Léon Gaumont, shed production units in favor of distribution and exhibition. Pathé's brand of Gallic modesty could be construed as a rationalization for his own too-hasty surrender.

Still, France had the worst cinema attendance of the major countries in western Europe, a condition aggravated by the persistence of the rural village. Urbanization marched at a much slower pace in France than in Germany and Great Britain, as the French countryside provided few outlets for cinema viewing. Parisians commonly posted an attendance rate six times higher than those dwelling in the provinces. A survey of 1937 indicated that 50 percent of Americans were regular cinemagoers; only 7 percent of the

French attained this distinction.[7] Thus, Pathé may have had grounds for his extravagant estimate that the United States, with a population quadruple that of France, possessed a cinema market perhaps forty to fifty times that of its once-feared competitor. French domestic market conditions were frustratingly inhospitable to an art form industrialized and plunged into competition on a global scale.

In the face of this handicap, France developed first ideological and later political ripostes to U.S. supremacy, a variety of responses that appeared to ripple in overlapping sequence: initially a public discourse in the 1920s and 1930s condemning the impending colonization of France and decolonization of the French Empire; then, the rise of artisanal populism as a defense of French culture against the industrialized assembly lines of Hollywood; and finally, the activist cultural intervention of Vichy that established the foundations of postwar French film policy. The last is one of the ironies of history long purged from memory by André Malraux, Jack Lang, and François Léotard, among the state ministers who have defined France's twentieth-century cultural mission.

FILM AND THE DECLINE OF FRANCE

French thinkers, bureaucrats, and politicians articulated a variety of themes on Hollywood's pernicious effects on national survival. However, three currents – sometimes overlapping – grew in momentum during the 1920s and 1930s. First and most simply, Hollywood had created a substantial body of work that made France look "bad." Reporting to Will Hays from Paris in May 1928, MPPDA representative Harold L. Smith observed that French cultural protectionists held "that American films inevitably show the French in a bad light when French plots are treated; and that our films always show a Frenchman as a 'gigolo' or other dispectable [sic] character and the French women as being '*légère*,' or women of easy virtue."[8] Earlier in the 1920s, the French had shared the complaints of other European powers that the United States crassly took all the credit for victory in World War I in such works as *The Big Parade* and *The Enemies of Women*. Soon many French became convinced that Hollywood actively targeted France for special denigration: for example, *Beau Geste*, *White Shadows in the South Seas*, and *Hot for Paris*, the last film provoking a riot of French soldiers that effectively stopped a theater in Beijing from further presentations. *Hot for Paris* featured an obnoxious Frenchman who spat in people's eyes while addressing them. Such complaints persisted throughout the interwar period. In 1938, France banned United Artists' film *The Hurricane* because, according to

Edwin Wilson, the U.S. chargé d'affaires ad interim in Paris, "the French Governor and colonial officials of the Pacific islands . . . were depicted as being unduly severe, both in speech and action." When the U.S. Embassy staff carefully explained to André-Léon Decloux, the acting chief of the American Section at the Quai d'Orsay, that the book inspiring the movie had been written by John Norman Hall, staunchly Francophile and an original member of the Lafayette Escadrille, the French relented, but with numerous demands. The Quai d'Orsay's representative on France's Board of Censors needed what the State Department called a "face saver" for the reversal, and the body suggested that

in all versions of the picture, both in France and abroad, deletion of (1) all reference to the French Government, the Ministry of Colonies and the fall of the Bastille; (2) all display of the French flag; (3) all reference to French colonies by name and the words, "French criminal code"; and (4) all scenes of violence, whipping, etc.[9]

Though Hollywood hardly complied with these demands, the U.S. film industry's 1939 release of a talking version of *Beau Geste* and *Devil's Island* ensured the renewal of charges of betrayal and the existence of a destructive agenda. Throughout the 1930s, France countered with its own imperial cycle of films glorifying *la mission civilisatrice*: Léon Poirier's *L'Appel du silence* (1936), Jacques de Baroncelli's *S.O.S. Sahara* (1938) and *L'Homme du Niger* (1939). Julien Duvivier directed *La Bandera* (1935), an *hommage* to the Spanish Legion in the Sahara and a work beloved by Franco. Despite a few films carrying a heavy pacifist aroma, such as Abel Gance's sound version of *J'accuse* (1937), over a third of France's movie output in 1938 treated the life and mission of its military. For anyone seeking to go beyond Gance's reproach of war, Edmond Sée, head of the *commission de contrôle*, left producers, exhibitors, and distributors with a stark warning on 25 October 1937: "A visa would be rigorously refused to . . . all films tending to bring the army into ridicule or to diminish its prestige. . . ."[10]

A second current of ideas fed fears that Hollywood resolutely worked against France in favor of the Anglo-Saxon fraternity of nations. The United States and the United Kingdom, *les pays Anglo-Saxons,* promoted each other's interests with a determination inimical to the French Empire. The noblesse oblige and flamboyant altruism of the British aristocracy pervaded *Beau Geste* at the expense of French imperialism; the *Tarzan* cycle of films promoted Edgar Rice Burroughs's notion that a boy of British noble extraction could still thrive when placed in the naked jungle, a victory of nature over nurture, superior breeding over upbringing. The French felt the weight of the Anglo-Saxon tyranny most acutely when Hollywood's imperial cycle of films put overripe Romanticism at the service of the British Empire. In a review of *Clive of India*, the critic for the French newspaper *Le Temps* (11 May 1935) enjoyed the movie, but ruefully admitted that Hollywood "appears particularly preoccupied at the moment in scanning the pages of English history and of exalting British genius." Comparing the film *Lives of a Bengal Lancer* with *Clive of India*, he notes a preference for treatments of "the apotheosis of British imperialism," featuring "the conquest of India." Declaring that "England may be proud of this new solemn homage which America has just rendered. Let us patiently await our turn," the French commentator left considerable doubt about Hollywood's good intentions:

It may be admitted that it is surprising to see the producers of the New World harness themselves to a task so contrary to their political gospel. We must resign ourselves to the inevitable. For the American scenario the Frenchman is an ugly puny little man, frivolous and debauched, while the Englishman is a superb and generous lion, whose feats of heroism are beyond count. Since today it is the magic lantern which writes history for the simple-minded, we may rightfully be slightly alarmed at this inequality of treatment.[11]

Though Jesse Isidor Strauss, representing the U.S. Embassy, suggested that Hollywood produce a "historical film based on the life of some distinguished Frenchman whose exploits . . . might *materially* contribute to solidifying the sympathy of the French cinemagoing public for American films," he inadvertently called attention to France's main vulnerability. Hollywood cared less about France, not because of an Anglo-Saxon cabal, but due to economics. As Harold Smith of the MPPDA coldly reminded lawyer Harold L. Williamson, second secretary of the U.S. Embassy in Paris: "the returns from the British market, insofar as our industry is concerned, are estimated at from 25 to 30 times the returns from the French market." This condition was certainly exacerbated by culture, the shared language, as Smith admitted with the verve of a latter-day cultural materialist:

[I]n England we are not handicapped with the difference in language. We do not have to spend Frs. 200,000 to dub a film before we can put it on the market. We do not have to spend any extra money to offer a film for sale in England.[12]

Anglophilia in U.S. culture undoubtedly has extraeconomic roots, and the preference for reactionary topics of feudal lineage cannot all be laid at the door of the cash nexus. Thus De Gaulle tapped a powerful thread of French *ressentiment* in his postwar foreign policy by opposing the symbiotic camarilla he called *les pays Anglo-Saxons*. Nonetheless, many French misdiagnosed the film situation and potential avenues for redress by believing that blood and nostalgia alone had predisposed Hollywood to foresake France. Seeking international solidarity, Yves Chataigneau of the Service des Oeuvres Française in the Ministry of Foreign Affairs had once saluted Lord Newton of Britain for awakening Europe from slumber on the U.S. film threat.[13] Subsequently Hollywood's empire cycle falsely convinced some French that Britain was safely back in America's camp. If economics helped weld Hollywood to the defense of the British Empire, Britons of the intellectual and political castes still shared with elite French a disdain for the U.S. film industry.

A third area of concern about the entertainment industry mirrored developments in most of interwar Europe: France assembled a cohort of ideologues who blamed Hollywood Jews and "Israelites" in France's domestic film industry for seeking the destruction of national culture and the empire. The literature bemoaning national decadence regularly encouraged this, most dramatically in the crass title *Uncle Shylock; or, American Imperialism in the Conquest of the World,* hatched by Radical Party deputy J. L. Chastanet. Modernity had begot decadence, and the Americans, through the Jews, were its chief agents. This constellation of ideas had such force that even a Jew such as Daniel Halévy endorsed the decadence school's oracular pronouncement that the city had been the incubator of national decline, and only a return to the healthy rural world of premodernity could arrest the rot.

French culture was seen as losing to American art forms, mental opiates that France's hard Right labeled "judéo–negro–américaine" jazz and "Israëlite cinéma." The most extreme agreed with Goebbels's characterization of American jazz as "the art of the sub-human." In 1933, the filmmaker and writer Yvan Noë wrote that "American cinema tends to imbecilize us and to destroy by its childishness and its wonderfully presented trifles our judgment, our good sense, and our critical spirit." Naturally he added a special reminder about the strategic power of the Jews in Hollywood:

American cinema is the property of a certain group of Israelite finance which leads the rest of America to the dramatic situation that it struggles against presently and maintains the bankruptcy of its economic and governing methods. But this finance is arrogant. . . . Like all of the arrogant, it is imperialist. It attempts to export the American spirit in order to put itself at ease and through some conquests to mask its bankruptcy.[14]

The fear of "Israelite finance" soon engulfed the Republic with a scandal involving Alexandre Stavisky, a Ukrainian Jew who had become a naturalized French citizen. Fresh accusations of swindling came crashing down on Stavisky in December 1933. Through bribes, bullying, and sweet cajoling of corrupt Radical Party politicians and magistrates, he had previously had his bail renewed nineteen times, allowing him to continue his swank and swinging life-style. On 9 January 1934, police headed to Stavisky's Alpine lair in hopes of arresting him on charges of issuing bogus bonds through his Crédit Municipal de Bayonne. When the gendarmes reported that the financier was in his death throes, through an act of hara-kiri, neither Left nor Right believed the police. The Left thought the police had iced Stavisky to cover up their own leadership's abetment of his misconduct; the Right immediately launched an attack on the foul stench of parliamentary corruption supposedly enveloping the Republic. Throughout January, the Camelots du Roi, a rightist organization founded in 1908, which as a side hobby had fomented disturbances at theatrical and cinema shows thought detrimental to France, staged a series of demonstrations against the rotten Republic. On 6 February, a convergence of many rightist organizations and rank-and-file citizens ignited violence at Place de la Concorde. Razor-blade-wielding rioters out to slash the legs of police horses and an assortment of rock-throwing hooligans encountered repressive counterattack: The melees left fifteen dead and perhaps two thousand wounded. Through the replacement of the Daladier cabinet by a government with former president Gaston Doumergue in the saddle, the Right once again rode back to power. The hard Right, however, lacked the unity and firepower of the German Nazis and Italian *fascisti* to impose full-blown fascism. The terrified Left soon reorganized to build the Popular Front as a prophylactic against future fascist triumph.[15]

The Stavisky affair gave French anti-Semites a new platform upon which to excoriate "Israelite finance," reflexively linked to a cinema industry that had carried the curse of France's moral and spiritual decline. While Hollywood Jews allegedly menaced the French Colonial Empire from without, Europeanized Jews bored their way from within, occupying important command posts in French cinema. A Roumanian Jew, Natan Tanenzapf, who Gallicized his name to Bérnard Natan, became the chief investor in the Pathé corporation and revived its production capabilities in the late 1920s and 1930s. Officially naturalized as French since 1921, he nevertheless had what the English politely call "a past." During the first six years of the 1920s, Natan had made pornographic films for what Ado Kyrou designates "the Marseille–Lyon–Paris axis" of clandestine theaters and bordellos. He found himself long paying bribes to old associates, who blackmailed him with clips of his earlier handiwork, and to journalists apparently ready to tell

about his choicest productions, such as *Le Moine* (The Monk, 1922) and
Le Canard (The Duck [U.S. title, *Fuck a Duck*], 1926). Delighting a clien-
tele thirsting for carnivals of wickedness, these films trafficked in the hell's
hollow of anticlerical imagery and bestial gluttony.[16]

Although Natan went mainstream with Pathé, enemies abounded with
allegations of his unscrupulous finance practice and condemnations of a
luxurious life-style designed to keep pace with other international movie
moguls. In addition to his background as a "Juif et pornocrate," in the
words of scholar Jean-Pierre Jeancolas, Natan faced constant comparison
with the free-wheeling playboy Stavisky.[17] During 1930–3, the big two,
Gaumont–Franco-Film–Aubert (formed 1928) and Pathé–Natan, produced
nearly a third of France's domestic films (i.e., GFFA 20 and Pathé–Natan
23 out of 157 French movies released in 1932). A financial crunch led Gaumont in 1934 and Pathé–Natan in 1936 to cease production, a crisis provoked by the escalating costs of the "talkie" revolution, declining attendance between 1932 and 1935, onerous state and municipal taxation, and
a Depression-era drying up of capital finance.[18] Meanwhile, charges flew
that Natan had issued a variant of Stavisky-style junk bonds. Irate investors
believed that he had taken a company with 200 million French francs (F)
in net worth and left it spilling 400 million F in red ink through an asset-
stripping operation that fed the coffers of Natan-owned affiliates. Indeed
the 600 million F in question represents a sum double that of the Stavisky
affair. The weekly newspaper *La Flèche* raised the damage assessment:
"the Pathé–Natan swindle is three times that of Stavisky. It affects 35 companies and subsidiaries with a deficit surpassing 900M Francs in six years."
Though more recent scholarship has repudiated claims that Natan had carried out an asset-stripping operation, few French journalists of the time
seemed prepared to look at a complex series of mergers and financial trans-
actions with a measure of dispassion.[19]

Arrested on fraud charges on 3 September 1936, Natan waged a losing
battle in French courts for the next two and a half years. In the public arena, critics of the French justice system mounted a defense that at best left
the movie producer underwhelmed with gratitude. The Marxist film commentator Georges Sadoul argued that Natan was both guilty and at the
same time a convenient scapegoat for more menacing elements in France's
business elite. From 1939 on, Natan languished in a maximum security
lockup in Paris. With ferocious enemies on the Right and others on the Left
appalled by this representative of finance capital, he had little hope. He was
soon to be deported by Nazi wolves, who exterminated the film financier
by 1943.[20]

Film financiers had long attracted hostile press in France. A commentator for *Monde* (7 July 1928), calling himself "Jim le Harponneur" after a controversial film of the same name (i.e., *The Sea Beast*), declared that "business and chicanery are not necessarily the same thing." Comparing the film financiers to the notorious Panama speculators of the late nineteenth century, he said that "consciously or not" the aspiring movie moguls have engaged in "escroquerie" (swindling). "Jim the Harpooner" avoided direct attacks on Jews and foreigners; but in the aftermath of the Stavisky affair, the Jewish and foreigner threat would become accented in French editorial commentary.[21]

Even a film weekly so prone to denounce Nazism as the Roman Catholic *Choisir* temporarily expressed sympathy with the German predicament in June 1934. "We have been surprised to learn," wrote its editorialist Jean Morienval, "when Hitler took his actions toward the Jews, that German cinema was going to cease to exist because it was all entirely in the hands of the Israelites." Noting that the German-Jewish film diaspora had headed to Paris, Morienval feared that: "at the risk of justifying Hitler, we see race solidarities manifesting themselves, not just for normal and natural assistance, but for restarting, consciously or not, the exclusive scheming about which the Germans themselves have moaned."[22]

Interwar French cinema had been revitalized by successive waves of immigrants. Initially the Bolshevik Revolution had brought a White Russian influx that gave many French silent films of the 1920s the themes of czarist and aristocratic intrigue. In the 1930s, fascism dislocated Central European directors, who temporarily relocated to Paris, among them Pabst, Ophüls, and, briefly, Fritz Lang. The latter, admired by Goebbels – whom Lang alleged had offered to put him in charge of German film production – wisely decided to cut and run to France's capital. The French government, notably the Ministry of Public Instruction and Fine Arts, received reports monitoring cinema personnel in France. Claiming the industry to be pervaded with odious riffraff, these undated dossiers from the 1930s give a flavor of the state's suspicions about film workers, three French, the rest foreigners:

1. Dhemont – French, 40 years old
   36 rue du Colisée
   the only honest one – possesses some capital with which he aids the combined
       producers Bianco-Pellegrin, etc. . . .
2. Blondy – French – a young and disturbed apache, supplier for the Germans –
   a trafficker in women.
3. Borowsky – Russian, 40 years old
   65, avenue de Champs Elysée
   on the blacklist of the Union des Artistes

4. Jack Darcy, 35 years old, without an address, on the blacklist . . .
5. Chemel – Swiss, 40 years old, on the blacklist . . .
6. Devalde, Jean – Belgian, 35 years old
   His collaborator Kassar, an Egyptian, has been deported from here at the end of last August.
7. Behars, Nicolas – Roumanian (?), 35 years old
   72, avenue des Champs Elysées
   spy, criminal, cocaine merchant, *formidable* bandit, works with the Germans and on special films (*La Garçonne*)[23]

The dossiers, riddled with misspellings of names, then held U.S. firms specially responsible for cheating French out of jobs in Paris, noting that the dubbing departments all had foreign directors. (At the very least, this subverted the intent of the French law that required the dubbing of foreign films in France.)

Dubbing Director

Paramount	M. Deutshner (Germans)
	Mlle Goldblatt
M-G-M	Mlle Irene Klaukowski (Russian)
	formidable
Warner Bros.	M. A. Woog (Dutch) the only suitable one.
Fox	M. Piperno . . . *formidable* for his "American stupidity"

NOT A SINGLE FRENCH PERSON!![24]

For most reactionary elements in interwar France, this foreign presence became an obsession, a pustulant sore in the body politic. Raymond Millet's *Trois millions d'étrangers en France – Les indésirables – Les bienvenus* (Paris: Médicis, 1938) sounded the general alarm, while Jean Giraudoux in *Pleins Pouvoirs* (1939) spoke specifically of "an infiltration" by "hundreds of thousands of Ashkenazim." In his multivolume work on the Jewish presence in France, fascist ideologue Lucien Rebatet broke down the personnel of the French film industry in the late hour of 1938: "80 percent Jewish, 10 percent émigrés without passports, and 10 percent French, authorized by their Marxist and Masonic attachments. . . ." Popularly known by his nom de plume François Vinneuil, he pointed out that "Those who settled in Paris were fundamentally the worst sort of scum, the lowest grade of con men, money-grubbing parasites, cold-shouldered even by their fellow Jews of any standing." (The cold-shouldering may have been an oblique reference to such notables as Baron Robert de Rothschild, president of the Paris Consistory of Israelites of France, who in a famous speech of May 1935 blamed the upswing of anti-Semitism on eastern European Jews. He accused them of being too prone to bad behavior and most ungracious with their radical attacks on the French government.)[25]

Rebatet belonged to a nucleus of radical Right intellectuals who kept a sharp eye on cinema for the newspapers *Action Française* and *Je suis partout*. Founded in 1930, *Je suis partout* became the house organ for Robert Brasillach, Maurice Bardèche, and Rebatet, thinkers committed to a house-cleaning of the foreign element that purportedly had brought on French national disgrace and the decay of empire. All three could rhapsodize about the artistry of Left directors such as Renoir, but elsewhere Rebatet warned the French director that his proper place might well be in a concentration camp. In their *Histoire du Cinéma* (1935), Brasillach and École Normale cohort Bardèche celebrated several foreign artists, including Eisenstein and Chaplin, as well as Left-leaning French directors. Many liberals hunt for fascist discourse in this book and come up mildly bewildered; not so for the second edition published in 1943, as the duo added a heavy dose of anti-Semitism. Bardèche claimed that he and his brother-in-law Brasillach were rational anti-Semites, while Rebatet and the novelist Céline, author of the notorious *Bagatelles pour un massacre* (1937), were instinctive anti-Semites. The distinction does not hold up so well under scrutiny. Heralding the Stavisky affair riots of February 1934 in terms akin to Wordsworth on the French Revolution ("Bliss was it to be alive . . . "), Brasillach spoke of that "exalting night" in which feeling triumphed over banal opinion. "That divine couple, Courage and Fear, had joined again and stalked the streets."[26] Later comparing the Jews to monkeys, he proudly justified their deportation after the Vel d'Hiv roundup of July 1942: "We must separate from the Jews en bloc and not keep any little ones." Never to be outdone with grotesque imagery, he regarded France's republic as "an old syphilitic whore stinking of patchouli and yeast infection."[27]

From 1932 to 1937, Brasillach had served as literary editor for the neo-royalist *Action Française* of Charles Maurras, who fulminated constantly against the *métèques* (dirty foreigners). In the course of joining Rebatet, Pierre Gaxotte, and P. A. Cousteau in seizing control of *Je suis partout* from its publisher, Fayard, in 1936, Brasillach became its editor-in-chief the following year. From that point on, the pages of *Je suis partout* dripped with fascist and anti-Semitic invective, hymns of hatred for the undesirables in France's midst. The anti-immigrant ferment appeared to have impact: The laws of 2 and 14 May 1938 subjected foreigners to tougher security and surveillance. Léon Blum's Popular Front government, victorious on 5 May 1936 and in complete collapse by 8 April 1938, had been relatively generous in allowing refugees, particularly republicans displaced by the carnage of civil-war Spain, to spill into France. That quickly came to a halt, as the new Daladier regime opened up concentration camps carrying such deceptively inviting names as "reception centers" and "supervised lodging centers." Arthur Koestler later wrote, in his autobiographical *Scum of the Earth* (1941), of his own four-month *séjour* in a Pyrenées-based "Concentration Camp for Undesirable Aliens" during the winter of 1939–40. Vichy then tightened the screws, setting up a "Revision of Naturalizations" process in the summer of 1940 that revoked citizenship from those allowed "to become French too easily" under a streamlined law of 1927.[28] Specific anti-Semitic legislation soon followed, as the state declared in October 1940:

The government in its task of national reconstruction has, from the very first day, studied the problem of the Jews and of certain foreigners, who, having abused our hospitality, have contributed to a significant degree to the defeat. Although there are some notable exceptions . . . the influence of the Jews has been undeniably corruptive and finally decaying.[29]

Brasillach, Bardèche, and Rebatet waged battle against the major French film directors for succumbing to insalubrious Jewish influences, and Hollywood for importing corrupting ideas into France. Brasillach and Bardèche saluted the great French director Marcel Carné as an artist of "talent"; but "in those years" bereft of "grandeur," he indulged in a debilitating "*judaïsante* aesthetic."[30] Referring to Carné's work with Jacques Feyder and briefly Arnold Pressburger, Lucien Rebatet explored the process by which a healthy Aryan cinéaste can become infected by Jewish bacilli:

Carné is an Aryan. But he has been imbued with many Jewish influences. He owes his success to Jews. Jews have coddled him. . . . Carné, who did not lack gifts, became the model of Jewified talent, as had Pabst in postwar Germany. Carné has been in France the most complete representative of that Marxist aestheticism which is, everywhere, one of the results of the proliferation of Jews and which is spontaneously engendered by the political, financial, and spiritual deliquescence which always follows the Jewification of a nation. Berlin experienced it from 1919 to 1930. It is rampant today in the theatre of the Jewish capital called New York, and it is beginning to penetrate Hollywood. This aestheticism is at once whining and brutal. It finds its subjects in filth and blood. It treats these with systematic naturalism accompanied by heavy social symbols of revolt and hatred – shifty and spineless symbols that evoke for the *goyim* the destructive enterprise of Jews, so willingly nihilistic, rather than the valor of an insurgent who protests proudly with gun in hand. . . . I am not a preacher. True artists must be free to depict the worst crimes. But Carné and his Jews have made the French cinema wallow in a degrading fatalistic determinism.[31]

Despite facing such punishing verbal abuse, Carné chose to continue working in France throughout the war. Right-wing director Julien Duvivier, who earned Rebatet's wrath by marrying a Jewish woman, prudently left for California. With the Vichy regime firmly in place, *Je suis partout* led a multipronged attack on those French filmmakers who fled in order to join the "'Colonie française' of Hollywood." Appalled by actor Charles Boyer, "deserter of the French cause," its correspondent noted how the "presse *judéo-américaine* piously reproduced" the star's words of joy upon betraying Vichy France. "I am the most happy of men since I am a citizen of the United States," declared Boyer, spoken at "the same moment," interjected *Je suis partout*, "when the Flying Fortresses of Mr. Roosevelt assassinate the French." Pointing out that the French colony in Hollywood contains such "names *bien français* as Adolphe Osso (his true name Ossoveltski), Robert Hakim, Gregor Rabinovitch, André Daven, Leonide Moguy, and Henri Diamant-Berger (this over-celebrated production shark who dared to confer on his odious co-religionist Samson Fainsilber the role of Richelieu in the film *The Three Musketeers*)," the newspaper wondered how Gentile French directors Jean Renoir, Julien Duvivier, and René Clair could join "this gallery," what it ridiculed as the "*golonie vranzaise.*"[32]

Je suis partout hailed the aftermath of 15 October 1942, the last day that "Anglo-Saxon films" could be shown in the nonoccupied zone of France. (The occupied zones of Paris and northern France had lived under a Hollywood ban since 1940.) "While the flying fortresses of Uncle Sam heave their bombs upon Brest, Rouen, and Lille, while American troops threaten or steal our colonies, the judeo-american films of Hollywood were still projected on the screens of Toulouse, Lyons, Nice, and Marseilles." Admitting that the U.S. films had arrived before the summer armistice with Nazi Germany, the newspaper noted that these works "had become for the Jews and the Gaullists a veritable political protest action." Sneering at the "*Juifs-juristes*" of Cannes who termed the ban "contrary to the Franco–American treaty of commerce," *Je suis partout* said it was instead overjoyed "to congratulate the director of the Cinématographe Nationale for having taken – at last . . ." this "necessary measure." Pleased that the minister of Information also banned many newspapers and magazines from speaking of Hollywood films and the actors and actresses *d'outre Atlantique,* its commentator noted that paper currently in short supply should not be "consecrated" to the scandalous tittle-tattle of "la colonie judéo–anglo-saxonne de Hollywood."[33]

What sickened the collaborationist newspaper was the many French who scurried to see their last American films the week of 9–15 October. "Du swing! du swing! Vrai swing américain," shouted one Marseilles venue, while a movie theater in Lyons announced: "Come see the last American film projected in France." Keeping "the *zazous* [hepcats] of the Côte d'Azure . . . heavily occupied," these last films provoked the Vichy organ to provide a typical dialogue from youthful partisans of American popular culture: "Mais oui, mon cher, I have to work like mad today, four American films to see here this evening!" The *zazous*, famous for their longish hair, British fashions, slacker demeanor, and passion for American jazz, sometimes faced reprisals from the Camelots du Roi, who pommeled these supposedly anti-French miscreants into the pavement. Such counterattack won immediate plaudits in *Je suis partout, Action française*, and *Appel*. For *Appel*, "the masses were made into morons, intoxicated, stripped of their reason, of their critical sense, by the Jews and the Anglo-Americans, allied for the subjugation of our race." According to its correspondent René Martel, the "perverted" film and the radio gave France "heroes" who fed the "degeneracy" of this generation: "singing stars, 'vamps' of cinema, grotesques of the music-hall."[34]

The Vichy regime pledged to put an end to all that. The exodus of French Jews, émigré artists, and dissident French directors became an occasion for celebration. L. C. Royer of *Le Matin* told of "a Son of Israel, a cinema magnate from the prewar period," who "arrogantly prophesied" that French cinema was finished. "You will not be able to do without us," allegedly bragged the Jewish movie chieftain in 1941, his words falsified the following year by robust production in 1942. Whereas just prior to 1939 France released an average of 125 films, Royer claimed that for May 1942– May 1943 the drop to 98 movies, of which 20 were Franco–German and 6 Franco–Italian coproductions, represented giant progress. The reason "is that our 98 films will no longer speak Yiddish," he explained. Thanks to the housecleaning, the French state could for the first time begin massive infusions of aid to France's movie industry, "65 percent of the cost of the film," added *Le Matin*. The goal, proclaimed Marcel Achard, representing Vichy's directors, producers, and scriptwriters, is to *viriliser* (strengthen) the French cinema.[35]

Vichy created a layer of institutions that would serve as the foundation for France's postwar resistance to Hollywood. During the occupation, Marcel Carné, a director vilified by Rebatet for his "Jewified" aesthetic, produced the masterpiece of French cinema *Les Enfants du Paradis* (*Children of Paradise*). Undoubtedly, many outsiders thought that Vichy's fumigation of both Hollywood and France's avant-garde would leave a parched cinematic landscape in its wake. The mediocrity of much cinema under Nazi Germany appeared to confirm this presumption. Instead Carné's nacreous genius prevailed, unsettling some partisans of the Resistance and Western liberals committed to the aesthetic ideology that artistic excellence best flourishes under freedom. In the dark shadow of repression, art oft delivers its most dazzling light.

THE RISE OF ARTISANAL POPULISM

When it came to discovering the wellsprings of cinematic genius, French artists and social critics early on fastened to a belief that France possessed a form of social organization superior to the U.S. culture that spawned Hollywood. The man of letters Georges Duhamel, who appeared to hate cinema entirely, elsewhere appealed to the individuality and creativity of the artisan, the small-scale craftsperson, over the industrialized machinery of the U.S. economy, the world of the faceless assembly line and the dictatorial monopoly capitalist. "I affirm that a people submitting to a half-century of the present regime of American cinema are headed toward the worst decadence," he wrote. Duhamel held up the danger of industrial methods in culture, as he spoke of how Americans "kill music" through the production of phonograph records, "music in tin-cans." Industrialized cinema, for him, became "A spectacle which demands no effort, which follows from no chain of ideas, raises no question, fails to attack seriously any problem, illuminates no desire, fails to arouse enlightenment, does not excite any hope save for the ridiculous one of someday being a 'star' in Los Angeles." In a moment of generosity, Duhamel noted that cinema requires "enormous capital," employing armies of talents, "countless, varied, amazing"; yet all their work stands as "pathetic" next to "a play of Molière . . . a painting of Rembrandt . . . a fugue of Bach."[36]

In order to "avoid the royal spanking which M. Georges Duhamel has publicly administered to us," the youthful director Jean Vigo advocated in 1930 the pursuit of "a social cinema," one able "to say something and to stimulate echoes other than those created by the belches of ladies and gentlemen who come to the cinema to help their digestion."[37] For Vigo, the artist in a small-scale cinema could take control and make a statement that Duhamel found so absent in industrialized entertainment. Others retained Duhamel's more pessimistic vision. The French Catholic intellectual Georges Bernanos wondered in 1931 if the inheritor of the next global upheaval would not be the followers of Lenin, but rather

some little Yankee shoe-shine boy, a kid with a rat's face, half Saxon, half Jew, with a trace of Negro ancestry in his maddened marrow, the future King of Oil, Rubber, Steel, creator of the Trust of Trusts, future master of a standardized planet, this god that the universe awaits, god of a godless universe.[38]

As for the partisans of French cinema, they kept a guarded faith that the artisan could carve out a space for creativity against the rampaging "future master of a standardized planet," industrialized Hollywood. In the phase between 1929 and 1939, 426 French producers created 681 French films, an average of one and a half movies per company. (In stark contrast, as Mae D. Huettig points out in her 1944 *Economic Control of the Motion Picture Industry*, the eight U.S. film majors in 1939 alone "released 396 or 82 percent of the 483 full-length feature pictures produced" by U.S. motion picture organizations.)[39]

During the advanced years of World War I, with Paris's screens filled with the gleaming smile of "the peerless, fearless girl" Pearl White, French film theoreticians began to formulate an alternative aesthetic to industrialized cinema. These dissidents thought that for cinema to become a true art it had to transcend the simplistic formulas of the commercial screen.

In 1917, Louis Delluc took the reins of the weekly film magazine *Le Film*, founded in 1914 and first edited by director Henri Diamant-Berger. Among the key writers in his stable, feminist filmmaker and theorist Germaine Dulac asserted the primacy of the critic in reorienting French cinema:

In the current state of cinematography, the work of criticism, analysis, and polemical exchange has as much productive value as the films themselves. I would even go so far as to say they have more value. . . . They direct the cinema toward a specific goal revealing its ideal form, an image of its perfection. . . .[40]

The American Marxist Harry Alan Potamkin hailed Delluc and his cohorts Léon Moussinac and Ricciotto Canudo for building "a body of critics, as authoritative as the critics of the other arts."[41] Delluc found much of value in commercial cinema, but he thought the medium needed to attract the best writers and intellectuals for it to attain the pinnacle of artistic achievement. He soon lured the poets Guillaume Apollinaire (1880–1918) and Louis Aragon, who published his first poetry in *Le Film*, "Charlot sentimental." Aragon candidly told director René Clair in 1923 what he expected from "the seventh art":

I like films without stupidity, the ones in which people kill each other and make love. I like films in which the characters are good-looking and have magnificent skin – you know that can be seen close up. I like Mack Sennett comedies with women in bathing suits, German films with magnificent romantic scenes, the films made by my friend Delluc, in which there are people who desire each other for a whole hour until the people in the audience make their seats rattle.[42]

Aragon argued that cinema had to achieve its own language, neither that of philosophy, theater, nor even poetry:

I like films in which there is no morality, in which vice is not punished, in which there are no fatherland or soldier boys, in which there is no Breton woman at the foot of an outdoor cross, in which there is no philosophy or poetry. Poetry isn't something you look for, it's something you find. . . .[43]

Cinema had begun by being treated as the inferior of literature and theater. The Toulouse-based critic Paul Souday confessed that "a serious critic cannot take an interest in cinema because cinema is less than goat dung."[44] In a symposium of 1912 in *Excelsior,* Xavier Roux bluntly argued that "Cinema favors mental sluggishness." Paul Margueritte suggested that "cinema is able to replace theatre . . . as in the colonies canned foods replace fresh milk and fresh meat." Maurice Leblanc observed that "Film will never be an artistic competitor of theatre. It is a commercial competitor. One quickly wearies of the childish dramas and vaudevilles presently projected on the screens." Albert Guinon, though favorable to the film medium, conceded that "cinema aristocracizes theatre."[45]

Delluc's body of intellectuals soon reversed this earlier debate by claiming the superiority of film over its predecessors in art. The novelist, poet, and director Jean Cocteau explained to Clair in 1923 that indeed cinema had slavishly and incorrectly followed the lead of the theater:

The cinema is in a blind alley. On the first day, since people were dazzled by the invention, the mistake began. They photographed stage plays. Gradually these plays became cinematic plays, but never pure cinema. Such progress can only be disastrous. Better and better: three-dimensionality, color, speech; we will soon have a cinema as dreary as our theatre.[46]

To the extent that U.S. film broke with theatrical conventions, it often won plaudits from the French critical community. D. W. Griffith's *Broken Blossoms* (1919), a title identical to a phrase in a poem of Apollinaire, featured Lillian Gish as a maltreated virgin who is killed by her abusive father. The Chinese man who adores her avenges the crime, but then commits suicide. The fog and shadows, the lyrical fatalism at work, led others to anoint this film the great ancestor of France's poetic realism of the 1930s; that is to say, the aesthetic of *Quai des brumes* and *Le Jour se leve,* those films that later incensed the Vichyite Right. Discussing *Broken Blossoms* in an unpublished lecture of 1926, Jean Grémillon hit on the terminology developed by Delluc's critical movement, the break from theatrical convention: "It is satisfying to find a work where such purely cinematographic means carry expression to its maximum intensity. . . ."[47]

Though they regularly rendered homage to Griffith, Chaplin, and Mack Sennett, the new French critics still saw the necessity for France to achieve a cultural space liberated from American suzerainty. Germaine Dulac made a forceful case in the early days of the Delluc regime, mixing appeals to cinema's higher calling with France's special mission in developing the art. While agreeing that cinema must transcend its theatrical influences and rise "among the superior forms of artistic expression," she soon confessed that "Oh! The Americans have shaken us up a bit!" Yet she remained defiant because:

When we've understood that the cinema is an art form, a French art form, . . . which can expand and affirm the great reputation of our literature in the world, reestablish the uncontested superiority of our taste, and *defend our culture,* we'll have achieved our real goal.[48]

Dulac made the case that the alternative to commercialized U.S. film is an art cinema, one able to mobilize the national culture against the current imposters at the gates. The avenue to achieve this goal became the ciné-club, a movement launched in theory during 1920 by Louis Delluc's *Le Journal du ciné-club* and in practice on 22 April 1921 by the Club des Amis du Septième Art (CASA), founded by Ricciotto Canudo. In the formation of the early ciné-club movement, Dulac propounded a central doctrine of artisanal populism, that film remain a popular art: "A ciné-club is a group of spectators who, without scorning those classic or popular works offered by the official circuits in commercial theaters, are interested in learning about and encouraging the technical and artistic progress of avant-garde films and films of quality, by means of special screenings at irregular intervals. . . ."[49] It sought to restore a dialogue, the communion between artist and audience, ruptured by the impersonal quality of industrial culture. In the last days of the occupation, André Bazin explained this persistent "desire to establish active relations between the work and the public." Though artists such as Brecht tried to rescue contemporary theater from passivity, Bazin held to the conventional wisdom that cinema was more prone to this danger:

Cinema has often been reproached for the passivity of its public, which is simultaneously individualistic and gregarious; this passivity has been contrasted with the communal response of a theatre audience – an audience dominated by the chandelier, that luminous, crystalline, circular, and symmetrical object so dear to Baudelaire – to the performance of actors. . . .[50]

He therefore sought new forms of cultural intervention: "it was . . . necessary that the work no longer be only a disembodied image but that it rediscover something of that human 'presence' of the theatre. This is why the authors, directors, and producers came in person to present their films."[51]

While Bazin was directly referring to the Vichy-era establishment of the Institut des Hautes Études Cinématographiques, his sentiments are in accord with Dulac on the early ciné-clubs. However, the ciné-clubs experienced such prodigious international growth in the 1920s that directors infrequently made it to sessions outside the major metropolitan centers. The clubs in Paris soon approached double figures, Ivor Montagu established the Film Society in London during 1925, and the Brussels ciné-club created its own rattle and gibble-gabble between Belgian and French cinéastes: In late 1926, Dulac, Epstein, Clair, Gance, and others gave lectures at Belgium's Salle de l'Union Coloniale.[52]

Most of the new Parisian clubs lost sight of Delluc's and Dulac's vision of alternative cinema as popular. According to Germaine Dulac, "Certainly we must not divide the cinema into an exceptional class and a commercial class. A popular art, it must reach both the general public and the elite."[53] Instead many clubs retreated into variants of aesthetic elitism. The new owner of Le Studio des Ursulines, established on 21 January 1926, spoke for this current among ciné-club activists: "We want to recruit our audience among the elite of the writers, the artistes, the intellectuals of the Latin quarter. . . ."[54] *Humanité* film critic Léon Moussinac stood out as the main figure who tried to keep the movement riveted to a popular mission. A founder of the Ciné-Club de France (merging his own Club Français du Cinéma with CASA) in 1924, the year Louis Delluc passed away, he soon established the first actively leftist ciné-club in 1928: Les Amis de Spartacus.

Les Amis de Spartacus began by acquiring the largest cinema in Paris's 15th *arrondissement,* the Casino de Grenelle. When it opened on 15 March 1928, the "comrades" were shocked that perhaps four thousand people showed up in hopes of occupying the two thousand seats. The membership rolls by early summer swelled beyond ten thousand and kept growing, estimates ranging from forty to eighty thousand. Logistically this overwhelming demand for Moussinac's cinematic stew posed many problems, at the very least subverting the intimacy necessary for dialogue between artist and audience. The theater responded with multiple screenings and promises of future innovations. Outposts of Les Amis de Spartacus sprung up in the Parisian *banlieu,* working-class suburbia. The organization's own provocative manifesto rallied the partisans of an alternative cinema:

To the public that loves and understands the cinema, that foresees its destiny, there remains only a single means of battling this dictatorship of money: to band together.

Henceforth, it is the purpose of "Amis de Spartacus," through the organization of restricted screenings, to ensure the distribution of major works of the French, German, American, and Soviet cinema.

The future of the cinematographe is certainly in the hands of the public.

It is indispensable that every film advocate work against commercial publicity, against French protectionism, against American colonization.[55]

Les Amis de Spartacus gained momentum during Moussinac's legal struggle with Jean Sapène, editor of the often pro-American French daily *Le Matin*, head of the Cinéromans film production company, and a mini-mogul with a wife who sought to become an international film star. The newspaper and wife-in-movies pairing occasioned comparisons of Sapène to U.S. press magnate William Randolph Hearst, with his mistress Marion Davies. On 15 October 1926, Moussinac had reviewed the American film *The Sea Beast,* starring John Barrymore and then playing in Sapène's Paris theaters. Popularly known by its French title, *Jim le Harponneur,* the *Moby-Dick* spectacle faced an onslaught of Moussinac's criticism on its utter banality, closed with his recommendation that this was a "spectacle cinéma-tographique à siffler sans hesitation" (a cinema show to boo without hesitation). Sapène pressed charges against Moussinac, claiming that the French communist had gone beyond the bounds of free speech by inciting riotous behavior among patrons. In the initial court case decided on 20 March 1928, Sapène prevailed, as Moussinac faced a fine of 500 F. French intellec-tuals and film workers – the first in a group calling itself the Association Amicale de la Critique Cinématographique, the second the Confédération des Travailleurs Intellectuels – rallied around Moussinac. An outpouring of public support came his way, an intervention condemning Sapène for be-traying press freedom and selling out to Hollywood vendors of screen rub-bish. A Paris-based dental surgeon named L. Chambrillon wrote Moussinac a representative letter, telling the indefatigable Marxist that if anyone "must be punished it well is the malefactor who abuses the public trust in produc-ing this con-artistry, because it is all simply a fraud."[56]

Moussinac eventually had this adverse decision reversed in the Court d'Appel de Paris on 12 December 1930. However, his own ciné-club long lay in shambles, the result of naked state repression and the rise of the sound revolution. In the first place, French police warned Moussinac that they would no longer tolerate his massive importation of Soviet films, banned by the rightist censorship board for commercial cinemas and permitted in the ciné-club only by the ruse that these were "private" presentations. The police placed underground infiltrators in Moussinac's club and promised to disrupt his presentations regularly if he failed to obey their cease and desist orders. Within six months, Moussinac and his cadres cracked, surrendering to the superior might of the French gendarmes. Les Amis de Spartacus shut down.

As for the sound revolution, the ciné-clubs had been able to provide a base of support for alternative cinema; but the talkie caused a giant leap in film costs as well as capital investment in retrofitting existing theaters with new equipment. The drain of resources for patent fees to mostly U.S.

and German firms pained French producers and exhibitors. Individual film houses continued to have success with silent works, but public demand overall drifted to the talkie. The increased capital costs extinguished several theaters and ciné-clubs.

Intellectually, however, many artists, filmmakers, and partisans of the ciné-club reacted with visceral hostility to the talkie, believing that it returned cinema to the retrograde standards of its predecessor, theater. In Clair's dialogues in 1923, Cocteau voiced fears of an imminent talkie revolution. The artist Fernand Léger affirmed his sentiments in observing that "As long as the film is based on fiction or the theatre, it will be nothing." He believed that voice annihilated the more authentic cinematic language, as he proclaimed that cinema will attain the artistic sublime when actors "learn to shut their mouths and make appropriate gestures." The writer Pierre Mac Orlan demanded that silent cinema capture art's "secret rhythms which music has already grasped, but which the art of writing cannot render because language imposes a rigid framework that cannot be dislocated." Léon Pierre-Quint explained that "The first automobile was indistinguishable from the horse-drawn cab. Film is too much like the theatre and newspaper serial, themselves outworn genres." Weary of having to repeat "a truism, but one that should be repeated at every opportunity and inscribed in every studio," Philippe Soupault lamented that "Filmmakers are making an effort to limit the cinema, to reduce it to the proportions of the theatre." Finally, in calling for "an art of pure cinema," the master of belles-lettres Paul Valéry proclaimed that "This art should steer clear of those – theatre or novel – that deal in speech." The politicized Left tended to focus on the talkie's increase of costs and strengthening of Hollywood-style monopoly capitalism; the literary avant-garde preferred to reject it on purely aesthetic grounds.[57]

Surrounded by a phalanx of intellectuals and artists once dedicated to the artistic integrity of silent cinema and its incommensurability with theater, the ciné-clubs now beat a temporary retreat from their hegemonic project of remaking the medium. During 1932–3, Moussinac largely abandoned cinema in order to study Soviet theater; even his colleague Georges Sadoul, once called "the Benedictine" of French cinema by René Clair for his seeming religious devotion to viewing all movies, took a hiatus from the silver screen.[58] He admitted that his exhaustion predated Al Jolson's talking debut in 1927: "I saw none of Vigo's films in the thirties (during the last years of his life) because I had more or less stopped being interested in the cinema between 1926 and 1934. . . ."[59] The ciné-clubs, though in retreat, did not completely expire; and Vigo's call for "a social cinema" in 1930 would later in the decade rally those committed to connecting art film with the popular audience. Even Clair, who had spoken of "the talking picture" as "a fearful monster, an unnatural creation, thanks to which the screen would become a poor theatre," soon mastered the art of combining image and dialogue.[60] He still kept up a furious debate with Marcel Pagnol, who offended the avant-garde with his belief in the primacy of dialogue and cinema's need to ape the theater.

While the avant-garde and the Left appeared to be temporarily derailed from their cinematic project, the group with new vitality in the 1928–35 conjuncture was the Roman Catholic Church. Following the Belgium-based OCIC's first international Catholic congress on cinema in April 1928 at The Hague (see Chapter 8), French Catholicism held its own Congress in Paris during early November 1928. Featuring reports on educational film (P. Jalabert), a Fédération des Salles Catholiques (Chanoine Simonin), and international aspects of the film problem (Monsignor Beaupin), the Congrès Catholique du Cinéma gave French Catholics an introduction to Chanoine Joseph Reymond, secretary general of the CCC (the Comité Catholique du Cinématographe, a name later changed to the Centrale Catholique de Collaboration). The Archbishop of Paris, Cardinal Dubois, held the first "Messe du Cinéma" (High Mass of Cinema), a ceremony marking the blessing of cinema by the church. This became an annual ritual in France, attracting thousands, including film producers who faced billingsgate from Moussinac and others loudly claiming hostility to medieval obscurantism. The French delegates proposed to reassemble at the next international cinema congress to be held in Munich in June 1929.[61]

Catholicism's Indian Summer in France radiated from a new array of publications: *Politique* founded in 1927; *La Vie intellectuelle*, 1928; *L'Aube, Esprit*, and *Choisir*, all three in 1932; and *Terre nouvelle*, 1935. In formulating Catholic thought on cinema, *Choisir* and *Esprit* were the most significant, the former family-oriented and conservative, the latter influencing the sophisticated intelligentsia and after World War II veering leftward.

Choisir and *Esprit* maintained a curious orientation to the ideological formation that has been designated "artisanal populism." *Esprit* made a strong push for the artisan against the dehumanizing industrial order, but its high-flown intellectualism generally avoided flights toward populism. *Choisir* by contrast made a distinctly populist appeal for the French public to rise up and demand better films; but in its embrace of modernity, the weekly rarely attacked industrial methods, and indeed praised the Hays Office and the American film majors for cleansing films of prurient filth. Although it encouraged Catholics to improve film as an art, *Choisir* did not

seek to drive a wedge between industrial and artisanal producers. While believing in the revival of French cinema and the promotion of nationalism,
delivered with a strong dash of anti-Soviet and anti-German populism,
Choisir found itself in a painful dilemma: Overwhelmingly it gave U.S. film
a higher moral rating than French film, thus discouraging family attendance
at the national cinema. According to figures assembled by Jean Morienval
in *Choisir* (9 August 1936), few French films were compatible with family
viewing:[62]

	French	U.S.
Able to be viewed by all	20%	50%
For adults only	25%	40%
À *rejeter* (rejected)	55%	10%

Ninety percent of U.S. films received full or qualified approval, double
the rate of France's domestic production. *Choisir* tried to counteract this
sad state of affairs by sponsoring its own films, in particular Léon Poirier's
L'Appel du silence, designed to give audiences a more favorable view of
French colonialism than what had been on display in Hollywood's Anglo-
phile imperial cycle. *Choisir* argued that in a France divided and on the
brink of civil war, perhaps the empire could rally all patriots to a renewal
of unified national purpose. Catholics used an advance subscription campaign to finance Poirier's production. Meanwhile, the Catholic film movement had built up a few hundred *salles des oeuvres,* rooms at small parishes
used for the projection of movies, and, more substantial, a circuit of *salles
familiales,* approximately 350 cinemas that presented morally wholesome
films fit for families. Assembled under regional associations, the *salles familiales* had the following distribution: 60 in the Parisian zone, which also
included the Ardennes and Vosge; 45 in Lille, linked to Nord, Pas-de-Calais,
and Somme; 130 in Franche-Comté, Alsace-Lorraine, Lyons, Savoie, and
Luxembourg; 50 in Rennes, including Brittany and Normandy; and 50 in
Bordeaux, including Bordelais, the Pyrenées, and the Vendée.[63] Referring
directly to *Choisir,* Léon Moussinac grudgingly admitted that the Catholic
movement had made an impact on both the government and domestic film
production:

The High Mass of Cinema, organized each year at the Church of the Madeleine by
the Catholic committee on the cinema [CCC], is turning out a considerable volume
of propaganda; all the official representatives of the cinema and the government participate in this ceremony to which the church gives a solemn character through the

presence of its highest prelates. The Catholic cinema produces a huge number of films with the collaboration of the industry, which finds it profitable to do so. . . . Catholic patronage chiefly uses 16mm films, whose network of distribution is organized to perfection.[64]

While it occasionally put forth Catholic social theory critical of the excesses of capitalism and communism, *Choisir* generally did not flinch in the face of industrialized culture. In contrast, *Esprit* adopted the consecrated task of healing the wounds of industrial civilization, an enterprise that would require new modalities of cultural expression. Its cinema critics, Roger Leenhardt and later André Bazin, emerged as seminal influences on the postwar European new wave, particularly in the latter's call for a "pure" cinematic language. Though counseling the avant-garde to embrace the talkie and raise cinema to a higher level of realism, Leenhardt devoted himself to restoring the link between artist and audience ruptured by industrial civilization. Foreshadowing Bazin's pronouncement on overcoming the loss of intimacy otherwise belonging to the live theater (see earlier in this section), Leenhardt in 1935 explained that obviously an audience

can be moved by a great film without knowing anything special about the cinema. But then a specific kind of beauty escapes you. . . . The modest, intimate school for spectators that I would like to initiate has no other pretention than to help those who love the cinema, in some small way, to seize that beauty "in the text itself."[65]

Bazin helped formulate the theory of the director as auteur, the artisan who produced texts almost as surely as the novelist through "the *caméra-stylo.*" As the scholar Dudley Andrew expressed it: "'*Le caméra-stylo*' was a battle cry demanding that the cinema of the future come not from an institutional factory, but directly from the mind and sensibility of the artist."[66] Bazin published in numerous forums, including the communist *L'Écran français,* where he delivered devastating attacks on the poverty of industrial culture. In the absurdly titled "Entomology of the Pin-Up Girl" (1946), he scientifically dissected the industrial manufacture of an artificial being with teeth perpetually gleaming and breasts of walloping size:

A wartime product created for the benefit of the American soldiers swarming to a long exile at the four corners of the world [who] soon became an industrial product, subject to well-fixed norms and as stable in quality as peanut butter or chewing gum. Rapidly perfected, like the jeep, among those things specifically stipulated for modern American military sociology, she is a perfectly harmonized product of given racial, geographic, social and religious influences.[67]

For defenders of French culture, its artisans of the screen would have to find avenues for creativity against industrial culture's unrelenting imposition of standardization and passive audiences. While the film critics, activists, and theoreticians formulated their prescriptions, French film producers early in the talkie revolution made a determined effort to distinguish their product from the industrialized Hollywood import. Less daunted by René Jeanne's claim in 1931 that soon all the world would be speaking "American," France's directors realized that the talking revolution could be turned to national advantage, as there were some audiences that craved representation of local culture.

The French producers relied on two claims to distinguish their product from industrialized Hollywood: (1) a more sustained output of works on provincial French themes and (2) a cinema of quality. Films on provincial French themes sometimes did well in the national market but posed challenges for export. Certain regions, notably Brittany, continued to protest against the dominant Parisian bias of French film; but Pagnol, among others, achieved international prominence with works set in southern France. Paramount, with its Paris affiliate, had Korda codirect Pagnol's *Marius* (1931), a belated recognition by Hollywood that "films with a strictly local background are preferred to those adapted," declared *Variety* (10 December 1930). "We are receiving increasing competition from native producers and will have to change."[68]

As for producing a cinema of quality,[69] this is an area where France tried to make a virtue of its handicap in capital and technological investment by stressing the creativity of its artisanal battalions. The distinguishing features of its cinema of quality included the prominence of its scriptwriters, Charles Spaak, Henri Jeanson, and Jacques Prévert, whose artistic integrity was respected by not subjecting their work to the sometimes dozens of rewrites by teams of script experts employed by Hollywood's machinery. Another distinguishing characteristic was set design much more faithful to France, an area mastered by the Polish-Russian Lazare Meerson and those other eastern European émigrés so detested by the shock troops of fascism. Though many Russian actors of the 1920s saw their careers shipwrecked in France by the talking revolution, the émigré set designers floated comfortably on currents favoring European forms of simplicity and authenticity. Meanwhile, French cinema attained a reputation for being an "actor's cinema," as its performers could move among different production houses and ateliers much more easily than the interwar Hollywood stars who lived a life of serfdom to the studios. French cinema in its desire for authenticity also made sustained use of nonprofessional actors, a practice of Renoir in movies like *Toni* (1935) that would receive later vindication in the craft of postwar Italy's neorealism (i.e., De Sica's rejection of proposals to use Cary

Grant as the star of *Ladri di biciclette* [*The Bicycle Thief*]). The prominence of the nonprofessional actor in many European art forms became one indicator of the break from manufactured aura and glamour. As Renoir expressed it:

Why do I avoid making films with actors? Because, with three exceptions, Wallace Beery, Eric von Stroheim, and Charlie Chaplin, the actor is a ruse; he who can develop several different characters is the exception. Amateurs well-used have a natural, unequalled sensitivity. The simpler, and permit me to say, the more unrefined they are, the more sincere they are. Education inhibits or destroys natural expression. That is why I prefer filming amateurs.[70]

Finally, quasi-documentary depiction and portrayals of everyday life, accenting the peculiarities of the French, were countered to Hollywood's cosmopolitan glamour and sometimes inauthentic sterotypes ill-suited to convey a sense of place. Again and again the German philosopher Theodor Adorno criticized the U.S. culture industry for being "destitute of meaning," a quality derived from the absence of authentic place:

A number of years ago in Los Angeles, I attended a performance of Johann Strauss' *La Chauve souris*, which I had loved so much for its music in Europe. Such a piece is related – not only in terms of its audience, but also in terms of its very form – to many conventions and traditions. When one sees it suddenly detached from its context, in Los Angeles, where no one knows about or even suspects the least "context," which is of course also communicated in the piece itself, then this work, in all its fallibility and feebleness, fades out on an impoverished stage, a bit pitiable and cold . . . one does not know what to do with it.[71]

French film production tried to show itself soaked in domestic traditions and conventions, infusing the work with the nuance and context that Adorno would later claim was stripped in the manufacture of processed culture.

Even the Marxist Left, which had started out the decade thoroughly alienated from the "social fascist" nature of France's bourgeois-democratic heritage, came to embrace French culture with a flag-waving passion and reverence, a transition from exclusive proletarian solidarity to a posture of Popular Front nationalist-populism. In 1931, Louis Aragon had regularly expressed prevailing contempt for French symbols such as the *tricouleur* and "La Marseillaise," reflected in his notorious verse "Front Rouge," which gained for him a five-year suspended prison sentence:

Bring down the cops . . .
Fire on Léon Blum
Fire on Boncour Frossard Déat
Fire on the trained bears of [. . .] social democracy . . .[72]

Starting in 1931, the head of the Parti Communiste Français, Maurice Thorez, recognizing the PCF's declining success, decided that culture would be a means for Marxist cadres to reconnect with French society. In 1932, the PCF supported the construction of the Association of Revolutionary Artists and Writers (AEAR), banding together all intellectuals seeking to arrest the spread of fascism. Nonparty intellectuals such as Malraux and André Gide signed its petitions against Nazism in 1933, and Gide himself joined the editorial board of its journal *Commune*. Though the journal in 1934 still portrayed itself as "against bourgeois culture; for revolutionary culture," the thaw continued in February of that year when the PCF's key spokesperson on cultural policy, Paul Vaillant-Couturier, said the AEAR sought "fraternally and objectively all intellectuals whatever your hesitations and objections" who seek "cultural combat" against the fascist menace. "We do not insist on a certificate of Marxist faith," he added in October. By August 1936 the AEAR had come full circle by defining itself simply as a "French literary review for the defense of culture." When the AEAR set up Maisons de Culture in 1935–8, eventually attaining ninety thousand members, *Commune* stipulated that they should exclude "political" issues in favor of culture. French ways of life became celebrated: Cathedrals were now part of the people's heritage, novels exhibited the true spirit of the French people, and Vaillant-Couturier hailed "the eternal France" of the countryside and the prehistoric paintings in the caves of Dordogne.[73]

Léon Moussinac, a schoolmate of Vaillant-Couturier, had a pivotal role in the AEAR. Assisting in the founding during November 1935 of its new cinema section, the Alliance du Cinéma Independent (ACI), he soon decried the French censorship board for banning its first major feature, *La Vie est à nous* (1936), a work that contrasted the richness of France – "A multitude of anonymous architects, sculptors, and builders in the Middle Ages built cathedrals, like those at Chartres, Rouen, Reims, Sens, Amiens, like Notre Dame in Paris, whose beauty is a tribute to the genius of our country" – with the perfidious selfishness of the two hundred families who purportedly rule France. Léon Blum's regime frustrated his Popular Front allies by not reversing the decision of the censorship board.[74]

The ACI thus changed its name to Ciné-Liberté in taking up the defense of cultural freedom and the production of new films. In the context of France's debate between industrial and artisanal methods in movie production, Ciné-Liberté led to an efflorescence of film and cultural discourse on the glories of the French artisan.

In anticipation of the 150th anniversary of the French Revolution, Ciné-Liberté led a subscription campaign for the production of *La Marseillaise* by Jean Renoir. Due to the growing unpopularity of Blum's government, the subscription drive fizzled, insufficient to cover enough of the production's costs. *Choisir* taunted the Left for failing to acknowledge that Catholics had pioneered this innovation in escaping the finance constraints of the commercial industry.[75] Nevertheless, Renoir completed the film, and it remains a central document in France's adoration of the heroic artisan, both in the memory of the revolution and in the strategy of motion-picture production.

Renoir declared that *La Marseillaise* has the simple aim of showing that "the Revolution was brought about by normal, intelligent, and pleasant people." The Right had constantly demonized the revolutionary as "a sort of ravenous, hirsute, dirty, ragged bandit who spends his days inflicting immoral, indecent, and bloody injuries." He denounced the royalist pamphleteer Jean Gabriel Peltier for feeding fears of foreigners with his claim that "The Revolution of August 10 was the product of a hundred conspiring brigands" who "called upon Maltese, Genoese, Piedmontese, upon some 250 Italians under the auspices of Petion and Santerre, who suddenly became masters of the General Assembly. . . ."[76]

Renoir sent Mme Jean-Paul Dreyfus to research the background of the five hundred volunteers in the Marseilles Battalion. Through her work, he showed that the members were hardly bandits but former military who had to show themselves free of debts and criminality. Its social base comprised military officers, public officials, all sorts of respectable artisans – carpenters, stonemasons, coopers, metalworkers – and numerous farmers and peasants.

Following the film's premiere, Louis Aragon hailed Renoir for his meticulous artisanal film craft in contrast to Hollywood's inauthentic industrialized methods:

Jean Renoir's great miracle – which by its mere existence shows up Hollywood-style "reconstructions" for academic fakery – is that despite the costumes and sets and the theme of *La Marseillaise,* he has made a film so current and powerful, so human that you are taken, carried away . . . as though it was our own life that was at issue. And, in fact, it is.[77]

In contrast to Alexander Korda, who declared that foreigners were better able to decipher the qualities of national character that could then appeal to international audiences, Renoir believed that a filmmaker's duty is to explode stereotypes. Korda stressed the standardization and stereotyping patterns identified with industrial cultural production; Renoir countered with the artisanal stamp of the unique individual, the hand-crafted article.

As he explained his distaste for the stereotyping and standardization of industrial cinema:

[T]hese simplifications are so facile. They enable people to recognize a Breton by his bag-pipes, an Alsatian by the ribbon in her hair, a Basque by his beret, China by its pagodas, America by its chewing-gum, Germany by its sauerkraut, Italy by its macaroni, Spain by its toreadors, the English by their big teeth. . . .
The misfortune is that these simplifications are borrowed from clichés which flower on the summits of history, like thick tufts of mistletoe, this parasitic plant which grows easily on a forgotten tree in a corner of the forest. And this is why we prefer little trees, with their true foliage.
In the case of the French Revolution which is the object of our film, these parasitic plants have reached vertiginous heights. . . .[78]

In his war against clichés and standardized, processed history, Renoir ended up angering certain left comrades by his self-described portrayal of Louis XVI as momentarily "poignant," other aristocrats as figures of good character, and a *citoyen* admonishing people to avoid automatically assuming that a priest is an enemy of the revolution by his cassock. Renoir believed in finding some redeeming qualities in everyone, save perhaps Marie-Antoinette, who is portrayed, declares Renoir protégé François Truffaut, as "beautiful, but something of a sourpuss." She even opposes Louis's decision to wield a toothbrush, a new hygienic fad of the late Enlightenment. "I will gladly attempt this brushing," he retorts.[79] In contrast to Renoir's self-portrayal as a meticulous researcher, however, Roger Leenhardt of *Esprit* railed against the film's reign of historical error: "He has faithfully followed, not history, but legend. His vision of the Revolution is that of our children's textbooks: a sentimental and idealized Jacobinism."[80]

While cinema of the Popular Front is sometimes seen as full of loving sentiments toward the proletariat, the reality is that very few films treated the industrial working class – a mere nine during the years 1936–9, according to a historical specialist on the period, Julian Jackson. Renoir and Carné were involved in the majority of them, but a closer examination shows a certain distance from proletarian solidarity. Renoir's *Crime de Monsieur Lange*, filmed in the autumn of 1935 and first shown in late January 1936, involves a small printing operation that is closer to an artisanal workshop than a large proletarianized factory. Carné and Renoir involve Jean Gabin as an apparent proletarian, but these films are predicated on his loner qualities and his trademark gestures, *la colère explosive* (the explosive anger), that are his signature of authenticity. He is no model of Popular Front solidarity and proletarian bonhomie, whether as an army deserter in *Quai des brumes*, a fugitive bunkered alone and against the police in *Le Jour se leve*, a locomotive engineer riddled with epilepsy as well as the avenging horror of his family's alcoholism in *La Bête humaine* (1938), or the vagabond figure of Pepel in *Les Bas-Fonds* (1936) – this last work populated by what Claude De Givray called two decades later "a remarkable gallery of dissatisfied, fiercely individualistic, nicely revolutionary characters, more sociable than socialist. . . ." None of these films has a protagonist with a prayer in hell of building socialism in this lifetime, much to the chagrin of those agitprop leftists who had collaborated with Renoir in the creation of *La Vie est à nous*.[81]

Renoir liked to claim that his favorite character in all his films was Boudu, the vagabond played by Marcel Simon who will not bathe, tears up books, spits in the house, and generally will not conform to bourgeois (let alone proletarian) standards of decorum. The director believed that the film *Boudu sauvé des eaux* (1932) defended an anarchic streak in human beings, the right to refuse to be part of a society that rigidly demanded compliance. Vigo, the son of the anarchist Miguel Almereyda (Eugène Vigo), also heralded the spirit of rebellion in *Zéro de conduite* (1933), albeit anarchy carried out with greater solidarity among the schoolchildren than could ever be salvaged from Boudu. Both Vigo and Renoir, then, combined a defense of artisanal cinema with the celebration of nonconformity and the spirit of anarchy.

Curiously on the French Right, Bardèche and Brasillach both championed artisanal over industrial methods in film, and both cited their devotion to anarchy as the foundation of this commitment. Though *Zéro de conduite* had been banned in France, with heavy support from rightist forces, they called it "a remarkable gesture of revolt, of sarcastic, humiliated and fun-loving youth."[82] Brasillach's constant calls in *Je suis partout* for an artisanal mode of production against the "modernist" Jewish forces often spilled over into his analysis of cinema. Among its virtues, artisanal production could best harness the energies of youth, otherwise dissipated and beaten down under industrial regimentation. François Vinneuil (Rebatet) blamed elements of the French film industry for forsaking the healthier artisanal mode in favor of "the big industry model of Hollywood," which he called a structure conducive to the rule of a "bunch of slick operators and *métèques* [dirty foreigners]."[83]

The social bases of anarchism are usually strong in European countries that have undergone mild industrialization and where protectionism typically maintains small-scale, artisanal factories. Italy and Spain are thus usually regarded as havens for anarchism. In contrast, those European nations with large-scale and advanced industries have a sizable proletariat that becomes the social base for socialist and social-democratic ideologies; for example, the Social Democratic Party (SPD) of Germany and the Labour Party of Great Britain. France is sometimes lumped in with Germany and Britain because of the strength of its socialist movements and an industrial might far ahead of its Latin neighbors to the south; but it should be observed how deeply entrenched artisanal methods and social organization permeated French capitalism. For instance, automobiles, one of the most advanced industries of the interwar period, had no large-scale producers in France with the exception of Citroën. Instead small firms dominated French auto manufacturing: 155 companies in 1914, 60 in 1932, and 31 in 1939.[84] There is a pattern toward rationalization, but it is clearly much slower than in Britain, Germany, and the United States. Anarchosyndicalism flapped and fluttered into decline in France during the opening two decades of the twentieth century, an outcome that may have been aided by the wild oscillations from socialism to fascism by its intellectuals, such as Georges Sorel, and its leadership's hardened devotion to productivist ideologies celebrating industrialism, themes prominent in the oratory of carpenter Léon Jamin of the Confédération Générale du Travail (CGT). Too quick to discard their artisanal birthright in favor of unleashing France's productive forces, Jamin and Sorel may have detached themselves from anarchosyndicalism's natural social base. The southern European communist parties, while still enthusiastic about the productive forces, learned to protect the small farmer and shopkeeper, gaining some unlikely political allies. In the field of culture, Communist Party theoreticians often spoke for the artisanal producer against the forces of monopoly capitalism, a thinly veiled reference to Hollywood.

When Gaumont and Pathé–Natan collapsed in the mid-1930s, PCF loyalist Sadoul later indicated that he much preferred the free hand given to the artisans over any restoration of France's aspiring monopoly capitalists:

The French monopolies and the international combines were succeeded by artisans without honesty or imagination, whose checks were issued with insufficient funds, whose fictitious companies were established in furnished rooms, who were involved in productions without capital or guarantors, in bankruptcies and even swindles.
  In fact, however, the reign of the hucksters had fewer disadvantages than that of those living corpses, the putrefying big companies. The film market enjoyed free, or at least relatively free, competition.[85]

In the absence of "putrefying big companies," French film production faced an array of challenges intrinsic to most artisanal regimes, hundreds of firms producing single or, at best, two to five pictures:[86]

1. The paucity of technical personnel with stable, long-term contracts and employment.
2. The failure to achieve strong capital investment because most fly-by-night operations simply rent studio space and equipment, typically on credit.
3. The drainage of wealth toward large foreign firms in the form of patent and other fees for technical expertise and gadgetry.
4. The weakness of coordination among distribution, exhibition, and production. The lack of deep advertising resources forces many movie enterprises to be dependent for promotion on exhibitors and other volatile forces: word of mouth and the generosity of critics. The unstable linkage between production and distribution, a handicap at home, is often deadly in export.

France's filmmakers fondly look back on the 1930s as the "Golden age of French film." Though Sadoul elsewhere found a mixture of delight in "the reign of the street vendors and speculators," the French state continued to fear the anarchic boom-and-bust cycles and the lurking prominence of the Hollywood colossus.[87] If the artists and intellectuals found in artisanal populism a legitimation for their production regime and resistance to Hollywood, the state sought a path toward order and stability – an elusive destination for the contentious French.

CHAPTER TEN

France and the Politics of State Intervention

Twentieth-century France frequently rallied to the defense of the small shop-keeper and the artisan, bulwarks of a distinctive French way of life. Laws requiring bakers to sell bread free of preservatives protect the baguette against the horror of Wonder Bread, regarded in France as a styrofoam block injected with minerals. Restrictions abound on vending machines, re-ducing the ubiquity of Coca-Cola and maintaining the friendly local tavern owner. All kinds of padlock laws stipulate who can sell certain goods.

The interwar artisans of film were handicapped in securing similar pro-tection. The hostility to the Jewish and émigré presence in France's industry left some political blocs less certain that protectionism in this sector de-fended the French way of life. Hence, the Vichyite Right's glee that only with the war's *épuration* (purging) of the industry could there ensue a full-blooded regime of both aid and protection. Even without the racialist back-lash, France's film industry remained wracked by divisions that spelled acri-mony when governments took bold action.

Well prior to the collapse of GFFA and Pathé–Natan in the mid-1930s, France had come to rely on the small company for the lion's share of domes-tic movies. Dozens of microfirms, some assembled for one picture, carrying such ephemeral titles as the "Société de production du film *Vidocq*" (1938) and "Société de production du film *Brazza*" (1939), generally backed pro-tection.[1] In the field of national distribution, seven of the thirteen active firms in France by 1935 were either U.S.-owned or adopted arrangements placing them in bed with U.S. interests.[2] This sector had trouble rallying in unison behind state activism. Finally, exhibitors regularly denounced the government and production interests for pursuing quotas through *con-tingentement* legislation. Calling proposed *contingentement* provisions in 1932 that would force foreign producers to import more French films "out-rageous, monstrous," Léon Brezillon, president of the Syndicat Français et de la Fédération Française des Directeurs de Théatres Cinématographiques, had his members flood the government with telegrams carrying predictions of rack and ruin.[3]

All three sectors agreed that the state overtaxed the exhibitors, resulting in diminished revenue for producers and distributors. During World War I, the French state required resources for the war emergency, but once these were in place it was hard to scale them back. Cinema owners had to pay both special national and municipal taxes, rates ratcheted progressively higher by the size of the venue and especially location in Paris. The U.S. Commerce Department's annual film report called "Cinema taxation in France . . . extremely high," ranging from 11 to 37 percent of total gross revenue.[4] Most large Parisian theaters paid well in excess of 30 percent. The French state in the interwar period barely gave any resources back to the industry, save for sponsoring a few educational films and works such as Renoir's *Le Bled* (1929), a feature glorifying the French conquest of Algeria on its hundredth anniversary. The national government in the mid-1930s granted non-Paris municipalities permission to reduce the taxation load on cinema, but with the proviso that it had to be replaced with new sources of local revenue. Many localities remained content to drain the entertainment vendors.

Though Parisians received no "state" tax relief, the "poor" tax of Paris, assessed on all amusements since the French revolution, was reduced from its historic level of 10 percent to 8.75 percent starting 28 March 1937. Meanwhile, the *patente* or license tax clearly sought to hit cinema harder than "legitimate theater": One owner explained that when he switched from a thespian stage to the silver screen, the state raised his *patente* from 1,400 F a year to 15,000–16,000 F. Overall, special cinema taxes (the poor and state taxes) plucked 70 million F from Paris and 110 million F from the rest of the country, thus raising 180 million F for the entire nation in 1937.[5]

Similar to many European countries, France witnessed outcries of an unchecked American rampage due to the extraordinary unity of its industry through the Hays Office. The German state established a mandatory Filmkammer designed to match swords with the Americans. The French sought organization to accomplish this end, though on the one issue on which there was unity – overtaxation – the state provided only cosmetic relief. During the 1920s, when the United States achieved a 75 percent share of the French market, the high taxation enjoyed support as a means of retaliating against the transatlantic invaders. However, in the 1930s, France built up considerable strength in its domestic market, going from 10 percent of the local

market in 1926 to 33 percent in 1936. Moreover, the lists of the most popular films overwhelmingly favored French movies: eighteen out of the top
twenty in 1936, nineteen out of twenty in 1937, and seveneen out of twenty
in 1938, according to the annual exhibitors' survey conducted by *La Cinématographie française*.[6] Thus the taxation policy, once an irritant to mainly
American producers and French exhibitors, now became for France's producers a clumsy redress, a means of shooting oneself in the foot.

The French state pressed on with schemes to attain industry unity. In
July 1936, Guy de Carmoy issued a report with a plan toward that end.
The industry set up that year a Confédération Générale du Cinéma (CGC)
close to his guideline, a kind of Filmkammer under private auspices, in contrast to Germany's heavy-handed statist approach. The CGC looked as
though it unified all French sectors with its four wings:

1. La Chambre Syndicale des Industries Techniques de Cinématographie,
   representing technicians and raw film manufacturers;
2. La Chambre Syndicale Française de la Production de Films, rallying the
   producers;
3. La Chambre Syndicale des Distributeurs de Films, which indeed included the U.S.-owned distributors in France's market; and
4. L'Union des Chambres Syndicales Françaises des Théâtres Cinématographiques, supposedly speaking for the exhibitors.[7]

Instead of bringing together the various branches, however, the CGC
encountered an industry sprouting and proliferating disunity, as exhibitors
declared that the organization spoke for the most protectionist wing of the
producers. The heated politics of the Popular Front soon dissipated any
good will among the industry's contending factions. Though the Popular
Front era witnessed a French film renaissance, the artistic triumphs did not
come from a state energized on behalf of national culture. Instead the highly charged politicization of all questions built support for ambitious demands followed by ferocious resistance from those outside the interventionist coalition. Socialist MP Paul Faure, a gifted orator, friend of Léon Blum,
and subsequently a roving minister of State without portfolio, proclaimed
to *Cinémonde* in April 1936 that

if one day our party acquired total control, it will make of the cinema a state institution. For it is impossible for a government that desires to initiate a new social
order to allow a means of propaganda as powerful as the cinema to remain in the
hands of groups who may well have interests opposed to its own.[8]

The Socialist Left spoke of nationalizing a fortified GFFA corporation,
which could allow for a vertically integrated firm to pursue a coordinated

policy in home and foreign markets. Low capital investment and continuous financial crisis in the industry kept alive this wager on the strong, a model appealing to those artisanal producers who blamed commercialization, not bigness, as the true enemy of art. Capitalist-oriented production shops and exhibitors spoke out angrily about their own fears of "Soviet-style" repression of freedom, especially when Robert Jarville of the Confédération Générale du Travail (CGT) unveiled before the Renaitour Senate inquiry of 1937 the union's scheme for a totally nationalized industry. Calling for a "Plan de construction économique pour la création d'un cinéma national," Jarville as secretary-general of the Syndicat Général des Travailleurs de l'Industrie du Film outlined the following program:[9]

1. *"Nationalization of the means of production"*: This would be carried out through "the total nationalization of laboratories, studios," followed by an indemnity paid over several years to their current owners.
2. *"Nationalized production"*: Through "an annual state credit," production would expand, "opposing . . . all conformist film." Because newsreels have such an impact on public opinion, a nationalized firm should replace the current five capitalist giants in the field: Éclair–Journal, Pathé–Natan, France–Actualités, Fox–Movietone, and Paramount.
3. *Control of private production:* In order to escape "the influence of forces hostile to social progress," scripts would be submitted for preproduction screening.
4. *Control of distribution:* Blaming distribution for a "great part of the responsibility in cinema's degradation," he called for a campaign against "scandalous" discounts and wheeling and dealing, as well as the creation of a body that could sell French films in foreign markets.
5. *Control over film exhibition:* Suggesting that some exhibitors cheated producers by dubious reporting of receipts, he also demanded a fairer process of programming and launching of films.
6. *State Institute of Cinematographic Technique:* A school for the training of directors and technicians was to be created.

Looming over this hexagonal assemblage was to be a tripartite management council called Le Conseil de Gestion de l'Industrie Nationalisée, representing producers (mainly from his Syndicat Général), consumers (Ciné-Liberté), and state personnel. Jarville argued that in the transitional phase to socialism the state should nationalize GFFA. He also asked for the government "to suppress the double program," as twin showing of films encouraged exhibitors to seek loads of cheap imports. For Jarville, the artisanal regime had flunked on one important count: Though France needed 450 films per year in its market, the slow-paced artisanal producers at home could only muster approximately 135. He believed that a muscularized GFFA and national production regime could make 240 films, substantially eroding Hollywood domination.

As the Popular Front continued to wither away, Jarville's proposals appeared dead on arrival. Long on providing forums for vaporous pronouncement and short on implementing cinema policy, the Blum government sat listlessly as the national censorship board threatened harsher crackdown on those films maligning the military and the imperial order. On 7 May 1936, two days after the Popular Front's electoral triumph, the censorship board fired a warning shot at foreign producers: A company that produced a film injurious to France would have the rest of its production barred completely from the national market – even if the offending movie had never appeared on French soil. On 25 October 1937, Edmond Sée, president of the Commission de Contrôle, gave his aforementioned directive announcing:

A. In the future visas will be absolutely refused by the Commission of Film Censorship for:
   1. Films having a tendency to ridicule the Army or capable of diminishing its prestige.
   2. Films liable to shock the national sentiments of foreigners and thereby bring about diplomatic incidents.
   3. Films showing armed attacks (hold-ups), burglaries with housebreaking, and any similar attempts which might have injurious influence on the minds of youths.
B. Visas will only in exceptional cases be granted for:
   1. War or spy films, which, for some time, have had a tendency to increase.
   2. All films based on military or police stories other than those mentioned above.[10]

Sée demanded that any production concerning "National Defense, great State institutions, French or foreign high officials" should be submitted to his office "before proceeding to produce the film." The partisans of Ciné-Liberté wearied of Blum's unwillingness to curb this zealotry. Catholic *Choisir*, in contrast, complained that the state had been willing to use censorship in defense of political institutions but let it lapse when it came to films of a sexually explicit nature. In relative terms, French censorship between the wars stood among the world's most libertarian on sexual matters, a stance that hurt its film industry's prospects in the export trade. Belgium and overseas Québec, two regions receptive to French film, regularly sent France's movies back to be sanitized. France's own treaties with the United States had been based on *contingentement*, an export strategy that forced Les États-Unis to take one French film for every seven licenses granted to

Hollywood products in France. The 1:7 ratio had been accepted in 1928, after previous French proposals for a 1:4 trading regime had met Hays's call for a total boycott. In any case, *contingentement* deteriorated into something of a joke, as U.S. firms imported the cheapest French works in order to grab licenses and, as noted, the sexual spiciness of the French product rendered numerous works unacceptable to both Joseph I. Breen of the MPPDA and any active state or city censorship boards. In film negotiations with the United States, France thus supplemented *contingentement* with tightened ceilings limiting the number of foreign film imports: A generous limit maximum of 500 foreign films from 1 March 1928 to 30 September 1930 was soon trimmed, at one point dwindling to a six-month quota of 70 non-French films starting on 1 July 1933. This eventually increased to a six-month *contingent* of 94 U.S. films on 21 July 1934. The 188 annual film limit by and large remained in place till the Second World War. In reality, the U.S. managed to export slightly over the limit for most of the decade. The French twice in the 1930s granted liberalized Hollywood access in exchange for freer importation of wines and champagnes, a post-Prohibition boom for France's wineries. A leading economic historian of the U.S. film industry estimates that in the 1930s Hollywood sent 85 percent of the potential number of films were no barriers in place, indicating that the quota had been far less onerous than claimed by Hays and his spokespeople.[11]

In spite of Paul Faure's tough talk on the eve of Popular Front victory, promising a socialist takeover of the film industry, Blum maintained business as usual. The Popular Front's greatest impact on filmmaking may have been the forty-hour workweek, an innovation that provoked hot debate in the industry on its artisanal nature. Many French movie firms denounced the forty-hour week by claiming that film artists were not proletarians per se, and that artisanal workers needed expansive hours when carrying out creative projects. Renoir countered that the forty-hour week was a great blessing to true artists and artisans who cry out for time off the set to read and ruminate over scripts, to make adjustments and innovations. Only the industrial machinery of Hollywood required eighteen-hour days as well as slavish obedience to delivered scripts and managerial diktats.

Oddly enough, the Popular Front did little to realize the communist Robert Jarville's plans for a nationalized film industry. Instead reactionary Vichy adopted several features of the leftist's program, including the Comité d'Organisation de l'Industrie Cinématographique (COIC), a state-run body that coordinated the activities of laboratories, studios, actors, directors, distribution, and exhibition; a training school, the Institut des Hautes Études Cinématographiques (IDHEC), opened on 6 January 1944; and a ban on the double program, an action that had been taken in Nazi Germany in hopes of helping short film, documentaries, and national production. In Germany, a Film Credit Bank had been established in 1933 with the cooperation of four Berlin banking institutions. Seven out of ten German films received advance funding to the tune of 68 percent of costs, an arrangement that forced artisanal producers to raise a healthy but not oppressive minority of early support for projects.[12] The COIC analogue under Vichy, as noted earlier, boasted of delivering a package with 65 percent support.

After an *épuration* of collaborationist elements, mild by the standards of 1940, the Centre National de la Cinématographie (CNC) replaced the COIC machinery in October 1946. The two bodies had quite similar functions, a state-run coordination of the industry. Those ashamed of the Vichy interlude like to claim the CNC's lineage in the proposals of Popular Front Education Minister Jean Zay and the report of Guy de Carmoy in 1936; nevertheless, the Zay and de Carmoy interventions had led to a private attempt at coordination, the CGC, a body immediately plunged during 1936 into paralyzing division. The CNC forms a closer parallel to the state-run blueprint of Vichy's COIC. Its main departure, as scholar Susan Hayward stresses, is conveyed in the title: The CNC accented the French nation as the Centre *National* de la Cinématographie; COIC saw itself as foremost an industrial body, the Comité de Organisation de *l'Industrie* Cinématographique. Goebbels in his diaries warned that he desired not strong *national* film production, but rather French works largely silly and frothy that would not threaten Germany's preeminence as the new European cinema power. An estimated twelve out of the twenty-three French comedies during World War II came from Continental, a firm established with Goebbels's blessing.[13] He appeared frustrated that some French films were perhaps too compelling and moving, not vacuous diversion appropriate for subaltern peoples. "If the French people are on the whole satisfied with light, corny stuff, we ought to make it our business to produce such cheap trash," he explained. "It would be a case of lunacy for us to promote competition against ourselves. We must proceed in our movie policies as the Americans do in their policies toward the North and South American continents."[14] Elsewhere Goebbels admitted that even his führer needed a large dosage of inanity. Recalling one such "wonderful day" in which "we watch a nice, funny old film," he noted that "The Führer does not want to watch any serious films at the moment. That is understandable. He has to preserve his nerves."[15]

France's film production in the early postwar period suffered several setbacks. COIC director Philippe Acoulon had since 10 April 1945 imposed a 7 percent tax on receipts designed to support cinema production. Angry exhibitors had the Conseil d'État in March 1946 block this program, an action that halted the renewal of industry aid until a law of September 1948.[16] In the winter of 1945–6, the Ministry of Foreign Affairs launched an effort against the Anglo-Saxon dominance of movie screens in Latin America, only to discover that in many markets well-educated elites and not the masses clamored for French films. "The welcome reserved for cinema in Peru is very favorable in Lima in first-run theatres [*les salles d'exclusivité*]," wrote French diplomat and commentator on Latin America Jean Supervielle. "It is less appreciated in neighborhood and provincial cinemas." While the United States had 50 percent of the Peruvian market in 1945, he observed that the Mexicans had made extraordinary gains there, from a 10 percent to a 40 percent share.[17] As the self-professed champions of the Latin peoples, he believed, France must find a way to a similar breakthrough. In Mexico itself, France's ambassador noted that in 1944 the United States had released 159 films; Argentina, 6; Russia, 1; and Mexico, 65. He asked whether "the Mexican public offers the slightest resistance to this American film invasion." His response: For "the people" he could respond "affirmatively," but "negatively" when it came to "la bourgeoisie." Thus for him the general public in Mexico might prove a better ally than the elite. He did concede that to tap this mass resistance, France would have to "sacrifice some pride" and dub its films in Spanish because only "the cultivated public" favors subtitles.[18]

Many French hated the idea of dubbing, believing that it defeated the purpose of expanding the diffusion of French films. France's *conseiller commercial* in Rio de Janeiro, Étienne de Croy, told the Ministry of Foreign Affairs that "cinema plays an essential role in the popular diffusion of our language and last year, the number of students at our Alliances [*françaises*] had nearly doubled upon the simple announcement of the return of French film."[19]

France set up a distribution network in Latin America, and a modest number of its films found screen time; but few inroads were made against U.S. domination. Doubtless some diplomats must have recoiled in horror when Henri-Georges Clouzot's *Le Corbeau* (1943) proved three times as popular as any other French film in Argentina during 1949. Henri Bonnet, France's ambassador to the United States, had in vain tried to block export visas for *Le Corbeau*, a work made during the fascist occupation that depicted vicious poison-pen letters and the foul underside of a small French village.[20]

The French foreign ministry's pursuit of film politics in Latin America was for the most part quiet diplomacy. Its film negotiations with the United

States, by contrast, regularly provoked hot and public debate. Those French clamoring to fortify the film industry regarded the Blum–Byrnes Accords of 28 May 1946 as a dagger to the heart of France's culture. For decades, this agreement has been scorned as the turning point ensuring that Hollywood controlled the destiny of French cinema.

The U.S. movie giants saw the end of the war as an opportunity to pursue a free-market frontier in France and its neighbors. With a backlog of over four years and two thousand films including *Gone with the Wind*, the Motion Picture Export Association of America pressured Washington to pry open the French market. In the spring of 1946, the elder statesperson Léon Blum, freed from Dachau just a year earlier by American troops, arrived in the United States to negotiate with Secretary of State James Byrnes an agreement reducing France's debts under Lend–Lease, establishing credit terms with the Export–Import Bank, and setting discounts on U.S. surplus items. While regarded in certain New Deal circles as a secular saint, Blum had to contend with a chilly reception from isolationists and the press organs of the corporate elite. "When Karl Marx Meets Santa Claus" is how the *Wall Street Journal* headlined its companion piece on his arrival.

Though Blum gave rather anemic support to French film as standard-bearer of the Popular Front, the MPEAA feared the socialist as committed to the restoration of restrictions on Hollywood's access to France. French negotiators had informed the State Department that they would seek an agreement guaranteeing domestic film exclusive access to the screen seven weeks per quarter, or seven of every thirteen weeks. Blum immediately lowered this demand to six, and soon retreated again to a five-per-thirteen week arrangement. The MPEAA finally offered a three-per-thirteen week package, as its representative, Carl Milliken, on 22 April 1946 indicated disenchantment with the French government's claim that it "might be persuaded to cut the quota from the seven weeks per quarter mentioned in their first discussions with us to four weeks per quarter," reported the State Department. Milliken "indicated that a four week quota would give the French a guaranty of 30 percent of the business and said this was too high," as Italy currently received two out of twelve (17 percent), Spain one out of five (20 percent), and Great Britain 22 percent.[21]

Léon Blum later stated that defending France's film industry had taken a diminished priority for him when it threatened the general interest, Europe's need for massive economic aid. After Washington at last offered four weeks of French film per thirteen weeks, he seized the initiative, aware that further intransigence could encourage the State Department to curtail generous terms in other domains. Able to attain the cancellation of $1.8 billion of debts and access to a $500 million credit line, Blum caved in, though gratified that France had greater screen time than Italy, Spain, and Britain: "I admit that if it had been necessary in the higher interests of France as a whole to sacrifice the French film industry, I would not have hesitated. . . . I underline that this accord guarantees 30 percent to national production." He called "seven weeks set aside for French films . . . impossible . . . because our American friends wanted a system based on the principle of free enterprise." The socialist newspaper *Le Populaire* predictably hailed Blum's handiwork as providing "the psychological impact necessary for rekindling French energies and permitting the definitive recovery of the European economy." Robert Buron, *député* of the Mouvement Républicain Populaire (MRP), thought Blum had improved substantially over the commerce treaty of 1936, when France's "cinema had been sacrificed then to other French products," namely wines and champagnes. *Le Populaire* later added that the injection of economic aid would allow for modernization of France's cinema industry.[22]

These cheerful sentiments became quickly smothered amid an avalanche of invective condemning the treaty. The secretary-general of France's Communist Party, Maurice Thorez, thundered that

The American film invading our screens thanks to Léon Blum is not only depriving our artists, our musicians, our workers, and our technicians, of their daily bread, it is literally poisoning the soul of our children, our young men and women, who are being turned into docile slaves of the American millionaires rather than French citizens, attached to the moral and intellectual values which constituted the grandeur and the glory of our homeland.[23]

At a meeting held in Paris on 15 June 1946, French actors, producers, union representatives, and technicians demanded the creation of a national defense committee for French cinema. According to U.S. ambassador Jefferson Caffery, the meeting called for nationalizing "former enemy and collaborationist" film interests, a refund to producers of the 17 percent luxury tax, export subsidies, bans on block booking, and increases in the annual 300 million F credit annually granted for the production of French film, as well as a trimming of its interest rates. Caffery ominously made note of "the support of Monsieur Bouzanguet, Secretary of the CGT[,] and of the Communist party through Monsieur Grenier, who assured the meeting that to defend the French movie industry was the same as defending France."[24] Fernand Grenier, who became a parliamentary deputy representing Seine, later spearheaded the French campaign against the Hollywood anticommunist film *The Iron Curtain*, which he labeled "Hitlerian garbage." "If the gov-

ernment does not know how to take indispensable measures" against Hollywood, he warned at this later date, "[the] people will take [the] government's place."[25]

Though the U.S. State Department reserved its heaviest attention for
communist attacks on the Blum–Byrnes accords, the movement for repudiation cut a wide swath across France's political culture. A limited communist–Catholic rapprochement ensued, as the Thomist intellectual Étienne
Gilson signaled in *Le Monde* the need to rebuff any movie agreement that
condemns "our people" to "absorbing practically unlimited dosages of this
narcotic." Gilson made a distinction between the industrial manufacture
of Hollywood and the artisanal craft of France:

[W]e have never confused in France the production of film with that of any manufactured product. Protected by their relative poverty, our studios have often desired
to make up for quantity by quality; that is to say, by making works of art. . . .
. . . [T]he average French film presentation is incomparably superior to that of
the American film. . . .[26]

The imagery of the U.S. industrial machinery swamping artisanal France
grew from resentment that in the nine-week phase per quarter open to foreign films, no numerical ceiling had been placed on U.S. imports. This represented a departure from the *contingentement* regime of the 1930s, with
its principle of 188 U.S. films per annum. The U.S. State Department called
quotas more faithful to GATT than ceilings. In the absence of a ceiling U.S.
film producers rained films on France, 338 during the first six months of
1947.[27] While the ten MPEAA companies remained relatively restrained
that year, sending fifteen films per firm (approximately 150 in total), the
independents went wild, opening their backlog for an opportunity at the
quarterly French bonanza of nine weeks of free enterprise. The French government later praised the MPEAA companies for not behaving like pigs at
the trough; but French film policymakers came to harbor anger at the independent producers. Often bitter that they had restricted access to MPEAA-
dominated foreign markets, the independents overplayed their hand. In a
speech in Nice, communist intellectual Georges Sadoul called this practice
"dumping," and he demanded that the state afford the film industry the
same protection granted agriculture and automobiles.[28] In reality, much of
the independent invasion received little or no screen time. France used dubbing laws and refused allocation of scarce film stock to keep U.S. works
out of circulation, a dexterous use of statutes requiring that both the recording of French language and copies of new prints be carried out on
France's soil. Thus U.S. Ambassador Caffery declared it shocking but un-

reported "that during 1947 French films obtained an average of 45 percent of total screen time in all French theaters," even though Blum–Byrnes guaranteed only four out of thirteen weeks or a 30.8 percent share of screen time.[29]

This points to perhaps the greatest misperception about Blum–Byrnes, the source of its status as a "black legend."[30] Most French commentators, including Sadoul, treated the 30.8 percent as a *ceiling,* when it was in fact a *minimum.* Total French film production indeed dropped from ninety-four long films in 1946 to seventy-two in 1947, though the shortage of film stock and importation of movies from non-U.S. sources (previously excluded by Vichy) probably accounted for a portion of the difficulty. Sadoul claimed in January 1948 that French studios were operating at 30–40 percent of capacity, and the unemployment of several hundred film workers built a base of cadres dedicated to protesting the accords. On 4 January 1948, French cinema stars Jacques Becker, Louis Daquin, Jean Marais, Simone Signoret, and Madeleine Sologne took to the streets *entre la Madeleine et la République,* serving notice that this capitulation to the American film lords would not stand.[31]

Blum–Byrnes had become such a badge of national shame that, Ambassador Caffery believed, the "French apparently feel that internal political importance of [the] film problem would justify any unfavorable international consequence which might result from unilateral action" against it. Judging the French reaction to be "psychological and political," he called attention to the absence of a vigorous film policy by the leadership of the Fourth Republic: "By placing major blame for present conditions of [the] French film industry on Blum–Byrnes understanding," the government "escapes its responsibility [for] lack of action in this field during [the] period since liberation."[32] The last point of Caffery's critique was indeed trenchant, though he failed to concede that the United States had threatened punishing consequences for nations pursuing too activist a film policy.

For Caffery, the rapprochement of previously antagonistic political forces spelled potentially grave danger. "This political situation has been created by Communist propaganda against American films," he cabled, "which has gained support from non-Communists who consider that American films are threatening French films as an art form and expression of French genius." The MPEAA's own ham-fisted diplomacy may have helped cement this alliance early on, as its Paris representative Harold Smith back in January 1947 had angered mainstream members of the government by his press release opposing French dubbing regulations, comparing them to the "type of pre-censorship" that "only existed before the war in Fascist countries in Europe."[33] When the French administration had defended it-self against the "fascist" accusation, Caffery had admitted "it will now be more difficult for [the] Foreign Office to accept our view of the regulations since to do so they will have to take a position contrary to official denial."[34]

In 1948, French politicians served notice that Blum–Byrnes had to be renegotiated with dispatch. U.S. Secretary of State George C. Marshall told the U.S. ambassador that concessions would be likely. He admitted that threats of withdrawing American aid had made the French cave in to the U.S. demands during 1946. "We agree that we were able to obtain Blum–Byrnes because it could be regarded as one segment within larger negoti-ations," but in the conjuncture of mid-1948 "film problems now stand by themselves and that films offer [the] only effective bargaining power."[35] On the latter point, French exhibitors stood as a lonely bloc opposed to new import restrictions.

The French negotiated a new regime, raising the quarterly quota of French film from four to five weeks, or from 30.8 percent of guaranteed playing time to 38.5. It restricted the U.S. film companies to 121 films per annum; non-U.S. foreign producers could bring in 65 films. Within the agreement, France granted 110 licenses to the MPAA companies (11 per firm) and 11 licenses to the entire membership of the Society of Indepen-dent Motion Picture Producers. The agreement, however, caused the U.S. State Department to seize the initiative for greater autonomy from the MPEAA. Independent Walt Disney waged a campaign in the French press and with France's government in opposition to MPEAA favoritism.[36] When Eagle–Lion Pictures lodged a legal complaint against U.S. negotiators for allegedly ignoring the several companies unaffiliated to either the MPEAA or SIMPP, the U.S. State Department wearied of having to adjudicate intra-capitalist feuding for market share. It sought to relinquish its position as the representative of U.S. film policy; in exchange, however, it granted the MPEAA extraordinary powers in conducting negotiations with foreign re-gimes. The MPEAA at first feared not having the intimidating effect of Washington directly at its side; but soon the industry adjusted, and the State Department could be counted on for backup *in the last instance*, checking regimes in wholesale trespass against what John Foster Dulles euphemis-tically called "the free flow of information."

For France in the course of 1948, the state put together the concrete film policy that U.S. Ambassador Caffery said was lacking at the time of the Blum–Byrnes accord. Predictably the U.S. State Department denounced the French initiatives, which included a compulsory levy on box-office tickets called the *soutien automatique*. This funneled support to French filmmakers at the rate of 15–25 percent of production costs throughout the 1950s. A far cry from Vichy's majority level of credit, it still repudiated the principle of vampire taxation of the 1930s; that is to say, the French state's previous tendency to suck the lifeblood from producers and exhibitors without injecting any resources back into the industry. The MPEAA and the State Department expressed their distaste for a measure that raised much of its revenue from U.S. films, largely transferred to French firms. The U.S. majors learned in due course how to set up postwar affiliates that swallowed a larger share of European aid. French film activists objected to the *soutien automatique* because it tended to reward those filmmakers whose previous work was a commercial success. They pressed for more aid programs based on criteria of artistic rather than commercial merit. The law of 6 August 1953 and the *avance sur recettes* program instituted in 1960, the latter with André Malraux as minister of Culture, gave primacy to artistic quality. While productions of Britain's film industry, for example, that can be distinguished from the Hollywood product have proven to be scant in many years, France has maintained a superior range of artistic diversity, even if the box-office record remains mixed. Of 970 films subsidized in France between 1960 and 1985, 550 could claim a total (94) or partial (456) reimbursement of the state. In addition, 112 films had audiences exceeding a million spectators; another 84 reached at least half a million. Of the 111 directors who had a "good" quality rating from the Centre National de la Cinématographie, 101 benefited from a subsidy, with 35 receiving one for their first long feature film – evidence that at least some new talent had been harvested by means of an activist cultural policy.[37] More recently, however, the aging of France's film avant-garde, with few youthful upstarts to supplant them, has led to calls for overhaul of the subsidy system. With 85 percent of registered French directors over age fifty in the mid-1990s, directorial greenness has been giving way to gerontocracy, as the average age of a director in France nearly doubled from twenty-eight years old in 1960 to fifty-five in 1993.[38]

The French New Wave emerged as the intellectual vanguard of French film during the 1950s, a movement that had an impact in several domains: economics, the stress on low-budget filmmaking, capitalizing on cheaper, hand-held cameras and use of 16mm; ideology, the youth generation against *le cinéma de papa;* and aesthetics, the celebration of the personal imprint of the lone artisan and opposition to the slick texture of industrial cinema.[39] Feminist Agnès Varda directed the first movie with an identifiable New Wave stamp, *La Pointe-Courte* (1954), a story – as fate would have it among groundbreaking works of cinema – about a fishing village. Varda contrasted the urban Parisian life-style of the wife with the simpler, fishing-village background of her husband, a source of conflict in their relationship that provides the backdrop for the filmmaker's artistry. From 1958 to 1961, the New Wave gained momentum and, though it paid homage to several celebrated Hollywood directors, it provided the intellectual foundations for an international resistance to replicating the Hollywood pattern of industrial cinema. With the notable exceptions of Renoir and Vigo, the New Wave treated France's filmmakers of the 1930s as too heavily weighed down by industrial conventions, a tired cinema of quality that needed to give way to the youthful artisans freed from studio discipline. The New Wave's brio and polemical fervor disposed of its predecessors of the 1930s as hopelessly tainted with industrial cinema's suppression of the creative genius at the heart of artistic innovation.

This interfamily French feud points to the historical fluidity of the very concepts "industrial" and "artisanal." France's film producers of the 1930s, who spent an estimated one-fifteenth as much per film as the average Hollywood production, may have been astonished to find themselves expelled from the artisanal Garden of Eden and assigned to a variety of industrial Purgatories and Hell.[40] Peering across the vast expanse of the Atlantic, the practitioners of *cinéma de papa* saw a land that by its industrial methods was sweeping away the simpler French way of life. In Duvivier's film *Pépé le Moko* (1936), the theme song "Où sont-ils donc" echoes from the gramophone telling one to beware of those who "speak to you about America / They have visions of cinema /They say to you, 'What a magnificent country'/Our Paris is nothing compared to that." The French person who runs to New York soon finds life there an empty existence, one lived in pursuit of the dollar and where émigrés have their hearts broken. Missing the Paris culture of "my *tabac* and my corner bistro," the singer longs to return to true friends, dancing, accordions, pastries, and bags of fresh *frites*. Only upon her return, the true Paris, "Montmartre seems to disappear." Old houses are bulldozed, and big heartless banks come in to replace them. The singer lets out a final lament, asking where are "my *tabac* and my corner bistro . . . ?" for the poor French will regret the loss of these great times from the past.[41]

The U.S. State Department and the MPEAA tried to argue that the French film protectionists were fighting over mere questions of market share. The artisans of the screen believed that to surrender the *tabac*, the corner bistro, the dance, the accordion, and now its distinctive cinema, meant that soon, like the singer in *Pépé le Moko*, Paris would go the way of heartless New York. Defense of the artisan, therefore, signified survival for a way of life, vindication of the communist deputé Fernand Grenier's extraordinary claim that to fight for French film is to fight for France. Less burdened by sentimentality and *cinéma de papa*'s mists of regret for the old France, France's New Wave, nevertheless, came to decry the destruction of Paris and the Americanization of French life. Attempting to convey the obscenity of late capitalism, the nation's most influential postwar director, Jean-Luc Godard, in *2 ou 3 choses que je sais d'elle* (*2 or 3 Things I Know about Her*, 1966), showed the uglification of Paris through housing-project suburbanization, a world of empty life-styles and consumerist excess that leads its protagonist to the terminus of prostitution. In the classic French cinema of the 1930s, Paris still can charm audiences; in Godard's most pessimistic work, the city has been hopelessly scarred by the depredations of property developers and banks.[42] In *Sauve qui peut (la vie)* (*Every Man for Himself,* 1979), the pimp forces the prostitute Isabelle to repeat over and over: "Only the banks are independent." Godard himself appears obsessed with prostitution as the model of life under capitalism. "I myself am a whore, fighting against the pimps of cinema," he declares.

The degradation of industrialization reaches its apogee in part four of *Sauve qui peut (la vie),* where he demonstrates the "Taylorization of sexual production," what Robert Stam calls the "technocrat's wet dream . . . sex . . . programmed and disciplined by the science of management":

The boss monopolizes the information, plans the work, and sets the procedure. . . . The orgy participants, like assembly line workers, are reduced to well-defined jerks, twists, moans, and quivers. The *cinéaste-patron* literally oversees a hierarchy of domination.[43]

The artisan of film has few means to rescue freedom, only ways of demonstrating industrial capitalism's daily degradation of life and labor. *Le Canard enchaîné* explained that

To be modern is to imitate the Americans. That's the French trouble: there is no modern way of being French. France, once the "mother of arts, letters, and science," has become a little copycat. Yesterday, we were the locomotive, today, the caboose.[44]

For Godard and France's artisans of film, their movies hold out thinning hope of derailing this locomotive, one that drags France to modernity's parched and empty abyss.

Conclusion

In the middle of World War II, future MPAA leader Eric Johnston wrote of his vision for postwar America: "I do not hesitate to say that the word upon which to fix the national mind at this time is simply, outrightly and frankly *capitalism*." Praised by *Reader's Digest* for his "leatherneck alertness when he landed on the shores of the District of Columbia," the former Marine captain in works such as "Utopia Is Production" (1946) proved to be a leading promoter of the idea that capitalist planning could allow for a growing economic pie that would stave off the horrors of class conflict and socialism. Johnston hailed the words of Justice Louis Brandeis: "The one final way in which we can improve the condition of the worker is to produce more, in order that there may be more to divide."[1] In the reconstruction of Western Europe, this idea became the simple selling point for American-style capitalism, and the Marshall Plan became the major means to achieve its triumph. At the same time, Johnston publicly sought to thwart communists who "spread the big lie that American recovery aid to Europe was a Wall Street plot aimed at capitalist domination of the continent."[2]

Historian Michael Hogan identifies four key business-oriented bodies that shaped and promoted the European Recovery Program or Marshall Plan: the Council on Foreign Relations (CFR), the Committee for Economic Development (CED), the Business Advisory Council (BAC), and the National Planning Association (NPA).[3] Eric Johnston belonged to all four bodies and was indeed a founding member of the CED, which had a chairman, Republican businessman and Studebaker executive Paul Hoffman, who headed the Economic Cooperation Administration (ECA). Looking over the large contingent of CED personnel in charge of the Marshall Plan (including as many as nine of the nineteen members of the "President's Committee on Foreign Aid"), David W. Eakins concluded: "Thus the officers of the Committee for Economic Development had not only helped to formulate the Marshall Plan, but were also almost uniquely responsible for carrying it out."[4]

The Marshall Plan spilled forth its largesse across Europe, only to leave a lingering resentment that it had been used to bully national governments into accepting unfettered importation of Hollywood culture. On 18 December 1947, at the National War College in Washington, D.C., George Kennan explained the workings of the Marshall Plan:

It doesn't work if you just send the stuff over and relax. It has to be played politically, when it gets over. It has to be dangled, sometimes withdrawn, sometimes extended. It has to be a skillful operation.[5]

Secretary of State George Marshall himself admitted that the United States had dangled the aid issue as a means of gaining French concessions on U.S. films in early 1946, over a year before his own plan had been unveiled; yet by 1948 even he counseled his ambassadors to restrain themselves from pressing too hard on films, a sensitive issue that could solidify opposition to the rest of U.S. foreign policy. Having secured a large market share for the MPEAA in most of Western Europe, the State Department did not want to badger governments into further humiliations, the complete crumbling of quotas. The State Department's tolerance toward France's and Britain's hikes in quota walls during 1948 inspired new occasions for MPEAA whining and wailing, but the U.S. film industry had more extraordinary challenges on the horizon: a loss in the U.S. antitrust suit that forced the majors to relinquish their exhibition network, and the rise of television.

The advanced penetration of commercial television in the United States brought the decline of regular family viewing of cinema, a demographic bulge that had sustained the moral regulation of film by the Hays Office. In the mid-1940s, total film admissions in the United States equaled that of Western Europe: around four billion per annum. By 1960, the U.S. was selling only 1.2 billion tickets; Western Europe, over three billion.[6] This substantial gap may have for a time nourished the cinematic New Wave in Europe, a movement that also gained minor market share in the United States through the GI bill and the gigantic postwar expansion of the higher education system. An eightfold increase in U.S. art theaters from 83 in 1950 to 664 in 1966 generated momentum for Europe's alternative cinema.[7] Some Hollywood elements in 1964 began a clamor for congressional subsidies, and in 1974 the *Los Angeles Times* even made a plea for tariffs against overseas productions.[8] Rarely a tremendous force at the box office, the cinematic New Wave eventually sputtered. Hollywood figured out new ways of conquering markets through the multiplex theater and blockbuster formulas predicated on the best of cold-war special effects and pyrotechnics.

Throughout postwar Europe, national governments stood determined to prevent broadcasting from becoming the commercialized circus that had subsumed international film production. State involvement in media had ample precedent in Europe, as most countries regarded post, telegraphs, radio, and then television as natural extensions of the public-service obligations of modern polities. The U.S. model of the viewer as consumer, to be entertained and delivered to the sellers of wares, came to be rejected in favor of a Europe-wide broadcasting model of the viewer as citizen, to be instructed and improved, shielded from those out to promote commerce over art. Explicitly comparing the state of broadcasting with that of film, Simon Rowson, former president of Britain's Kinematograph Renters Society, testified before the Moyne committee back in the mid-1930s that

It is conceivable, of course, that the cinema might have developed in the same way as broadcasting. Commercial interest would have in that case have been confined to the sale of apparatus of various kinds, and a quasi-public authority would have supplied the programmes. Had this been the case, there is no room for doubt that development would have been along totally different lines. . . . Instruction and non-entertainment would have been the dominating principle of the programmes, and the devotees would have been numbered by thousands instead of millions. Chaplin, Disney, Garbo, Shearer, Laughton would probably have been names unknown, whilst the great mass of pleasure which millions of people of all classes throughout the world have felt would not have been experienced. The guiding conception of all those who have been responsible for its development is the same as was described by the late Mr. Henry Labouchere in connection with the novel: It is not intended to instruct or improve – only to amuse![9]

Will Hays, opposing "those who would use the films to bemuse, rather than amuse, the American public," proclaimed that "The great function of the entertainment screen is to entertain. Entertainment and recreation might be likened to machine tools necessary to bring human machinery to the height of its efficiency."[10] The U.S. culture industry promoted an ideology of the good life as freedom from politics, a negation of the classical European and civic humanist ideal of political engagement as essential to human fulfillment. In October 1947, Marshall McLuhan recalled greeting an American official who expressed discontent that Italians were not sufficiently absorbing the gospel of consumer affluence and individualism proffered by U.S. entertainment:

[T]he Italians can tell you names of the ministers in the government but not the names of the favourite products of the celebrities of their country. In addition, the walls of the Italian cities are plastered more with political slogans than with commercial ones. According to the opinion of this officer there is little hope that the Italians will achieve a state of prosperity and internal calm until they start to be more interested in the respective merits of different types of cornflakes and cigarettes rather than the relative abilities of their political leaders.[11]

Commercialism in broadcasting remained one of the flashpoints for European debate on the survival of national culture. Belgium and France initially banned commercial broadcasting; Britain after a wrenching debate in 1954 split between a commercial-free BBC and a sponsored ITV network. Italy also decided to compromise, allowing in 1957 no television advertising except for one thirty-minute show called *Carosello,* by 1960 the nation's most viewed program. Through a telegram in 1957, Pope Pius XII told the Catholic association of peasant proprietors, the Coldiretti, of his disenchantment with the destruction of rural culture by "changing times, materialist propaganda, and audiovisual communications." Pier Paolo Pasolini regretted that the Holy See failed to seize the day by fighting consumerism with the tenacity it had mistakenly mustered against salacity:

[T]he Vatican never understood what it should or should not have censored. For example, it should have censored *Carosello* because it is in the all-powerful *Carosello* that the new type of life which the Italians "must" lead explodes on to our screens with absolute, peremptory clarity. And nobody can tell me we're talking about a way of life in which religion counts for very much. On the other hand, the purely religious broadcasts are so tedious and so repressive in spirit that the Vatican would have done well to have censored the lot.[12]

As Pasolini's and the pope's interventions suggest, the culture industry remorselessly sweeps away centuries-old ways of life. European intellectuals sounded desperate sometimes in trying to stem the tide. Milan Kundera depicts a character in one novel who declares that her real enemy "is Kitsch, not communism."[13] High culture remained a refuge for some Europeans seeking to validate the superiority of their civilization; yet Soviet polemicists in the furious early days of the cold war began to lump together American and Western European artistic work as unified in their capitalist promotion of decadent culture. During the World Congress of Intellectuals held in 1948 at Wrocław, Poland, Alexander Fadeyev, general secretary of the Union of Soviet Writers, inveighed against Western culture for yielding "disgusting filth." While focusing heavily on writers with American backgrounds – John Dos Passos, T. S. Eliot, Henry Miller, and Eugene O'Neill – he charged artists of their ilk with fomenting "aggressive propaganda": "if hyenas could type and jackals use fountain pens, they would write like them." Hungarian Marxist philosopher György Lukács made the cryptic claim that "Russian culture and Soviet culture are beyond Western intelligence." The exasperated head of UNESCO, Julian Huxley, soon regularly called a lackey of the British Foreign Office by Soviet writers, delivered one of the best of his *bons mots:* "Workers of the world unite! You have nothing to lose but your brains."[14]

Unimpressed that Huxley had for such outbursts been vilified as "the specious director of UNESCO" in Soviet literacy publications, the U.S. national-security apparatus kept his operation under surveillance, as cold warriors remained suspicious for his support of leftist poet Pablo Neruda and of his cinema advisor John Grierson. Huxley angered the U.S. State Department with his complaint that UNESCO had been too pervaded by "Anglo-Saxonism." Huxley's recommendation of French leadership indicated that he had been sympathetic to France's cultural criticism of Anglo-Saxonism. State Department officials such as Walter Kotschnig, the author of *Slaves Need No Leaders* (1943), condemned efforts at "gallicizing UNESCO." The prevailing wisdom should hold: "Any active leadership in UNESCO would have to come from the Anglo-Saxon rather than the French speaking world." Somewhat surprisingly the United States later in 1948 backed Mexico's Jaime Torres-Bodet, said approvingly to be "susceptible to political influence (applied appropriately) on the most vital matters." Longtime U.S. academic and cultural policymaker Waldo Leland had earlier ruled out an Indian sympathetic to U.S. interests, because "It would be difficult for an oriental to be Director General of an international organization which is mainly occidental in composition and which must rely almost entirely on occidental support and interest."[15]

The U.S. film industry chose in its own productions to reply to Soviet and European views that U.S. popular culture destroyed true civilization. In *Silk Stockings* (1957), the remake of *Ninotchka* (1939), Cyd Charisse as Ninotchka tells Fred Astaire (Steve Canfield), who is producing a film of *War and Peace,* that he is vandalizing the cultural heritage of Russia. "We have just witnessed the most insulting travesty of Russian culture," declares Ninotchka, as Canfield turns a solemn Russian classical composition into a gaudy theatrical number about Napoleon and Josephine. The lyrics are undoubtedly of unmatched vulgarity: "Josephine, commonly called Jo . . . she had agitating eyes, titilating thighs, lubricating lips, undulating hips." As the Russian composer named Boroff (Wim Sonneveld) cries out, "They cannot do this to me," Canfield proudly says of Americans: "We do this sort of thing all the time. . . . Who cares." When Ninotchka responds that "I care very much about something that is part of the Russian heritage," Canfield tells her that he had been wrong to believe that the ultraserious, communist Ninotchka, once "a carefully trained robot," had turned into "a woman"; her inability to lighten up and laugh at American entertain-

ment is proof that she still suffers from totalitarian indoctrination. The rest
of the film leaves the challenge: Will Ninotchka win the victory over herself and love silk stockings, that is to say, American opulence and entertainment? Just as British propagandists portrayed the Nazis as incapable of a
sense of humor, the U.S. film depicts those questioning the values of the entertainment industry as deficient in this most human of qualities. Until Steve
Canfield "saves" her, Ninotchka remains one of communism's countless
victims: a woman turned masculine, rendered bereft of feminine warmth,
unable to savor the cornucopia of capitalism displayed in U.S. entertainment.

Boosters of American popular culture such as Will Hays and Eric Johnston liked to claim that its worldwide success was partly due to its promotion of a superior way of life. Nonetheless, many ordinary Europeans who
voted for anticapitalist and social-democratic parties also proved loyal devotees of American popular culture. This sort of cognitive dissonance caused
problems for the parliamentary Left. The British Labour Party, in debates
on film quotas in 1927 and 1938 and over commercial television in 1954
and 1963, faced splits between the vast majority of its backbenchers seeking
to contain American imports and a minority urging surrender, "to let the
people have what they want." The success of the British Tories in the 1950s
and early 1960s may have been due to the party cleverly casting aside its
paternalistic tradition in favor of populist appeals to consumer affluence
and individualist freedom of choice.

Still no major European country succumbed to the temptation of an
American-style cultural free marketplace. Government protection starting
with quotas in the late 1920s probably succeeded in increasing European
production, with the sound revolution also raising public yearnings to hear
national artistes. In the postwar period, aid to cinema producers brought
more fruitful results in France than in Britain. The British state, despite
claiming to back "independent" cinema, probably put too much stress on
rewarding commercial and industrial producers. The French learned to
strengthen artistic and artisanal cinema, and granted support to provincial
exhibitors whose decline would otherwise extinguish cinema viewing in
many rural zones. The British state long seemed content with the "fleapit-
ization" of the country's exhibition sector, a secular decay that converted
filmgoing into what Martin Dale cites as "a slum activity watched in slum
conditions."[16] The average Briton attended 29 cinema shows per year in
1950; the French attended 8.9 times. By 1985, British viewers were going
to the cinema only once annually; the French, 3.4 times.[17] Cinema policy
appeared to have kept France as a player in world cinema, though some

Britons said their Gallic neighbor succeeded largely through the ennui of French television. Britain boasted of possessing the world's "least worst television."

In several years of the postwar period, France's national producers held a plurality of the national market, an impressive accomplishment when measured by the interwar yardstick and against that of its European neighbors. With the exception of a few tiny regional markets such as Belgium's Wallonia, however, France never could compete with the Americans in any sphere of the international trade. For many critics, this again raised the age-old question of why it is American popular culture alone that seems to export well practically everywhere.

The size of America's market and its immigrant composition have been central components of the nation's ability to produce culture for a global market. Less explored is the manner in which class, generational, and regional cleavages usually redound to the benefit of U.S. popular culture.

In terms of class and cultural creation, European critics and American dissidents such as the "aristocratic" radical essayist Dwight Macdonald scorned U.S. elites for sharing too much of the culture of the assimilated immigrant masses. "The problem is especially acute" in the United States, bemoaned Macdonald, "because class lines are especially weak here. If there were a clearly defined cultural elite here, then the masses could have their Kitsch and the classes could have their High Culture with everybody happy."[18] Instead the urban bourgeoisie in the U.S. Northeast and the plantation aristocracy in the South feel at home in mass culture. Biographer Matthew Josephson liked to portray industrialist Henry Clay Frick as parked in his Renaissance throne amid walls graced with paintings by Velásquez, Van Dyck, Holbein, and El Greco, yet something was terribly wrong with this picture: The philanthropist and avid art collector is earnestly absorbed in reading the *Saturday Evening Post*.[19] For Macdonald, there were two preconditions for the successful creation of commercial popular culture, or what he preferred to call Kitsch and Masscult. "One is that the producer must believe in what he is doing," he wrote. Macdonald featured the story of Norman Rockwell who, after a short Picasso phase, returned with gusto to his *Saturday Evening Post* clichés. "Maybe it isn't the highest form of art, but it's art nevertheless, and it's what I love to do," explained Rockwell. "I feel that I am doing something when I paint a picture that appeals to most people. This is a democracy, isn't it?" Macdonald jeeringly retorts, "'Yep, sure is.'" He then adds that "The other condition for success in Masscult is that the writer, artist, editor, director or entertainer must have a good deal of the mass man in himself. . . ." He gives as an example his own boss, journalistic entrepreneur Henry Luce, who proclaimed the twentieth to be "The American Century":

I was struck by three qualities he had as an editor: his shrewdness as to what was and was not "a story," his high dedication to his task, and his limited cultural background despite, or perhaps because of, his having attended Yale College. All three are closely interrelated in his success: a more sophisticated editor would have gotten out of step with his millions of readers, a less idealistic one would have lacked the moral oomph to attract them, and he knew a "story" when he saw one because what interested them interested him.[20]

In contrast, the European cultural elite is so soaked in classical and high culture that an artifact like *The Saturday Evening Post* or *Reader's Digest* could be created only with a certain cynicism or lack of authenticity. Education at the Gymnasium, the public school, the École Normale, Oxbridge, or a similar setting creates too impenetrable a boundary between high culture and mass culture. Europe produces its share of cultural and media entrepreneurs, but too many artists are divorced from popular tastes. J. Arthur Rank came to be regarded as a philistine laughingstock among the cultural establishment for his innocent query, "Who is Thomas Hardy?" Hollywood filmmakers register success by commercial sales; European directors, by the approval and admiration of fellow directors. The artisanal populism of the Popular Front can easily succumb to artisanal elitism in such a truncated conception of the "true" audience. Godard later took this to the far side of the extreme in proclaiming that "films are made for one or maybe two people."

An important area in which the European artisanal producer abdicated to Hollywood culture was in the creation of children's entertainment. According to the Catholic Church's cinema ratings of 1951–2 for the French market, France produced only two films suitable for children, whereas Hollywood sent over twenty-two.[21] Annoyed that secular and leftist forces might scoff at Catholic-supported entertainment as "childish" (*enfantin*), Chanoine Joseph Reymond of *Choisir* reminded France in 1932 that "it is a fact that youth and children are the most faithful clients of the movie theatres . . . it is clear that the cinema has an immeasurable influence since it commands the future."[22] When J. Arthur Rank tried to create cinema productions for his children's clubs, he faced lampoon and contempt from intellectuals such as J. P. Mayer, who worried that he sought to indoctrinate the youngsters into becoming life customers of commercial cinema [Fig. 12]. He was accused of profiteering off the most vulnerable segment of the population. Though Rank may have provoked cynicism by his constant profes-

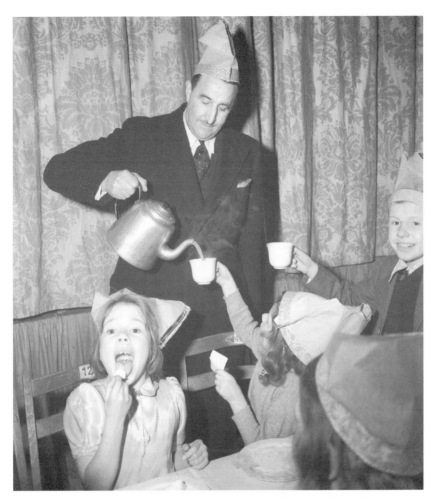

FIGURE 12. In a festive mood at a Christmas party of 1948 at Lime Grove Baths, Hammersmith, British film magnate J. Arthur Rank pours tea for the children of his staff. Though often mocked by intellectuals for his brand of youth entertainment, Rank worried that movie industries outside of Hollywood neglected children. *Source:* Hulton|Archive.

sions of public service and the inanity of many of the weekly rituals at the Saturday performances, he did take the entertainment needs of youth more seriously than the avant-garde and the many partisans of the documentary movement, who instead waxed enthusiastically about creating educational films.

Later on, teenagers and young adults would adopt American movies and music as a form of generational solidarity and revolt against parental control and national culture. In understanding the latest American music and popular culture, youth from Toulouse to Tokyo may have more in common with each other than with adults from their own nation. Even when their politics were nominally leftish during the 1960s, this generation had been transformed into what Godard called "the children of Marx and Coca-Cola." The irony of the worker and student demonstrations of May 1968, argued Régis Debray, was their transformation of France from a paternalistic culture of *travail, famille, et patrie* to a California-style capitalism that venerates cultural commodities, the moveable feast of merchandise.[23] The abdication of the children's market to American producers creates loyalties and tastes that are in the last analysis less receptive to the established national culture. When their own children become troubled and obstreperous, which can conveniently be blamed on the American culture they are imbibing, the erstwhile rebels sometimes rediscover appreciation for the national culture, but by then it is too late. Older adults attend cinema less often, buy fewer CDs, and become the market for so-called high culture.

A case could be made that U.S. capitalism has often achieved dominance through skilled cultivation of the child market, and this is not just confined to movies. Riesman and his collaborators in *The Lonely Crowd* (1950), perhaps the most influential twentieth-century book on American social character, expressed trepidation about how business seemed to target children as a means of securing adult acquiescence in major household spending decisions.[24] With television advertising in its infancy, these social critics could barely have had a foretaste of what was to come. The global leader in fast food, McDonald's, is blatant in using children to disrupt home eating patterns through spasmodic demands for Happy Meals, Chicken McNuggets, and rendezvous with the fantasy heaven of Ronald McDonald. Disney has built its theme-park empire around making the dream come true for millions of prepubescent Mouseketeers, many of whom are snared through early exposure to its cartoon, video, and multimedia carnival shows. The current computer and video-games revolution has developed considerable momentum from the U.S. subteen market, as generational hierarchies are upset by youth's superior mastery of the medium in relation to their hapless adult overlords. Surprisingly to those who regard American domination as a foregone conclusion, the U.S. culture industry has ceded significant global market share in these newer fields to the comic-book empires and Poké-mon–Play Station syndrome of postmodern Japan. Asada Akira, a leading Japanese social critic, assails the manner in which Japan has descended into

"infantile capitalism," a social order in which the worlds of work and leisure meld: "Japanese engineers are cleverly manoeuvred into displaying a
childlike passion whereby they are easily obsessed by machines . . . children
are running around, each one as fast as possible, at the front lines of capitalism as infantilization proceeds."[25]

To return, however, to the question of film during the interwar and early
postwar periods, it is more than just class and generational rifts in the production and reception of culture that secured Hollywood's seeming impreg-
nability to outside challenge. Regional differences within nations fragment
audiences in ways that have long frustrated proponents of a national cultural policy. Frequently missing or misrepresented in domestic cultural works,
the provinces tend to settle for Hollywood over national film producers. In
the 1930s, John Grierson attacked what he called the West London bias of
most British films, the absence of representations of Scotland, Wales, Northern Ireland, and the rest of England. In France, *Choisir* expressed "regret"
that so much "French intelligence may appear congested" in Paris, so that
the nation is not creating "films Norman and Gascon, Lorraine and Pro-
vençal."[26] The Parisian bias of its national producers met storms of protest
in regions such as Brittany. In response to the 1936 comedy *Tout va très
bien madame la marquise* – identical in title to a French popular song from
the same year – the province rose up against this production of a Paris company that, according to the American consul in Nantes, B. M. Hulley, "represents the male Breton as a village idiot type and the female as a person
[of] light morals." He added that the feature "which seems to arouse most
resentment is that restaurants of the region are shown as serving rotten fish"
– an unsavory characterization that could kill Brittany's summer tourist
trade. Banned by the mayors of Nantes and Le Havre, exhibitors refused
to show the film in Rennes, Quimper, Concarneau, and Vannes. Two Breton parliamentary deputies asked a Paris theater to cease exhibiting it, and
the minister of the Navy, who also served as mayor of St. Malo, demanded
that the Ministry of Education make further presentations illegal.[27]
    Films of the European metropolis (Paris and London), then, are some-
times regarded in the provinces as more alien than the products of Hollywood. Several European countries possess a plurality of languages and
communal identities, a powerful source of resistance to the urban cultures
of Paris, London, and Madrid. In Belgium, the Flemings flee the French-
speaking films so popular in Brussels and Wallonia; they absorb Hollywood
films in their wake, sometimes 80 percent of the Flanders market. In turn,
the communal and provincial rebels from the national or metropolitan cul-

ture have trouble gaining a wider audience for their own artists. The French
nouveau philosophe Bernard Henri-Lévy accused the Mitterrand-era Minister of Culture Jack Lang of waging "a war of berets, bourrées, and Breton
bagpipes" against U.S. popular culture, while another skeptical French critic, Guy Konopnicki, declared in *Le Monde* the futility of efforts at promoting communal culture: "The worst Broadway revue will always outclass
the pathetic spectacle of folkloric dances in clogs."[28]

From a distance, then, U.S. popular culture continues its inexorable
march. If ever weakened in the metropolis, it gains new adherents in the
provincial peripheries. Still, postwar Europe has provided many surprises
for those who believed that Hollywood has imposed a suffocating unifor-
mity and standardization on the globe. Amid the ubiquity of American popular culture, Europe has witnessed the efflorescence of all sorts of neo-
nationalisms, separatist movements, and seekers of regional autonomy:
Scots, Flemings, Bretons, Occitans, Catalonians, Basques, Corsicans, Ca-
nary Islanders, and on and on. Gigantism in economic organization and
Americanization of popular culture have coexisted with all sorts of redis-
coveries and inventions of tradition, struggles and microresistances against
what British writer Digby Anderson calls "a Europe no longer of disparate,
strange, even feuding countries, but one happy family of nations living in
harmony. How convenient. How ghastly."[29] Beyond the frontiers of western Europe, Iranian leaders fight what they call "Westoxification," while
proponents of so-called samurai capitalism in Japan, kinship capitalism
among the Chinese diaspora, and the *chaebol* (interlocking conglomerate)-
dominated economic order of Korea try to argue for paths to modernity that depart from American-style universalism. The anti-Enlightenment
political philosopher John Gray observes that "The growth of the world
economy does not inaugurate a universal civilization, as Smith and Marx
thought it must." Instead he finds that "It creates regimes that achieve modernity by renewing their own cultural traditions, not by imitating western
countries. There are many modernities, and as many ways of failing to be
modern."[30]

The greatest director of Hollywood's silent era, D. W. Griffith, admonished his actors and actresses to speak of film with reverence, to repudiate
vulgar labels assigned to it such as "the flickers." For Griffith, film was the
universal language prophesied by Scripture, the means by which the Kingdom of God would be realized on earth. America had been chosen to sum-
mon its powers. "The motion picture will do three things as no other instrument will do," echoed Will Hays during a speech in Paris. "It will entertain
– an essential service; it will instruct – a divine opportunity; and greater than

any other instrument in the world today, it will promote understanding between men and men and between nation and nation." Calling films "the universal language," able to reach "Eskimos" in "the Arctic" and "aborigines" in "Arizona," Hays declared that once people "know each other they cannot hate each other, and they cannot make war."[31]

Hays would be neither the first nor the last to herald new means of communication as harbingers of perpetual peace. With the first transatlantic telegraph cable in 1858, Victorian boosters proclaimed: "It is impossible that old prejudices and hostilities should longer exist, while such an instrument has been created for the exchange of thought between all nations of the earth." Later proponents of radio touted its pacific wonders, as the BBC World Service adopted the motto: "Nation shall speak peace unto nation." With the invention of the Internet, media guru Nicholas Negroponte of MIT speaks of how children "are not going to know what nationalism is." The high-tech genius Michael Dertouzos speculates about the rise of "computer-aided peace," which "may help stave off future flare-ups of ethnic hatred and national break-ups."[32] Perhaps boldest of all, Pulitzer Prize–winning journalist Thomas Friedman propounded the Golden Arches theory of pacifism: No two countries that possess a McDonald's fast-food franchise have ever gone to war against one another.

"Presumption," thought Montaigne, "is our natural and original malady." That was said to be the reason God scattered hundreds of languages at Babel, and perhaps explains why ethnicity and communal identity are once again on the march. In confronting the global impact of American popular culture, Europeans have shown that there are still wells of resistance, that Hays's and Griffith's celluloid-delivered heaven is not about to be realized on this twenty-first-century Earth.

Notes

INTRODUCTION

1. Sydney Smith, review of Adam Seybert, *Statistical Annals of the United States of America, Edinburgh Review* 33 (January 1820): 69–80, at pp. 79–80.
2. Charles Pomaret, *L'Amérique à la conquête de l'Europe* (Paris: Librairie Armand Colin, 1931), p. 284.
3. Editorial, "Home Rule for Britain," *World Film News* 2(8) (November 1937): p. 5. This is also quoted by Margaret Dickinson and Sarah Street, *Cinema and State: The Film Industry and the British Government, 1927–1984* (London: British Film Institute, 1985), p. 58.
4. *Bioscope* quoted by Rachael Low, *The History of the British Film, 1918–1929* (London: Allen & Unwin, 1971), p. 16. Luchaire testimony in William Marston Seabury, *Motion Picture Problems: The Cinema and the League of Nations* (New York: Avondale Press, 1929), p. 236, see appendix. Stalin quoted by Anthony Smith, *The Shadow in the Cave: The Broadcaster, His Audience, and the State* (Urbana: University of Illinois Press, 1973), p. 187.
5. Besides transnational approaches, my work has obviously benefited from histories and film studies based on national cinema. Cinema and state studies have received major impetus from the national studies of Margaret Dickinson, Sarah Street, Andrew Higson, James Chapman, Mariel Grant, James Robertson, Annette Kuhn, Rachael Low, Jeffrey Richards, Ian Aitken, Paul Swann, D. L. LeMahieu, and Duncan Petrie on Britain; Colin Crisp, Richard Abel, Susan Hayward, Evelyn Ehrlich, René Bonnell, René Prédal, Paul Leglise, Alan Williams, and Ginette Vincendeau on France; and Richard Maltby, David Culbert, Thomas Doherty, Douglas Gomery, Tino Balio, Robert Sklar, Leslie Midkiff DeBauche, Garth Jowett, Clayton Koppes, Gregory Black, and Lary May on the United States. I have also made extensive use of more traditional genres such as biography, particularly Karol Kulik on Korda as well as Geoffrey Macnab, Michael Wakelin, and Alan Wood on Rank.
6. For a discussion of these concepts, see Randal Johnson, "In the Belly of the Ogre: Cinema and State in Latin America," in John King, Ana M. Lopez, Manuel Alvarado, eds., *Mediating Two Worlds: Cinematic Encounters in the Americas* (London: British Film Institute, 1993), pp. 204–13, at p. 210, and

Jorge Schnitman, *Film Industries in Latin America: Dependency and Development* (Norwood, N.J.: Ablex, 1984), p. 46.

7. Poulantzas wrote an essay on Miliband's *The State in Capitalist Society* for Britain's leading Marxist journal, *New Left Review*. Their exchange was reprinted as "The Problem of the Capitalist State," in Robin Blackburn, ed., *Ideology in Social Science* (Glasgow: Fontana/Collins, 1979 [1972]), pp. 238–62.

8. Some instrumentalists will argue that the very presence of corporate lawyers such as Dulles and McCloy in the state apparatus confirms their model against Poulantzas's view that "the capitalist State best serves the interests of the capitalist class only when the members of this class do not participate directly in the State apparatus." However, Poulantzas also clarifies that "direct participation of members of the capitalist class . . . in the government, even where it exists, is not the important side of the matter" (ibid., pp. 245–6). Others will point to Washington's intervention on behalf of United Fruit in Guatemala during 1954 as evidence of little shift in capitalist control over the state. Nevertheless, it has been suggested that the Eisenhower administration stepped up antitrust investigations of United Fruit precisely because of fears that the principle of autonomy appeared to be breached in the crushing of Arbenz.

9. Data from Andrew Higson and Richard Maltby, eds., *"Film Europe" and "Film America": Cinema, Commerce, and Cultural Exchange, 1920–1939* (Exeter: University of Exeter Press, 1999), pp. 13 and 20.

10. Ursula Hardt, *From Caligari to California: Eric Pommer's Life in the International Film Wars* (Providence and Oxford: Berghahn Books, 1996), pp. 88–9.

11. The critic Frédéric-Philippe Amiguet, *Cinema! Cinema!* (1923) quoted by Siegfried Kracauer, *From Caligari to Hitler: A Psychological History of the German Film* (Princeton: Princeton University Press, 1974 [1947]), p. 3.

12. Besides the valuable collection of Higson and Maltby and the biography of Pommer by Hardt cited above (see n. 10), there is also Klaus Kreimeier's *Die Ufa-Story: Geschichte eines Filmkonzerns* (Munich: Carl Hanser Verlag, 1992), now available in English translation as *The UFA Story: A History of Germany's Greatest Film Company 1918–1945*, trans. Robert and Rita Kimber (New York: Hill & Wang, 1996; Berkeley: University of California Press, 1999). Thomas Saunders, Joseph Garncarz, and Heide Fehrenbach have also produced works with insights into UFA. A central controversy that needs to be resolved: Kristin Thompson and Garncarz have widely varying estimates of how much U.S. film occupied German screens in the interwar period. See their contributions to Higson and Maltby.

13. Kristin Ross, *Fast Cars, Clean Bodies: Decolonization and the Reordering of French Culture* (Cambridge, Mass.: MIT Press, 1998 [1995]), p. 37.

14. Alan Wood, *Mr. Rank: A Study of J. Arthur Rank and British Films* (London: Hodder & Stoughton, 1952), p. 48.

15. This is a central argument of Jeremy Tunstall, *The Media Are American: Anglo-American Media in the World* (New York: Columbia University Press, 1977).

16. Walter Lippmann, *Men of Destiny* (New York: Macmillan, 1927), pp. 215–16.

17. For those seeking a more robust condemnation of censorship than represented in my work, see the meticulous scholarship of Gregory D. Black, *Hollywood Censored: Morality Codes, Catholics, and the Movies* (New York: Cambridge University Press, 1994). He regularly accuses Breen and his cohorts of "mutilating" works of cinema. Two other exemplary works are Frank Walsh, *Sin and Censorship: The Catholic Church and the Motion Picture Industry* (New Haven: Yale University Press, 1996), and Thomas Doherty, *Pre-Code Hollywood: Sex, Immorality, and Insurrection in American Cinema, 1930–1934* (New York: Columbia University Press, 1999). Doherty in his conclusion humbly points out that much film produced without censorship controls since the 1960s has lacked aesthetic worth.

18. MIT social scientist Walter Dean Burnham has conducted several transnational studies and surveys that indicate a major decline of religious belief in all advanced capitalist societies, except Canada and especially the United States. In many measures of "intensity" of religious belief, the United States rivals Bangladesh rather than its affluent first-world counterparts. See also Roger Finke and Rodney Stark, *The Churching of America, 1776–1990: Winners and Losers in Our Religious Economy* (New Brunswick: Rutgers University Press, 1992), described on its front jacket flap as a book explaining how the U.S. "religious environment" is "a free market economy, where churches compete for souls. . . . In 1776, fewer than 1 in 5 Americans were active in church affairs. Today church membership includes about 6 out of 10 people." In Europe, where churches receive state support, religious organizations long lost the recruiting drive of America's free-enterprise religious bodies. Finke and Stark's model is vulnerable, however, when it comes to Poland, where the absence of religious competition did not appear to erode the vitality of Roman Catholicism.

19. Perry Anderson, lecture of 20 October 1985, New School for Social Research, New York, reprinted in "Agendas for Radical History," *Radical History Review* 36, September 1986, pp. 35–6.

20. Figures from (U.K.) Board of Trade, *Tendencies to Monopoly in the Cinematograph Industry: Report of a Committee Appointed by the Cinematograph Films Council* (London: HMSO, 1944), p. 28, para. 100.

1. THE DOMESTIC ROOTS OF HOLLYWOOD'S FOREIGN POLICY

1. Will H. Hays, "What Is Being Done for Motion Pictures," p. 8, speech of 5 October 1923, Will Hays Papers, I, reel 12, microfilms division, Rutgers University.

2. Ibid.

3. Press release of 16 October 1923, Hays Papers, I, reel 12.

4. Richard Schickel, *D. W. Griffith: An American Life* (New York: Simon & Schuster, 1984), pp. 486–502.

5. For details on this episode, see James C. Robertson, *The Hidden Cinema:*

British Film Censorship in Action, 1913–1972 (London: Routledge, 1989), pp. 26–7 (Routledge also published an updated paperback [*–1975*] in 1993), and list of films banned in the United Kingdom, James C. Robertson, *The British Board of Film Censors: Film Censorship in Britain, 1896–1950* (London: Croom Helm, 1985), app. 3, p. 186. See also John Walker, ed., *Halliwell's Film Guide*, 8th ed., revised and updated (New York: HarperCollins, 1992), p. 34.

6. Ernest Betts, *Heraclitus, or the Future of Films* (London: Dutton, 1928), pp. 44–6. For this and similar quotations of disdain for Hollywood, see Rachael Low, *The History of the British Film, 1918–1929* (London: Allen & Unwin, 1971), pp. 17–19.

7. Hays Papers, II, reel 19, frame 1167ff.

8. "Good Cheer Wanted," *Moving Picture World*, 20 February 1909, p. 196.

9. Martin Quigley, "Radicalism – An Industry Peril," *Motion Picture Herald*, 11 December 1937, pp. 17–18. In a companion piece to Quigley's speech, the *MPH* reports that the Theatre Owners of North and South Carolina on "the second day of the convention [in Pinehurst, N.C.] . . . aligned themselves with other southern exhibitors by adopting a resolution protesting against indiscriminate intermingling of the white and Negro races in motion pictures."

10. Elliot Paul and Luis Quintanilla, *With a Hays Nonny Nonny* (New York: Random House, 1942), p. 178.

11. Henry Lehrman quoted by Laurence Greene, *The Era of Wonderful Nonsense: A Casebook of the 'Twenties* (New York: Bobbs–Merrill, 1939), p. 65.

12. Neal Gabler, *An Empire of Their Own: How the Jews Invented Hollywood* (New York: Crown, 1988), pp. 277 and 460n. Gabler argues that in spite of his rhetoric, Crafts was probably less animated by anti-Semitism than Ford and others. The expression "500 un-Christian Jews" appeared to be common among moral crusaders. Dr. James Empringham complained to the *New York World*: "I attended a meeting of motion picture owners in New York, and I was the only Christian present. The remainder of the company consisted of 500 un-Christian Jews." Empringham quoted in Henry Ford, *The International Jew: The World's Foremost Problem*, vol. II (Dearborn, Mich.: Dearborn Publishing, April 1921; reprint, Reedy, W.V.: Liberty Bell Publications, 1976), p. 119.

13. Crafts's press release is reproduced in Terry Ramsaye, *A Million and One Nights: A History of the Motion Picture*, 2 vols. (New York: Simon & Schuster, 1926; reprint 2 vols. as 1, New York: Touchstone, 1986), 2: 483. Ramsaye observed that Crafts "should . . . have realized that if the movie men of 1920 had surrounded $40,000,000 they would have gone to Albany and incorporated a new company, not to Washington to spend it." For Crafts's testimony before the U.S. Congress on "crime-breeding films," see *Hearings before the Committee on Education, House of Representatives, Sixty-fourth Congress, First Session of H.R. 456 . . . January 13, 14, 15, 17, 18, and 19, 1916* (Washington, D.C.: U.S. GPO, 1916; reprint, New York: Arno Press, 1978), p. 66.

14. "Jewish Control of the American Theater," in Ford, *International Jew*, II: 88.

15. Ford, *International Jew*, II: 91, 94, and 110.

16. See "Jewish Jazz Becomes Our National Music" (6 August 1921) and "How the Jewish Song Trust Makes You Sing" (13 August 1921), reprinted in Ford, *International Jew*, III: esp. 74–5.

17. Quotation of *Dearborn Independent* and Frederick Boyd Stevenson from "The Jewish Aspect of the 'Movie' Problem" (12 February 1921), reprinted in Ford, *International Jew*, II: 118.

18. Ramsaye has a photograph of the actual letter in *A Million and One Nights*, 2: 812–13, interleaf.

19. Ibid., p. 815. For Hays on his "tenderfoot" status, see text of London speech in Hays Papers, as well as his memoirs. Hays's salary figures are sometimes disputed, but Frederick C. Munroe, a former board member of the MPPDA, gave the following specifics: "[Hays] was invited to become 'Czar' of the 'Movies' on a three-year contract at $100,000 per year. At the expiration of this contract he calmly asked for a cast-iron ten-year contract at a salary of $150,000 plus an expense allowance of $100,000 a year, the latter not to be accounted for. In other words, he was to be paid $250,000 a year. . . ." Letter of Frederick C. Munroe, National Economy League, Massachusetts branch, to Arthur B. Emmonds II, American Red Cross, 20 July 1933, file Advisory Council – Boston, box 3, Motion Picture Research Council files, Hoover Institution Archives, Stanford University [hereafter MPRC files].

20. For Crafts and Ford reactions, see Will H. Hays, *The Memoirs of Will H. Hays* (Garden City, N.Y.: Doubleday, 1955), p. 326. For an essay that discusses WASP disdain for the urban culture of the newer immigrants, see Richard Maltby, "The Production Code and the Hays Office," in Tino Balio, *Grand Design: Hollywood as a Modern Business Enterprise, 1930–1939* (History of the American Cinema, no. 5) (New York: Charles Scribner's, 1993), 37–72.

21. "Jewish Control of American Theater," in Ford, *International Jew*, II: 96.

22. Joseph Jefferson O'Neill, "They Call Him 'Bill Hays' Now That He's in the Movies – *Globe* Man Interviews G.O.P. Postmaster General, Who Got a Raise from $12,000 to $150,000," *Boston Sunday Globe*, 9 April 1922.

23. Hays, *Memoirs*, pp. 327 and 336.

24. Hays placed Moley's quotations prominently in his *Memoirs*, pp. 335 and 337.

25. Ibid., p. 334.

26. Among contemporary scholars, Ian Jarvie follows Moley as the leading proponent of the corporatist interpretation for the foundation of the Hays Office. While Jarvie remains the most knowledgeable scholar of the documents concerning state–MPPDA relations, I believe his decision to downplay censorship issues too drastic, and I have sought to restore them to a central place in the MPPDA's history. Try as he might, Hays rarely found himself free of controversy on this front, and he had to adjust political and corporatist strategy accordingly. In Jarvie's defense, the MPPDA certainly had more far-reaching obligations than, say, the British Board of Film Censors, a body purer in its censorship function and less corporatist in its ambitions. See Ian Jarvie, *Hollywood's Overseas Campaign: The North Atlantic Movie Trade, 1920–1950* (New York: Cambridge University Press, 1992).

27. Allen L. Woll, *The Latin Image in American Film* (Los Angeles: UCLA Latin American Center Publications, 1977), especially chap. 2, "The Attack of the Greasers," pp. 6–28.

28. Hays, *Memoirs*, p. 334.

29. "Movies," *Atlantic Monthly*, July 1921, p. 28. This quotation figured prominently in a legal brief against the film industry. See Connecticut brief, 3 October 1927, in MPRC files, box 59.

30. Hughes quoted in "American Foreign Relations and American Reputation Abroad as Affected by Motion Pictures," Exhibit "A" in MPRC files, box 58. See also *Film Daily*, 13 October 1923.

31. This listing builds upon Tino Balio's structure of censorship introduced in his "Introduction" to *Grand Design*, pp. 3–5.

32. Fred Eastman and Edward Ouellette, *Better Motion Pictures* (Boston and Chicago: Pilgrim Press, 1936), p. 38.

33. Sabine Hake, *The Cinema's Third Machine: Writing on Film in Germany, 1907–1933* (Lincoln: University of Nebraska Press, 1993). See the brief but informative entry of Joseph Garncarz, Michael Wedel, and Thomas Elsaesser, "Kino Reform Movement," in Ginette Vincendeau, ed., *Encyclopedia of European Cinema* (New York: Facts on File, 1995), pp. 241–2.

34. The IAKM interview with Samuel quoted by Neville March Hunnings, *Film Censors and the Law* (London: Allen & Unwin, 1967), p. 61n. He lists the source as PRO HO45/10811/312397/1, though a brief search of this Home Office file did not turn up this record.

35. Hortense Powdermaker, *Hollywood, the Dream Factory: An Anthropologist Looks at the Movies* (Boston: Little, Brown, 1950), p. 64.

36. Mexican censorship announcement sent to Joseph I. Breen, 26 November 1937, *Lawless Riders* file, Production Code Administration [hereafter PCA], American Academy of Motion Picture Arts and Sciences [hereafter AAMPAS], Beverly Hills, California. This film later received Mexico's approval on 5 January 1939.

37. Conversation: Major Herron with the Office of the Economic Advisor, 13 February 1928, U.S. National Archives [henceforth U.S. NA], Record Group [henceforth RG] 59, 800.4061/96.

38. Woll, *Latin Image*, p. 34. League of Nations Treaty Series, vol. 165 (1935), no. 3818.

39. PCA files on *The Boudoir Diplomat*, *Dracula*, and *Her Man* quoted and discussed by Ruth Vasey, *The World According to Hollywood, 1918–1939* (Madison: University of Wisconsin Press, 1997), pp. 115–22. She indicates that the problem of locale was hardly confined to foreign regimes. Hollywood had to be cautious about offending southerners; hence, *I Am a Fugitive from a Chain Gang* (1932) intentionally avoided the Georgia locale of Robert E. Burns's autobiographical *I Am a Fugitive from a Georgia Chain Gang!* (New York: Grosset & Dunlap, 1932), a work serialized in *True Detective* during 1931.

40. Hays, *Memoirs*, p. 433.

41. Ibid., p. 434.

42. Ibid.

43. Joy quoted by Maltby, "Production Code and the Hays Office," p. 40.
44. Text of the Production Code available in Hays Papers and Martin Quigley, *Decency in Motion Pictures* (New York: Macmillan, 1937), pp. 52–70; see especially pp. 59–60.
45. For a concrete case of this part of the code, see letter of James B. M. Fisher to Dr. Wingate, 27 May 1933, *Ann Vickers* file, PCA, AAMPAS.
46. In recent times, the film scholar Thomas Doherty deserves credit for bringing attention to the formulation of a Jewish-owned industry selling Catholic theology to Protestant America. There have been several close variants. The historian of movie censorship Francis G. Couvares gives it a social-class spin: "An industry largely financed by Protestant bankers, operated by Jewish studio executives, and policed by Catholic bureaucrats, all the while claiming to represent grass-roots America. . . ." See his essay "Hollywood, Main Street, and the Church: Trying to Censor the Movies before the Production Code," in Francis G. Couvares, ed., *Movie Censorship and American Culture* (Washington, D.C.: Smithsonian Institution Press, 1996), 129–58, at p. 152.
47. Parsons quoted by *New York Herald Tribune*, 7 July 1934; see Hays Papers, II, reel 12, frame 163. For Hays on Catholics, see *Memoirs*, pp. 449–50. For *The Churchman*, see Maltby, "Production Code and the Hays Office," pp. 45–6.
48. A. H. Giannini of the Bank of America took special pains to remind Hays of Pius XI's approval of the document and subsequent disappointment with its violation. See Hays, *Memoirs*, p. 440.
49. Letter and *New York Times* article in *Scarface* file, PCA, AAMPAS.
50. *Scarface* file, PCA, AAMPAS.
51. *Variety* and James Shelley Hamilton quoted by Walker, ed., *Halliwell's Film Guide*, p. 977.
52. *Scarface* file, PCA, AAMPAS.
53. Ibid.
54. Ibid.
55. For a listing of films deleted or banned in interwar Italy, see James Hay, *Popular Film Culture in Fascist Italy: The Passing of the Rex* (Bloomington: University of Indiana Press, 1987), pp. 86–8.
56. Wanger quoted by Matthew Bernstein, *Walter Wanger: Hollywood Independent* (Berkeley: University of California Press, 1994), p. 126.
57. *Scarface* file, PCA, AAMPAS. Lea Jacobs, *The Wages of Sin: Censorship and the Fallen Woman Film, 1928–1942* (Madison: University of Wisconsin Press, 1991), has shown how accentuating transgression might in specific cases be the logic of the PCA's regime of precensorship. Along with Richard Maltby and Annette Kuhn, she has reshaped the understanding of censorship. While Kuhn and Jacobs have thoroughly explored the terrain of sexuality, I am suggesting that their insight might be useful in understanding the moral regulation of other genres, particularly crime films.
58. *Scarface* file, PCA, AAMPAS.
59. For British policy on crime films, see Robertson, *British Board of Film Censors*, pp. 78–9. He notes that some local authorities decried the BBFC's lax

policy on *Scarface,* and in Birmingham they outright banned the film. He shows that from 1932 to 1934 the BBFC often opposed films depicting crime in the United Kingdom itself. The body proved more amenable to such works in the 1940s and 1950s.

60. *Public Enemy* file, PCA, AAMPAS.
61. *Frankenstein* file, PCA, AAMPAS.
62. Hays letter of 29 September 1932, quoted by Vasey, *World According to Hollywood,* p. 124.
63. *Possessed* file, PCA, AAMPAS; also quoted by Maltby, "Production Code and the Hays Office," p. 52.
64. For an account that finds Mae West to be the inspiration of much of the agitation, see Gerald C. Gardner, *The Censorship Papers: Movie Censorship Letters from the Hays Office, 1934–1968* (New York: Dodd, Mead, 1987), pp. 139–47. For a more detailed account of West's battles with censors, see George Eels and Stanley Musgrove, *Mae West: A Biography* (New York: Morrow, 1982).
65. *Hot for Paris* file, PCA, AAMPAS.
66. Letter of Breen to Hays, 25 August 1931, Hays Papers, II, reel 5, frame 1273ff.
67. Letter of Joseph Breen to Martin Quigley, 1 May 1932, Martin Quigley Papers, box 1, folder 3, Georgetown University, Lauinger Library, Special Collections.
68. Ibid.
69. Letter of Joseph Breen to Wilfrid Parsons, S.J., 10 October 1932, Wilfrid Parsons Papers, Georgetown University, Lauinger Library, Special Collections.
70. Letter of Wilfrid Parsons, S.J., to Joseph Breen, 25 August 1933, Parsons Papers.
71. Father Daniel A. Lord on the origins of the Legion of Decency, quoted by Eastman and Ouellette, *Better Motion Pictures,* pp. 40–1.
72. Cantwell and Cicognani quoted by Hays, *Memoirs,* pp. 450–1.
73. Paul W. Facey, *The Legion of Decency: A Sociological Analysis of the Emergence and Development of a Social Pressure Group* (New York: Arno Press, 1974) (reprint of his Ph.D. diss., Department of Political Philosophy, Fordham University, 1945).
74. Hays Papers, II, reel 12, frame 2.
75. Ibid., reel 11, frame 1036. *Chicago Herald–Examiner,* 14 June 1934.
76. Ibid., frame 866. "NonCatholics Join Campaign on Dirty Films," *Chicago Daily News,* 6 June 1934.
77. "Protestantism and Jewry Join Catholics on Movie Ban," *Christian Century,* 4 July 1934, pp. 884–5.
78. For these press clips, see Hays Papers, II, reel 12, frames 9, 176–7.
79. Letter of E. W. Burgess to William H. Short, 17 March 1932, file "Chicago – March 16th to 23 1932," box 3, MPRC files.
80. Lowell quoted in letter of William H. Short to Ambassador Alanson B. Houghton, Washington, D.C., 14 October 1933, box 3, MPRC files.
81. For quotations of Ross, Blumer, et al., see file "Columbus Conference: Résumés of Findings," especially "The Motion Picture as a Molder of National

Character," box 57, and file "Résumé of Payne Fund Findings," box 60, MPRC files.

   Among the more celebrated of the Payne Fund/MPRC books are the following (all with the same publication information – New York: Macmillan, 1933): Herbert Blumer and Philip M. Hauser, *Movies, Delinquency, and Crime;* George D. Stoddard, *Getting Ideas from the Movies;* James Henry Forman, *Our Movie Made Children;* Ruth Peterson and L. L. Thurstone, *Motion Pictures and the Social Attitudes of Children;* Herbert Blumer, *Motion Pictures and Conduct;* W. W. Charters, *Motion Pictures and Youth;* Mark A. May, *The Social Conduct and Attitudes of Movie Fans;* and Wendell S. Dysinger and Christian A. Ruckmick, *The Emotional Responses of Children to the Motion Picture Situation;* and Dorothy F. Marquis, Vernon L. Miller, and Samuel Renshaw, *Children's Sleep.*

82. For quotations of Moley and MPRC fund-raising appeals, see memo of Raymond Norr to Will Hays, 19 March 1938, Hays Papers, II, reel 20, frame 667ff., especially pp. 4–7.

83. Letter of Armstrong Perry to William H. Short, no date (ca. August 1929), box 58, file "Industry Study," MPRC files.

84. Letter of William H. Short to Armstrong Perry, 4 September 1929, box 58, MPRC files.

85. For quotation of MPRC minutes, see memo of Norr to Hays, 19 March 1938, Hays Papers, II, reel 20, frame 667ff.

86. "Editorial Comment on Church Action," 6 July 1934, mimeographed memorandum, Hays Papers, II, reel 12, frames 147ff.

87. Hays Papers, II, reel 12, frame 164.

88. Ibid., reel 11, frame 1020.

89. Pelley quoted by Leo P. Ribuffo, *The Old Christian Right: The Protestant Far Right from the Great Depression to the Cold War* (Philadelphia: Temple University Press, 1983), pp. 61–2, 295.

90. Dayton *News-Week,* 7 July 1934. Hays Papers, II, reel 12, frame 166 for Chicago archdiocese rating and frame 177 for West statement.

91. Gardner, *Censorship Papers,* pp. 143–5.

92. Hays Papers, II, reel 12, frame 67ff.

93. Ibid., frame 6.

94. Maltby, "Production Code and the Hays Office," p. 61; see also his note 54 for further background.

95. Hays, *Memoirs,* pp. 453–4.

96. Hays Papers, II, reel 12.

97. *Mutual Film Corporation v. Ohio Industrial Commission,* 236 U.S. 230, U.S. Supreme Court (1915), p. 230. For a cogent discussion of this landmark case, see Richard S. Randall, *Censorship of the Movies* (Madison: University of Wisconsin Press, 1970), p. 19.

98. "Boycott on Fan Mags," *Daily Variety,* 6 March 1935, and "Appendix 2: Fan Magazines," in Anthony Slide, ed., *International Film, Radio, and Television Journals* (Westport, Conn.: Greenwood Press, 1985), pp. 383–8.

99. Maltby, "Production Code and the Hays Office," p. 67. See "Whose Business Is the Motion Picture?" *Motion Picture Herald,* 22 February 1936.

100. Hays Papers, II, frames 1013–15. This abbreviated text is slightly different from the actual twenty-page code. For instance, it directly mentions "Communistic propaganda," which is only implied in the actual code. Breen and Quigley were more preoccupied with anticommunism in the 1930s than Hays and are the likely source of its accentuation in this abbreviated text.

101. Paul and Quintanilla, *With a Hays Nonny Nonny*, p. 3.

102. John Stuart Mill's argument that the best art and ideas are created when there is a free marketplace of ideas may be a weak basis upon which to ground the principles of civil liberties; that is to say, the view that freedom of speech is the best order because of outcomes. When addressing outcomes, Nietzsche may have been more accurate in regarding certain repressive regimes as beneficial to great art. Civil libertarians then would have to ground arguments on behalf of liberty on its intrinsic value, rather than on by-products or outcomes. In making this point, it should be added that repression often leads to enormous sterility in artistic production, though rarely without isolated pockets of resistance. Repression concentrates the energies of the creative class on the artistic sublime, powers dissipated when everything goes and nothing matters, the predicament under libertarian late capitalism. George Steiner is among the most profound contemporary thinkers discussing the paradox of liberty and artistic decline. See his contribution to the panel discussion with Conor Cruise O'Brien, Leszek Kolakowski, and Robert Boyers, "The Responsibility of Intellectuals," *Salmagundi*, nos. 70–1 (Spring–Summer 1986): 164–95.

103. The text of *Vigilanti Cura: Encyclical Letter on Improper Motion Pictures* (1936) that I have quoted is available in five languages at the official Web site of the Vatican at www.vatican.va. The Paulist Press long circulated a very similar English translation of this text (still available through a link at www.pilgrims.org/edmedia.htm). See also Hays Papers, II, reel 12, starting at frame 898. It is believed Martin Quigley helped the papacy in composing this document. There are perhaps three different English translations of it that still circulate.

104. Msgr. Louis Picard, *Un Pionnier: Le Chanoine Brohée* (Brussels: Éditions Universitaires, 1949), p. 108.

105. For data on the Chicago archdiocese, see *New York Herald–Tribune*, 8 July 1934. For Legion of Decency data, consult *Motion Picture Daily*, 18 November 1941. Cf. Hays Papers, II, reels 12 and 29. For the view that the Chicago archdiocese was more stringent than other Catholic officials, see *Private Life of Henry VIII* file, PCA, AAMPAS, in which Hays officialdom complains vigorously about its rejection of films approved elsewhere. In a letter of 22 January 1935, Breen told Martin Quigley of his disenchantment with the Chicago Legion of Decency: "I am thoroughly disgusted with the Legion of Decency, and more especially with that branch which holds forth on the South Shores of Lake Michigan." Quigley Papers, box 1, folder 3.

106. The legal departments of the movie majors were on the alert about such legislative scares. For the Illinois text, see "Motion Picture Producers Association – General" file, Records of the Legal Department, Twentieth Century–Fox Film Corporation [hereafter TCF], Special Collections, University of Cal-

ifornia at Los Angeles [hereafter UCLA]. The legislation stipulated a fine of at least $1,000 for a first offense, escalating to $10,000 or imprisonment not to exceed five years for subsequent offenses. For a leading tract that decried the divorce menace to U.S. civilization, see John R. Rice, *What Is Wrong with the Movies?* (Grand Rapids, Mich.: Zondervan Publishing House, 1938), especially chap. 2, entitled "Movies Are Made by Sinful, Wicked People, Unfit to Be Examples." It cites the work of MPRC scholar Edgar Dale.

107. Breen letter of 31 October 1936, *Charge of the Light Brigade* file, PCA, AAMPAS.

108. Letter of Martin Quigley to Joseph Breen, 30 March 1934, Quigley Papers, box 1, folder 3. Kenneth G. Crawford, *The Pressure Boys: The Inside Story of Lobbying in America* (New York: Julian Messner, 1939) expresses suspicion of Hays for taming pesky critics by quietly putting them on the MPPDA payroll.

109. Kennedy's observations are discussed in Chapter 2.

110. Glyn Roberts, "The Hitler of Hollywood," *Film Weekly*, 31 August 1934. For an account of film censorship that agrees with Roberts's assessment, Leonard J. Leff and Jerold L. Simmons, *The Dame in the Kimono: Hollywood, Censorship, and the Production Code from the 1920s to the 1960s* (New York: Grove Weidenfeld, 1990). Commenting on the title "Hitler of Hollywood," they write: "By 1935, Breen had earned it." Notwithstanding Breen's anti-Semitic utterances in private correspondence and his sympathy for some rightist regimes, this sobriquet does little to illuminate his practice of film regulation.

111. Arthur Schlesinger, "History of the Week," *New York Post*, 10 January 1954. Denying any vestige of anti-Catholicism in his intervention, Schlesinger pointed approvingly to his earlier writings that became a selection of the Catholic Book Club. In a hostile reply to Schlesinger, Martin Quigley tried to downplay Catholic influence over the code by saying that it is based on "the basic moral charter of all of the religions of the Judean-Christian Civilization." Letter of Quigley to Schlesinger, 12 January 1954, Quigley Papers, box 1, folder 39.

112. See "Factors Affecting the Motion Picture Business in the Netherlands," 15 March 1926, in U.S. NA RG59 856.4061. After making some adjustments in the Bioscope Bill (Netherlands), the conservative forces finally overcame the defeats of previous years by passing it in the First Chamber on 12 May 1926 by a 24–15 vote.

113. See *Hearings before the Committee on Education, House of Representatives, 20 March 1914* (Washington, D.C.: U.S. GPO, 1914), p. 18. For libertarian approval of Gaynor, see Robert M. Thornton, "William Jay Gaynor: Libertarian Mayor of New York," *The Freeman* 20(3) (March 1970): 156–64. The staunchest critics of censorship typically accepted the principle that immoral or indecent speech was subject to legal redress. When asked back in 1916 by U.S. Representative John W. Abercrombie of Alabama if he favored "the elimination of all censoring everywhere," J. W. Binder, a Pennsylvania Dutchman serving as executive secretary of the Motion Picture Board of Trade, said: "Absolutely, everywhere, except in war." But he soon clarified that just as

newspapers hire proofreaders to avoid "any action for libel for printing anything that was libelous, indecent, or immoral," he believed ". . . it is to the interest of every manufacturing moving-picture concern to see that nothing goes out which might subject him to action for libel, indecency, or immorality. . . . Consequently it is to the interest of the manufacturer to protect the public by making high-grade clean pictures. . . ." *Hearings before the Committee on Education, House of Representatives, Sixty-fourth Congress, First Session of H.R. 456* . . . (Washington, D.C.: U.S. GPO, 1916), pp. 17–19.

114. Letter of Jason Joy to Joseph Breen, 15 December 1931, *Possessed* file, PCA, AAMPAS.

115. Gregory D. Black, *Hollywood Censored: Morality Codes, Catholics, and the Movies* (New York: Cambridge University Press, 1994), pp. 287, 291n100, cites the *PCA Annual Reports, 1935–1940* as the source for Breen's destruction of social content. Lary May, *The Big Tomorrow: Hollywood and the Politics of the American Way* (Chicago: University of Chicago Press, 2000), provides somewhat more optimistic data about the presence of social content in movies of the 1930s.

116. *Mildred Pierce* file, PCA, AAMPAS. For a wider context on this film, see Andrea Walsh, *Women's Film and Female Experience, 1940–1950* (New York: Praeger, 1984).

117. Newark *Star–Ledger*, 4 December 1944. See also "Objective Burma" file, PCA, AAMPAS.

118. Letter of Breen to Quigley, 25 September 1937, Quigley Papers, box 1, folder 3.

119. Shurlock admitted: "No, we never refused seals. We were in the business of granting seals. The whole purpose of our existence was to arrange pictures so that we could give seals. You had to give a seal." Jacobs, *Wages of Sin*, p. 20. For an inside view of the process, see Jack Vizzard, *See No Evil: Life Inside a Hollywood Censor* (New York: Simon & Schuster, 1970).

120. Letter of Quigley to Breen, 10 January 1939, Quigley Papers, box 1, folder 3. See also Maltby, "Production Code and the Hays Office," pp. 68–70, and Marjorie A. Valleau, *The Spanish Civil War in American and European Films* (Ann Arbor, Mich.: UMI Research Press, 1982).

121. Zanuck quoted by Leonard Mosley, *Zanuck: The Rise and Fall of Hollywood's Last Tycoon* (Boston: Little, Brown, 1984), p. 188. In 1950, Hortense Powdermaker challenged the conventional wisdom that message pictures do not sell. Noting that *Crossfire* on anti-Semitism and *Home of the Brave, Lost Boundaries,* and *Pinky* on racism flourished, she showed how abruptly the postwar industry "changed its formula to 'Any message picture will make money' and produced a cycle of anti-Communist pictures." When *I Married a Communist, The Iron Curtain, Red Menace,* and *The Red Danube* then flopped at the box office and with critics, *Variety* (5 October 1949) observed: "The public will buy 'message' pix, but they gotta be good." See Powdermaker, *Hollywood, the Dream Factory,* chap. 2 (quotes are on p. 41).

122. Wanger quoted by Bernstein, *Walter Wanger*, p. 138.

123. Maltby has been the most effective commentator on the economic roots of moral regulation. My work seeks to place the economic interpretation in a more global context.
124. Lord memo, "The Code – One Year Later," Hays Papers, II, reel 5, frame 715.
125. Philip French, *The Movie Moguls: An Informal History of the Hollywood Tycoons* (London: Weidenfeld & Nicolson, 1969), p. 59.
126. *Scarface* file, PCA, AAMPAS.
127. *Captain Blood* file, PCA, AAMPAS. See also "An Entertaining *Nell Gwyn*," *The Times* (London), 24 September 1934.
128. *Pygmalion* file, PCA, AAMPAS.
129. For this episode, see French, *Movie Moguls*, p. 47.
130. "'Catholic Action' Backed by Women," *New York Times*, 23 February 1936, secs. 2 and 3, p. 1. Father Daniel Lord also joined Protestant reformers in seeking legislative remedies for block booking, in contrast to former Catholic allies such as Martin Quigley. See Black, *Hollywood Censored*, p. 168.
131. Letter of Bishop John J. Cantwell to Patrick Joseph Casey, 2 September 1933 in OF73, box 2, Franklin D. Roosevelt Library [hereafter FDR Library], Hyde Park, N.Y. Cantwell's initial strategy was to apply organized pressure on New York bankers: "They do not desire to run the risk of . . . lending money to an industry that in many instances is undermining the sanctity of the home and the sacredness of marriage."
132. For a harsh assessment of U.S. Catholic suspicion of state intervention on these issues prior to World War I, see David R. Roediger and Philip S. Foner, *Our Own Time: A History of American Labor and the Working Day* (New York: Verso, 1989), p. 229.

2. HOLLYWOOD AND THE STATE DEPARTMENT

1. William Victor Strauss, "Foreign Distribution of American Motion Pictures," *Harvard Business Review* 8(3) (April 1930): 307–15, at p. 307.
2. For background on Creel, see Emily Rosenberg, *Spreading the American Dream: American Economic and Cultural Expansion, 1890–1945* (New York: Hill & Wang, 1991 [1982]), pp. 79–86.
3. For the expansion of the BFDC, see ibid., pp. 140–1.
4. Klein's testimony became cited liberally by critics of Hollywood's expansion. See Sir Philip Cunliffe-Lister's quotation of this testimony before the British parliament in *Parliamentary Debates* (House of Commons), 16 March 1927, vol. 203, col. 2040, and documents supporting the Moyne committee (1934–6) at the Public Record Office / U.K. Board of Trade [hereafter, PRO BT], BT55/3.
5. North letter to Miller, 30 August 1928, and Miller reply of 2 October 1928, North acknowledgment of 18 October 1928, U.S. NA RG151, Records of the Bureau of Foreign and Domestic Commerce, General Records, 1914–55 400.2, Trade Promotion – Motion Pictures. Belgium file in box 1649.
6. (U.K.) Board of Trade, *Report of a Committee Appointed by the Board of Trade to Consider the Position of British Films*. Rt. Hon. Lord Moyne (chairman), Cmd. 5320 (London: HMSO, 1936), p. 7, para. 12.

7. Will H. Hays, *The Memoirs of Will H. Hays* (Garden City, N.Y.: Doubleday, 1955), p. 508.
8. Letter of Will Hays to Joseph C. Grew, Under Secretary of State, 7 January 1926, U.S. NA RG59, 800.4061, 1910–29.
9. Letter of Leland Harrison ("For the Secretary of State [Frank B. Kellogg]") to "Certain American Diplomatic and Consular Officers," 30 January 1926 [To American Embassies, Legations, and High Commissions in Buenos Aires, Vienna, Brussels, Rio de Janeiro, Sofia, Santiago, Peking, Prague, Copenhagen, Cairo, Budapest, Rome, Tokyo, Riga, Mexico City, The Hague, Oslo, Teheran, Lima, Warsaw, Helsingfors, Paris, Berlin, London, Athens, Lisbon, Bucharest, Belgrade, Madrid, Stockholm, Berne, Constantinople], in U.S. NA RG59 800.4061/34, 1910–29.
10. See Berlin memorandum of Jacob Gould Schurman to U.S. Secretary of State, 6 August 1926, U.S. NA RG59, 800.4061, 1910–29.
11. Ibid.
12. See Oslo memorandum of Lauritz S. Swenson to U.S. Department of State, 9 July 1926, U.S. NA RG59, 800.4061/84, 1910–29.
13. For the exchange with van Karnebeek, see note of Richard M. Tobin, Legation of the USA, The Hague, to the Secretary of State, 19 April 1926 in U.S. NA RG59, 856.4061/9. See also George E. Anderson, "Moving Pictures in the Netherlands" (27 February 1922) and "Factors Affecting the Motion Picture Business in the Netherlands" (15 March 1926) in the same RG59 file.
14. London memorandum of 2 March 1926, U.S. NA RG59, 800.4061/36, 1910–29.
15. Melbourne memorandum of Walter T. Costello to U.S. Department of State, 6 August 1926, U.S. NA RG59, 800.4061/89.
16. Madrid memorandum of Ogden H. Hammond to U.S. Secretary of State, 5 May 1926, U.S. NA RG59, 800.4061/73.
17. H. S. Villard, Office of the Economic Adviser, Department of State, "Foreign Restrictions on American Films," 25 March 1929, U.S. NA RG59, 800.4061, Motion Pictures/4½, 1910–29. Villard is also quoted by Ian Jarvie, *Hollywood's Overseas Campaign: The North Atlantic Movie Trade, 1920–1950* (New York: Cambridge University Press, 1992), pp. 325–6. He lists its location as follows: "Memorandum, 'Foreign Restrictions on U.S. Films,' 25 March 1929, U.S. NA RG59 1940–1944 [*sic*] 800.4061 Motion Pictures/4½" (the [*sic*] being his). I was unable to retrieve this document by using his citation of the 1940–4 box. Jarvie's scholarship is marked by meticulous accuracy in the labeling of documents, so I am puzzled by this seemingly cryptic coding. (The National Archives may have refiled it since Jarvie's consultation, or he may have seen a carbon copy of it in another RG59 box. The file I found in the 1910–29 box contains stamps from the Department of State's Division of Communications and Recording on 1 November 1932 and is initialed with the date of 10-29-43 by "DCR," so it is likely Villard's intervention continued to be consulted by policymakers into the 1940s.)
18. Father McLaughlin statement to an unnamed New Haven newspaper quoted in "Memorandum to Board of Directors," a collection of press clippings to the MPPDA, May 1926, Hays Papers, I, reel 27. The context for McLaugh-

lin's comment was the voicing of opposition to the construction of a movie theater in New Haven in April 1926. The founding pastor of Saint Brendan's from 1913 to 1960, Father McLaughlin served parishioners from a relatively affluent zone of New Haven that included a large component of successful professionals. My thanks to Father Donald French of Saint Brendan's for some of this background.

In her letter to the State Department of 15 January 1944, Cornelia A. Gibbs mentioned the DAR attack of 1922, and she enclosed an undated text of her attack on Hollywood and *Hot for Paris* for the *Baltimore Catholic Review* of the early 1930s. See U.S. NA RG59, 800.4061, 1940–4.

19. Fred Eastman, *The Menace of the Movies: A Series of Five Articles Studying an Urgent American Problem* (Chicago: Christian Century reprint, ca. 1930), supplied in Gibbs letter of 15 January 1944 in U.S. NA RG59, 800.4061, 1940–4. The five articles from this booklet are "The Menace of the Movies," "Our Children and the Movies," "Ambassadors of Ill Will," "Who Controls the Movies?" and "What's To Be Done with the Movies?" Eastman admitted that many others had already produced similar critiques. Perhaps he was thinking of the two pamphlets from the late 1920s produced by Clifford Gray Twombly, *The Moving Picture Menace* (Lancaster, Penn.: no publisher, ca. 1928), 11 pp., and *The Moving Picture Menace Grows* (Lancaster, Penn.: no publisher, 1929), 8 pp. The only copy of the former is held by Franklin and Marshall College library, and of the latter by the University of Notre Dame library.

20. Kennedy letter in Raymond Moley Papers, box 27, file 56, Hoover Institution Archives, Stanford University. Ian Jarvie in *Hollywood's Overseas Campaign* discusses this document at length on pp. 340 and 361n. According to Jarvie, "What Kennedy may have been referring to were attacks on Hays from within his own membership. Evidence of these was a *New York Times* story reporting Hollywood as outraged at Hays's spineless attitude toward overseas protests about U.S. films and at his failure to extract support from the State Department." The trouble with this account is that the article appeared on 24 November 1935, almost a year and a half later. Jarvie's stress on corporatism in MPPDA politics to the exclusion of domestic censorship campaigns causes him to miss the Legion of Decency campaign in mid-1934 as the immediate context for the anti-Hays agitation referred to by Kennedy.

21. Data from Robert B. Ray, *A Certain Tendency of the Hollywood Cinema, 1930–1980* (Princeton: Princeton University Press, 1985), pp. 25–6. Thomas Doherty, *Projections of War: Hollywood, American Culture, and World War II* (New York: Columbia University Press, 1993), cites a U.S. Department of Commerce estimate in 1944 that 80 cents of each dollar spent on "spectator amusement" went to the film industry. "U.S. Survey Shows Films Get 80% to 85% of Amusement Coin," *Variety*, 19 July 1944. See also George W. Hunt, "Of Many Things," *America*, 5 March 1994.

22. For Wheeler, Nye, and Lindbergh quotations, see dossier in Hays Papers, II, reel 29. Wheeler quoted by *New York Times*, 17 January 1941.

23. Charles Higham, *Warner Brothers – A History of the Studio: Its Pictures, Stars, and Personalities* (New York: Scribner's, 1975), p. 141.

24. Letter of B. K. Wheeler to Will Hays, 13 January 1941, President's Personal Files [hereafter PPF] 1945, FDR Library Hyde Park, N.Y.
25. Hilaire Belloc, *The Jews* (Boston: Houghton Mifflin, 1922), p. 156.
26. U.S. Congress, Senate, *Propaganda in Motion Pictures: Hearings before a Subcommittee of the Committee on Interstate Commerce, Seventy-Seventh Congress, First Session on S. Res. 152: A Resolution Authorizing an Investigation of Propaganda Disseminated by the Motion-Picture Industry and of Any Monopoly in the Production, Distribution or Exhibition of Motion Pictures, September 9 to 26, 1941* (Washington D.C.: U.S. GPO, 1942), p. 11. Part of this report has been reprinted in David Culbert, ed.-in-chief, *Film and Propaganda in America: A Documentary History*, vol. II, pt. 1, "World War II" (Westport, Conn.: Greenwood Press, 1990), pp. 3–77.
27. U.S. Congress, Senate, *Propaganda in Motion Pictures*, p. 391.
28. See MPPDA press summary of 23 January 1941, pp. 27–8, Hays Papers, II, reel 27.
29. Mayer quoted by Otto Friedrich, *City of Nets: A Portrait of Hollywood in the 1940's* (New York: Harper & Row, 1987), p. 49.
30. Jarratt memorandum in PRO INF1/600. Two recent studies that explore this activity: Nicholas John Cull, *Selling War: The British Propaganda Campaign against American "Neutrality" in World War II* (Oxford: Oxford University Press, 1995), and Thomas E. Mahl, *Desperate Deception: British Covert Operations in the United States, 1939–44* (Washington, D.C.: Brassey's, 1998).
31. "Movies Not Inciting to War, says Will H. Hays in Film Analysis Sent to Senator Wheeler" (16 January 1941) including letter to Wheeler (14 January 1941), PPF 1945, Will H. Hays file.
32. Willkie quoted by Doherty, *Projections of War*, p. 42.
33. For a commentary that identifies the thinly veiled Anglophilia of interwar films, see Gore Vidal's discussion of the Alexander Korda–executive-produced film *Fire Over England* (1937) in *Screening History* (Cambridge, Mass.: Harvard University Press, 1992), chap. 2. Although some scholars believe that Korda's film was just a good yarn and did not have a full-blown interventionist agenda, Vidal argues for the close similarities between this production and the Korda-directed *That Hamilton Woman* (1941), perhaps Winston Churchill's favorite movie for rallying the world to the defense of Britain. One of Vidal's most profound insights about U.S. films is the relative scarcity and inept handling of actual U.S. history, especially concerning American presidents. Hollywood characteristically displaces political history into European epic, the British and Roman imperial dramas, rather than engaging with the nation's own past. This traditional blockage gave Hays the space to claim that the studios were not trying to shape political debate in the United States.
34. Reinhardt quoted by Ruth Vasey, *The World According to Hollywood, 1918–1939* (Madison: University of Wisconsin Press, 1997), p. 156.
35. U.S. Congress, Senate, *Propaganda in Motion Pictures*, p. 389.
36. For a discussion of Nye's words, see H. Mark Glancy, *When Hollywood Loved Britain: The Hollywood "British" Film, 1939–45* (Manchester: Manchester University Press, 1999), pp. 61–6.
37. Hon. Lowell Mellett, Office of Government Reports, 27 August 1941, memo

to FDR, PPF 1945, Will H. Hays file. This document appears to be incorrectly filed in Hays–FDR correspondence from the period 1942–5.
38. Some of this conjecture is reinforced by Glancy, *When Hollywood Loved Britain,* pp. 61–6. His account is especially useful for understanding Chaplin's parody of the Production Code in *The Great Dictator.* On p. 57, he writes: "Chaplin actually follows these rules . . . by referring to Germany as 'Tomania,' Italy as 'Bacteria,' by redesigning the swastika as the 'double cross,' and referring to the Fuhrer as 'The Phooey.' Adolf Hitler is 'Adenoid Hynkel,' Benito Mussolini is 'Benzino Napoloni,' Goebbels is 'Garbage,' and Göring is 'Herring.' But rather than seeing this as a satire on his own policies, Breen may have taken some comfort in these thinly veiled allusions."
39. U.S. Congress, Senate, *Propaganda in Motion Pictures,* pp. 338–9.
40. Zanuck quoted by Mel Gussow, *Don't Say Yes Until I Finish Talking: A Biography of Darryl F. Zanuck* (New York: Pocket Books, 1972), p. 112. For an account of the hearings that credits Willkie with the industry's victory over the isolationists, see Thomas Schatz, *Boom and Bust: America Cinema in the 1940s* (Berkeley: University of California Press, 1999 [1997]), pp. 39–40. After failing to secure his renomination as Republican presidential standard-bearer in 1944, Willkie perished from a heart attack on 8 October 1944.
41. Testimony of First Lieutenant Milton Sperling, USMCR, First Amphibious Corps, Combat Photographic Company, taken at Warner Brothers–First National Studios, Burbank, California, on 18 December 1942, by Major John H. Amen, IGD, U.S. NA Suitland, RG159, box 1165, 333.9, p. 765. The actual text of this testimony has been reproduced in Culbert, *Film and Propaganda in America,* pp. 251–67.
42. Testimony of Sperling, p. 756.
43. Ibid.
44. Ibid., p. 759.
45. Doherty, *Projections of War,* pp. 41–2.
46. Their report and the primary documents on this investigation have been assembled in Culbert, *Film and Propaganda in America,* pp. 95–147.
47. *Congressional Record,* 30 June 1943, pp. 6883, 6885, 6891. See also pamphlet by War Activities Committee, *Movies at War,* vol. II (New York and Hollywood, 1943) in U.S. NA RG59, 800.4061, 1940–4, Motion Pictures. For background on the government and the film industry during World War II, particularly the Office of War Information (OWI), the Bureau of Motion Pictures (BMP), and the Office of Censorship, see Doherty, *Projections of War,* chap. 3, especially pp. 42–3, and Clayton R. Koppes and Gregory D. Black, *Hollywood Goes to War: How Politics, Profits, and Propaganda Shaped World War II Movies* (New York: Free Press, 1987).
48. Jack Warner, *My First Hundred Years in Hollywood: An Autobiography* (New York: Random House, 1965).
49. Presidential memorandum for Hon. Lowell Mellett, PPF 1050, Warner Brothers Film Co. file. Harry Warner also wrote an angry letter (dated 25 August 1943) to Henry Luce about the "public rumbleseating" remark in *Time,* a letter that he passed on to FDR. See OF73, box 3, Warner file, also at the FDR Library.

50. Flowers quoted by David Culbert, "American Film Policy in the Re-education of Germany," in Nicholas Pronay and Keith Wilson, eds., *The Political Re-education of Germany and Her Allies after World War II* (London: Croom Helm, 1985), pp. 173–202, at p. 193. He lists this document as coming from box 684, Warner Brothers Archives, USC Special Collections [hereafter WB Archives].

51. Ibid., p. 180.

52. For discussions of the significance of *The Stranger,* see Friedrich, *City of Nets,* p. 266, and Michael Wood, *America in the Movies* (New York: Columbia University Press, 1989 [1975]), pp. 122–4. Edward G. Robinson thought little of the film and his own performance: "It was bloodless, and so was I." Quoted by Andrew Sinclair, *Spiegel: The Man Behind the Pictures* (Boston: Little, Brown, 1987), pp. 44–5.

53. When screenwriter Hecht asked Selznick to contribute to Jewish political charities in the 1940s, Selznick responded: "I'm an American and not a Jew. . . . It would be silly of me to pretend suddenly that I'm a Jew, with some sort of full-blown Jewish psychology." Hecht then wagered him to name any three people in Hollywood, and he would ask them whether they regard Selznick to be "an American or a Jew." Hecht called up Martin Quigley of the *Motion Picture Exhibitors Herald* and met the response: "I'd say David Selznick was a Jew." Selznick's second choice was the screenwriter Nunnally Johnson, who "hemmed a few moments but finally offered the same reply." In desperation, Selznick told Hecht to put Selznick's own agent Leland Hayward on the line. He replied: "For God's sake, what's the matter with David? He's a Jew and he knows it." Friedrich, *City of Nets,* pp. 359–60.

54. Leonard Mosley, *Zanuck: The Rise and Fall of Hollywood's Last Tycoon* (Boston: Little, Brown, 1984), pp. 210–11.

55. Friedrich, *City of Nets,* pp. 365–6. Paraphrase of Lardner in Nora Sayre, *Running Time: Films of the Cold War* (New York: Dial Press, 1982), p. 40. Elia Kazan, *Elia Kazan: A Life* (New York: Anchor Books, 1989), p. 333.

56. Walter Millis, ed., *The Forrestal Diaries* (New York: Viking Press, 1951), pp. 242–3. Forrestal's swipe at communist attorneys may have been a reference to Alger Hiss.

57. Rankin quoted by Friedrich, *City of Nets,* p. 321n.

58. Ibid., pp. 299–300.

59. Taylor quoted by Doherty, *Projections of War,* p. 144.

60. For Rand's and Mayer's testimony, see Friedrich, *City of Nets,* pp. 316–20, and House Committee on Un-American Activities, *Hearings Regarding the Communist Infiltration of the Motion Picture Industry . . . before the Committee on Un-American Activities. House of Representatives, 80th Congress, Pursuant to H. Res. 111* (Washington, D.C.: U.S. GPO, 1947). For selected excerpts from HUAC testimony including that of Rand, see Eric Bentley, ed., *Thirty Years of Treason: Excerpts from Hearings before the House Committee on Un-American Activities, 1938–1968* (New York: Viking Press, 1971), esp. pp. 111–19.

61. Winnington quoted by John Walker, ed., *Halliwell's Film Guide,* 8th ed., revised and updated (New York: HarperCollins, 1992), p. 1037.

62. See Charles Oliver, "Beyond Taste: The Perils of Defining Art," *Reason* 32(10) (March 2001): 57–61, a review essay on Louis Torres and Michelle Marder Kamhi's *What Art Is: The Esthetic Theory of Ayn Rand* (Chicago: Open Court, 2000).
63. Ludwig von Mises, "Why 'Intellectuals' Hate Capitalism," *Human Events*, 14(11) (16 March 1957): sec. II. This article was an extract from his book *The Anti-Capitalistic Mentality* (Princeton: D. Van Nostrand, 1956). Ronald Reagan claimed to be a devoted reader of the newsletter *Human Events*.
64. Friedrich, *City of Nets*, p. 318.
65. Zanuck quoted by Mosley, *Zanuck*, p. 188.
66. Butler quoted by Richard Barnet, *The Roots of War* (New York: Penguin, 1972), p. 58.
67. Edwin Kiester, *The Case of the Missing Executive* (New York: American Jewish Committee, Institute of Human Relations, 1972), pp. 10–11, and G. William Domhoff and Richard Zweigenhaft, *Jews in the Protestant Establishment* (New York: Praeger, 1982), pp. 22–3.
68. A. A. Berle, Assistant Secretary of State, "American Motion Pictures in the Postwar World," 22 February 1944, in U.S. NA RG59, 800.4061, 1940–4 Motion Pictures.
69. Ibid.
70. Hays address in *Motion Picture Herald*, 31 March 1945, and Hays Papers, II, reel 35.
71. Eric Johnston, *America Unlimited* (Garden City, N.Y.: Doubleday, Doran, 1944), p. 245, and his "Utopia Is Production," *Screen Actor* 14(9) (August 1946): 14–15, at p. 15. I am grateful to Valerie Yaros, historian and archivist for the Screen Actors Guild, who managed to track down this article, even though previous historians have incorrectly listed the date of publication as either 1945 or April 1946. See Lary May's otherwise skillful dissection of these texts in *The Big Tomorrow: Hollywood and the Politics of the American Way* (Chicago: University of Chicago Press, 2000), chap. 5. Johnston had delivered the "Utopia Is Production" speech to a convention held in Chicago's Stevens Hotel for the International Alliance of Theatrical Stage Employees and Motion Picture Machine Operators (IATSE). Speculation that Johnston might receive the Republican nomination for president of the United States had begun as early as 1943. Finding Johnston freer of the "heavy-jowled, paunchy, fish-eyed, cautious, stuffy, overbearing, tired or combative" qualities of other business leaders, George Soule wrote that "Mr. Johnston obviously does not sound like a candidate. Perhaps it is because he does not spread the odor of the traditional politician that a number of his acquaintances would like to see him running things." See George Soule, "Eric Johnston: Knight-Errant of Main Street," *New Republic*, no. 1515 [aka 109(24)] (13 December 1943), pp. 841–4.

3. THE MPAA AND THE STATE DEPARTMENT

1. Hays letter of 21 October 1943 to Cordell Hull and memo of 18 October 1943 in U.S. NA RG59, 800.4061, 1940–4 Motion Pictures; italics his.

2. Ibid.
3. Allport memorandum of 14 July 1944, U.S. NA RG59, 800.4061, 1940–4 Motion Pictures.
4. Letter of Cornelia A. Gibbs to Joseph C. Grew, Department of State, 28 June 1945, U.S. NA RG59, 800.4061, 1945–9 Motion Pictures.
5. For a discussion of Brown's and Deming's responses to Disney's film, see Julianne Burton, "Don (Juanito) Duck and the Imperial–Patriarchal Unconscious: Disney Studios, the Good Neighbor Policy, and the Packaging of Latin America," in Andrew Parker, Mary Russo, Doris Sommer, and Patricia Yaeger, eds., *Nationalisms and Sexualities* (New York: Routledge, 1992), pp. 21–41, at p. 31.
6. Leo Rosten, *Hollywood: The Movie Colony, the Movie Makers* (New York: Harcourt, Brace, 1941), p. 356. The sudden fear of supposed revolutionary themes may have caught Hollywood by surprise, even if it was the leftist Paul Robeson singing "Ol' Man River." Only two years before, Poland's Ministry of Interior clamped bans on three Hollywood studios for allegedly calling a boxer "Pulaski" and a thuggish gangster "Kosciuszko," names for characters that were a slur on the Polish nation and two of the most beloved heroes of the American Revolution, Count Casimir Pulaski and General Tadeusz Kosciuszko. See "Poles Bar Films of 3 Studios Here," *New York Times*, 25 May 1934. Back in 1928, Poland had established a Central Committee on Film and Cinema lodged in the Ministry of Interior, a centralization of administration that an unnamed German newspaper praised as setting a good example for the rest of Europe. See *World-wide Motion Picture Developments* (Motion Picture Section, U.S. Department of Commerce), 3 October 1928, p. 2.
7. Duggan letter of 19 December 1929, box 58, MPRC files.
8. Ulyses Petit de Murat, "Discusses American Film," *Detroit Free Press*, 9 November 1941. See MPPDA press summary of 21 November 1941, p. 395, Hays Papers, II, reel 29.
9. Rosten, *Hollywood*, p. 356.
10. Elbert G. Matthews memorandum of 26 October 1944, Kabul, U.S. NA RG59, 800.4061, 1940–4 Motion Pictures. In the 1940s, Sunni Islam was glibly condemned as "fanatical," while Shiite Islam was thought closer to the putative moderation of Western religion. In the 1980s, the State Department simply reversed this demonology, as Shiism emerged as its leading symbol for rampaging fundamentalism and terrorism. In the wake of the World Trade Center catastrophe, it remains to be seen whether anti-Sunni brands of Islamophobia will have a resurgence.
11. James W. Gantenbein memorandum of 22 May 1944, Quito, U.S. NA RG59, 800.4061, 1940–4 Motion Pictures.
12. Boaz Long memorandum of 28 September 1944, Guatemala City, U.S. NA RG59, 800.4061, 1940–4 Motion Pictures.
13. Carlton J. H. Hayes memorandum of 14 February 1944, Madrid, U.S. NA RG59, 800.4061, 1940–4 Motion Pictures. Judging by its date, he sent this without Berle's prompting.
14. "ICD Joins Military Government," *Military Government Bulletin*, 22 December 1945, p. 5, in GAD-Suitland, RG-260, Records of the United States

Occupation Headquarters, WWII, box 242, Office of Military Government, Information Control Division. This newsletter is also reproduced in Lawrence H. Suid, ed., *Film and Propaganda in America: A Documentary History*, vol. IV: *1945 and After* (Westport, Conn.: Greenwood Press, 1991), pp. 48–53.

15. See MPPDA press summary of 27 May 1943, pp. 83–4, Hays Papers, II, reel 31.

16. Breen quoted by Thomas Doherty, *Projections of War: Hollywood, American Culture, and World War II* (New York: Columbia University Press, 1993), p. 38.

17. Martin Quigley, Jr., and Richard Gertner, *Films in America, 1929–1969: A Panoramic View of Four Decades of Sound* (New York: Golden Press, 1970), p. 171.

18. American Consul General, Munich, 26 February 1947, no. 428, to U.S. Department of State, U.S. NA RG59, 862.4061, 1945–9 Motion Pictures.

19. HICOG memorandum of 25 July 1950, "German Press Comments on Status of Film Industry in Germany," U.S. NA RG59, 862A.452, 1950–4 Motion Pictures.

20. See Enclosure no. 2 to Despatch no. 428, American Consul General Munich, dated 26 February 1947, "German Attitudes toward American Motion Pictures," U.S. NA RG59, 862.4061, 1945–9 Motion Pictures. The writer for the *Mittag* appears to hold the common but mistaken belief that *Bengali* (the German release title for *Lives of a Bengal Lancer*) is an English movie rather than a Hollywood production. This cinematic celebration of British imperialism enjoyed significant popularity in Nazi Germany, but the U.S. occupation regime did not permit it to be released again until 1951. My thanks to Prof. Eric Rentschler for this background.

21. Eugene Anderson memorandum to John Begg, 7 February 1946, "Acquisition of Movie Theatres in Germany by Paramount Pictures," U.S. NA RG59, 862.4061, 1945–9 Motion Pictures.

22. J. K. Galbraith reply of 27 March 1946 to Bernard Bernstein, U.S. NA RG59, 862.4061, 1-3062, 1945–9 Motion Pictures. Bernstein's letter is dated 30 January 1946.

23. Letter of J. J. McCloy to Harry Hopkins, 8 January 1944, re "Motion Picture Production in Post-war Germany," U.S. NA RG59, 862.4061, 1945–9 MP1-1145 (1944 document filed in 1945–9 box under collection "Motion Picture Production in Post-war Germany").

24. "Crisis in the Bavarian Film Industry," report of 15 March 1951, U.S. NA RG59, 862A.452, 1950–4 Motion Pictures.

25. Theodore Smith letter of 23 March 1951 to Isaiah Frank, U.S. NA RG59, 862A.452, 1950–4 Motion Pictures.

26. HICOG Frankfurt, "Motion Picture Entertainment, 35mm, 00038, first calendar quarter 1952," Foreign Service Serial no. 725, U.S. NA RG59, 862A.452/6-1752, 1950–4 Motion Pictures.

27. Department of State memorandum of conversation, "Disposition of Former Reich-Owned Motion Picture Properties under Allied High Commission Law Number 32," U.S. NA RG59, 862A.452/10-2352, 1950–4 Motion Pictures.

28. Dean Acheson, Department of State airgram, 13 September 1951, U.S. NA RG59, 862A.452, 1950–4 Motion Pictures.

29. See HICOG, Frankfurt memorandum of 12 October 1951, despatch no. 1080, in NA RG59, 862A.452, 1950–4.
30. Dean Acheson, Department of State, outgoing airgram to HICOG, Frankfurt, A-467, 8 August 1951, U.S. NA RG59, 862A.452, 8-851 1950–4 Motion Pictures.
31. Cf. HICOG Frankfurt memorandum of 9 November 1950, U.S. NA RG59, 862A.452/11-950 with U.S. NA RG59, 862A.452/4-1051.
32. Dean Acheson, outgoing telegram, Department of State, to HICOG Frankfurt, 19 October 1950, U.S. NA RG59, 862A.452/10-1950, 1950–4 Motion Pictures.
33. "Importation of U.S. Films to Germany," memorandum of 28 March 1951, U.S. NA RG59, 862A.452, 1950–4 Motion Pictures.
34. Theodore Kaghan, Chief, Information Services Division, Office of Public Affairs, HICOG Frankfurt, to the Department of State, "Financial Assistance for German Film Industry," despatch no. 1080, October 1951, U.S. NA RG59, 862A.452/10-1251, 1950–4 Motion Pictures.
35. For background on the German Right and film, see the article in the *Münchener Allgemeine* (18 June 1950) headlined "Hugenberg's UFA Plans" by Edmund Schopen, chairman of the Bavarian Theatre Organization. He charged that the "Dusseldorf circle" of Hugenberg, Groven, Dr. Winkler, and Dr. Dahlgren was engineering a plot against UFA decartelization. U.S. NA RG59, 862A.452/7-2550, 1950–4 Motion Pictures.
36. Major General Smedley D. Butler, "America's Armed Forces," pts. I–III, in *Common Sense* 4(10) (October 1935): 6–10, 4(11) (November 1935): 8–12, 4(12) (December 1935): 10–14; the quotation is from pt. II: 8. In a letter to FDR, Josephus Daniels sounded almost as alarmed as Butler when he complained that the oil executives "would like to have an Ambassador who would be a messenger boy for their companies." Josephus Daniels, letter to FDR of 7 October 1937, PSF (President's Secretary's File) Mexico, FDR Library. My thanks to Andrew C. Tripp for this reference.
37. North quoted by Ian Jarvie, *Hollywood's Overseas Campaign: The North Atlantic Movie Trade, 1920–1950* (New York: Cambridge University Press, 1992), p. 323.
38. Sayre quoted in ibid., p. 345.
39. Letter of Ellis Arnall, President of the Society of Independent Motion Picture Producers, to Henry J. Kellerman, Officer in Charge, German and Austrian Public Affairs, Department of State, 10 March 1950, U.S. NA RG59, 862A.452/3-1050, 1950–4 Motion Pictures.
40. Dean Acheson, Department of State, outgoing airgram of 7 November 1950, U.S. NA RG59, 862A.452/11-750, 1950–4 Motion Pictures.
41. Alfred V. Roemer, HICOG Frankfurt, 1717, "Film Daily Article" to State Department, 21 November 1950, U.S. NA RG59, 862A.452/11-2150, 1950–4 Motion Pictures.
42. F. McCracken Fisher memorandum to Herbert T. Edwards, 24 September 1951, U.S. NA RG59, 862A.452/9-2451, 1950–4 Motion Pictures.
43. According to Leo P. Crespi, Chief, Reactions Analysis Staff, Office of Public Affairs, HICOG, in a memorandum of 2 August 1950 entitled "German

Reactions to the American-Sponsored Newsreel – *Welt im Film*," "Among the
small minority of U.S. Zone respondents who have seen newsreels other than
Welt im Film – and who can hence make a comparative judgment – prefer-
ences seem pretty well divided at this time between *Welt im Film* and Fox
Movie Tone News. Among Berliners, however, – the majority of which have
had the opportunity to see more than one newsreel – preference for *Welt im
Film* leads by a wide margin." U.S. NA RG59, 862A.452/8-250.

44. Henry P. Pilgert, *Press, Radio and Film in West Germany, 1945–1953* (n.l.:
Historical Division, Office of the Executive Secretary, Office of the U.S. High
Commissioner for Germany, 1953), p. 97.

45. State Department minutes of 22 January 1952, U.S. NA RG59, 862A.452/1-
2252, 1950–4 Motion Pictures.

46. Data and quotation in Thomas Guback, "Shaping the Film Business in Postwar Germany: The Role of the U.S. Film Industry and the U.S. State," in
Paul Kerr, ed., *The Hollywood Film Industry: A Reader* (London and New
York: Routledge/British Film Institute, 1986), pp. 245–75, at p. 261. This
essay refines arguments developed in his book *The International Film Industry: Western Europe and America since 1945* (Bloomington: Indiana
University Press, 1969). Gross's statement appeared in debate on the United States Information Agency (USIA) in the *Congressional Record, Proceedings and Debates of the 86th Congress, 1st Session, 1959*, vol. 105, pt. 7,
p. 9128.

47. John Foster Dulles, Department of State instruction no. A-783, 6 January
1954, "Film Agreement between United States and Germany," to HICOG,
Bonn, RG59, 862A.452/12-1653, 1950–4 Motion Pictures.

48. Jack Valenti, "The 'Foreign Service' of the Motion Picture Association of
America," *Journal of the Producers Guild of America* 10(1) (March 1968):
21–5, at p. 22. Will H. Hays, *The Memoirs of Will H. Hays* (Garden City,
N.Y.: Doubleday, 1955), p. 334. For a discussion of Valenti's remark and its
wider context, see Thomas Guback, "Hollywood's International Market,"
in Tino Balio, ed., *The American Film Industry*, rev. ed. (Madison: University
of Wisconsin Press, 1985), pp. 463–86, at p. 471.

4. GRIERSON, THE DOCUMENTARY SPIRIT, AND THE PROJECTION OF BRITAIN

1. Owen Young quoted in Gleason Archer, *History of Radio to 1926* (New
York: American Historical Society, 1938), p. 164.

2. Confidential memorandum of Neville Kearney, Federation of British Industries, to A. Willert, Foreign Office, PRO FO395/452, especially pp. 263–9.

3. *Parliamentary Debates (Commons)*, 22 March 1927, vol. 204, col. 259.

4. "Number 9. The Association of Cine-Technicians Evidence Submitted to the
Board of Trade," Moyne committee files, PRO BT55/3.

5. See the editors' introduction to Justine Ashby and Andrew Higson, eds., *British Cinema, Past and Present* (London: Routledge, 2000), p. 14.

6. "Number 6. Cinematograph Films Act, 1927," Board of Trade memorandum
to the Moyne committee, 14 May 1936, PRO BT55/3. See also Margaret

Dickinson and Sarah Street, *Cinema and State: The Film Industry and the British Government, 1927–1984* (London: British Film Institute, 1985), pp. 42 and 64. They rely on U.S. Department of Commerce figures, which are slightly different from the Board of Trade numbers; i.e., the Board of Trade said Britain produced 26 films in 1926, while the U.S. Department of Commerce put the figure at 4.8 percent out of 742 films (approximately 36). The discrepancy likely results from some films that were produced elsewhere in the empire or Commonwealth, movies that the Board of Trade did not count as British films.

7. For *Evening Standard* and similar articles from U.K. press, see clip file in box 4, Paul Rotha Papers, UCLA Special Collections.

8. See J. M. Keynes, "The Arts Council: Its Policy and Hopes," *The Listener,* 12 July 1945; letter of J. Pole, director of publicity, United Artists, *The Times* (London), 11 July 1945; letter of J. M. Keynes apologizing to Pole, *The Times* (London), 12 July 1945; and memorandum on the affair by Richard Johnson, Third Secretary of U.S. Embassy, London, 14 July 1945, NA RG59, 841.403/7-1445.

9. The film league, as well as the British Films Week, undergo treatment in my forthcoming volume on cinema and empire (working title: *Hollywood and the Decline of European Imperialism*).

10. *Parliamentary Debates (Commons)*, 29 June 1925, vol. 185, col. 2018.

11. Ibid., col. 2084, and *Manchester Guardian*, 30 June 1925, the latter reporting the interruption of cheers.

12. *Manchester Guardian*, 20 June 1925. Ian Jarvie, *Hollywood's Overseas Campaign: The North Atlantic Movie Trade, 1920–1950* (New York: Cambridge University Press, 1992), p. 131n, attacks Dickinson and Street's study of cinema and the British state for allegedly "misattribut[ing] the letter to the *Daily Telegraph*, a paper with which the *Morning Post* later merged." On pp. 106–7, he also implies that the elites who wrote this letter chose the *Morning Post* instead of *The Times* and other outlets. *The Times* (London), 20 June 1925, p. 11, published it within an article headlined "Future of British Films: A Plea for Inquiry." The letter was released to numerous newspapers.

13. *Parliamentary Debates (Lords)*, 14 May 1925, vol. 61, cols. 273 and 277.

14. "Home Film Industry in Jeopardy," *Manchester Guardian*, 4 June 1925, p. 13.

15. These public inquiries will undergo exploration in my forthcoming book on film and imperialism (see note 9).

16. For figures on EMB budget, see Dickinson and Street, *Cinema and State,* p. 28, which cites PRO DO [Dominions Office] 35/203. Paul Rotha, *Documentary Diary: An Informal History of the British Documentary Film, 1928–1939* (London: Secker & Warburg/New York: Hill & Wang, 1973), p. 21, claims the overall EMB budget was higher, though he does not cite any source. On p. 41, in a rare loss for words, he writes that EMB equipment "scratched negative like – well, like what?" Amery testimony from *Parliamentary Debates (Commons)*, 28 March 1927, vol. 204, col. 846.

17. Tallents quoted by Rotha, *Documentary Diary*, pp. 25–6; Amery quoted by Dickinson and Street, *Cinema and State,* p. 28.

18. See Paul Swann, *The British Documentary Film Movement, 1926–1946* (Cambridge: Cambridge University Press, 1989); cf. the critique of Swann in Ian Aitken, *Film and Reform: John Grierson and the Documentary Film Movement* (London: Routledge, 1990), especially pp. 13–14.
19. Forsyth Hardy, ed., *Grierson on Documentary* (London: Faber & Faber, 1966), pp. 207, 290–1. Rotha, *Documentary Diary*, pp. 20–1. See also Paul Rotha, with Sinclair Road & Richard Griffith, *Documentary Film[: The Use of the Film Medium to Interpret Creatively and in Social Terms the Life of the People as It Exists in Reality]* (New York: Hastings House, 1968 [1935; 3d ed., 1952]), pp. 203–4.
20. Rotha, *Documentary Diary*, pp. 20–1. Grierson interviewed in Elizabeth Sussex, *The Rise and Fall of British Documentary* (Berkeley: University of California Press, 1975), p. 3.
21. Rotha, *Documentary Diary*, pp. 43–4.
22. Hoare quoted by Philip M. Taylor, "British Official Attitudes towards Propaganda Abroad, 1918–39," in Nicholas Pronay and D. W. Spring, eds., *Propaganda, Politics, and Film, 1918–45* (London: Macmillan, 1982), pp. 23–49, at pp. 38–9.
23. Taylor, "British Official Attitudes," pp. 41–2, 44–5, and D. W. Ellwood, "'Showing the World What Is Owed to Britain': Foreign Policy and Cultural Propaganda, 1935–45," also in Pronay and Spring, *Propaganda, Politics, and Film*, pp. 50–73, at pp. 52 and 69.
24. Graham Greene, "*Song of Ceylon*," *The Spectator*, 4 October 1935, reprinted in John Russell Taylor, ed., *The Pleasure Dome: Graham Greene – The Collected Film Criticism, 1935–40* (Oxford: Oxford University Press, 1980), p. 25.
25. For a cogent analysis of Jennings's later work, as well as that of Benjamin Britten, see Peter Stansky and William Abrahams, *London's Burning: Life, Death, and Art in the Second World War* (Stanford: Stanford University Press, 1994).
26. See Watt interview in Sussex, p. 49; Rotha, *Documentary Diary*, pp. 132–3. On pp. 231–2, Rotha fiercely disagrees with Watt giving Cavalcanti priority over Grierson's contribution to documentary film. This debate "smouldered" from the late 1930s to well into the postwar period. Aitken, *Film and Reform*, p. 127, attacks the quality of the equipment, and D. L. LeMahieu in *A Culture for Democracy: Mass Communication and the Cultivated Mind in Britain between the Wars* (Oxford: Oxford University Press / Clarendon Press, 1988), p. 221, decries Rotha's *Contact* as archaic, a "relic." Gavin Lambert's essay "Sight and Sound" (1950), reprinted in Richard Dyer MacCann, ed., *Film: A Montage of Theories – 42 Film Makers and Critics Discuss the Art and Theory of Film* (New York: E. P. Dutton, 1966), pp. 45–52, openly admits: ". . . the senior generation of film theorists in this country – Rotha, Lindgren, Manvell . . . – had their ideas and standards formed and fixed by the silent cinema. . ." (p. 45).
27. Lancelot Hogben, "The New Visual Culture: A Review," *Sight and Sound* 5(17) (Spring 1936): 6–9, at p. 7. Claiming that documentary holds the promise of rendering complex mathematics intelligible to people of average intelligence, Hogben believed this film genre "could make the bugbear of the class-

room the most breathless adventure of the curriculum" (p. 9). *The Cinema* cited in "Number 8. Memorandum on Documentary and Cultural Films . . . Submitted by the Associated Realist Film Producers, Ltd.," esp. Annex III, pp. 24–6, 12 May 1936, PRO BT55/3.

28. Sussex, *Rise and Fall of British Documentary*, p. 3.
29. Dickinson and Street, *Cinema and State*, p. 65; Swann, *British Documentary Film Movement*, p. 15.
30. PRO BT55/3.
31. Roger Manvell, *Film* (Harmondsworth: Penguin, 1950 [1944]), p. 199. Please see Chapter 9 for further background on the rise of the ciné-club movement.
32. Rotha, *Documentary Diary*, p. 116.
33. Joyce Nelson, *The Colonized Eye: Rethinking the Grierson Legend* (Toronto: Between the Lines, 1988), pp. 34–5.
34. Gary Evans, *John Grierson and the National Film Board: The Politics of Wartime Propaganda* (Toronto: University of Toronto Press, 1984), pp. 242–7, 266–7.
35. Forsyth Hardy, *John Grierson: A Documentary Biography* (London: Faber & Faber, 1979), pp. 87–8.
36. Letter of David Schrire to Paul Rotha, 11 July 1934, Rotha Papers, box 70, file 7. His "bitch" remark may confirm documentary director Muriel Box's view that the "progressive" boys club in the vanguard of the documentary movement often practiced a Cro-Magnon sexism. See her *Odd Woman Out* (London: Leslie Frewin, 1974).
37. Letter of Schrire to Rotha, op. cit. Rotha ended up working with Ralph Bond and admiring him; but Bond was usually the Grierson associate most accused of Stalinist tendencies. There were vague accusations that Bond diverted information on the BBC to Moscow, while working on a documentary. See Hardy, *John Grierson*, pp. 87–8.
38. Rotha, *Documentary Diary*, p. 143.
39. The critique of Auden appears in "Meetings and Acquaintances," *World Film News* 1(1) (April 1936): 13. The author is listed as "All Hands," suggesting that the entire editorial board of WFN opposed Auden's critique. Auden had slipped his attack on the class bases of the documentary film movement into an unsigned book review of Rotha's *Documentary Film* for the BBC house organ *The Listener* 15(371) (19 February 1936): 368–9.
40. "Meetings and Acquaintances," op cit.
41. For the Grierson–Jennings clash, see Aitken, *Film and Reform*, p. 147. Joyce Nelson, *Colonized Eye*, pp. 116–17, cites Canadian film historians Peter Morris and Gary Evans on the Griersonian obsession with work and the rarity of leisure themes. An NFB filmmaker spoke of hundreds of films about work, whereas scholar Evans could find only two World War II–era NFB films about sport and leisure: *Hot Ice* (1940) and *Ski in the Valley of the Saints* (1944).
42. Walter Lippmann, *Public Opinion* (New York: Macmillan, 1957 [1922]), pp. 31, 236, and 248.
43. H. L. Mencken, "Katzenjammer," *American Mercury*, January 1926, quoted and discussed by Ronald Steel, *Walter Lippmann and the American Century* (Boston: Little, Brown, 1980), p. 214.

44. Tallents list reprinted in Roy Armes, *A Critical History of the British Cinema* (New York: Oxford University Press, 1978), p. 133.
45. Watt quoted in ibid., p. 133.
46. Paul Rotha, *Rotha on the Film: Selection of Writings about the Cinema* (Fair Lawn, N.J.: Essential Books, 1956), p. 26.
47. Schrire letter of 25 November 1935 quoted by Rotha, *Documentary Diary*, p. 30.
48. Rotha quoted and Soviet film discussed by LeMahieu, *Culture for Democracy*, pp. 215–20 (quote at p. 219). Stephen C. Shafer, *British Popular Films, 1929–1939: The Cinema of Reassurance* (London: Routledge, 1997), chap. 3, gives a sense of the wide range of opinions on "escapist versus realistic" portrayals of the working class in British films. A typist testified in *Picturegoer Weekly* (30 July 1932) that "it does not follow that because I am a typist I want to see films about typists." She added: "on the contrary, I like my heroines to be . . . one of the thousands of things I am not." Another film fan expressed the reasons she spent her leisure time at the cinema in a letter to *Film Pictorial* (22 July 1933): "To see our ordinary lives portrayed on the screen over and over again? Emphatically not! What we want is to be carried right away from our own sphere of life – we see and hear enough about that! – and be taken to realms which have hitherto existed only in our imagination."
49. Régis Debray, *Charles de Gaulle: Futurist of the Nation* (London: Verso, 1994), pp. 45–6.
50. Harry Alan Potamkin, "Grierson's *Drifters*," *Close Up* (Switzerland), October 1930, reprinted in Lewis Jacobs, ed., *The Documentary Tradition, from Nanook to Woodstock* (New York: Hopkinson & Blake, 1971), pp. 64–5.
51. Stephen Tallents, *The Projection of England* (London: Faber & Faber, 1932), p. 32. See also Swann, *British Documentary Film Movement*, p. 46.
52. For the seminal influence of Turin over Grierson, see Aitken, *Film and Reform*. For the distinction between human and social documentary, see William Stott, *Documentary Expression and Thirties America* (New York: Oxford University Press, 1973).
53. Bertolt Brecht, "The Popular and the Realistic," in John Willett, ed. and trans., *Brecht on Theatre: The Development of an Aesthetic* (New York: Hill & Wang, 1992 [1964]), pp. 107–12.
54. Grierson quoted by K. J. Coldicutt, "*Turksib*: Building a Railroad," in the bulletin of the Realist Film Association in Melbourne, Australia, April 1933, reprinted in Jacobs, *Documentary Tradition*, pp. 45–8, at p. 48.
55. "British Film Success at Venice: *Man of Aran*," *The Times* (London), 17 September 1934; and Ivor Montagu, *Film World* (Baltimore: Penguin, 1964), pp. 281–5.
56. John Grierson, "Flaherty's Poetic *Moana*," *New York Sun*, 8 February 1926, reprinted in Jacobs, *Documentary Tradition*, pp. 25–6.
57. *Observer*, 21 August 1932, and Aitken, *Film and Reform*, p. 8.
58. Rotha, *Documentary Diary*, pp. xxii–xxiii.
59. "Plight of British Film," *South Wales News*, 25–26 February 1926, in report of A. B. Cooke, Swansea, to U.S. Department of State, 12 March 1926, NA RG59, 841.4061/56.

60. John Grierson, "The Future for British Films," *Spectator*, 14 May 1932; and Jarvie, *Hollywood's Overseas Campaign*, pp. 78–9.
61. Grierson letter to Elton of 28 January 1941, copy received by Basil Wright, box 70, file 2, Rotha Papers.
62. Letter of David Schrire to Paul Rotha, 4 January 1946, box 70, file 7, Rotha Papers.
63. John Grierson, minutes of evidence, Moyne committee, 30 June 1936, PRO BT55/4 CCF2. Also cited by Swann, *British Documentary Film Movement*, p. 15.
64. John Grierson, "The Film in International Relations," 21 November 1944, speeches and articles for vol. II, box 70, file 3, Rotha Papers.

5. THE KORDA ROAD TO RICHES, RECOVERY, AND RUIN

1. *Parliamentary Debates (Lords)*, 6 July 1925, vol. 61, col. 1055. At that time Newton attacked the Federation of British Industries for "purely dilatory" tactics in attempting to forestall state intervention by developing plans among private film interests. As the situation for British film worsened, the Federation of British Industries became receptive to state action.
2. *Parliamentary Debates (Commons)*, 22 March 1927, vol. 204, col. 238.
3. Letter of A. Fletcher to Rowland Kenney, Esq., News Dept., Foreign Office, 7 September 1934, PRO FO395/517, p. 327 of file.
4. Letter of Sir Arthur Willert, News Department, Foreign Office, to Lord Tyrrell, British Embassy, Paris, 25 March 1931, PRO FO395/452.
5. See the extensive correspondence in PRO FO395/452.
6. Foreign Office minute of Sir A. Willert, 27 November 1930, P2214/17/150, PRO FO395/441. For further background on British censorship, especially of *How Lord Kitchener Was Betrayed*, see James Robertson, *The Hidden Cinema: British Film Censorship in Action, 1913–1972* (London: Routledge, 1993 [1989]), especially chap. 1.
7. See my forthcoming book (working title: *Hollywood and the Decline of European Imperialism*) on film and imperialism for more details on the *Gunga Din* episode.
8. Bernard Charman, "Britain Must Develop Stars to Stay in Race, Says Charman," *Motion Picture Herald*, 22 October 1932, p. 11. He quotes Wilcox from the *Daily Mail*.
9. PRO FO395/517. See documents numbered 317, 329, 331. I am grateful to Jarvie's work for helping me to locate these sources.
10. British audiences flocked to hear such lines as Charles II declaring, "The King is father to his people . . . ," while Nell interjects: "Well, of a good many of them." Unfortunately for Wilcox, heavy-handed censorship of cleavage and wisecracks may have greatly diminished the film's appeal to U.S. audiences.
11. Paul Tabori, *Alexander Korda: A Biography* (London: Oldbourne, 1959), pp. 129–30.
12. *Motion Picture Herald*, quoted by Alexander Korda in letter to Martin Quigley, 16 June 1932, box 3, folder 22, Quigley Papers. The film was known as *Service for Ladies* in the United Kingdom.

13. For these and similar examples, see evidence of the Association of Cine-Technicians submitted to Board of Trade, PRO BT55/3.
14. Translated and quoted by Tabori, *Alexander Korda*, p. 51.
15. Ibid., p. 51.
16. See Lewis Lapham, *Lapham's Rules of Influence* (New York: Random House, 1999), p. 90.
17. Letter of Alexander Korda to Martin Quigley, 16 June 1932, box 3, folder 22, Quigley Papers.
18. For Balcon and Priestley attacks, see H. Mark Glancy, *When Hollywood Loved Britain: The Hollywood "British" Film, 1939–45* (Manchester: Manchester University Press, 1999), pp. 168–9.
19. Vansittart (who cowrote *Sixty Glorious Years*) quoted by Jeffrey Richards, *Visions of Yesterday* (London: Routledge & Kegan Paul, 1973), p. 4. In his entry for Wilcox in the *Dictionary of National Biography, 1971–1980* (Oxford: Oxford University Press, 1986), Richards denies Wilcox's claim that he was born in Cork County, Eire. Richards states that, despite Wilcox's Irish pride, he was actually born in Norwood, London.
20. Graham Greene review of *Nurse Edith Cavell* in *The Spectator*, 27 October 1939, reprinted in John Russell Taylor, ed., *The Pleasure Dome: Graham Greene – The Collected Film Criticism, 1935–40* (Oxford: Oxford University Press, 1980), pp. 247–8.
21. Michael Korda, *Charmed Lives* (New York: Random House, 1979), p. 84.
22. Cohn quoted by Paul F. Boller Jr. and Ronald L. Davis, *Hollywood Anecdotes* (New York: William Morrow, 1987), pp. 63–4. For a full portrait of Cohn, see Bernard F. Dick, *The Merchant Prince of Poverty Row: Harry Cohn of Columbia Pictures* (Lexington: University Press of Kentucky, 1993).
23. This correspondence can be found in box 814, file 621 (Korda), Records of the Legal Department, TCF.
24. Korda, *Charmed Lives*, pp. 84–5.
25. Ibid., p. 85, and Records of the Legal Department, TCF.
26. W. B. Courtney, "New Worlds for Alexander," *Collier's* 97(7) (15 February 1936): 25, 48–52, at 25; quoted by Karol Kulik, *Alexander Korda: The Man Who Could Work Miracles* (New Rochelle: Arlington House, 1975), p. 118.
27. "British Films: 'Closed House Policy' Effect in Germany and Russia/A Lesson for Europe," *Morning Post*, 25 February 1929; also available in NA RG59, 841.4061, 1910–29 [frame 911].
28. Kulik, *Alexander Korda*, p. 160.
29. Korda quoted by Stephen Watts, "Alexander Korda and the International Film," *Cinema Quarterly* 2(1) (Autumn 1933): 12–15, at 14. Kulik, *Alexander Korda*, pp. 97–8.
30. Korda quoted by Watts, pp. 14–15. The Feyder film in question was *L'Image* (*Das Bildnis*).
31. I have expanded upon the examples in Michael Korda's *Charmed Lives*, p. 81.
32. Sue Harper, "Studying Popular Taste: British Historical Films in the 1930s," in Richard Dyer and Ginette Vincendeau, eds., *Popular European Cinema* (London: Routledge, 1992), pp. 101–11. See also Sue Harper, *Picturing the*

Past: The Rise and Fall of the British Costume Film (London: British Film Institute, 1994).

33. Perry Anderson, "Components of the National Culture," in Alexander Cockburn and Robin Blackburn, eds., Student Power: Problems, Diagnosis, Action (Harmondsworth: Penguin Books, 1969), pp. 214–84.

34. Cripps quoted by Political and Economic Planning (PEP), The British Film Industry (London: PEP, 1952), p. 71.

35. Ibid., p. 72.

36. Kulik, Alexander Korda, p. 168.

37. John Grierson, introduction to F. D. Klingender and Stuart Legg, Money behind the Screen: A Report Prepared on Behalf of the Film Council (London: Lawrence & Wishart, 1937). Korda did not like the Wardour Street locale of most of Britain's film industry and headquartered his operation elsewhere.

38. PEP, British Film Industry, pp. 70–3.

39. Letter of Gradwell Sears to Jack Warner, 14 August 1939, reprinted in full in Randy Behlmer, ed., Inside Warner Brothers (1935–1951) (New York: Viking Press, 1985), p. 100. For more details on this film, see [The Private Lives of] Elizabeth and Essex file, 18027, WB Archives.

40. Ibid. The film had been adapted from Maxwell Anderson's 1930 verse play Elizabeth the Queen, a title retained in U.K. prints and sometimes used when the film is broadcast on television.

41. Warner letters to Sears, 14 July and 16 August 1939, in Behlmer, Inside Warner Brothers, pp. 98 and 100.

42. Peter Hay, Hollywood Anecdotes (New York: Oxford University Press, 1990), p. 144.

43. Quoted by Kulik, Alexander Korda, pp. 173–4n.

44. Balcon quoted in ibid., p. 169.

45. Hay, Hollywood Anecdotes, p. 164.

46. Wright quoted by Kulik, Alexander Korda, p. 173.

47. Marcel Ermans, "Alexander le Magnifique," trans. and reprinted (with commentary) in World Film News 2(3) (June 1937): 6–7. I discovered this article through Kulik's biography.

48. Ibid.

49. Ibid.

50. Tabori, Alexander Korda, p. 266. Some render Korda's statement on his blunders as follows: "If I make one, it's a beaut."

51. Parliamentary Debates (Commons), 4 November 1937, vol. 328, col. 1162.

52. Parliamentary Debates (Lords), 3 March 1938, vol. 107, col. 991. Cunliffe-Lister had been created Viscount Swinton in 1935 (and would become the 1st Earl of Swinton in 1955).

53. Parliamentary Debates (Commons), 4 November 1937, vol. 328, col. 1275.

54. Parliamentary Debates (Lords), 3 March 1938, vol. 107, cols. 996–8.

55. Sir Adrian Baillie, in Parliamentary Debates (Commons), 4 November 1937, vol. 328, col. 1204.

56. Stanley, in ibid., col. 1173.

57. Parliamentary Debates (Commons), 7 April 1937, vol. 322, col. 205, cited again in ibid., 4 November 1937, vol. 328, col. 1226.

58. Ibid., 4 April 1937, vol. 322, cols. 206–7, cited in ibid., 4 November 1937, vol. 328, col. 1226.
59. Ibid., 4 November 1937, vol. 328, col. 1231.
60. Ibid., cols. 1230–1.
61. For background on Arnold Wilson, see Simon Haxey, *England's Money Lords* (New York: Harrison–Hilton Books, 1939), pp. 24, 197, 211, and 214. See *The Times* (London), 24 September 1935 and 20 December 1938, and the *Manchester Guardian,* 10 October 1936 and 11 June 1938.
62. *Parliamentary Debates (Commons),* 4 November 1937, vol. 328, cols. 1233–6.
63. Ibid., col. 1248.
64. (U.K.) Board of Trade, *Report of a Committee Appointed by the Board of Trade to Consider the Position of British Films.* Rt. Hon. Lord Moyne (chairman), Cmd. 5320 (London: HMSO, 1936), p. 16, para. 44, which gives the figure of 147 defaults. For the leap to 350, see testimony of Captain David Euan Wallace in *Parliamentary Debates (Commons),* 24 February 1938, vol. 332, col. 630.
65. *Parliamentary Debates (Commons),* 4 November 1937, vol. 328, col. 1161.
66. "British Films: Interest in G.H.Q. Scheme, Need for a Great Leader," *Morning Post,* 19 March 1929, and "British Film: The Growth of Gaumont," *Morning Post,* 19 February 1929. See also NA RG59, 841.4061, 1910–29 [microfilm frames 900–1, 918].
67. *Parliamentary Debates (Lords),* 3 March 1938, vol. 107, col. 1004.
68. Ibid., col. 1019.
69. "Memorandum of Motion Producer Distributors of America, Inc.," p. 12, in Hays Papers, II, reel 19, frames 864–77.

6. THE AGE OF RANK

1. "British Films: Problem of Home Productions," *Morning Post,* 22 February 1929. See NA RG59, 841.4061, 1910–29, frame 908.
2. Robert Murphy, "Rank's Attempt on the American Market, 1944–1949," in James Curran and Vincent Porter, eds., *British Cinema History* (London: Weidenfeld & Nicolson/Totowa, N.J.: Barnes & Noble, 1983), pp. 164–78, at p. 165. Murphy then refutes the belief that Rank was so "stupid."
3. Alan Wood, *Mr. Rank: A Study of J. Arthur Rank and British Films* (London: Hodder & Stoughton, 1952), p. 75.
4. Ibid., pp. 80–1.
5. F. D. Klingender and Stuart Legg, *Money behind the Screen: A Report Prepared on Behalf of the Film Council* (London: Lawrence & Wishart, 1937), pp. 37–8. D. L. LeMahieu, *A Culture for Democracy: Mass Communication and the Cultivated Mind in Britain between the Wars* (Oxford: Oxford University Press/Clarendon Press, 1988), p. 230n, warns that this reference must be used "with caution," and Ian Jarvie in *Hollywood's Overseas Campaign: The North Atlantic Movie Trade, 1920–1950* (New York: Cambridge University Press, 1992), p. 153, calls their work "a simple Communist 'conspiracy' view of American machinations." While I can concur with LeMahieu that this

book exhibits "facile versions of economic determinism" (p. 309), I wish that he and Jarvie would provide more precise examples of factual errors in Klingender and Legg, who provide a large catalog of stock ownership and financial maneuverings in the film industry. See also Geoffrey Macnab, *J. Arthur Rank and the British Film Industry* (London: Routledge, 1993), p. 19.

6. Wilcox quoted by Margaret Dickinson and Sarah Street, *Cinema and State: The Film Industry and the British Government, 1927–1984* (London: British Film Institute, 1985), p. 81.

7. Ibid., pp. 81–3. As the Bank of England came under increasing pressure to promote industrial investment during the 1930s, Norman "always thought the Bank should restrict its interest to what he thought were 'basic' industries" such as steel, notes historian R. S. Sayers, *The Bank of England, 1891–1944,* 2 vols. (Cambridge: Cambridge University Press, 1986 [1976]), vol. 2, p. 550n. "When the film industry needed reconstruction, he would not touch it."

8. Wood, *Mr. Rank,* p. 111, and Macnab, *J. Arthur Rank,* p. 33.

9. Wood, *Mr. Rank,* pp. 68, 71, and 276; for further background on Wesley, see William Speck, *Stability and Strife: England, 1714–1760* (Cambridge, Mass.: Harvard University Press, 1979), pp. 116–18.

10. Wesley quoted by Speck, *Stability and Strife,* pp. 114–15. Ironically Joseph Rank, J. Arthur's father, was said to be a good dancer, but he did so only at home, in private.

11. John Wesley, *Sermons on Several Occasions,* 2 vols. (New York: T. Mason and G. Lane, 1839), vol. II, p. 415. See Sermon CXVII, "The Rich Man and Lazarus."

12. Wood, *Mr. Rank,* p. 223.

13. "King Arthur & Co.," *Time* 49(24) (19 May 1947): 87–94. Francis Sill Wickware, "J. Arthur Rank," *Life* 19(15) (8 October 1945): 107–21. Though "a very popular member of the sergeants' mess" during World War I, according to Michael Wakelin in *J. Arthur Rank: The Man behind the Gong* (London: Lion Publishing, 1996), p. 36, Rank eventually rose to his highest position of the war, the modest post of deputy-lieutenant.

14. G. A. Atkinson in *The Methodist Times,* quoted by R. J. Burnett and E. D. Martell, *The Devil's Camera: Menace of a Film-Ridden World* (London: Epworth Press, 1932), p. 12. See also Macnab, *J. Arthur Rank,* pp. 12–13.

15. Atkinson quoted by Burnett and Martell, *Devil's Camera,* pp. 36–7.

16. PRO HO45/15208.

17. Ibid.

18. Quoted by Burnett and Martell, *Devil's Camera,* pp. 10 and 58.

19. Ibid., p. 11. Atkinson quoted on p. 36.

20. Rank quoted by Wood, *Mr. Rank,* p. 69.

21. Film Council, "Cinema in the Service of Religion," *World Film News* 2(2) (May 1937): 10–11.

22. T. W. C. Curd, "Catholic Inaction!" *The Month,* March 1935, p. 257.

23. Film Council, "Cinema in the Service of Religion," loc. cit.

24. The Arts Enquiry, *The Factual Film* (London: PEP/Oxford University Press, 1947), p. 162.

25. John Grierson, "Filming the Gospel: A Dangerous Policy," *World Film News* 1(2) (May 1936): 23.
26. "King Arthur & Co.," 89.
27. Macnab, *J. Arthur Rank*, pp. 27–30, 205, and Wood, *Mr. Rank*, pp. 87–8.
28. Speech of 29 January 1902 quoted by Paul Foot, *Immigration and Race in British Politics* (Baltimore: Penguin, 1965), p. 88.
29. The purchase of Beaverbrook's chain of theaters in the late 1920s became a substantial minority of its circuit.
30. Wood, *Mr. Rank*, pp. 84, 86–7, 107.
31. Mary Field, "Children's Entertainment Films," in Peter Noble, ed., *British Film Yearbook, 1947–48* (London: Skelton Robinson), pp. 75–7.
32. Oath quoted by Macnab, *J. Arthur Rank*, p. 150.
33. Field, "Children's Entertainment Films," pp. 76–7.
34. Ibid., p. 77.
35. Ibid., p. 76, and Macnab, *J. Arthur Rank*, p. 235. See her memoir *Good Company: The Story of the Children's Entertainment Film* (London: Longmans, Green, 1952).
36. J. P. Mayer, *British Cinemas and Their Audiences: Sociological Studies* (London: Dennis Dobson, 1948), pp. 4–5, 276–7. See also Jakob Burckhardt, *Briefe an seinen Freund Friedrich von Preen* (Stuttgart: Deutsche Verlags-Anstalt, 1922), p. 130. Seneca, *Ad Lucilium Epistulae Morales,* 3 vols., trans. Richard M. Gunmere (Loeb Classical Library, London: William Heinemann, 1942 [1920]), I: 29–37. Blaise Pascal, *Pascal's Pensées,* trans. W. F. Trotter (New York: E. P. Dutton, 1958), p. 39. I have slightly revised Mayer's translations of Burckhardt and Pascal.
37. Mayer, *British Cinemas*, pp. 151–2.
38. Ibid., p. 152.
39. Breen letter to Johnston, 22 March 1946, *Wicked Lady* file, PCA, AAMPAS.
40. "King Arthur & Co.," 90.
41. Wood, *Mr. Rank*, p. 150.
42. Breen letter of 22 March 1946 to Eric Johnston, *Wicked Lady* file.
43. Letter of Breen to Eric Johnston, 13 February 1946, *Wicked Lady* file.
44. Quoted by Sheridan Morley, *James Mason: Odd Man Out* (London: Weidenfeld & Nicolson, 1984), pp. 61–2.
45. Mayer, *British Cinemas*, p. 8.
46. *Objective Burma* file, WB Archives.
47. "War Office 'Blow Up' U.S. Burma Film Fake," *Daily Sketch*, 25 September 1945; "Films and the Allies," *The Times* (London), 25 September 1945. Taylor made this remark in *SEAC: The Services Newspaper of South East Asia Command*. For these and numerous other clippings, see *Objective Burma* file, WB Archives.
48. *The Times* (London), 25 September 1945.
49. Letter of Max Milder to Jack Warner, 26 September 1945, in *Objective Burma* file, WB Archives.
50. Quoted in despatch of Richard K. Johnson, Third Secretary of London Embassy, to U.S. Department of State, 26 October 1945, in NA RG59, 841.4061, 1945–9.

51. Reg Whitley, "A-Bomb Film Toned Down," *Daily Mirror*, 6 October 1945. See Richard K. Johnson, despatch to U.S. Secretary of State, 22 October 1945, in NA RG59, 841.4061, 1945–9.
52. Paul Hunter, "Uncle Shylock Again?" *Liberty*, 9 February 1946, in *Objective Burma* file, WB Archives.
53. F. W. Allport, "Memorandum for Mr. Eric Johnston," 24 September 1946, p. 4, in NA RG59, 841.4061, 1945–9.
54. Ibid., p. 3.
55. Ibid., pp. 5–6. For data, see F. W. Allport, memorandum of 10 October 1946, NA RG59, 841.4061, 1945–9.
56. A. G. White, memorandum to R. J. Shackle, 11 July 1946, PRO BT64/2229.
57. This report was often consulted by the Board of Trade; see PRO BT64/2188.
58. PRO BT64/61/12979 XC9292. See also Dickinson and Street, *Cinema and State*, p. 127.
59. PRO BT64/2283 XC9253, p. 325 of file. Attached to memorandum of 14 May 1947. Jarvie, *Hollywood's Overseas Campaign*, p. 226, lists this document as 28 April 1947, although he may be citing a previous draft of Rowe-Dutton's memorandum.
60. PRO BT64/2283 XC9253, pp. 319 and 323.
61. Eric Johnston quoted in "Film 'Big 8' Bans Movies for Britain," *New York Times*, 9 August 1947, p. 5.
62. U.S. Senator Kenneth McKellar of Tennessee sent the *Washington Times Herald* editorial to Secretary of State George C. Marshall. See NA RG59, 841.4061, 8-1847, 1945–9.
63. Rundall memorandum of 23 February 1947 in PRO FO371/61064. For some reason his name is spelled "Rundle" on this document and elsewhere "Rundall."
64. Memorandum of conversation, 12 August 1947, NA RG59, 841.4061, 1945–9.
65. Wilfrid Eady, memorandum of conversation with Eric Johnston on 23 August in Washington, signed 27 August 1947, PRO BT64/2283, pp. 24–6 of file.
66. Ibid.
67. Minutes, United Kingdom Films Tax, 10 February 1948, PRO BT64/2370.
68. Ibid.
69. Ibid.
70. Macnab, *J. Arthur Rank*, p. 179.
71. "Can Film-makers Approach the Chancellor: Arguments against the New Tax," *Manchester Guardian*, 24 July 1947.
72. Breen letter of 14 September 1948, *Oliver Twist* file, PCA, AAMPAS. For general background, Macnab, *J. Arthur Rank*, p. 70.
73. See Breen letter to Jock Lawrence, 22 November 1950, *Oliver Twist* file.
74. ADL quoted in telegram of Francis S. Harmon to Eric Johnston in Paris, 7 September 1948; Julius Streicher, of course, was the self-proclaimed "Jew-baiter Number One" of Nazi Germany. Clipping from *Independent Film Journal* (2 December 1950) in *Oliver Twist* file.
75. Letter of Everett R. Clinchy, National Conference of Christians and Jews, to Nate Spingold, Columbia Pictures, 5 January 1951, in *Oliver Twist* file. See

this file for Gordon item dated 28 November 1950 and Hogan correspondence.

76. Breen letter to Sidney Schreiber, Esq., follow-up from a 22 November 1950 letter to Jock Lawrence, *Oliver Twist* file.

77. Letter of Eleanor Lewis to Miss Taylore, July 1947, *Black Narcissus* file, PCA, AAMPAS. This file also contains a clipping of Tomlinson's article entitled "*Black Narcissus* – Black Calumny."

78. Article from *The Tablet*, n.d., dateline 25 July 1947, *Black Narcissus* file.

79. Dickinson and Street, *Cinema and State*, pp. 155–6.

80. Ayn Rand, "Screen Guide for Americans," *Plain Talk* 2(1)(November 1947): 37–42.

81. For data on the decline of the businessman as villain and the wealthy as decadent, see tables provided by Lary May, *The Big Tomorrow: Hollywood and the Politics of the American Way* (Chicago: University of Chicago Press, 2000), pp. 273–4. His data show, however, that the consensus era of World War II had already created the decline in this movie character type. Johnston did what he could to prevent the reemergence of any vaguely anticapitalist rumblings. For the Rand and Johnston quotations, see Murray Schumach, *The Face on the Cutting Room Floor: The Story of Movie and Television Censorship* (New York: Da Capo Press, 1975 [1964]), p. 139; May, *Big Tomorrow*, p. 203; and Thomas Schatz, *Boom and Bust: America Cinema in the 1940s* (Berkeley: University of California Press, 1999 [1997]), p. 382.

82. Eric Johnston, *America Unlimited* (Garden City, N.Y.: Doubleday, Doran, 1944), p. 152. He uses the term "crackpots" on pp. 58, 152, and 244, although the very last reference on p. 244 focuses on preachers of "group and race hatreds."

83. *Parliamentary Debates (Commons)*, 21 January 1948, vol. 446, col. 218.

84. Walter Millis, ed., *The Forrestal Diaries* (New York: Viking Press, 1951), pp. 132–3. Forrestal made this observation much earlier than the film crisis; see entry of 8 February 1946. Bevin's reliability to U.S. capitalism had long been celebrated in such elite journalistic forums as the *New York Times,* which on 27 September 1936, sec. 4, p. 6, saluted his election as president of the Trades Union Congress (TUC): "Mr. Bevin is as good a Tory as Winston Churchill, so far as foreign affairs are concerned and his autocratic power over the workers . . . is now formally recognized. . . . The Spanish question is only one of several on which the Baldwin government and the nominal Labour opposition are in accord. They see eye to eye on the colonial problem. . . . The Labour party hates communism as bitterly as does the government."

85. Telegram of L. Douglas to Robert Lovett, 2 March 1948, U.S. NA RG59, 841.4061, 1945–9.

86. Quoted by Dickinson and Street, *Cinema and State,* p. 190.

87. Letter of Tom O'Brien to E. Bevin, 2 March 1948, PRO BT64/2370. An anonymous Board of Trade functionary evidently judged this plea to be groveling to Bevin, as the official placed an ironic exclamation point (!) after the reference to Bevin's "great mind."

88. Alexander Walker, *Hollywood England: The British Film Industry in the Sixties* (London: Michael Joseph, 1974; reprint London: Harrap, 1986).

89. For these quotations, see Dickinson and Street, *Cinema and State*, p. 190.
90. "Dollars and Films," *The Times* (London), 12 March 1948, p. 5.
91. "The Film Agreement," *Manchester Guardian*, 13 March 1948. See also "American Films," *Manchester Guardian*, 12 March 1948, p. 4.
92. See excerpts from articles in PRO BT64/2374.
93. George Perry, *The Great British Picture Show* (New York: Hill & Wang, 1974), p. 137.
94. Dickinson and Street, *Cinema and State*, p. 191.
95. More recently film historians have demoted Friese-Greene by arguing that British patriots exaggerated his contribution to the invention of cinema.
96. Wood, *Mr. Rank*, pp. 124 and 269. Swann, *The Hollywood Feature Film in Postwar Britain* (London: Croom Helm, 1987), pp. 130–1. The Friese-Greene and Rank family anecdotes are taken from Swann.

7. THE U.S.–U.K. FILM CONFLICT

1. "Motion Picture Policy," memorandum of Don Bliss to U.S. Secretary of State, 16 January 1948, NA RG59, 841.4061, 1945–9.
2. E. Bevin to Lewis Douglas, 18 August 1947, *Foreign Relations of the United States (FRUS), 1947* (Washington, D.C.: U.S. GPO), vol. 3, p. 60, cited by Alan Bullock, *Ernest Bevin: Foreign Secretary, 1945–1951* (New York: W. W. Norton, 1983), p. 452.
3. "Film Financial Problem," memorandum of Don Bliss to Lewis Douglas, 22 September 1947, NA RG84, 840.4, reproduced in full by Ian Jarvie, *Hollywood's Overseas Campaign: The North Atlantic Movie Trade, 1920–1950* (New York: Cambridge University Press, 1992), pp. 238–41.
4. R. G. Somervell to Ernest Rowe-Dutton, 11 September 1947, PRO BT64/2283, p. 4 of file.
5. R. G. Somervell memorandum of 2 April 1948, PRO BT64/2370.
6. For quotations of Foot and Wilson, see Geoffrey Macnab, *J. Arthur Rank and the British Film Industry* (London: Routledge, 1993), pp. 188 and 197.
7. See Board of Trade memorandum of conversation with E. H. Lever, 20 October 1939, PRO BT64/94/50054/40.
8. Margaret Dickinson, ed., *Rogue Reels: Oppositional Film in Britain, 1945–90* (London: British Film Institute, 1999), pp. 18–23, presents the arguments of these unions and their allies. A skeptical Ian Jarvie worries that such state activism may have saddled the government with many theaters that would soon be money losers in the postwar epoch, with the rise of new leisure activities.
9. Macnab, *J. Arthur Rank*, pp. 229–30, in a section entitled "Davis the Ogre," takes up some of these legends.
10. Data from Milton Moskowitz, Michael Katz, and Robert Levering, eds., *Everybody's Business, an Almanac: The Irreverent Guide to Corporate America* (New York: Harper & Row, 1980), p. 415; American billions.
11. For Xerox–Apple comparison, see David A. Kaplan, *The Silicon Boys and Their Valley of Dreams* (New York: William Morrow, 1999), pp. 99 and 103.
12. Matthew Bernstein, the biographer of Walter Wanger, makes a similar point about UA: "Wanger discovered that the problem lay closer to home – at Unit-

ed Artists. Like Selznick and Korda, he felt the distributor, while charging him a 30 percent distribution fee, simply lacked the negotiating power to get the best play dates and rental income for his releases, regardless of their quality." Wanger himself complained of UA's inability to break into first-run theaters: "Because of the United Artists sales set-up, and the fact that they have no circuit of theatres, they cannot demand their prices from the exhibitors and not give them leading attractions." Matthew Bernstein, *Walter Wanger: Hollywood Independent* (Berkeley: University of California Press, 1994), p. 157.

13. Betty Lasky, *RKO: The Biggest Little Major of Them All* (Englewood Cliffs, N.J.: Prentice–Hall, 1984), p. 205.

14. Scholars such as Sue Harper have done much to debunk the constant claim that realism permeated British film output. The tenacity of the realism ideology may require further exploration.

15. Margaret Dickinson and Sarah Street, *Cinema and State: The Film Industry and the British Government, 1927–1984* (London: British Film Institute, 1985), p. 225, express it this way: "Whereas the British officials favoured a policy of minimal inteference and had confidence in the operation of market forces, their continental counterparts had a more *dirigiste* approach. The subsidy in France was used as an instrument of policy to encourage certain developments in the industry." Cf. Chapter 10 on France.

16. Jeffrey Dell, *Nobody Ordered Wolves* (London: William Heinemann, 1939), p. 297. For the cow and sheep destruction, see p. 295. Macnab, *J. Arthur Rank*, pp. 18–19, makes the connection between Dell's novel and the industry going to the dogs.

8. BELGIUM AND THE MAKING OF AN INTERNATIONAL CATHOLIC FILM MOVEMENT

1. Jules Michelet, *Histoire de la révolution française*, vol. II (Paris: Pléiade, 1939), p. 123. This quotation, notorious in Belgium, is discussed by Jean Stengers, "La Belgique de 1830, une 'nationalité de convention'?" in Hervé Hasquin, ed., *Histoire et historiens depuis 1830 en Belgique* (Brussells: Éditions de l'Université de Bruxelles, 1981) (special issue, *Revue de l'université de Bruxelles,* nos. 1–2, 1981), pp. 7–19, at p. 7.

2. Letter of Otto von Bismarck to Goltz, 8 August 1866, quoted by Stengers, "La Belgique de 1830," p. 9.

3. George Louis Beer, diary entry of 14 February 1919, quoted by Sally Marks, *Innocent Abroad: Belgium at the Paris Peace Conference of 1919* (Chapel Hill: University of North Carolina Press, 1981), p. 96.

4. Jules Destrée, *La Lettre au Roi* (Charleroi: Institut Jules Destrée, 1981 [1912]), pp. 14–16.

5. For a summary of this episode, see Georges Sadoul, *Dictionary of Films,* ed. and trans. Peter Morris (Berkeley: University of California Press, 1972), pp. 174–5.

6. Val R. Lorwin, "Belgium: Religion, Class, and Language in National Politics," in Robert A. Dahl, ed., *Political Oppositions in Western Democracies* (New Haven: Yale University Press, 1966), pp. 147–87.

7. Nathan D. Golden, chief of Motion Picture Division, U.S. Department of Commerce, *Review of Foreign Film Markets during 1937* (Washington, D.C.: U.S. GPO, 1938), p. 27.
8. Francis Bolen, *Histoire authentique du cinéma belge* (Brussels: Éditions Memo & Codec, 1978), and Paul Davay, *Cinéma de Belgique* (Gembloux: Duculot, 1973), provide essential background on Belgian film.
9. Nadine Lubelski-Bernard, "Up to the Year 1914: A Certain Indifference," in Albert d'Haenens, ed., *150 Years of Communities and Cultures in Belgium* (Brussels: Ministry of Foreign Affairs, 1980), pp. 232–5, at pp. 234–5.
10. "Lettre de S.E. le Cardinal Pacelli au Président de l'OCIC," 27 April 1934, in AKF 40, Archive of the Katholieke Film Liga, held at KADOC (Katholiek Documentatie- en Onderzoekscentrum), Louvain, Belgium.
11. Mercier quoted by Archbishop Barry J. Hickey, "Fulton J. Sheen: Prophetic Inspiration for Today's New Evangelisation," *AD2000: A Journal of Religious Opinion* 13(2) (March 2000): 12–13, at p. 12.
12. Jacques Cleynen, "La Politique du cinéma Français: Stratégies et réalisations, 1929–1935," Ph.D. thesis, 1983, École des Hautes Études en Sciences Sociales, Paris, p. 285n.
13. Ibid., pp. 285–91. Cleynen conducted interviews with Monsignor Stourm and Father Leo Lunders, both active in OCIC, to confirm that Reymond and Ernst had been too bogged down in national film activism. For the Internationaler Katholischer Filmkongress and Internationaler katholischer Rundfunk-kongress in Munich, see Georg Ernst and Bernhard Marschall, eds., *Film und Rundfunk* (Munich: Verlag Leohaus, 1929).
14. For background on Brohée's activism, see Msgr. Louis Picard, *Un Pionnier: Le Chanoine Brohée* (Brussels: Éditions Universitaires, 1949).
15. OCIC, "L'Office Catholique International du Cinématographe: Son histoire, sa mission" (n.d.), and Cardinal Pacelli, letter to OCIC, 27 April 1934, AKF 40.
16. For Breen's assertion, see Gregory D. Black, *Hollywood Censored: Morality Codes, Catholics, and the Movies* (New York: Cambridge University Press, 1994), p. 238.
17. Picard, *Un Pionnier*, p. 120.
18. For the proceedings of the 1947 congress, see OCIC, *Les Catholiques parlent du cinéma* (Paris–Brussells: Éditions Universitaires, 1948). See also Rev. John A. V. Burke, *Why a Catholic Film Society: The Story of the Film Apostolate in England* (London: Catholic Film Society pamphlet, 1949), p. 5.
19. Litvinov and Muckermann quoted in OCIC brochure, "Je suis le maître du monde" (printed in Liège, n.d.), in AKF 42, KADOC.
20. Porfirio quoted in ibid. Fayard, Wong Quincey, and the unnamed Malaysian sultan are also cited in this document. The congress alluded to was the International Congress of Educational and Instructional Cinematography held in Rome in April 1934.
21. See AKF 42 file, KADOC. While DOCIP itself claimed forty Belgian newspapers loyal to its network, *World Film News* 1(3) (June 1936) estimated that sixty newspapers and magazines in Belgium and foreign countries regularly used DOCIP's information.

22. "Catholic Agency Uses Press as Film Censorship Weapon," *World Film News* 1(3) (June 1936): 9.
23. Ibid.
24. For the details of Lunders's biography, see AKF 21, KADOC, which holds his résumé. The Flemish priest Father Damien (1840–89) lived and died among those suffering with leprosy on the Pacific island of Molokai; hence, the title *Le Pèlerin de l'enfer (Pilgrimage to Hell)*. Two works that provide brief background on this film are Marianne Thys, *Belgian Cinema / Le Cinéma Belge / De Belgische Film* (Ghent: Ludion, 1999), and Paul Thomas, *Un Siècle de cinéma belge* (Ottignies: Quorum, 1995). Johnson quoted in John Walker, ed., *Halliwell's Film Guide*, 8th ed., revised and updated (New York: Harper-Collins, 1992), p. 819. Les Keyser and Barbara Keyser, *Hollywood and the Catholic Church: The Image of Roman Catholicism in American Movies* (Chicago: Loyola University Press, 1984), p. 151.
25. See entry for *The Singing Nun* in John Walker, ed., *Halliwell's Film Guide*, p. 1017.
26. "Les Classiques Français," *Choisir*, 7 January 1934, p. 15. I am grateful to Mark Sourian for this citation.
27. Leo Lunders O.P., "La Classification des films," in OCIC, *Les Catholiques parlent du cinéma*, pp. 176–88.
28. "Une Enquête sur la Comission de Contrôle des Films: Une Entrevue avec M. Gombault, président de la Commission de contrôle," pt. III, *Le Soir*, 25 December 1936, p. 6.
29. "Film Censors," *New York Times*, 13 October 1935, sec. 9, p. 5.
30. Wets quoted in AKF 42, KADOC. Wets, a juvenile judge in Brussels, published some of his inquiry in the *Bulletin de la Société pour la Protection de l'enfance* (May 1920), declared Vandervelde in *Sénat – Annales Parlementaires*, séance du mardi 15 juin [session of Tuesday, 15 June] 1920, p. 396. For a colorful account of the revolution of 1830, see Cleveland Moffett, "Two Cheers for the Revolution," *Bulletin* (Brussels), 4 January 1980.
31. Hoover quoted by Thomas Doherty, *Teenagers and Teenpics: The Juvenilization of American Movies in the 1950s* (Boston: Unwin Hyman, 1988), p. 120. See "Hoover Again Aims Fire at Crime Films," *Motion Picture Herald*, 10 May 1958, p. 20. Hoover added, "Not since the days when thousands passed the bier of the infamous John Dillinger and made his home a virtual shrine have we witnessed such a brazen affront to our national conscience."
32. File 95, Publiciteit/Radio Vlaanderen, AMSAB (Archief en Museum voor de Socialistische ArbeidersBeweging/national partij-archief), Ghent. See also Rik Stallaerts, *Rode Glamour: Bioscoop, film en socialistische beweging* (Bijdragen Museum van de Vlaamse Sociale Strijd, no. 6; Ghent: Provinciebestuur Oost-Vlaanderen, 1989), especially p. 41. I have relied on Doherty's summary (*Teenagers and Teenpics*, pp. 78–9) of the plot of *Teenage Crime Wave*, a film sadly not available in local film archives.
33. Doherty, *Teenagers and Teenpics*, pp. 75–6, 117–18, and appendix, pp. 245–61. For Luce, see also Hy Hollinger, "Controversial Pic Backfire," *Variety*, 14 September 1956, p. 5.

34. Dave H. Morris, "Dubbing of Foreign Films in Belgium," memorandum of 8 March 1935, U.S. NA RG59, 855.4061, 1930–9.
35. For background to this dispute, see Harold Smith, MPPDA overseas representative, letter to U.S. State Department of 22 November 1935, in U.S. NA RG59, 855.4061, 1930–9.
36. R. Walton Moore, letter of 6 September 1939, to Orme Wilson, American chargé d'affaires ad interim, Brussels, U.S. NA RG59, 855.4061, 1930–9.
37. For a summary of the plot of *Nudist Land,* I have relied on the account of Eric Schaefer, *"Bold! Daring! Shocking! True!" A History of Exploitation Films, 1919–1959* (Durham, N.C.: Duke University Press, 1999), p. 296. Schaefer indicates that there were several versions of this movie. Also, the anthropological footage was recycled in a variety of pronudist films of the postwar epoch.
38. Orme Wilson, "Certain American Films Criticized on the Grounds of Immorality," memorandum no. 397 of 14 July 1939 to U.S. Secretary of State, U.S. NA RG59, 855.4061, 1930–9.
39. For report on the Belgian parliamentary session of 22 June 1939, see U.S. NA RG59, 855.4061, 1930–9.
40. U.S. NA RG59, 855.4061, 1930–9.
41. There will be much more on the Belgian Congo in my forthcoming volume on film and imperialism (working title: *Hollywood and the Decline of European Imperialism*).
42. Jaco van Dormael, "L'Essential de la vie d'un artiste est le stade de l'incompetence," *Revue Belge du Cinéma,* April 1994, p. 72. See also Keith Reader, "Belgian Film Comedy and National Identity," in Joe Andrew, Malcolm Crook, Diana Holmes, and Eva Kolinsky, eds., *Why Europe? Problems of Culture and Identity,* vol. 2: *Media, Film, Gender, Youth and Education* (New York: St. Martin's Press / London: Macmillan, 2000), pp. 27–36, at p. 29.

9. FRANCE AND RESISTANCE TO HOLLYWOOD

1. Susan Hayward, *French National Cinema* (New York: Routledge, 1993), p. 20.
2. Richard Abel, *The Red Rooster Scare: Making Cinema American, 1900–1910* (Berkeley: University of California Press, 1999), especially pp. 120–6.
3. "Lettre du colonel Marchand," *Le Film,* 7 March 1914, reprinted in René Prédal, *La Société française (1914–1945) à travers le cinéma* (Paris: Armand Colin, 1972), pp. 57–8.
4. "Extrait du discours de M. Demaria," in Prédal, *La Société française,* pp. 58–60. See also Marcel L'Herbier, *Intelligence du cinématographe* (Paris: Buchet/Chastel, 1946), especially pp. 93, 98–9, 450–1.
5. Elmer Tracey Barnes, *The Motion-Picture Comrades in African Jungles; or, Camera Boys in Wild Animal Land* (New York: New York Book Co., 1917), p. 37. By 1917, few Western audiences could remember the brief fright that ensued during the initial exposure of Europeans to motion pictures. Louis Lumière's presentation in Paris of a harmless short, *Arrivée d'un train à La Ciotat (Arrival of a Train at La Ciotat,* 1895), sent some of the uninitiated

flinching in fear that the train would come careening off the screen and into the seats à la Woody Allen's *The Purple Rose of Cairo*.

6. Charles Pathé, "De Pathé frères à Pathé cinéma," *Premier Plan*, no. 55, quoted by Francis Bordat, "Le Cinéma américain en France: Histoire et Bilan," in C.-J. Bertrand and F. Bordat, *Les Médias américains en France: Influence et pénétration* (Paris: Belin, 1989), pp. 93–4.

7. See *La Cinématographie française*, no. 973 (25 June 1937).

8. Harold Smith, confidential memorandum on France of 1 May 1928, Hays Papers, I, reel 40, frames 755ff., p. 10 of document.

9. "Embassy Obtains Authorization for Showing of American Film, *Hurricane*," memorandum no. 1856, 8 March 1938, U.S. NA RG59, 851.4061, 1930–9.

10. Prédal, *La Société française*, pp. 165–83, and Colin Crisp, *The Classic French Cinema, 1930–1960* (Bloomington: Indiana University Press, 1993), pp. 250–2.

11. See memorandum of U.S. Embassy in Paris, "American Films in France," no. 1871, U.S. NA RG59 851.4061, 1930–9.

12. Letter of Harold Smith to Harold Williamson, 10 September 1935, see especially "Enclosure no. 3 to Despatch no. 2162 dated 12 September 1935 from the Embassy at Paris," in U.S. NA RG59 851.4061, 1930–9.

13. Yves Chataigneau, "L'Influence internationale du cinématographe," n.d. (probably 1928), in RK786, Rondel collection, Bibliothèque de l'Arsenal, Paris.

14. Yvan Noë, *L'Épicerie des rêves* (1933), quoted by J.-P. Jeancolas, "Cinéma des années trente: La Crise et l'image de la crise," *Le Mouvement social* no. 154 (January–March 1991): 173–95, at p. 183.

15. Philippe Bernard and Henri Dubief, *The Decline of the Third Republic, 1914–1938*, trans. Anthony Forster (Cambridge: Cambridge University Press, 1985), especially pp. 224–9.

16. For the background and details on Natan's pornographic past, see Joseph W. Slade, "Bernard Natan: France's Legendary Pornographer," *Journal of Film and Video* 45(2–3) (Summer–Fall 1993): 72–90. See also Ado Kyrou and Paul Caron, "D'un Certain Cinéma clandestin," *Positif* nos. 61–3 (June–August 1964): 209–23. Caron summarizes many of the film plots. Kyrou referred to the Marseilles–Lyons–Paris axis in his *Amour-érotisme et cinéma* (Paris: Éric Losfield, 1967 [1957]), pp. 196. Slade believes that Natan was rapidly winding down his career in pornography during 1926, and he disagrees with film historians and French antiquarian dealers who often attribute the film *Soeur Vaseline* (1926) to Natan.

17. J.-P. Jeancolas, *15 ans d'années trente: Le Cinéma des français, 1929–1944* (Paris: Stock, 1983), p. 31n.

18. Elizabeth Grottle Strebel, *French Social Cinema of the Nineteen Thirties: A Cinematographic Expression of Popular Front Consciousness* (New York: Arno Press, 1980), pp. 56, 114–16 (after Ph.D. thesis, Department of History, Princeton University, 1973). Strebel may overestimate the number of films created by the two giants. Crisp suggests that Gaumont's production was much weaker at this juncture (*Classic French Cinema*, p. 29).

19. Calling for a dramatic reevaluation of Natan's role in French film history and criticizing most film historians for largely accepting the swindling charges against Natan, Gilles Willems has created a new climate for understanding the financial behavior of Pathé–Natan. See G. Willems, "Aux origines du groupe Pathé–Natan," in Pierre-Jean Benghozi and Christian Delage, eds., *Une Histoire économique du cinéma français, 1895–1995: Regards croisés franco–américains* (Paris: L'Harmattan, 1997), pp. 93–110.

20. Crisp, *Classic French Cinema*, pp. 30–2. See J.-Ch. Marie, "Les gangsters du cinéma," *La Flèche de Paris* 3(3) (7 March 1936): 6. A Popular Front organ, *La Flèche* called itself the newspaper for "all those who desire to liberate France from the tyranny of money." Slade, "Bernard Natan," pp. 80 and 85, discusses Natan's imprisonment. For Sadoul's ambivalent condemnation of the affair, see his column "En marge de l'Affaire Pathé–Natan" for *Regards* 262 (19 January 1939), later reprinted in *Chroniques du cinéma français, 1939–1967* (Paris: Éditions Union Générale d'Éditions, 1979), pp. 37–8. Overall Sadoul regarded Natan as partly responsible for the decadence of French cinema in the early 1930s, and he again accused the movie producer of chicanery in *French Film* (London: Falcon Press, 1953; reprint, New York: Arno, 1972), pp. 69–70.

21. See Rondel collection, RK638, Bibliothèque de l'Arsenal, Paris.

22. "Des films français réalisés par des français," *Choisir*, 10 Juin 1934, p. 16.

23. F21/4697, Archives nationales (AN), Paris.

24. Ibid. See also memorandum of the Directeur Général de la Sureté Nationale, file 5, F21/4691. This corrects the spellings on the "list of personalities . . . suspect or undesirable . . . from the national point of view" and/or "morality." "Behar y Stroumsa, Nicolas dit 'Behars' / Blondy, Maurice dit 'Raymond'/Boronski (et non Borowsky), Georges/Dewalde, Jean/Goldblatt, née Blumenfeld, Ilse / Katkoff (et non Kartkoff), Nicolas / Kirshner (et non Deutschner), Alfred/Piperno, Joseph/Woog, Roger/. . . ."

25. Jean Giraudoux, *Pleins Pouvoirs* (Paris: NRF Gallimard, 1939), p. 66. Lucien Rebatet (aka François Vinneuil), *Les Tribus du cinéma et du théâtre*, vol. IV: *Les Juifs en France* (Paris: Nouvelles Éditions Françaises, 1941), p. 65. Jacques Cleynen, "La Politique du cinéma français: Stratégies et réalisations, 1929–1935," Ph.D. thesis, 1983, École des Hautes Études en Sciences Sociales, Paris, pp. 461–3. The first Rebatet translation is mine, the second is by Crisp, *Classic French Cinema*, p. 147. Rothschild speech discussed by Richard I. Cohen, *The Burden of Conscience: French Jewry's Response to the Holocaust* (Bloomington: Indiana University Press, 1987), p. 9.

26. Brasillach from *Notre avant-guerre* quoted by Robert O. Paxton, *Vichy France: Old Guard and New Order, 1940–1944* (New York: Columbia University Press, 1972), p. 245. For background on Brasillach, Bardèche, and Rebatet, see Richard Abel, *French Film Theory and Criticism, 1907–1939*, vol. II: *1929–1939* (Princeton: Princeton University Press, 1993 [1988], especially pp. 168n–172n; Michel Laval, *Brasillach, ou, la trahison du clerc* (Paris: Hachette, 1992); Alice Kaplan, *The Collaborator: The Trial and Execution of Robert Brasillach* (Chicago: University of Chicago Press, 2000); Alice Yae-

ger Kaplan, *Reproductions of Banality: Fascism, Literature, and French Intellectual Life* (Theory and History of Literature, no. 36) (Minneapolis: University of Minnesota Press, 1986); and William R. Tucker, *The Fascist Ego: A Political Biography of Robert Brasillach* (Berkeley: University of California Press, 1975).

27. Brasillach quoted by literary scholar Susan Rubin Suleiman in her review of Kaplan's *The Collaborator:* "55 Years after His Execution, a French Traitor Is Very Much Alive," *Forward*, 4 August 2000, p. 11.

28. Paxton, *Vichy France*, pp. 170–1, and Cohen, *Burden of Conscience*, p. 8.

29. Quoted by Jacques Adler, *The Jews of Paris and the Final Solution: Communal Response and Internal Conflicts, 1940–1944* (Oxford: Oxford University Press, 1987), p. 16.

30. Maurice Bardèche and Robert Brasillach, *Histoire du cinéma*, rev ed. (Paris: Éditions André Martel, 1948 [1935]), quoted by Prédal, *La Société française,* p. 219.

31. Rebatet, *Les Tribus*, pp. 86–7. I have generally relied on the expressive translation of Edward Baron Turk, *Child of Paradise: Marcel Carné and the Golden Age of French Cinema* (Cambridge, Mass.: Harvard University Press, 1989), p. 187. Rebatet's text on Carné has been reprinted in several works, including in Jeancolas, *15 ans d'années trente* (pp. 306–7), and in the appendix to Jacques Siclier, *La France de Pétain et son cinéma* (Paris: Henri Veyrier, 1981), pp. 459–60. It was also published in *Le Film*, 16 June 1941.

32. These press clips appear in F42/123, AN. The *Je suis partout* clip is marked 6 November 1942.

33. F42/123 AN.

34. René Martel, "Les Anglo-Américains et la France," *Appel*, 12 November 1942, in F42/123.

35. See "Le Renouveau du cinéma français," *Le Matin*, 17 August 1942, and the interview of Achard conducted by René Michel, "M. Marcel Achard veut viriliser le cinéma français," *Le Matin*, 11 June 1942.

36. Georges Duhamel, *Scènes de la vie future* (Paris: Mercure de Paris, 1930), pp. 52–3, 58–60.

37. Jean Vigo, "Vers un cinéma social," lecture delivered at Théâtre du Vieux Colombier (14 June 1930), later reprinted in *Ciné-Club* 5 (February 1949). An English translation by Stuart Liebman is available in Abel, *French Film Theory and Criticism*, II: 60–3, and Strebel quotes it at length with her own translation (*French Social Cinema*, p. 97).

38. Georges Bernanos, *La Grande Peur des bien-pensants* (Paris: Grasset, 1931), p. 454, quoted by Paxton, *Vichy France*, p. 146.

39. See Raymond Borde, "'The Golden Age': French Cinema of the 1930s," in Mary Lea Bandy, ed., *Rediscovering French Film* (New York: Museum of Modern Art, 1983), pp. 67–81. He relies on Raymond Chirat, *Catalogue des films français de long métrage: Films sonores de fiction 1929–1939* (Brussels: Cinémathèque Royale de Belgique, 1975). Mae D. Huettig, *Economic Control of the Motion Picture Industry: A Study in Industrial Organization* (Philadelphia: University of Pennsylvania Press, 1944), p. 1.

40. Dulac quoted by Sandy Flitterman-Lewis, *To Desire Differently: Feminism and the French Cinema* (Urbana and Chicago: University of Illinois Press, 1990), p. 82.
41. H. A. Potamkin, "The Plight of the European Movie," *National Board of Review Magazine* 2 (December 1927): 4–6, at 6. Richard Abel, *French Cinema: The First Wave, 1915–1929* (Princeton: Princeton University Press, 1984), p. 263.
42. Louis Aragon interview reprinted in René Clair, "An Opinion Poll," in R. Clair, *Cinema Yesterday and Today*, ed. and intro. R. C. Dale, trans. Stanley Appelbaum (New York: Dover, 1972), 19–22, at p. 19.
43. Ibid.
44. Souday quoted by André Bazin, "Let's Rediscover Cinema!" in A. Bazin, *French Cinema of the Occupation and Resistance: The Birth of a Critical Esthetic*, comp. and intro. François Truffaut, trans. Stanley Hochman (New York: Ungar, 1981), 25–8, at p. 28. Bazin's article appeared originally in *L'Echo des étudiants*, 26 June 1943.
45. *Excelsior* forum quoted by René Jeanne and Charles Ford, *Le Cinéma et la presse, 1895–1960* (Paris: Armand Colin, 1961), pp. 41–2.
46. Cocteau interview reprinted in Clair, "Opinion Poll," p. 19.
47. For Grémillon and the reception of *Broken Blossoms* in France, see Dudley Andrew, *Mists of Regret: Culture and Sensibility in Classic French Film* (Princeton: Princeton University Press, 1995), pp. 36–40.
48. Germaine Dulac, "Mise en Scène," *Le Film*, 12 November 1917, quoted by Flitterman-Lewis, *To Desire Differently*, pp. 83–4.
49. Dulac quoted in ibid., pp. 86–7.
50. André Bazin, "To Create a Public," 18 March 1944 (in a French student publication), reprinted in A. Bazin, *French Cinema*, 68–70, at p. 69.
51. Ibid.
52. Abel, *French Cinema: The First Wave*, p. 264.
53. Dulac quoted by Flitterman-Lewis, *To Desire Differently*, p. 87.
54. Quoted by Prédal, *La Société française*, p. 107.
55. Manifesto reprinted in Abel, *French Cinema: The First Wave*, p. 265.
56. Chambrillon letter, press clippings, and letters of support for Moussinac in the Fonds Moussinac, Bibliothèque de l'Arsenal, Paris. These papers were in the process of being recataloged when I examined them in the summer of 1992, but the *Jim le Harponneur* files were then listed as LM16 (001–014). The Chambrillon letter of 11 January 1929 is contained in LM16 (010).
57. All quotations from Clair, *Cinema Yesterday and Today*, pp. 19–20.
58. Ibid., pp. 38–9.
59. P. E. Salles Gomes, *Jean Vigo*, trans. Allan Francovich (Berkeley: University of California Press, 1971 [1957]), p. 245n.
60. Clair, *Cinema Yesterday and Today*, p. 120.
61. "Le Congrès Catholique du Cinéma," *La Cinématographie française*, no. 523 (10 November 1928): 14, located on RK577, no. 30 of microfilm, Bibliothèque de l'Arsenal.
62. Jean Morienval, "L'Encyclique du Pape de l'industrie cinématographique," *Choisir*, 9 August 1936. Data were culled from ratings in both *Choisir* and

La Documentation cinématographique. Morienval responded to a critique of Catholics by Pierre Autré in *La Cinématographie française,* no. 924 (18 July 1936): 5–6.

63. Data from Cleynen, "La Politique du cinéma français," p. 293.

64. Léon Moussinac, "État du cinéma international" (1933), reprinted in Léon Moussinac, *L'Âge ingrat du cinéma* (Paris: Les Éditeurs Français Réunis, 1967), 331–54, at p. 349. I have relied on a translation of this essay by Richard Abel, *French Film Theory and Criticism,* II: 105–11.

65. Roger Leenhardt, "Où l'on ouvre l'école du spectateur," *Esprit* 3(38) (November 1935): 332–3. This is another text translated by Abel, *French Film Theory and Criticism,* II: pp. 194–5. Leenhardt and Bazin both had a certain distance from Catholicism, the former regarding agnosticism to be the proper theological orientation for *Esprit,* the latter criticizing his closest friend, Guy Léger, for becoming a priest, an action he attacked for necessitating belief in "invisible things." See the Dudley Andrew biography cited in note 66.

66. Dudley Andrew, *André Bazin* (New York: Oxford University Press, 1978), p. 188. Alexandre Astruc pioneered the concept in a famous essay, "Naissance d'une nouvelle avant-garde: la caméra-stylo," *L'Écran français* no. 144 (30 March 1948). See Alexandre Astruc, "The Birth of a New Avant-Garde: Le Caméra-Stylo," in Peter Graham, ed., *The New Wave: Critical Landmarks* (Garden City, N.Y.: Doubleday, 1968), pp. 17–23.

67. André Bazin, "Entomologie de la pin-up girl," *L'Écran français,* 17 December 1946, quoted by Andrew, *André Bazin,* p. 100.

68. Andrew, *Mists of Regret,* p. 97.

69. The discussion that follows owes much to Dudley Andrew, *Mists of Regret,* and Flitterman-Lewis, *To Desire Differently,* especially pp. 175–85.

70. "Quand Jean Renoir Met en Scène *Toni* aux Martigues," *Pour Vous,* 10 January 1935, p. 14, quoted by Strebel, *French Social Cinema,* p. 238. Renoir's observation should be taken with a certain bucket of salt. The reality is that most of Renoir's films were dominated by professionals. He also two years earlier stated his preference for professionals in "Comment j'anime mes personnages," *Pour Vous,* 6 July 1933, reprinted in his *Écrits, 1926–1971* (Paris: Pierre Belfond, 1974), pp. 223–5. In the earlier essay he does allow a place for the nonprofessional – "It doesn't matter whether these people come off the street or whether they are professionals" – yet he opted for the latter, "especially given that the exigencies of the industry force us to make films very quickly."

71. See debate of Adorno with Lucien Goldmann, reprinted in L. Goldmann, *Cultural Creation in Modern Society,* trans. Bart Grahl (Saint Louis: Telos Press, 1976), p. 135.

72. Louis Aragon, "Front Rouge," translated by E. E. Cummings in George J. Firmage, ed., *E. E. Cummings: Complete Poems, 1904–1962* (New York: Liveright, 1991), pp. 880–97, at p. 885.

73. Julian Jackson, *The Popular Front in France: Defending Democracy, 1934–1938* (Cambridge: Cambridge University Press, 1990), pp. 118–21.

74. Jonathan Buchsbaum, *Cinéma Engagé: Film in the Popular Front* (Urbana: University of Illinois Press, 1988), p. 92.

75. "Entre les films," *Choisir,* 25 April 1937, p. 45. As the newspaper put it: "Les lanceurs du film *La Marseillaise,* qui sont communistes comme on sait, cé-lèbrent la formule 'absolument nouvelle' de la réalisation d'un film par voie de souscription populaire. Mais on sait que c'est ainsi qu'a été réalisé *L'Appel du silence,* avec la participation, disait le générique, 'de 100.000 Français et Belges.'"
76. Jean Renoir, "Honneur aux Marseillais," *Regards,* 10 February 1938, quoted by Strebel, *French Social Cinema,* pp. 224–5.
77. Aragon review in *Ce Soir,* 10 February 1938, quoted by Célia Bertin, *Jean Renoir: A Life in Pictures,* trans. Mireille and Leonard Muellner (Baltimore: Johns Hopkins, 1991 [1986]), p. 146.
78. Renoir quoted by Strebel, p. 221. She cites the Georges Sadoul Papers as the source.
79. Review of Truffaut published in appendix to André Bazin, *Jean Renoir,* ed. François Truffaut, trans. W. W. Halsey II and William H. Simon (New York: Simon & Schuster, 1986 [1973]), p. 251. In the original French edition, see A. Bazin, *Jean Renoir* (Paris: Éditions du Champ Libre, 1971), pp. 240–1.
80. Roger Leenhardt, "*La Marseillaise,*" *Esprit* 4(66) (March 1938): 957–8, re-printed and trans. Abel, *French Film Theory and Criticism,* II: 245–6.
81. De Givray quoted in Bazin, *Jean Renoir,* p. 247. This paragraph takes most of its analysis from Jackson, *Popular Front in France,* p. 145.
82. Quoted by Salles Gomes, *Jean Vigo,* pp. 209–10.
83. Abel, *French Film Theory and Criticism,* II: 152–3, 172.
84. Data from Crisp, *Classic French Cinema,* p. 40.
85. Sadoul quoted by Clair, *Cinema Yesterday and Today,* pp. 168–9.
86. The analysis that follows is derived from Crisp, *Classic French Cinema.*
87. Georges Sadoul, *Le Cinéma français 1890–1962* (Paris: Flammarion, 1962), p. 67.

10. FRANCE AND THE POLITICS OF STATE INTERVENTION

1. Colin Crisp, *The Classic French Cinema, 1930–1960* (Bloomington: Indiana University Press, 1993), p. 38.
2. Victoria de Grazia, "Mass Culture and Sovereignty: The American Challenge to European Cinemas, 1920–1960," *Journal of Modern History* 61 (March 1989): 53–87, at p. 71.
3. For telegrams and Brezillon message from the newsletter *l'Écran: Pour la défense des intérêts cinématographiques,* 4 June 1932, see the records held in F21/4696, AN Paris.
4. Nathan D. Golden, chief of Motion Picture Division, U.S. Department of Commerce, *Review of Foreign Film Markets during 1938* (Washington, D.C.: GPO, 1939), p. 71.
5. Nathan D. Golden, *Review of Foreign Film Markets during 1937* (Washington, D.C.: U.S. GPO, 1938), p. 138.
6. See issues of *La Cinématographie française,* no. 960 (26 March 1937), no. 1012 (25 March 1938), and no. 1065 (31 March 1939). The MPPDA and the U.S. State Department regularly cited the annual exhibitor survey as proof

that France required no protection of its film market. See U.S. NA RG59, 851.4061, 1930–9. Many of the top scholars of French cinema, for instance Ginette Vincendeau, accept the veracity of this survey, but I wonder if the exhibitors favored listing French films to avoid protectionist backlash. It is probably fair to concede that French films were more popular than the U.S. product.

7. Paul Leglise, *Histoire de la politique du cinéma français,* vol. 1: *Le Cinéma et la Troisième République, 1895–1940* (Paris: Filmeditions/Pierre Lherminier, 1969), chaps. 12 and 15, for the evolution of corporative institutions in the mid-1930s. Nathan D. Golden, *Review of Foreign Film Markets during 1936* (Washington, D.C.: U.S. GPO, 1937), pp. 69–70.

8. Leglise, *Politique du cinéma français,* 1: 120.

9. Jarville testimony, séance de la sous-commission du 24 mars [session of the subcommittee of 24 March] 1937, reprinted in Jean-Michel Renaitour, *Où va le cinéma français?* (Paris: Éditions Baudinière, 1937), pp. 388–99.

10. Sée quoted by Golden, *Review . . . 1937,* pp. 134–5.

11. See Leglise, *Politique du cinéma français,* 1: 261–7, and the useful appendix on French film legislation in Ginette Vincendeau, "French Cinema in the 1930s: Social Text and Context of a Popular Entertainment Medium," unpublished Ph.D. diss., Department of English and American Studies, University of East Anglia, 1985, pp. 98–102. Though some of it has appeared in short articles, Vincendeau's important thesis has yet to be published. Douglas Gomery is the leading economic historian who gives the 85 percent figure, cited by Vincendeau, "French Cinema in the 1930s," p. 66. For fuller analysis of the economics of Hollywood, see D. Gomery, *The Hollywood Studio System* (New York: Saint Martin's Press, 1986).

12. Crisp, *Classic French Cinema,* p. 41.

13. Susan Hayward, *French National Cinema* (New York: Routledge, 1993), pp. 43–5, 157. Evelyn Ehrlich, *Cinema of Paradox: French Filmmaking under the German Occupation* (New York: Columbia University Press, 1985), shows, however, the diversity of Continental's productions, reflected in Clouzot's *Le Corbeau.* She also discusses Guy de Carmoy's role in early Vichy film policy, perhaps supporting those who link the CNC more to initiatives in 1936 than from Vichy. He was active in the Resistance.

14. See Goebbels's entry of 19 May 1942 in J. Goebbels, *The Goebbels Diaries 1942–1943,* trans. Louis P. Lochner (Garden City, N.Y.: Doubleday, 1948), p. 221.

15. New entries from Goebbels's diaries quoted by *Guardian* (London), 13 July 1992, p. 3.

16. René Prédal, *Cinéma français depuis 1945* (Paris: Éditions Nathan, 1991), p. 36.

17. Jean Supervielle, memorandum of 27 March 1946, in B Amérique, 1944–52, Generalités, vol. 99, Ministère des Affaires Étrangères [hereafter MAE], Quai d'Orsay, Paris.

18. "Extrait d'un rapport de notre Ambassade à Mexique concernant le marché cinématographique et en Amérique central," 20 March 1946, MAE.

19. M. Croy, memorandum from Rio de Janeiro, 27 July 1946, MAE.

20. See Henri Bonnet telegram of 20 January 1948 from Washington consulate to Quai d'Orsay in B Amérique, 1944–52, vol. 277, MAE. According to the clipped prose of Bonnet's telegram, "ce film présente vie française sous un jour extremement défavorable est de nature à (causer) un grand tort à notre pays. . . . S'il est possible, d'empêcher la diffusion de ce film aux États-Unis." Bonnet was rebuffed by France's Commission de Contrôle Cinématographique, which ruled that Le Corbeau should be exported because of its artistic merit. Some viewers of Le Corbeau regard it as a camouflaged critique of collaborationist elements under the occupation.

21. Memorandum of conversation, 22 April 1946, U.S. State Department, "French Motion Pictures," U.S. NA RG59, 851.4061, 1945–9.

22. Crisp, Classic French Cinema, p. 74. Leglise, Histoire de la politique du cinéma français, vol. II: Entre deux républiques, 1940–1946 (Paris: Filmeditions / Pierre Lherminier, 1977), p. 171. For press reaction, see "L'Opinion de la presse parisienne," Le Monde, 30 May 1946, p. 3, and memorandum of U.S. Ambassador Jefferson Caffery to U.S. State Department, 18 June 1946, U.S. NA RG59, 851.4061, 1945–9. Blum's meeting with cinema professionals on 21 June 1946 is discussed by Jacques Thibau, La France colonisée (Paris: Flammarion, 1980), p. 69.

23. Thorez quoted by Crisp, Classic French Cinema, p. 75.

24. See J. Caffery memorandum of 18 June 1946, U.S. NA RG59, 851.4061, 1945–9.

25. Grenier quoted in Bruce memorandum to U.S. Secretary of State, 23 June 1949, U.S. NA RG59, 851.4061, 1945–9.

26. Étienne Gilson, "Une Erreur Franco-Américaine," Le Monde, 12 June 1946, p. 3.

27. Prédal, Le Cinéma français depuis 1945, p. 34, gives the figure of 338; Sadoul gave 328 in his speeches of 1947.

28. "Communist attack on Blum–Byrnes agreement . . . ," memorandum of American Consulate, Nice, 20 January 1948, U.S. NA RG59, 851.4061, 1945–9. See the local communist daily in Nice, Le Patriote, 4 January 1948, for a report on Sadoul's address.

29. Memorandum of J. Caffery to U.S. Secretary of State, 9 April 1948, U.S. NA RG59, 851.4061, 1945–9.

30. See Jacques Portes, "Les Origines de la légende noire des accords Blum–Byrnes sur le cinéma," Revue d'histoire Moderne et Contemporaine 33 (April–June 1986): 314–29.

31. Prédal, Le Cinéma français depuis 1945, p. 35. On the unemployment of French film workers, Alexander Cockburn largely agrees with Sadoul's estimates, as he recently wrote: "Half the studios closed and unemployment in the industry soon reached 75 percent. The number of workers employed in the French film industry dropped from 2,132 in 1946 to 898 in 1947. Another round of layoffs in 1948 chopped 60 percent of the remaining workforce." A. Cockburn, "Two Way Street," Guardian (London), 12 May 1995.

32. Caffery telegram to U.S. Secretary of State, 8 July 1948, U.S. NA RG59, 851.4061, 1945–9.

33. For Caffery's attack on communists, see airgram of 9 April 1948 to U.S. Secretary of State, U.S. NA RG59, 851.4061, 1945–9. For the Smith flap, see "New French Rule on Dubbing Film Dialogue Irks Hollywood," *New York Herald–Tribune* (Paris), 5 January 1947, and the French rejoinder in the 7 January 1947 issue, "French Deny Film Accord Is Violated."

34. Caffery telegram of 7 January 1947 to U.S. Secretary of State, U.S. NA RG59, 851.4061, 1945–9.

35. George C. Marshall, U.S. Department of State outgoing telegram of 21 July 1948, U.S. NA RG59, 851.4061, 1945–9.

36. Memorandum, "Accords sur le cinéma," Bonnet à Schumann, 25 August 1948, B Amérique, 1944–52, vol. 277, MAE. For U.S complaints that Disney was ruining the confidential nature of the negotiations, see Caffery memorandum of 23 August 1948 on *Le Monde*'s coverage of Disney, U.S. NA RG59, 851.4061, 1945–9. The State Department's problems with Eagle–Lion Pictures soon eclipsed the Disney issue in these RG59 files.

37. For background on these subsidies, see Hayward, *French National Cinema*, pp. 46–7, and for data on producers, see Conseil de l'Europe, *La Politique culturelle de la France: Programme européen d'évaluation*, Strasbourg (Robert Wangermée, "Rapport du groupe d'experts européens"; Bernard Gournay, "Rapport national") (Paris: La Documentation française, 1988), pp. 324–6.

38. For data and critique of the graying of European talent, see Martin Dale, *The Movie Game: The Film Business in Britain, Europe, and America* (London: Cassell, 1997), p. 161.

39. These categories come from the work of Bernard Eisenschitz, ably discussed by Sandy Flitterman-Lewis, *To Desire Differently: Feminism and the French Cinema* (Urbana and Chicago: University of Illinois Press, 1990), p. 254. She also provides valuable insight on the oeuvre of Varda.

40. During the Renaitour hearings of 1937, Gabriel Signoret estimated that the average French film cost 2.0–2.5 million F. "Think that the same film is made in America with at least 40 million F!" he exclaimed. See Renaitour, *Où va le cinéma français?*, p. 175. Guy de Carmoy in 1936 set French film costs in the 1.2–1.7 million F range. Vincendeau, "French Cinema in the 1930s," p. 92n.

41. Vincendeau provides the lyrics in ibid., p. 176. Earlier in her chapter she discusses *Pépé le Moko* and the song.

42. Pierre Sorlin, *European Cinemas, European Societies, 1939–1990* (London: Routledge, 1991), chap. 4, discusses what he calls "the end of cities" in postwar European cinema.

43. Robert Stam, "Jean-Luc Godard's *Sauve qui peut (la vie),"* *Millenium Film Journal* nos. 10–11 (Fall–Winter 1981–2): 194–9, quoted by Claire Pajaczkowska, "'Liberté! Egalité! Paternité!': Jean-Luc Godard and Anne-Marie Miéville's *Sauve qui peut (la vie)* (1980)," in Susan Hayward and Ginette Vincendeau, eds., *French Film: Texts and Contexts* (London: Routledge, 1990), pp. 241–55, at p. 247.

44. *Le Canard enchaîné*, 31 August 1977, quoted by Richard Kuisel, *Seducing the French: The Dilemma of Americanization* (Berkeley: University of California Press, 1993), p. 219.

CONCLUSION

1. Eric Johnston, "Your Stake in Capitalism," *Reader's Digest* 42 (February 1943): 1–6. See also his "Utopia Is Production," *Screen Actor* 14(9) (August 1946): 14–15. For more on productivity as a means of overcoming class conflict, see Charles S. Maier, *In Search of Stability: Explorations in Historical Political Economy* (New York: Cambridge University Press, 1987), especially pp. 121–52.
2. Eric Johnston, *We're All In It* (New York: Dutton, 1948), p. 168.
3. Michael J. Hogan, *The Marshall Plan: America, Britain, and the Reconstruction of Western Europe, 1947–1952* (New York: Cambridge University Press, 1989 [1987]), pp. 97–8.
4. David W. Eakins, "Business Planners and America's Postwar Expansion," in David Horowitz, ed., *Corporations and the Cold War* (Studies in Imperialism and the Cold War, no. 2) (New York: Monthly Review Press, 1970), pp. 143–71, at p. 166.
5. Kennan quoted by John Lewis Gaddis, *Strategies of Containment: A Critical Appraisal of Postwar American National Security Policy* (New York: Oxford University Press, 1982), p. 38n.
6. Data from Martin Dale, *The Movie Game: The Film Business in Britain, Europe, and America* (London: Cassell, 1997), p. 171. Pierre Sorlin remarks that the decline in Britain and the U.S. during the 1950s was markedly steep: "between 1951 and 1960, British audiences diminished by 60 percent. During the same period, Continental audiences increased by 16 percent." P. Sorlin, "From *The Third Man* to *Shakespeare in Love*: Fifty Years of British Success on Continental Screens," in Justine Ashby and Andrew Higson, eds., *British Cinema, Past and Present* (London: Routledge, 2000), pp. 80–91, at p. 82.
7. See Tino Balio, "Introduction to Part I," in Balio, ed., *Hollywood in the Age of Television* (Boston: Unwin Hyman, 1990), pp. 3–40, at p. 7.
8. Richard Schickel, "Cinema Paradiso," *Wilson Quarterly* 23(3) (Summer 1999): 56–70. On p. 67, he estimates that "In the period between 1950 and the early 1970s, the number of theaters playing 'art' films in the United States rose from 100 to more than 700."
9. "Testimony No. 22 . . . ," Moyne committee hearings, PRO BT55/3.
10. "Film Propaganda Is Barred by Hays," *New York Times*, 21 July 1941, p. 17.
11. Marshall McLuhan, "American Advertising," *Horizon* 93(4) (October 1947): 132–41, quoted by Paul Ginsborg, *A History of Contemporary Italy: Society and Politics, 1943–1988* (London: Penguin, 1990), pp. 247–8.
12. Pasolini quoted by Ginsborg, *History of Contemporary Italy*, p. 241. See Pasolini's *Scritti corsari* (Milano: Garzanti, 1975), pp. 69–70.
13. Milan Kundera, *The Unbearable Lightness of Being*, trans. Michael Henry Heim (New York: Harper & Row, 1985), p. 254.
14. Frank A. Ninkovich, *The Diplomacy of Ideas: U.S. Foreign Policy and Cultural Relations, 1938–1950* (New York: Cambridge University Press, 1981), pp. 160–1.

15. Ibid., pp. 149–51.
16. Dale, *Movie Game*, p. 173. Dale does not give the original source of the slum quotation.
17. Data from René Bonnell, *La Vingt-cinquième image: Une Économie de l'audiovisuel* (Paris: Gallimard/FEMIS, 1989), p. 20. The introduction of a movie channel on French television caused a massive drop to 2.3 shows per year in 1987, still double that of Britain, but an indication of the delicate ecology of visual media.
18. Dwight Macdonald, "Masscult & Midcult," *Partisan Review* 27 (Spring 1960): 203–33, reprinted in D. Macdonald, *Against the American Grain: Essays on the Effects of Mass Culture* (New York: Da Capo, 1983 [1962]), pp. 3–75, especially pp. 31–4.
19. Matthew Josephson, *The Robber Barons* (New York: Harcourt, Brace, & World, 1962 [1934]), pp. 345–6. For Josephson, the U.S. robber barons in their art and literature collections "had the droll aspect of the aborigine who decorates his person with the *disjecta membra* of Western civilization, with pieces of tin cans for his earrings, or a rubber tire for a belt."
20. Macdonald, *Against the American Grain*, pp. 31–4.
21. Irwin Wall, *The United States and the Making of Postwar France, 1945–1954* (New York: Cambridge University Press, 1991), pp. 120–1. Wall uses data from the Catholic *Repertoire Générale des Films*. He notes that the failure to create children's culture loses the youth generation to Hollywood.
22. Reymond clarified in "Aux parents et aux éducateurs," *Choisir*, January 1932 (first issue, as a monthly), that the Catholic film movement sought entertainment that was family-oriented, rather than works to be narrowly regarded as "childish." His statement on youth and cinema's future appeared in "Qui va au cinéma?" *Choisir,* 4 December 1932.
23. Régis Debray, *Modeste contribution aux discours et cérémonies officiels du dixième anniversaire* (Paris: Maspero, 1978). An extract and translation is available in R. Debray, "A Modest Contribution to the Rites and Ceremonies of the Tenth Anniversary," *New Left Review* no. 115 (May–June 1979): 45–65.
24. David Riesman, with Nathan Glazer and Reuel Denney, *The Lonely Crowd A Study of the Changing American Character* (New Haven: Yale University Press, 1961 [1950]), pp. 96–9. For a work that makes note of Riesman's critique of child-targeted advertising, see Margaret J. King, "Empires of Popular Culture: McDonald's and Disney," in Marshall Fishwick, ed., *The World of Ronald McDonald* (special issue of *Journal of American Culture*, n.d., ca. 1977–8; Bowling Green, Ohio: Popular Culture Press, 1978), pp. 424–37, at p. 434.
25. Asada Akira, interview, "In the Place of Nothingness," *New Left Review,* 2d ser., no. 5 (September–October 2000): 15–40, at 38–9.
26. Jean Morienval, "Des Films français réalisés par des français," *Choisir,* 10 June 1934, p. 16.
27. Memorandum of B. M. Hulley, "A French Film Boycotted in Brittany," 6 January 1937, U.S. NA RG59, 851.4061, 1930–9. Newspaper accounts of the conflict appeared on the following dates: *Nouvelliste Morbihannais,* 20, 22,

25, 30 December 1936, and 5 January 1937; *Ouest Éclair,* 23, 26, 27, 20 December 1936, and 1, 4 January 1937; *Le Phare,* 1 January 1937.

28. Bernard Henri-Lévy, "Anti-américanisme primair," *Le Matin de Paris,* 3 August 1982, and Guy Konopnicki, "À des années-lumières," *Le Monde,* 7 August 1982. See discussion of these two texts in Armand Mattelart, Xavier Delcourt, and Michèlle Mattelart, *International Image Markets: In Search of an Alternative Perspective,* trans. D. Buxton (London: Comedia, 1984), p. 15, originally published in France as *La Culture contre la Democratie? L'audiovisuel à l'heure transnationale* (Paris: Éditions La Découverte, 1983).

29. Digby Anderson, "Tasteless Dutch Tomatoes and Waiters Named Terry," *New York Times Magazine,* 3 December 1989, p. 60.

30. For a discussion of this portion of John Gray's *False Dawn: The Delusions of Global Capitalism* (London: Granta, 1998), see Fredric Jameson, "Globalization and Strategy," *New Left Review,* 2d ser., 4 (July/August 2000): 49–68, at 61.

31. "World Credit and Movies Called U.S. 'Ambassadors,'" *New York Herald* (Paris), 20 April 1928, p. 7. Lillian Gish recounts Griffith's ideas on film and Scripture in the documentary *Henri Langlois* (1970), directed by Roberto Guerra and Eila Hershon, on the founder of the Cinémathèque Française.

32. Quotations from "What the Internet Cannot Do," *The Economist* 356(8184) (19 August 2000): 11–13, at p. 11.

Selected Bibliography

UNITED STATES

Archives

American Academy of Motion Picture Arts and Sciences [AAMPAS], Beverly Hills
(Production Code Administration [PCA] files; George Stevens Papers)
Franklin D. Roosevelt [FDR] Library, Hyde Park, N.Y. (Official File [OF]; Presi-
dent's Personal Files [PPF], President's Secretary's File [PSF])
Georgetown University, Lauinger Library, Special Collections, Washington D.C.
(Rev. Wilfrid Parsons Papers; Martin Quigley Papers)
Herbert H. Hoover Presidential Library (HHH Commerce Department documents)
Hoover Institution Archives, Stanford University (Motion Picture Research Council
[MPRC] files; Raymond Moley Papers)
National Archives [U.S. NA], Washington, D.C. (RG59, RG151)
Rutgers University microfilms (Will Hays Papers)
University of California at Los Angeles, Special Collections (legal records of Twen-
tieth Century–Fox [TCF]; Paul Rotha Papers)
Warner Brothers [WB] Archives, Doheny Library, University of Southern California
(production files; Wolf Cohen Papers)

Books

Balio, Tino. *Grand Design: Hollywood as a Modern Business Enterprise, 1930–
1939.* (*History of the American Cinema,* no. 5.) New York: Charles Scribner's,
1993.
Basinger, Jeanine. *The World War II Combat Film.* New York: Columbia Univer-
sity Press, 1986.
Baxter, John. *The Hollywood Exiles.* New York: Taplinger Publishing, 1976.
Berg, A. Scott. *Goldwyn: A Biography.* New York: Knopf, 1989.
Bernstein, Matthew. *Walter Wanger: Hollywood Independent.* Berkeley: University
of California Press, 1994.
Black, Gregory D. *The Catholic Crusade against the Movies, 1940–1975.* New
York: Cambridge University Press, 1998.

Hollywood Censored: Morality Codes, Catholics, and the Movies. New York: Cambridge University Press, 1994.

Bowser, Eileen. *The Transformation of Cinema, 1907–1915.* (*History of the American Cinema*, no. 2.) New York: Charles Scribner's, 1990.

Ceplair, Larry, and Steven Englund. *The Inquisition in Hollywood: Politics in the Film Community, 1930–1960.* Berkeley: University of California Press, 1983 [1980].

Christensen, Terry. *Reel Politics: American Political Movies from "Birth of a Nation" to "Platoon."* New York: Blackwell, 1987.

Couvares, Francis G., ed. *Movie Censorship and American Culture.* Washington, D.C.: Smithsonian Institution Press, 1996.

Crafton, Donald. *The Talkies: American Cinema's Transition to Sound, 1926–1931.* (*History of the American Cinema*, no. 4.) Berkeley: University of California Press, 1997.

Crawford, Kenneth G. *The Pressure Boys: The Inside Story of Lobbying in America.* New York: Julian Messner, 1939.

Creel, George. *How We Advertised America: The First Telling of the Amazing Story of the Committee on Public Information That Carried the Gospel of Americanism to Every Corner of the Globe.* New York: Harper, 1920.

Cripps, Thomas. *Slow Fade to Black: The Negro in American Film, 1900–1942.* New York: Oxford University Press, 1977.

Culbert, David, ed.-in-chief. *Film and Propaganda in America: A Documentary History.* 4 vols. Westport, Conn.: Greenwood Press, 1990.

Dates, Jannette L., and William Barlow, eds. *Split Image: African Americans in the Mass Media.* Washington, D.C.: Howard University Press, 1990.

DeBauche, Leslie Midkiff. *Reel Patriotism: The Movies and World War I.* Madison: University of Wisconsin Press, 1997.

Dick, Bernard F. *The Merchant Prince of Poverty Row: Harry Cohn of Columbia Pictures.* Lexington: University Press of Kentucky, 1993.

Doherty, Thomas. *Pre-Code Hollywood: Sex, Immorality, and Insurrection in American Cinema, 1930–1934.* New York: Columbia University Press, 1999.

Projections of War: Hollywood, American Culture, and World War II. New York: Columbia University Press, 1993.

Teenagers and Teenpics: The Juvenilization of American Movies in the 1950s. Boston: Unwin Hyman, 1988.

Dooley, Roger. *From Scarface to Scarlett: American Films in the 1930s.* New York: Harcourt Brace Jovanovich, 1979.

Ernst, Morris, and Pare Lorentz. *Censored: The Private Life of the Movie.* New York: Jonathan Cape & Harrison Smith, 1930.

Facey, Paul W., S.J. *The Legion of Decency: A Sociological Analysis of the Emergence and Development of a Social Pressure Group.* New York: Arno Press, 1974.

Feldman, Charles. *The National Board of Censorship of Motion Pictures, 1909–1922.* New York: Arno Press, 1975.

Forman, Henry James. *Our Movie Made Children.* New York: Macmillan, 1933.

French, Philip. *The Movie Moguls: An Informal History of the Hollywood Tycoons.* London: Weidenfeld & Nicolson, 1969.

Friedman, Lester. *Hollywood's Image of the Jew*. New York: Ungar, 1982.

Friedrich, Otto. *City of Nets: A Portrait of Hollywood in the 1940's*. New York: Harper & Row, 1987.

Gabler, Neal. *An Empire of Their Own: How the Jews Invented Hollywood*. New York: Crown, 1988.

Gardner, Gerald C. *The Censorship Papers: Movie Censorship Letters from the Hays Office, 1934–1968*. New York: Dodd, Mead, 1987.

Glancy, H. Mark. *When Hollywood Loved Britain: The Hollywood "British" Film, 1939–45*. Manchester: Manchester University Press, 1999.

Gomery, Douglas. *The Hollywood Studio System*. New York: St. Martin's Press, 1986.

Guback, Thomas. *The International Film Industry: Western Europe and America since 1945*. Bloomington: Indiana University Press, 1969.

Hale, Georgia. *Charlie Chaplin: Intimate Close-Ups*. H. Kiernan, ed. Metuchen, N.J.: Scarecrow Press, 1995.

Hamilton, Ian. *Writers in Hollywood, 1915–1951*. New York: Harper & Row, 1990.

Haskell, Molly. *From Reverence to Rape: The Treatment of Women in the Movies*. Chicago: University of Chicago Press, 1987 [1974].

Hays, Will. *The Memoirs of Will H. Hays*. Garden City, N.Y.: Doubleday, 1955.

Inglis, Ruth. *Freedom of the Movies*. Chicago: University of Chicago Press, 1947.

Isenberg, Michael T. *War on Film: The American Cinema and World War I*. Rutherford, N.J.: Fairleigh Dickinson University Press, 1981.

Izod, John. *Hollywood and the Box Office, 1895–1986*. London: Macmillan, 1988.

Jacobs, Lea. *The Wages of Sin: Censorship and the Fallen Woman Film*. Madison: University of Wisconsin Press, 1991.

Jowett, Garth, Ian C. Jarvie, and Kathryn H. Fuller. *Children and the Movies: Media Influence and the Payne Fund Controversy*. New York: Cambridge University Press, 1996.

Kerr, Paul, ed. *The Hollywood Film Industry*. London: Routledge & Kegan Paul/British Film Institute, 1986.

Keyser, Les, and Barbara Keyser. *Hollywood and the Catholic Church: The Image of Roman Catholicism in American Movies*. Chicago: Loyola University Press, 1984.

King, John, Ana M. Lopez, and Manuel Alvarado. *Mediating Two Worlds: Cinematic Encounters in the Americas*. London: British Film Institute, 1993.

Kirkpatrick, Sidney. *A Cast of Killers*. New York: Dutton, 1986.

Koppes, Clayton R., and Gregory D. Black. *Hollywood Goes to War: How Politics, Profits, and Propaganda Shaped World War II Movies*. New York: Free Press, 1987.

Leff, Leonard J., and Jerold L. Simmons. *The Dame in the Kimono: Hollywood, Censorship, and the Production Code from the 1920s to the 1960s*. New York: Grove Weidenfeld, 1990.

Maltby, Richard. *Harmless Entertainment: Hollywood and the Ideology of Consensus*. Metuchen, N.J.: Scarecrow Press, 1983.

May, Lary. *The Big Tomorrow: Hollywood and the Politics of the American Way*. Chicago: University of Chicago Press, 2000.

Screening Out the Past: The Birth of Mass Culture and the Motion Picture Industry. Chicago: University of Chicago Press, 1983 [1980].

Moley, Raymond. *Are We Movie Made?* New York: Macy–Masius, 1938.

The Hays Office. New York: Bobbs–Merrill, 1945.

Mock, James R., and Cedric Larson. *Words That Won the War: The Story of the Committee on Public Information 1917–1919.* Princeton: Princeton University Press, 1939.

Navasky, Victor. *Naming Names.* New York: Viking Press, 1980.

Powdermaker, Hortense. *Hollywood, the Dream Factory: An Anthropologist Looks at the Movies.* Boston: Little, Brown, 1950.

Pronay, Nicholas, and Keith Wilson, eds. *The Political Re-education of Germany and Her Allies after World War II.* London: Croom Helm, 1985.

Quigley, Martin. *Decency in Motion Pictures.* New York: Macmillan, 1937.

Ramsaye, Terry. *A Million and One Nights: A History of the Motion Picture.* New York: Simon & Schuster, 1926; reprint, New York: Touchstone, 1986.

Roddick, Nick. *A New Deal in Entertainment: Warner Brothers in the 1930s.* London: British Film Institute, 1983.

Rosenberg, Emily. *Spreading the American Dream: American Economic and Cultural Expansion, 1890–1945.* New York: Hill & Wang, 1991 [1982].

Ross, Steven J. *Working-Class Hollywood: Silent Film and the Shaping of Class in America.* Princeton: Princeton University Press, 1998.

Rosten, Leo. *Hollywood: The Movie Colony, the Movie Makers.* New York: Harcourt, Brace, 1941.

Schaefer, Eric. *"Bold! Daring! Shocking! True!" A History of Exploitation Films, 1919–1959.* Durham, N.C.: Duke University Press, 1999.

Schatz, Thomas. *Boom and Bust: American Cinema in the 1940s. (History of the American Cinema, no. 6.)* Berkeley: University of Californiia Press, 1999 [1997].

The Genius of the System: Hollywood Filmmaking in the Studio Era. New York: Pantheon, 1988.

Seabury, William Marston. *Motion Picture Problems: The Cinema and the League of Nations.* New York: Avondale, 1929.

The Public and the Motion Picture Industry. New York: Macmillan, 1926.

Segrave, Kerry. *American Films Abroad: Hollywood's Domination of the World's Movie Screens.* Jefferson, N.C.: McFarland, 1997.

Shohat, Ella, and Robert Stam. *Unthinking Eurocentrism: Multiculturalism and the Media.* New York: Routledge, 1994.

Skinner, James M. *The Cross and the Cinema: The Legion of Decency and the National Catholic Office for Motion Pictures.* Westport, Conn.: Praeger, 1993.

Sklar, Robert. *Movie Made America: A Cultural History of American Movies.* New York: Harper & Row, 1975.

Staiger, Janet, ed. *The Studio System.* New Brunswick, N.J.: Rutgers University Press, 1995.

Taylor, John Russell. *Strangers in Paradise: The Hollywood Emigrés.* London: Faber & Faber, 1983.

Thompson, Kristin. *Exporting Entertainment: America in the World Film Market, 1907–1934.* London: British Film Institute, 1985.

Tunstall, Jeremy. *The Media Are American: Anglo-American Media in the World*. New York: Columbia University Press, 1977.
Vasey, Ruth. *The World According to Hollywood, 1918–1939*. Madison: University of Wisconsin Press, 1997.
Vizzard, Jack. *See No Evil: Life Inside a Hollywood Censor*. New York: Simon & Schuster, 1970.
Walsh, Andrea. *Women's Film and Female Experience, 1940–1950*. New York: Praeger, 1984.
Walsh, Frank. *Sin and Censorship: The Catholic Church and the Motion Picture Industry*. New Haven: Yale University Press, 1996.
Winkler, Alan M. *The Politics of Propaganda: The OWI, 1942–1945*. New Haven: Yale University Press, 1978.

GREAT BRITAIN

Archives

British Film Institute, London (Ivor Montagu Papers, newspaper and microfilm collections)
Public Record Office [PRO], London (Board of Trade [BT]; Cabinet [CAB]; Colonial Office [CO]; Dominions Office [DO]; Foreign Office [FO]; Home Office [HO]; Ministry of Information [INF])
University of California at Los Angeles special collections (Paul Rotha Papers)

Books

Aitken, Ian. *Film and Reform: John Grierson and the Documentary Film Movement*. London: Routledge, 1990.
Aldgate, Anthony. *Britain Can Take It: British Cinema in the Second World War*. Oxford: Blackwell, 1986.
Censorship and the Permissive Society: British Cinema and Theater, 1955–1965. Oxford: Clarendon Press, 1995.
Aldgate, Anthony, and Jeffrey Richards. *The Best of British: Cinema and Society, 1930–70*. Oxford: Blackwell, 1983.
Armes, Roy. *A Critical History of the British Cinema*. New York: Oxford University Press, 1978.
Arts Enquiry, The. *The Factual Film*. London: PEP/Oxford University Press, 1947.
Ashby, Justine, and Andrew Higson, eds. *British Cinema, Past and Present*. London: Routledge, 2000.
Atwell, David. *Cathedrals of the Movies: A History of their Audiences*. London: Architectural Press, 1980.
Barnouw, Erik. *Documentary: A History of the Non-Fiction Film*. New York: Oxford University Press, 1974.
Barr, Charles. *Ealing Studios*. New York: Overlook, 1980.
Betts, Ernest. *The Film Business: A History of British Cinema, 1896–1972*. London: Allen & Unwin, 1973.
Inside Pictures. London: Cresset Press, 1960.

Board of Trade (U.K.). Lord Moyne, committee chairman. *Report of a Committee Appointed by the Board of Trade to Consider the Position of British Films.* London: HMSO, 1936.

Albert Palache, committee chairman. *Tendencies to Monopoly in the Cinematograph Industry: Report of a Committee Appointed by the Cinematograph Films Council.* London: HMSO, 1944.

Bond, Ralph. *Monopoly: The Future of British Films.* London: Association of Cine-Technicians, 1946.

Box, Muriel. *Odd Woman Out.* London: Leslie Frewin, 1974.

Bullock, Alan. *Ernest Bevin: Foreign Secretary, 1945–1951.* New York: W. W. Norton, 1983.

Chanan, Michael. *The Dream That Kicks: The Prehistory and Early Years of Cinema in Britain.* London: Routledge & Kegan Paul, 1980.

Chapman, James. *The British at War: Cinema, State, and Propaganda, 1939–1945.* London: I. B. Tauris, 1998.

Cook, Pam. *Fashioning the Nation: Costume and Identity in British Cinema.* London: British Film Institute, 1996.

Cull, Nicholas John. *Selling War: The British Propaganda Campaign against American "Neutrality" in World War II.* New York: Oxford University Press, 1995.

Curran, James, and Vincent Porter, eds. *British Cinema History.* London: Weidenfeld & Nicolson/Totowa, N.J.: Barnes & Noble, 1983.

Denny, Ludwell. *America Conquers Britain: A Record of Economic War.* New York: Alfred Knopf, 1930.

Dickinson, Margaret, ed. *Rogue Reels: Oppositional Film in Britain, 1945–90.* London: British Film Institute, 1999.

Dickinson, Margaret, and Sarah Street. *Cinema and State: The Film Industry and the British Government, 1927–1984.* London: British Film Institute, 1985.

Dixon, Wheeler Winston, ed. *Re-Viewing British Cinema, 1900–1992.* Albany: State University of New York Press, 1994.

Docherty, David, David Morrison, and Michael Tracey. *The Last Picture Show? Britain's Changing Film Audiences.* London: British Film Institute, 1987.

Durgnat, Raymond. *A Mirror for England: British Movies from Austerity to Affluence.* London: Faber & Faber, 1970.

Foot, Paul. *The Politics of Harold Wilson.* Harmondsworth: Penguin, 1968.

Gledhill, Christine, ed. *Home Is Where the Heart Is: Studies in Melodrama and the Woman's Film.* London: British Film Institute, 1987.

Grant, Mariel. *Propaganda and the Role of the State in Inter-War Britain.* Oxford: Oxford University Press, 1994.

Grantley, Lord. *Silver Spoon.* London: Hutchinson, 1954.

Harper, Sue. *Picturing the Past: The Rise and Fall of the British Costume Film.* London: British Film Institute, 1994.

Higson, Andrew. *Waving the Flag: Constructing a National Cinema in Britain.* Oxford: Oxford University Press, 1995.

Hill, John. *Sex, Class, and Realism.* London: British Film Institute, 1986.

Hogenkamp, Bert. *Deadly Parallels: Film and the Left in Britain, 1929–1939.* London: Lawrence & Wishart, 1986.

Hunnings, Neville March. *Film Censors and the Law*. London: Allen & Unwin, 1967.

Jarvie, Ian. *Hollywood's Overseas Campaign: The North Atlantic Movie Trade, 1920–1950*. New York: Cambridge University Press, 1992.

Jones, Stephen G. *The British Labour Movement and Film, 1918–1939*. London: Routledge, 1987.

Klingender, F. D., and Stuart Legg. *Money behind the Screen: A Report Prepared on Behalf of the Film Council*. London: Lawrence & Wishart, 1937.

Korda, Michael. *Charmed Lives*. New York: Random House, 1979.

Kuhn, Annette. *Cinema, Censorship, and Sexuality, 1909–1925*. London: Routledge, 1988.

Kulik, Karol. *Alexander Korda: The Man Who Could Work Miracles*. New Rochelle, N.Y.: Arlington House, 1975.

Landy, Marcia. *British Genres: Cinema and Society, 1930–1960*. Princeton: Princeton University Press, 1991.

Lant, Antonia. *Blackout: Reinventing Women for Wartime British Cinema*. Princeton: Princeton University Press, 1991.

LeMahieu, D. L. *A Culture for Democracy: Mass Communication and the Cultivated Mind in Britain between the Wars*. Oxford: Oxford University Press / Clarendon Press, 1988.

Low, Rachael. *Documentary and Educational Films of the 1930s*. London: Allen & Unwin, 1979.

Film Making in 1930s Britain. London: Allen & Unwin, 1985.

The History of the British Film, 1918–1929. London: Allen & Unwin, 1971.

Mackenzie, John, ed. *Imperialism and Popular Culture*. Manchester: Manchester University Press, 1986.

Macnab, Geoffrey. *J. Arthur Rank and the British Film Industry*. London: Routledge, 1993.

Mayer, J. P. *British Cinemas and Their Audiences: Sociological Studies*. London: Dennis Dobson, 1948.

Sociology of Film: Studies and Documents. London: Faber & Faber, 1946.

Montagu, Ivor. *The Political Censorship of Films*. London: Gollancz, 1929.

Murphy, Robert. *Realism and Tinsel: Cinema and Society in Britain, 1939–1948*. London: Routledge, 1989.

National Council on Public Morals. Commission of Inquiry on Cinema. *The Cinema: Its Present Position and Future Possibilities*. London: Williams & Norgate, 1917; reprint, New York: Arno Press, 1970.

Nelson, Joyce. *The Colonized Eye: Rethinking the Grierson Legend*. Toronto: Between the Lines, 1988.

Perry, George. *The Great British Picture Show*. New York: Hill & Wang, 1974.

Petrie, Duncan. *Creativity and Constraint in the British Film Industry*. London: Macmillan, 1991.

Political and Economic Planning (PEP). *The British Film Industry*. London: PEP, 1952.

Pronay, Nicholas, and D. W. Spring, eds. *Propaganda, Politics, and Film, 1918–45*. London: Macmillan, 1982.

Richards, Jeffrey. *The Age of the Dream Palace: Cinema and Society in Britain, 1930–1939.* London: Routledge, 1984.

Visions of Yesterday. London: Routledge, 1973.

Rigby, Jonathan. *English Gothic: A Century of Horror Cinema.* Richmond, Surrey: Reynolds & Hearn, 2000.

Robertson, James C. *The British Board of Film Censors: Film Censorship in Britain, 1896–1950.* London: Croom Helm, 1985.

The Hidden Cinema: British Film Censorship in Action, 1913–1972. London: Routledge, 1989; 1993 (updated paperback, –1975).

Rotha, Paul. *Documentary Diary: An Informal History of the British Documentary Film, 1928–1939.* London: Secker & Warburg/New York: Hill & Wang, 1973.

Shafer, Stephen C. *British Popular Films, 1929–1939: The Cinema of Reassurance.* London: Routledge, 1997.

Short, K. R. M., ed. *Feature Films as History.* Knoxville: University of Tennessee Press, 1981.

Slide, Anthony. *Banned in the USA: British Films in the United States and Their Censorship, 1933–60.* London: I. B. Tauris, 1998.

Stead, Peter. *Film and the Working Class.* London: Routledge, 1989.

Street, Sarah. *British National Cinema.* London: Routledge, 1997.

Sussex, Elizabeth. *The Rise and Fall of British Documentary.* Berkeley: University of California Press, 1975.

Swann, Paul. *The British Documentary Film Movement, 1926–1946.* Cambridge: Cambridge University Press, 1989.

Taylor, Philip M. *The Projection of Britain: British Overseas Publicity and Propaganda, 1919–1939.* Cambridge: Cambridge University Press, 1981.

Wakelin, Michael. *J. Arthur Rank: The Man behind the Gong.* London: Lion Publishing, 1996.

Wood, Alan. *Mr. Rank: A Study of J. Arthur Rank and British Films.* London: Hodder & Stoughton, 1952.

BELGIUM

Archives

Archief en Museum voor de Socialistische Arbeidersbeweging / national partij-archief (AMSAB), Ghent (Radio Vlaanderen files)

Archives Générales du Royaume, Brussels (papers of Charles de Broqueville)

Bibliothèque Royale Albert, Brussels (newspaper and microfilms)

Katholiek Documentatie-en Onderzoekscentrum (KADOC), Louvain, Belgium (Archives of the Katholieke Film Liga [AKF])

Books

Bolen, Francis. *Histoire authentique du cinéma belge.* Brussels: Éditions Memo et Codec, 1978.

CRISP (Centre de Recherche et d'Information Socio-Politiques). *Morphologie des Groupes Financiers.* Brussels: CRISP, 1962.

Dahl, Robert A., ed. *Political Oppositions in Western Democracies.* New Haven: Yale University Press, 1966.

Davay, Paul. *Cinéma de Belgique.* Gembloux: Duculot, 1973.

Depraetere, Hans, and Jenny Dierickx. *La Guerre froide en Belgique: La Répression envers le PCB et le FI.* Antwerp: Éditions EPO, 1986.

d'Haenens, Albert, ed. *150 Years of Communities and Cultures in Belgium.* Brussels: Ministry of Foreign Affairs, 1980.

Fournet, Eric. *Quand Hergé découvrait l'Amérique: Rêves et cauchemars d'un petit européen dans les années trente.* Brussels: Didier Hatier, 1992.

Gérard-Libois, Jules, and José Gotovitch. *L'An 40, la Belgique occupée.* Brussels: CRISP, 1971.

Gérard-Libois, Jules, and Rosine Lewin. *La Belgique entre dans la guerre froide et l'Europe, 1947–1953.* Brussels: Politique et Histoire, 1992.

Jungblut, Guy, Patric Leboutte, and Dominique Paini, eds. *Une Encyclopédie des cinémas de Belgique.* Paris: Musée d'Art Moderne de la Ville de Paris, 1990.

Marks, Sally. *Innocent Abroad: Belgium at the Paris Peace Conference of 1919.* Chapel Hill: University of North Carolina Press, 1981.

Office Catholique International du Cinéma (OCIC). *Les Catholiques parlent du cinéma* (Actes du 4e congrès international de l'OCIC tenu à Bruxelles du 16 au 22 juin 1947). Paris–Brussels: Éditions Universitaires, 1948.

Picard, Louis, Msgr. *Un Pionnier: Le Chanoine Brohée.* Brussels: Éditions Universitaires, 1949.

Ramirez, Francis, and Christian Rolot. *Histoire du cinéma colonial au Zaïre, au Rwanda et au Burundi.* Tervuren: Musée Royal de l'Afrique Centrale, 1985.

Sojcher, Frédéric. *La Kermesse heroïque du cinéma belge.* Paris: Harmattan, 1999.

Stallaerts, Rik. *Rode Glamour: Bioscoop, film en socialistische beweging.* Bijdragen Museum van de Vlaamse Sociale Strijd no. 6. Ghent: Provinciebestuur Oost-Vlaanderen, 1989.

Stephany, Pierre. *Nos années 50: Une Histoire (belge) de l'après-guerre.* Paris: Éditions Duculot, 1987.

Thomas, Paul. *Un Siècle de cinéma belge.* Ottignies: Quorum, 1995.

Thys, Marianne. *Belgian Cinema/Le Cinéma Belge/De Belgische Film.* Ghent: Ludion, 1999.

Van Bever, L. *Le Cinéma pour Africains.* Brussels: G. Van Campenhout, 1952.

Witte, Els, and Jan Craeybeckx. *La Belgique politique de 1830 à nos jours: Les Tensions d'une démocratie bourgeoise.* Brussels: Éditions Labor, 1987.

FRANCE

Archives

Archives Nationales [AN], Paris (F21 Beaux-Arts; F42 Cinéma)

Bibliothèque de l'Arsenal, Paris (Fonds Moussinac; Rondel collection; newspapers and microfilms)

Institut des Hautes Études Cinématographiques (IDHEC), Paris (dissertations, clip files)

Ministères des Affaires Étrangères (MAE), Quai d'Orsay, Paris (B Amérique files)

Books

Abel, Richard. *The Ciné Goes to Town: French Cinema, 1896–1914.* Berkeley: University of California Press, 1994.
———. *French Cinema: The First Wave, 1915–1929.* Princeton: Princeton University Press, 1984.
———. *French Film Theory and Criticism, 1907–1939.* 2 vols. Princeton: Princeton University Press, 1993 [1988].
———. *The Red Rooster Scare: Making Cinema American, 1900–1910.* Berkeley: University of California Press, 1999.
Andrew, Dudley. *André Bazin.* New York: Oxford University Press, 1978.
———. *Mists of Regret: Culture and Sensibility in Classic French Film.* Princeton: Princeton University Press, 1995.
Arletty. *La Défense.* Paris: La Table Ronde, 1971.
Aron, Robert. *Histoire de l'épuration,* vol. 2: *Le Monde de la presse, des arts, des lettres.* Paris: Fayard, 1975.
Bazin, André. *French Cinema of the Occupation and Resistance: The Birth of a Critical Esthetic.* Comp. and intro. François Truffaut. Trans. Stanley Hochman. New York: Ungar, 1981.
———. *Jean Renoir.* Ed. François Truffaut. Trans. W. W. Halsey II and William H. Simon. New York: Simon & Schuster, 1986 [1973].
Benghozi, Pierre-Jean, and Christian Delage, eds. *Une Histoire économique du cinéma français: Regards croisés franco-américains.* Paris: L'Harmattan, 1997.
Bertin, Célia. *Jean Renoir: A Life in Pictures.* Trans. Mireille and Leonard Muellner. Baltimore: Johns Hopkins University Press, 1991.
Bertin-Maghit, J.-P. *Le Cinéma sous l'Occupation.* Paris: Olivier Orban, 1989.
Bertrand, C.-J., and Francis Bordat, eds. *Les Médias américains en France: Influence et pénétration.* Paris: Belin, 1989.
Bonnell, René. *Le Cinéma exploité.* Paris: Seuil, 1978.
———. *La Vingt-cinquième Image: Une Économie de l'audiovisuel.* Paris: Gallimard / FEMIS, 1989.
Buchsbaum, Jonathan. *Cinéma Engagé: Film in the Popular Front.* Urbana: University of Illinois Press, 1988.
Clair, René. *Cinema Yesterday and Today.* Ed. and intro. R. C. Dale. Trans. Stanley Appelbaum. New York: Dover, 1972.
Courtade, Francis. *Les Malédictions du cinéma français.* Paris: Alain Moreau, 1978.
Crisp, Colin. *The Classic French Cinema, 1930–1960.* Bloomington: Indiana University Press, 1993.
Darmon, Pierre. *Le Monde du cinéma sous l'Occupation.* Paris: Stock, 1997.
Debray, Régis. *Teachers, Writers, Celebrities: The Intellectuals of Modern France.* London: Verso, 1981.
Degand, Claude. *Le Cinéma . . . cette industrie.* Paris: Éditions techniques et économiques, 1972.
Durand, Jacques. *Le Cinéma et son public.* Paris: Sirey, 1958.
Dyer, Richard, and Ginette Vincendeau, eds. *Popular European Cinema.* London: Routledge, 1992.

Ehrlich, Evelyn. *Cinema of Paradox: French Filmmaking under the German Occupation.* New York: Columbia University Press, 1985.

Ferro, Marc. *Cinéma et histoire.* Paris: Denoel, 1977.

Flitterman-Lewis, Sandy. *To Desire Differently: Feminism and the French Cinema.* Urbana and Chicago: University of Illinois Press, 1990.

Ford, Charles. *Histoire du cinéma français contemporain, 1945–1977.* Paris: Éditions France-Empire, 1977.

Garçon, François. *De Blum à Pétain: Cinéma et société française, 1936–1944.* Paris: Éditions du Cerf, 1984.

Gaston-Mathé, Catherine. *La Société française au miroir de son cinéma: De la débâcle à la décolonisation.* Paris: Diffusion, Le Seuil, 1997.

Ghali, Noureddine. *L'Avant-garde cinématographique en France dans les années vingt: Idées, conceptions, théories.* Paris: Éditions Paris experimental, 1995.

Greene, Naomi. *Landscapes of Loss: The National Past in Postwar French Cinema.* Princeton: Princeton University Press, 1999.

Guillaume-Grimaud, Geneviève. *Le Cinéma du Front populaire.* Paris: Lherminier, 1986.

Hayward, Susan. *French National Cinema.* London: Routledge, 1993.

Higson, Andrew, and Richard Maltby, eds. *"Film Europe" and "Film America": Cinema, Commerce, and Cultural Exchange, 1920–1939.* Exeter: University of Exeter Press, 1999.

Hubert-Lacombe, Patricia. *Le Cinéma français dans la guerre froide: 1946–1956.* Paris: L'Harmattan, 1996.

Jackson, Julian. *The Popular Front in France: Defending Democracy, 1934–1938.* Cambridge: Cambridge University Press, 1990.

Jeancolas, Jean-Pierre. *Histoire du cinéma français.* Paris: Nathan, 1995.

15 Ans des années trente: Le Cinéma des français, 1929–1944. Paris: Stock, 1983.

Jeanne, René, and Charles Ford. *Le Cinéma et la presse, 1895–1960.* Paris: Armand Colin, 1961.

Kuisel, Richard. *Seducing the French: The Dilemma of Americanization.* Berkeley: University of California Press, 1993.

Leglise, Paul. *Histoire de la politique du cinéma français,* 2 vols. Paris: Filmeditions/Pierre Lherminier, 1969 and 1977.

Lindeperg, Sylvie. *Les Écrans de l'ombre: La Seconde Guerre mondiale dans le cinéma français, 1944–1969.* Paris: CNRS Éditions, 1997.

McMillan, James F. *Dreyfus to De Gaulle: Politics and Society in France 1898–1969.* London: Edward Arnold, 1985.

Moussinac, Léon. *L'Âge ingrat du cinéma.* Paris: Éditeurs français réunis, 1967.

Ory, Pascal. *L'Aventure culturelle française: 1945–1989.* Paris: Flammarion, 1989.

Pathé: Premier empire du cinema. Paris: Centre Georges Pompidou, 1994.

Porcile, François. *Défense du court métrage français.* Paris: Éditions du Cerf, 1965.

Prédal, René. *Le Cinéma français depuis 1945.* Paris: Éditions Nathan, 1991.

La Société française (1914–1945) à travers le cinéma. Paris: Armand Colin, 1972.

Renaitour, Jean-Michel. *Où va le cinéma français?* Paris: Éditions Baudinière, 1937.

Ross, Kristin. *Fast Cars, Clean Bodies: Decolonization and the Reordering of French Culture.* Cambridge, Mass.: MIT Press, 1998 [1995].

Sadoul, Georges. *Le Cinéma français 1890–1962*. Paris: Flammarion, 1962.

Salles Gomes, P. E. *Jean Vigo*. Trans. Allan Francovich. Berkeley: University of California Press, 1971 [1957].

Sesonske, Alexander. *Jean Renoir: The French Films, 1924–1939*. Cambridge, Mass.: Harvard University Press, 1980.

Siclier, Jacques. *La France de Pétain et son cinéma*. Paris: Henri Veyrier, 1981.

Sorlin, Pierre. *European Cinemas, European Societies, 1939–1990*. London: Routledge, 1991.

The Film in History: Restaging the Past. Totowa, N.J.: Barnes & Noble, 1980.

Strauss, David. *Menace in the West: The Rise of French Anti-Americanism in Modern Times*. Westport, Conn.: Greenwood Press, 1978.

Strebel, Elizabeth Grottle. *French Social Cinema of the Nineteen Thirties: A Cinematographic Expression of Popular Front Consciousness*. New York: Arno Press, 1980 [1973].

Thibau, Jacques. *La France colonisée*. Paris: Flammarion, 1980.

Turk, Edward Baron. *Child of Paradise: Marcel Carné and the Golden Age of French Cinema*. Cambridge, Mass.: Harvard University Press, 1989.

Vincendeau, Ginette, and Susan Hayward, eds. *French Film: Texts and Contexts*. London: Routledge, 1990.

Wall, Irwin. *The United States and the Making of Postwar France, 1945–1954*. New York: Cambridge University Press, 1991.

Williams, Alan. *Republic of Images: A History of French Filmmaking*. Cambridge, Mass.: Harvard University Press, 1992.

Filmography

N.B.: An attempt has been made to use *release* dates consistently.

Aero-Engine, dir. Arthur Elton, prod. John Grierson (U.K., EMB Film Unit, 1933–4)

All Quiet on the Western Front, dir. Lewis Milestone, prod. Carl Laemmle Jr. (U.S., Universal Pictures, 1930)

America (aka *Love and Sacrifice; Pour Indépendance*), dir. & prod. D. W. Griffith (U.S., D. W. Griffith Prods./United Artists, 1924)

Americans All, prod. Louis de Rochemont (U.S., *March of Time* newsreel, Time, Inc., 1941) (*N.B.*: Another *March of Time* newsreel with the same title and producer, re U.S. racial prejudice and anti-Semitism, was released in 1944. Also, export versions of *Americans All* differ from the U.S. releases of the newsreel.)

Andy Hardy's Dilemma, dir. George B. Seitz (U.S., MGM, 1938)

Ann Vickers, dir. John Cromwell, prod. Pandro S. Berman (U.S., RKO Radio Pictures, 1933)

Appel du silence, L', dir. Léon Poirier (France, Léon Poirier, 1936)

Arrivée d'un train à La Ciotat (*Arrival of a Train at La Ciotat,* aka *Train Arriving at a Station*), dir. Auguste and Louis Lumière (France, 1895)

Attack of the Crab Monsters, dir. & prod. Roger Corman (U.S., Allied Artists/Los Altos, 1957)

Bandera, La (*Escape from Yesterday*), dir. Julien Duvivier (France, Société nouvelle de cinématographie, 1935)

Bas-Fonds, Les (*The Lower Depths,* 1937), dir. Jean Renoir, prod. Alexandre Kamenka (France, Albatros, 1936)

Battle of Russia, dir. & prod. Frank Capra (U.S., War Department, 1944), in series *Why We Fight*

BBC: The Voice of Britain, dir. & prod. John Grierson and Alberto Cavalcanti (U.K., GPO Film Unit for the BBC, 1934–5)

Beau Geste, dir. Herbert Brenon, prod. Jesse L. Lasky and Adolph Zukor (U.S., Paramount Pictures, 1926)

Beau Geste, dir. & prod. William A. Wellman (U.S., Paramount Pictures, 1939)

Belle of the Nineties (aka *It Ain't No Sin* [working title]), dir. Leo McCarey, prod. William LeBaron (U.S., Paramount Pictures, 1934)

Bête humaine, La (*The Human Beast*, 1939), dir. Jean Renoir, prod. Robert Hakim (France, Paris Film Production, 1938)
Big Parade, The, dir. King Vidor, prod. Irving Thalberg (U.S., MGM, 1925)
Birth of a Nation, The (aka *The Clansman*), dir. D. W. Griffith, prod. D. W. Griffith and Harry E. Aitken (U.S., D. W. Griffith Corp. / Epoch Producing Corp., 1915)
Black Narcissus, dir. and prod. Michael Powell and Emeric Pressburger (U.K., Independent Producers / The Archers, 1947)
Blackboard Jungle, dir. Richard Brooks, prod. Pandro S. Berman (U.S., MGM, 1955)
Bled, Le, dir. Jean Renoir (France, Société des Films historiques [with French government], 1929)
Bonnie Prince Charlie, dir. Anthony Kimmins, prod. Edward Black (U.K., London Film Prods. / British Lion, 1948)
Boudoir Diplomat, The, dir. Malcolm St. Clair, prod. Carl Laemmle Jr. (U.S., Universal Pictures, 1930)
Boudu sauvé des eaux (*Boudu Saved from Drowning*, 1967), dir. Jean Renoir, prod. Michel Simon and Jean Gehret (France, Société Sirius, 1932)
Brazza ou l'épopée du Congo, dir. Léon Poirier (France, Société de production du film Brazza, 1940)
Bride of Frankenstein, dir. James Whale, prod. Carl Laemmle Jr. and James Whale (U.S., Universal Pictures, 1935)
Brighton Rock (aka *Young Scarface* [U.S.]) dir. John Boutling, prod. Roy Boulting (U.K., Associated British Picture Corp., 1947)
Broken Blossoms (aka *The Chink and the Child; Scarlet Blossoms; The Yellow Man and the Girl*), dir. & prod. D. W. Griffith (U.S., D W. Griffith Prods., 1919)
Broncho Billy and the Greaser, dir. & prod. Gilbert M. Anderson (U.S., Essanay, 1914)
Bronenosets Potemkin (*Battleship Potemkin;* aka *Potemkin*), dir. Sergei Eisenstein (USSR, Goskino / Mosfil'm, 1925)
Bucket of Blood, A, dir. & prod. Roger Corman (U.S., Alta Vista, 1959)
Burma Victory, dir. Roy Boulting, prod. David MacDonald (U.K., British Army Film Unit, 1945)
Cabinet des Dr. Caligari, Das (aka *Das Kabinett des Dr. Caligari; The Cabinet of Dr. Caligari* [U.S., 1921]), dir. Robert Wiene, prod. Rudolf Meinert and Erich Pommer (Germany, Decla–Bioscop AG, 1920)
Canard, Le (The Duck; U.S. title *Fuck a Duck*), prod. Bérnard Natan (France, clandestine production, 1926)
Captain Blood, dir. Michael Curtiz, prod. Hal B. Wallis [uncred.] (U.S., Cosmopolitan Prods. / First National Pictures / Warner Bros., 1935)
Catherine the Great (aka *The Rise of Catherine the Great*), dir. Paul Czinner, prod. Alexander Korda [and Ludovico Toeplitz, uncred.] (U.K., London Film Prods., 1934)
Charge of the Light Brigade, dir. Michael Curtiz, prod. Hal B. Wallis [uncred.] (U.S., Warner Bros., 1936)
Chienne, La, dir. Jean Renoir, prod. Pierre Braunberger (France, Braunberger–Richebé, 1931)

Children at School, dir. Basil Wright (U.K., Realist Film Unit for the British Commercial Gas Association, 1937)

Citizen Kane, dir. & prod. Orson Welles (U.S., Mercury Prods./RKO Radio Pictures, 1941)

Clive of India, dir. Richard Boleslawski, prod. William Goetz and Raymond Griffith (U.S., Twentieth Century Pictures/United Artists, 1935)

Coal Face, dir. Alberto Cavalcanti (U.K., GPO Film Unit, 1935)

Confessions of a Nazi Spy, dir. Anatole Litvak (U.S., First National Pictures/Warner Bros., 1939)

Contact, dir. Paul Rotha (U.K., British Instructional Pictures, 1933)

Corbeau, Le (The Raven), dir. Henri-Georges Clouzot, prod. René Montis (France, Continental, 1943)

Crime de Monsieur Lange, Le (The Crime of Monsieur Lange, 1964), dir. Jean Renoir, prod. André Halley des Fontaines (France, Obéron, 1936)

Crossfire, dir. Edward Dmytryk, prod. Dore Schary (U.S., RKO Radio Pictures, 1947)

Crybaby Killer, The, dir. Jus Addiss, prod. Roger Corman (U.S., Allied Artists, 1958)

Dancing Gob, The (U.S., Paramount/Christie Talking Plays, 1929)

Dead of Night, dir. Alberto Cavalcanti, Charles Crichton, Basil Dearden, and Robert Hamer, prod. Michael Balcon (U.K., Eagle–Lion Films/Ealing Studios/GCF, 1945)

Death Mills, in series Orientation Films (U.S., Signal Corps, 1945)

Desert Fox, The, dir. Henry Hathaway, prod. Nunnally Johnson (U.S., Twentieth Century–Fox, 1951)

2 ou 3 choses que je sais d'elle (2 or 3 Things I Know about Her), dir. Jean-Luc Godard (France, Anouchka Films/Argos Films/Les Films du Carosse/Parc Film, 1966)

Devil's Island (aka *Song of Hell),* dir. William Clemens (U.S., Warner Bros., 1939)

Dominicans of Woodchester, prod. Dominican Fathers of Woodchester (U.K., Catholic Film Society, 1936)

Double Indemnity, dir. Billy Wilder, prod. Buddy G. DeSylva (U.S., Paramount Pictures, 1944)

Dove, The, dir. Roland West, prod. Joseph M. Schenck (U.S., Norma Talmadge Film Corp./United Artists, 1928); cf. *Girl of the Rio*

Dr. Jekyll and Mr. Hyde, dir. Rouben Mamoulian, prod. Rouben Mamoulian and Adolph Zukor (U.S., Paramount Pictures, 1931)

Dracula, dir. Tod Browning, prod. Tod Browning and Carl Laemmle Jr. (U.S., Universal Pictures, 1931)

Dragstrip Riot, dir. David Bradley, prod. O'Dale Ireland (U.S., American International Pictures, 1958)

Drifters, dir. John Grierson (U.K., New Era Films for the EMB, 1929)

Eastern Valley, dir. Paul Rotha and Donald Alexander, prod. Stuart Legg (U.K., GPO Film Unit, 1937)

Enemies of Women, dir. Alan Crosland (U.S., Cosmopolitan Pictures, 1923)

Enfants du Paradis, Les (Children of Paradise [U.S., 1946]), dir. Marcel Carné, prod. Raymond Borderie and Fred Orain (France, Pathé Cinéma, 1945)

Enough to Eat?, dir. Edgar Anstey (U.K., Gas, Light, and Coke Co., London, 1936)

Eureka Stockade (aka *Massacre Hill*), dir. Harry Watt, prod. Leslie Norman (U.K.– Australia, Ealing Studios, 1948)

Extase (*Ecstasy*; aka *Symphony of Love*), dir. Gustav Machaty (Czechoslovakia, Electra / Jewel, 1932)

Face of Britain, dir. Paul Rotha (U.K., G.B. Instructional, Ltd., 1935)

Farewell to Arms, A, dir. Frank Borzage, prod. Edward A. Blatt (U.S., Paramount Pictures, 1932)

Fire Over England, dir. William K. Howard, prod. Erich Pommer (U.K., London Film Prods., 1937)

Franciscans of Guildford (U.K., Catholic Film Society, 1936)

Frankenstein, dir. James Whale, prod. Carl Laemmle Jr. (U.S., Universal Pictures, 1931)

Garçonne, La (The Tomboy), dir. Jean de Limur (France, Franco London Films, 1936)

Gaslight (*Murder in Thornton Square* [U.K.]), dir. George Cukor, prod. Arthur Hornblow Jr. (U.S., MGM, 1944)

Gefangene von Shanghai, Die, dir. Géza von Bolváry (Germany, Nero-Film GmbH, 1927)

Gentleman's Agreement, dir. Elia Kazan, prod. Darryl F. Zanuck (U.S., Twentieth Century–Fox, 1947)

Gilda, dir. Charles Vidor, prod. Virginia Van Upp (U.S., Columbia Pictures, 1946)

Girl of the Rio (aka *The Dove*), dir. Herbert Brenon, prod. Louis Sarecky (U.S., RKO Radio Pictures, 1932)

Going My Way, dir. & prod. Leo McCarey (U.S., Paramount Pictures, 1944)

Gone with the Wind, dir. Victor Fleming [George Cukor et al., uncred.], prod. David O. Selznick (U.S., MGM / Selznick Internationl Pictures, 1939)

Grapes of Wrath, The, dir. John Ford, prod. Darryl F. Zanuck (U.S., Twentieth Century–Fox, 1940)

Greaser's Revenge, The (U.S., Frontier, 1914)

Great Awakening, The, prod. Terence McArdle (U.K., Catholic Film Society, 1934)

Great Dictator, The, dir. & prod. Charles Chaplin (U.S., Charles Chaplin Prods. / United Artists, 1940)

Great Expectations, dir David Lean, prod. Ronald Neame (U.K., Cineguild, 1946)

Green Goddess, dir. Alfred E. Green (U.S., Vitaphone–Warner Bros., 1930)

Gunga Din, dir. George Stevens, prod. George Stevens and Pandro S. Berman (U.S., RKO Radio Pictures, 1939)

Hello Sweetheart, dir. Monty Banks, prod. Irving Asher (U.S., First National Pictures / Teddington Studios / Warner Bros., 1935)

Henri Langlois (aka *Langlois*), dir. & prod. Roberto Guerra and Eila Hershon (U.S., Hershon and Guerra independent production, 1970)

Henry V (aka *Henry the Fifth* [U.S., 1946]), dir. Laurence Olivier and Reginald Beck, prod. Laurence Olivier and Fillippo Del Guidice (U.K., Two Cities Film, 1944)

Her Man, dir. Tay Garnett, prod. E. B. Derr (U.S., Pathé Entertainment,1930)

Hitler's Children, dir. Edward Dmytryk, prod. Edward A. Golden (U.S., RKO Radio Pictures, 1943)

Home of the Brave, dir. Mark Robson, prod. Stanley Kramer (U.S., Screen Plays Corp., 1949)

Homme du Niger, L' (*Forbidden Love*), dir. Jacques de Baroncelli (France, SPFLH, 1939)

Hot for Paris, dir. Raoul Walsh (U.S., Fox Film, 1929)

Hot Ice (aka *Glace vive*), dir. Irving Jacoby (Canada, National Film Board, 1940)

Hot Rod Girl, dir. Leslie H. Martinson, prod. Norman T. Herman (U.S., American International Pictures, 1956)

House on 92nd Street, The, dir. Henry Hathaway, prod. Louis De Rochemont (U.S., Twentieth Century–Fox, 1945)

Housing Problems, dir. Arthur Elton and Edgar Anstrey (U.K., British Commercial Gas Association 1935)

How Lord Kitchener Was Betrayed (aka *The Betrayal of Lord Kitchener*), dir. Percy Nash (U.K., Screenplays, 1921)

Hunchback of Notre Dame, The, dir. William Dieterle, prod. Pandro S. Berman (U.S., RKO Radio Pictures, 1939)

Hurricane, The, dir. John Ford, prod. Samuel Goldwyn (U.S., United Artists / Goldwyn Pictures, 1937)

I Am a Fugitive from a Chain Gang, dir. Mervyn LeRoy, prod. Hal B. Wallis (U.S., Vitaphone / Warner Bros., 1932)

I Married a Communist (aka *The Woman on Pier 13* [U.K.]), dir. Robert Stevenson, prod. Sid Rogell (U.S., RKO Radio Pictures, 1949)

I Was a Teenage Frankenstein (aka *Teenage Frankenstein* [U.K.]), dir. Herbert L. Strock, prod. (U.S., American International Pictures / Santa Rosa Prods., 1957)

Ideal Husband, An, dir. & prod. Alexander Korda (U.K., London Film Prods. / British Lion / Twentieth Century–Fox, 1947)

I'm No Angel, dir. Wesley Ruggles, prod. William LeBaron (U.S., Paramount Pictures, 1933)

Image, L' (aka *Das Bildnis*), dir. Jacques Feyder (Austria: Vita-Film, 1925)

Iron Curtain, The (aka *Behind the Iron Curtain*), dir. William A. Wellman, prod. Sol. C. Siegel (U.S., Twentieth Century–Fox, 1948)

It Can't Happen Here (U.S., MGM, 1936 – unproduced)

J'accuse (aka *I Accuse; That They May Live* [U.S., 1939]), dir. & prod. Abel Gance (remake of his 1919 silent film) (France, Forrester–Parrant Prods., 1937)

Jew Süss (aka *Power* [U.S.]), dir. Lothar Mendes, prod. Michael Balcon (U.K., Gaumont–British, 1934)

Jour se leve, Le (aka *Daybreak* [U.S.]), dir. Marcel Carné (France, Sigma / Vauban Prods., 1939)

Juarez, dir. William Dieterle, prod. Hal B. Wallis, and Henry Blanke (U.S., First National Pictures / Warner Bros., 1939)

Kabinett des Dr. Caligari, Das, see Cabinet des Dr. Caligari, Das

Kermesse heroïque, La (aka *Carnival in Flanders* [U.S., 1936]), dir. Jacques Feyder, prod. Pierre Guerlais (France, Films Sonores Tobis, 1935)

Key Largo, dir. John Huston, prod. Jerry Wald (U.S., Warner Bros., 1948)

Kid, The, dir. & prod. Charles Chaplin (U.S., Chaplin / First National Pictures, 1921)

Kind Hearts and Coronets, dir. Robert Hamer, prod. Michael Balcon (U.K., Ealing Studios, 1949)

Knute Rockne – All American (aka *A Modern Hero* [U.K.]), dir. Lloyd Bacon, prod. Robert Fellows (U.S., Warner Bros., 1940)

Ladri di biciclette (*Bicycle Thieves;* aka *The Bicycle Thief* [U.S., 1949]), dir. &
prod. Vittorio De Sica (Italy, PDS–ENIC, 1948)
Lawless Riders, dir. Spencer Lawless Bennet, prod. Larry Darmour (U.S., Columbia
Pictures, 1935)
Little Caesar, dir. Mervyn LeRoy, prod. Hal B. Wallis [and Darryl F. Zanuck, un-
cred.] (U.S., First National Pictures/Warner Bros., 1930)
Lives of a Bengal Lancer, The, dir. Henry Hathaway, prod. Louis D. Lighton (U.S.,
Paramount Pictures, 1934)
Lost Boundaries, dir. Alfred Werker, prod. Louis De Rochemont (Louis De Roche-
mont Assoc./RD–DR Prods., 1949)
Love Finds Andy Hardy, dir. George B. Seitz, prod. Lou L. Ostrorw and Carey Wil-
son [uncred.] (U.S., MGM/Loew's, 1938)
Madame Butterfly, dir. Marion Gering, prod. B. P. Schulberg (U.S., Paramount Pic-
tures, 1932)
Madonna of the Seven Moons, dir. Arthur Crabtree, prod. Maurice Ostrer (U.K.,
Gainsborough Pictures, 1944)
Maltese Falcon, The, dir. John Huston, prod. Hal B. Wallis (U.S., First National
Pictures/Warner Bros., 1941)
Man of Aran, dir. Robert J. Flaherty, prod. Michael Balcon (U.K., Gainsborough
Pictures/Gaumont–British/Rank Organisation, 1934)
Man Who Could Work Miracles, The, dir. Lothar Mendes, prod. Alexander Korda
(U.K., London Film Prods., 1936)
Marius, dir. Alexander Korda and Marcel Pagnol (France, Les Films Marcel Pagnol,
1931)
Marseillaise, La, dir. & prod. Jean Renoir (France, CGT, then Société de Produc-
tion et d'exploitation du film La Marseillaise, 1937)
Men in Her Life, The, dir. & prod. Gregory Ratoff (U.S., Columbia Pictures, 1941)
Mildred Pierce, dir. Michael Curtiz, prod. Jack L. Warner (U.S., First National Pic-
tures, 1945)
Mine Own Executioner, dir. Anthony Kimmins, prod. Anthony Kimmins and Jack
Kitchin (U.K., London Film Prods., 1947)
Mission to Moscow, dir. Michael Curtiz, prod. Robert Buckner (U.S., Warner Bros.,
1943)
Moana: A Romance of the South Seas, dir. Robert J. Flaherty, prod. Robert J. Fla-
herty, Frances Hubbard Flaherty, Adolph Zukor, and Jesse L. Lasky (U.S., Fa-
mous Players–Lasky Corp., 1926)
Moine, Le (The Monk), prod. Bérnard Natan (France, clandestine production,
1922)
Monster on the Campus (aka *Monster in the Night; Stranger on the Campus*), dir.
Jack Arnold, prod. Joseph Gershenson (U.S., Universal, 1958)
Mr. Blabbermouth, dir. Basil Wrangell (U.S., MGM, 1942)
Mrs. Miniver, dir. William Wyler, prod. William Wyler and Sidney Franklin (U.S.,
MGM, 1942)
Murders in the Rue Morgue, dir. Robert Florey, prod. Carl Laemmle Jr. (U.S., Uni-
versal Pictures, 1932)
Nanook of the North, dir. & prod. Robert Flaherty (U.S., Les Frères Revillon /
Pathé Exchange, 1922)

Nell Gwyn, dir. & prod. Herbert Wilcox (U.K., British & Dominion Film Corp./ United Artists, 1934)

Night Mail, dir. & prod. Basil Wright and Harry Watt, prod. John Grierson (U.K., GPO Film Unit, 1936)

Ninotchka, dir. & prod. Ernst Lubitsch (U.S., MGM–Loew's, 1939)

North Sea, dir. Harry Watt, prod. Alberto Cavalcanti (U.K., GPO Film Unit, 1938)

North Star, The (aka *Armored Attack* [recut]), dir. Lewis Milestone, prod. Samuel Goldwyn (U.S., Goldwyn Pictures Corp., 1943)

Nosferatu, a Symphony of Horror [or, . . . *the Vampire*] (*Nosferatu – Eine Symphonie des Grauens*), dir. F. W. Murnau, prod. Enrico Dieckmann and Albin Grau (Germany, Prana-Film, 1922)

Nudist Land, dir. Royal Horter, prod. Royal Horter and Harry Rice (U.S., Horter/ Rice, 1937)

Nun's Story, The, dir. Fred Zinnemann, prod. Henry Blanke (U.S., Warner Bros., 1959)

Nurse Edith Cavell, dir. & prod. Herbert Wilcox (U.S., Imperadio Pictures/Imperator, 1939)

Objective Burma, dir. Raoul Walsh, prod. Jack L. Warner (U.S., Warner Bros., 1945)

Oliver Twist, dir. David Lean, prod. Ronald Neame [and Anthony Havelock-Allen, uncred.] (U.K., Cineguild/J. Arthur Rank Films, 1948)

Outlaw, The, dir. Howard Hughes [and Howard Hawks, uncred.], prod. Howard Hughes (U.S., Howard Hughes, 1943)

Overlanders, The, dir. Harry Watt, prod. Michael Balcon and Ralph Short (U.K.– Australia, Ealing Studios/First Australian, 1946)

Ox-Bow Incident, The (aka *Strange Incident* [U.K.]), dir. William A. Wellman, prod. Lamar Trotti (U.S., Twentieh Century–Fox, 1943)

Pélerin de l'enfer, Le (*Pilgrimage to Hell; De Pelgrim der verdoemden*), dir. Henri Schneider (asst. dir. Henri Storck), prod. Robert Lussac (Belgium, Étendard Films, 1945)

Pépé le Moko, dir. Julien Duvivier, prod. Raymond and Robert Hakim (France, Paris Film/Pathé Studios, 1936)

Pett and Pott: A Fairy Story of the Suburbs, dir. Alberto Cavalcanti (U.K., GPO Film Unit, 1934)

Phantom of the Opera, dir. Rupert Julian [and Lon Chaney and Edward Sedgwick, uncred.], prod. Carl Laemmle (U.S., Universal Pictures, 1925)

Pimpernel Smith, dir. & prod. Leslie Howard (U.K., London Film Prods., 1941)

Pinky, dir. Elia Kazan [and John Ford, uncred.], prod. Darryl F. Zanuck (U.S., Twentieth Century–Fox, 1949)

Pointe-Courte, La, dir. Agnès Varda, prod. Alain Resnais (France, Ciné-Tamaris, 1954)

Possessed, dir. & prod. Clarence Brown (U.S., MGM, 1931)

Potemkin, see Bronenosets Potemkin

Potomok Chingis-Khana (*Storm over Asia; aka The Heir to Genghis Khan*), dir. Vsevolod Pudovkin (USSR, Mezhrabpomfilm, 1928)

Prince and the Pauper, The, dir. William Keighley, prod. Hal B. Wallis [uncred.] (U.S., Warner Bros., 1937)

Princess and the Plumber, dir. Alexander Korda [and John G. Blystone, uncred.] ,
    prod. Al Rockett (U.S., Fox Film, 1930)
Prisonnière de Changhai, La, see Gefangene von Shanghai, Die
Private Life of Don Juan, The (aka *Don Juan*), dir. & prod. Alexander Korda (U.K.,
    London Film Prods., 1934)
Private Life of Henry VIII, The, dir. & prod. Alexander Korda (U.K., London Film
    Prods., 1933)
Private Life of the Gannets, The, dir. Julian Huxley (U.K., Skibo Prods., 1934)
Private Lives, dir. & prod. Sidney Franklin (U.S., MGM, 1931)
Private Lives of Elizabeth and Essex, The (aka *Elizabeth the Queen*), dir. Michael
    Curtiz, prod. Hal B. Wallis (U.S., Warner Bros., 1939)
Public Enemy, The, dir. William A. Wellman, prod. Darryl F. Zanuck (U.S., Warner
    Bros., 1931)
Purple Rose of Cairo, The, dir. Woody Allen, prod. Robert Greenhut (U.S., Rollins–
    Joffe, 1985)
Pygmalion, dir. Leslie Howard and Anthony Asquith, prod. Gabriel Pascal (U.K.,
    Pascal Film Productions, 1938)
Quai des brumes (Port of Shadows), dir. Marcel Carné, prod. Gregor Rabinowitch
    (France, Ciné-Alliance, 1938)
Red Danube, The, dir. George Sidney, prod. Carey Wilson (U.S., MGM, 1949)
Red Menace, dir. R. G. Springsteen, prod. Herbert J. Yates (U.S., Republic Pictures,
    1949)
Rembrandt, dir. & prod. Alexander Korda (U.K., London Film Prods., 1936)
Reserved for Ladies, see Service for Ladies
Retreats for Boys (U.K., Catholic Film Society, 1936)
Riot in Juvenile Prison, dir. Edward L. Cahn, prod. Robert E. Kent (U.S., Vogue
    Pictures, 1959)
Room at the Top, dir. Jack Clayton, prod. James and John Woolf (U.K., Remus,
    1959)
Sacrament of Baptism, prod. Ferdinand Valentine (U.K., Catholic Film Society,
    1936)
Sacrament of Holy Matrimony (U.K., Catholic Film Society, 1936)
Sail Ho (U.S., *Sports Parade* series, Warner Bros., 1941)
Salt of the Earth, dir. Herbert J. Biberman, prod. Adolfo Barela, Sonja Dahl Biber-
    man, and Paul Jarrico (U.S., Independent Prods./International Union of Mine,
    Mill & Smelter Workers, 1954)
Satan's Sister, dir. George Pearson, prod. Betty Balfour and George Pearson (U.K.,
    BWP Films, 1925)
Sauve qui peut (la vie) (Every Man for Himself, aka *Slow Motion),* dir. Jean-Luc
    Godard, prod. Alain Sarde, Jean-Luc Godard (France, Sara Films/MK2/Saga
    Productions/Sonimage/CNC/ZDF/SSR/ORF, 1979)
Scarface[: Shame of the Nation], dir. Howard Hawks, prod. Howard Hughes (U.S.,
    Caddo/United Artists, 1932)
Scarlet Pimpernel, The, dir. Harold Young, prod. Alexander Korda [and Grace
    Blake, uncred.] (U.K., London Film Prods., 1934)
Scarlet Street, dir. Fritz Lang, prod. Fritz Lang and Walter Wanger (U.S., Diana
    Production Co./Universal Pictures, 1945)

Sea Beast, The (aka *Jim le Harponneur* [France]), dir. Millard Webb (U.S., Warner Bros., 1926)

Sea Hawk, dir. Michael Curtiz, prod. Hal B. Wallis (U.S., Warner Bros.,1940)

Sergeant York, dir. Howard Hawks, prod. Howard Hawks, Jesse L. Lasky, and Hal B. Wallis (U.S., Warner Bros., 1941)

Service for Ladies (aka *Reserved for Ladies* [U.S.]), dir. & prod. Alezander Korda (U.K., Paramount British, 1932)

Seventh Veil, The, dir. Compton Bennett, prod. Sydney Box (U.K., Ortis Films, 1946)

Show Boat, dir. James Whale, prod. Carl Laemmle Jr. (U.S., Universal, 1936)

Silk Stockings, dir. Rouben Mamoulian, prod. Arthur Freed (U.S., MGM, 1957)

Singing Nun, The, dir. Henry Koster, prod. John Beck (U.S., MGM, 1966)

Sixty Glorious Years (aka *Queen of Destiny* [U.S.]), dir. & prod. Herbert Wilcox (U.K., Imperator Film Prods., 1938)

Ski in the Valley of the Saints, prod. Graham McInnes (Canada, National Film Board/Crawley Films Ltd., 1944)

Soeur Vaseline, prod. attributed to Bérnard Natan (France, clandestine production, 1926)

Song of Bernadette, The, dir. Henry King, prod. William Perlberg (U.S., Twentieth Century–Fox, 1943)

Song of Ceylon, dir. Basil Wright, prod. John Grierson (U.K., EMB/GPO Film Unit for the Ceylon Tea Propaganda Board, 1934)

Song of Russia, dir. Gregory Ratoff, prod. Sandro S. Berman and Joe Pasternak (U.S., MGM, 1943)

S.O.S. Sahara, dir. Jacques de Baroncelli (France, A.C.E.. 1938)

Spare Time, dir. Humphrey Jennings (U.K., Mass Observation/GPO Film Unit, 1939)

State Fair, dir. Henry King, prod. Winfield R. Sheehan (U.S., Fox Film, 1933)

Storm in a Teacup, dir. Ian Dalrymple and Victor Saville, prod. Alexander Korda (U.K., United Artists/Victor Saville Prods., 1937)

Stranger, The (aka *Date with Destiny* [working title]), dir. Orson Welles, prod. Sam Spiegel (U.S., Haig Corp./International Pictures/RKO, 1946)

Sun Valley Serenade, dir. H. Bruce Humberstone, prod. Milton Sperling (U.S., Twentieth Century–Fox, 1941)

Tarzan and His Mate, dir. Cedric Gibbons [and Jack Conway, uncred.], prod. Bernard H. Hyman (U.S., MGM, 1934)

Tarzan, the Ape Man, dir. W. S. Van Dyke, prod. Bernard H. Hyman [and Irving Thalberg, uncred.] (U.S., MGM, 1932)

Teen-age Crime Wave (aka *La Rage du Crime; Drang Naar Misdaad* [both Belgium], dir. Fred F. Sears, prod. Sam Katzman (U.S., Clover / Columbia Pictures, 1955)

That Hamilton Woman (aka *Lady Hamilton*), dir. & prod. Alexander Korda (U.K., Alexander Korda Films, 1941)

Thérèse Raquin (aka *Shadows of Fear; Thou Shalt Not*), dir. Jacques Feyder (France–Germany, DEFU/Deutsche First National, 1928)

Things to Come, dir. William Cameron Menzies, prod. Alexander Korda (U.K., London Film Prods., 1936)

Third Man, The, dir. Carol Reed, prod. David O. Selznick and Hugh Perceval (U.K., Selznick International/British Lion, 1949)

This Is the Army, dir. Michael Curtiz, prod. Jack L. Warner and Hal B. Wallis (U.S., Warner Bros., 1943)

Three Caballeros, The, dir. Norman Ferguson, prod. Walt Disney (U.S., Walt Disney Prods., 1945)

Tobacco Road, dir. John Ford, prod. Darryl F. Zanuck (U.S., Twentieth Century–Fox, 1941)

Today We Live, dir. Ruby Grierson and Ralph Bond (U.K., Strand Film Co., 1937)

Toni, dir. Jean Renoir, prod. Pierre Gaut (France, Films d'Audjourd'hui, 1935)

Tony the Greaser (U.S., Star Films–Méliès Co., 1911; remake Vitagraph, 1914)

Tout va très bien madame la marquise, dir. Henry Wulschleger (France, France Prods., 1936)

Trois mousquetaires, Les (*The Three Musketeers*) (pt. 1, *Les Ferrets de la reine;* pt. 2, *Milady*), dir. Henri Diamant-Berger, prod. Fernand Méric (France, Films Diamant, 1933)

Turksib, dir. Victor A. Turin (USSR, Vostokkino, 1929)

Turn of the Tide, dir. Norman Walker, prod. John Corfield (U.K., British National/Gaumont, 1935)

Underground, dir. Vincent Sherman, prod. William Jacobs and Jack L. Warner (U.S., Warner Bros., 1941)

Union Pacific, dir. & prod. Cecil B. DeMille (U.S., Paramount Pictures, 1939)

Victoria the Great, dir. & prod. Herbert Wilcox (U.K., Imperator Film Prods., 1937)

Vidocq, dir. Jacques Daroy (France, Les Films Agiman/Société de production du film Vidocq, 1938)

Vie est à nous, La (*People of France,* 1937), dir. Jean Renoir (France, Parti Communiste Français, 1936)

Welt im Film, weekly newsreel, 369 issues, prod. U.S. and U.K. military occupation governments in Germany (joint U.S.–U.K prod. 18 May 1945–1 June 1950; U.S. prod., 1 June 1950–27 June 1952)

White Heat, dir. Raoul Walsh, prod. Louis F. Edelman (U.S., Warner Bros., 1949)

White Shadows in the South Seas, dir. W. S. Van Dyke [and Robert J. Flaherty, uncred.], prod. Hunt Stromberg (U.S., Cosmopolitan Pictures/MGM, 1928)

Who's Afraid of Virginia Woolf?, dir. Mike Nichols, prod. Ernest Lehman (U.S., Chenault Prods./Warner Bros., 1966)

Wicked Lady, The, dir. Leslie Arliss, prod. Maurice Ostrer (U.K., Gainsborough Pictures, 1945)

Wizard of Oz, The, dir. Victor Fleming [and Richard Thorpe and King Vidor, uncred.], prod. Victor Fleming and Mervyn LeRoy (U.S., MGM, 1939)

Yankee Doodle Dandy, dir. Michael Curtiz, prod. Hal B. Wallis and William Cagney (U.S., Warner Bros., 1942)

Zéro de conduite (*Zero for Conduct*), dir. & prod. Jean Vigo (France, Argui-Films, 1933)

Zum goldenen Anker (*The Golden Anchor*), dir. Alexander Korda, prod. Marcel Pagnol (France, Marcel Pagnol/Paramount Publix Corp., 1931)

Index

Field, Mary, 179–80
Film Council, 156
Filmleidung, 218
Filmrundschau, 215
Financial Times, 158, 198–9
Finke, Roger, 291n18
Fire over England, 304n33
First Amendment, 52
Fisher, F. McCracken, 112
Fisher, James B., 32
Flaherty, Robert, 134, 137–8
Flèche de Paris, La, 233, 330n20
Fletcher, Angus 141
Flowers, W. F., 83
Flynn, Errol, 60, 157, 183
Foot, Michael, 203, 206
Ford, Henry, 21, 23
Fordism, 8
Foreign Office (U.K.), 6, 66, 141–5; *see also*
    Bevin, Ernest
"Formula, The," 32–3
Forrestal, James, 85, 196
France, 4, 65, 70, 93, 187, 223, 278, 280–1
    cinema attendance, 227–8, 280–1
    domination of global cinema lost, 226–7
    film criticism in reviving cinema, 241–5
    Hollywood angers, 70, 228–31
    vs. Jews and foreigners, 231–9
    Latin America strategy, 265
    postwar state support, 264–5, 270–1
    Vichy support of film, 6, 239, 263–4
Franciscans of Guildford, 174
Frank, Isaiah, 104
Frankenstein, 39
free flow of information, 116
Frick, Henry Clay, 281
Friedrich, Otto, 87
Friedman, Thomas, 287
Friese-Greene, William, 199, 324n95

Gabin, Jean, 254–5
Gainsborough Films, 178, 182, 205
Galbraith, John Kenneth, 102–3
Gamble, Snowden, 132
Gance, Abel, 229
gangster cycle, 34–9, 60, 75, 98–9
Garçonne, La, 235
Gaslight, 100
Gatenbein, James W., 97
Gaumont (France), 256, 258
Gaumont–British, 129, 145, 157, 169,
    177–8, 179

Gaumont–Franco–Film–Aubert (GFFA),
    233, 261
Gavaerts, 223
Gaxotte, Pierre, 236
Gay, Edwin F., 45
Gaynor, William J., 57
Geddes. Auckland Sir, 144
General Agreement on Tariffs and Trade
    (GATT), 104, 111, 116, 195
General Cinema Finance Corporation
    (GCFC), 169, 175; *see also* Rank,
    J. Arthur
General Film Distributors, 169, 175
General Post Office (GPO) Film Unit,
    126–40; *see also* Grierson, John
Geneva, *see* League of Nations, Conference
    on the Abolition of Import and Export
    Prohibitions and Restrictions
Gentleman's Agreement, 84
German-American Bund, 75
Germany
    anti-Nazi films, 77–9, 81, 98
    decartelization, 103, 105
    double-program ban, 264
    expressionism, 19
    Film Credit Bank, 264
    film industry, 7–8
    Filmkammer, 104, 259
    import restrictions, 93
    Kino Reform Movement, 30
    Kontingent system, 4, 65
    moral crusaders, 30, 44
    newspapers attack Hollywood, 66–7
    U.S. occupation regime, 98–107, 110–14
    and WWI, 63–4; as film villain, 28;
        Korda on, 147–8
    see also Goebbels, Joseph; High Commis-
        sion in Germany
Gerould, Kathleen, 28–9
Gibbs, Cornelia A., 71, 94
Gibbs, William F., 55
Gide, André, 252
Gilda, 183
Gillies, Stewart, 170
Girl of the Rio, 31
Gilson, Etienne, 268
Giraudoux, Jean, 235
Gish, Lillian, 242, 340n31
Glancy, H. Mark, 2
globalization, 8
Godard, Jean-Luc, 273, 282, 284
Goddard, Paulette, 160